Methodologies and Use Cases on Extended Reality for Training and Education

Anacleto Correia
Naval Academy, Portugal

Vitor Viegas
Naval Academy, Portugal

A volume in the Advances in Educational Technologies and Instructional Design (AETID) Book Series

IGI Global
PUBLISHER of TIMELY KNOWLEDGE

Published in the United States of America by
IGI Global
Information Science Reference (an imprint of IGI Global)
701 E. Chocolate Avenue
Hershey PA, USA 17033
Tel: 717-533-8845
Fax: 717-533-8661
E-mail: cust@igi-global.com
Web site: http://www.igi-global.com

Library of Congress Cataloging-in-Publication Data

Names: Viegas, Vitor, 1976- editor. | Correia, Anacleto, 1961- editor.
Title: Methodologies and use cases on extended reality for training and education / Vitor Viegas and Anacleto Correia, editors.
Description: Hershey, PA : Information Science Reference, 2022. | Includes bibliographical references and index. | Summary: "The objective of this book is to describe, for the domain of education and training, the current research status of extended reality usage, discuss the foreseen advancements in the design and development of various types of immersive learning environments, as well as the emerging pedagogical innovations in the field"-- Provided by publisher.
Identifiers: LCCN 2022021396 (print) | LCCN 2022021397 (ebook) | ISBN 9781668433980 (hardcover) | ISBN 9781668433997 (paperback) | ISBN 9781668434000 (ebook)
Subjects: LCSH: Virtual reality in education. | Artificial intelligence--Educational applications.
Classification: LCC LB1044.87 .M48 2022 (print) | LCC LB1044.87 (ebook) | DDC 371.33/468--dc23/eng/20220623
LC record available at https://lccn.loc.gov/2022021396
LC ebook record available at https://lccn.loc.gov/2022021397

This book is published in the IGI Global book series Advances in Educational Technologies and Instructional Design (AETID) (ISSN: 2326-8905; eISSN: 2326-8913)

British Cataloguing in Publication Data
A Cataloguing in Publication record for this book is available from the British Library.

All work contributed to this book is new, previously-unpublished material.
The views expressed in this book are those of the authors, but not necessarily of the publisher.

For electronic access to this publication, please contact: eresources@igi-global.com.

Advances in Educational Technologies and Instructional Design (AETID) Book Series

ISSN:2326-8905
EISSN:2326-8913

Editor-in-Chief: Lawrence A. Tomei Robert Morris University, USA

MISSION

Education has undergone, and continues to undergo, immense changes in the way it is enacted and distributed to both child and adult learners. In modern education, the traditional classroom learning experience has evolved to include technological resources and to provide online classroom opportunities to students of all ages regardless of their geographical locations. From distance education, Massive-Open-Online-Courses (MOOCs), and electronic tablets in the classroom, technology is now an integral part of learning and is also affecting the way educators communicate information to students.

The **Advances in Educational Technologies & Instructional Design (AETID) Book Series** explores new research and theories for facilitating learning and improving educational performance utilizing technological processes and resources. The series examines technologies that can be integrated into K-12 classrooms to improve skills and learning abilities in all subjects including STEM education and language learning. Additionally, it studies the emergence of fully online classrooms for young and adult learners alike, and the communication and accountability challenges that can arise. Trending topics that are covered include adaptive learning, game-based learning, virtual school environments, and social media effects. School administrators, educators, academicians, researchers, and students will find this series to be an excellent resource for the effective design and implementation of learning technologies in their classes.

COVERAGE

- Web 2.0 and Education
- Social Media Effects on Education
- Instructional Design Models
- Adaptive Learning
- K-12 Educational Technologies
- Curriculum Development
- Collaboration Tools
- Higher Education Technologies
- Online Media in Classrooms
- Game-Based Learning

IGI Global is currently accepting manuscripts for publication within this series. To submit a proposal for a volume in this series, please contact our Acquisition Editors at Acquisitions@igi-global.com or visit: http://www.igi-global.com/publish/.

The Advances in Educational Technologies and Instructional Design (AETID) Book Series (ISSN 2326-8905) is published by IGI Global, 701 E. Chocolate Avenue, Hershey, PA 17033-1240, USA, www.igi-global.com. This series is composed of titles available for purchase individually; each title is edited to be contextually exclusive from any other title within the series. For pricing and ordering information please visit http://www.igi-global.com/book-series/advances-educational-technologies-instructional-design/73678. Postmaster: Send all address changes to above address.

Titles in this Series

For a list of additional titles in this series, please visit:
http://www.igi-global.com/book-series/advances-educational-technologies-instructional-design/73678

Guide to Integrating Problem-Based Learning Programs in Higher Education Classrooms Design, Implementation, and Evaluation
Pam Epler (Youngstown State University, USA) and Jodee Jacobs (Youngstown State University, USA)
Information Science Reference • © 2022 • 246pp • H/C (ISBN: 9781799881773) • US $205.00

EdTech Economy and the Transformation of Education
Sara Fazzin (Xenophon College London, UK)
Information Science Reference • © 2022 • 294pp • H/C (ISBN: 9781799889045) • US $215.00

English as a Foreign Language in a New-Found Post-Pandemic World
Walaa M. El-Henawy (Port Said University, Egypt) and Maria del Mar Suárez (Universitat de Barcelona, Spain)
Information Science Reference • © 2022 • 335pp • H/C (ISBN: 9781668442050) • US $215.00

Handbook of Research on Learner-Centered Approaches to Teaching in an Age of Transformational Change
Billi L. Bromer (Brenau University, USA) and Caroline M. Crawford (University of Houston-Clear Lake, USA)
Information Science Reference • © 2022 • 385pp • H/C (ISBN: 9781668442401) • US $270.00

Handbook of Research on Teacher and Student Perspectives on the Digital Turn in Education
Sviatlana Karpava (University of Cyprus, Cyprus)
Information Science Reference • © 2022 • 586pp • H/C (ISBN: 9781668444467) • US $270.00

For an entire list of titles in this series, please visit:
http://www.igi-global.com/book-series/advances-educational-technologies-instructional-design/73678

IGI Global
PUBLISHER of TIMELY KNOWLEDGE

701 East Chocolate Avenue, Hershey, PA 17033, USA
Tel: 717-533-8845 x100 • Fax: 717-533-8661
E-Mail: cust@igi-global.com • www.igi-global.com

Table of Contents

Detailed Table of Contents

the domain of CBRN (chemical, biological, radiological, nuclear), who need high-quality training to avoid fatal errors and ensure the success of operations. However, CBRN practice sessions can reproduce only approximated, low-fidelity versions of real scenarios, whereas highly detailed simulations should be preferred. To address this issue, the authors developed a prototype of an immersive virtual reality (VR) training platform in cooperation with CBRN experts from the Italian Air Force. The devised platform is an improved version of an existing tool and offers a digital training ground where operators can learn CBRN procedures and test their abilities in a realistic virtual environment without facing the risks normally associated with real hazardous scenarios.

Traditional evacuation training is ineffective as it does not simulate decision making against tough disaster situations. Therefore, evacuation training should be significantly enhanced to offer realistic simulated evacuation experiences, entailing decision making. A promising approach to the enhancement is to introduce virtual reality (VR) into evacuation training, and there have been numerous VR-based evacuation training systems. The authors launched the project Evacuation Training in Metaverse (ETM) considering the recent surge of interest in the metaverse as a VR extension. The ETM system is being developed based on the design principle: gathering numerous participants, pursuing high fidelity, and simulating a sudden earthquake. The ETM system transforms ordinary time to emergency time by creating a sudden earthquake, allowing participants to experience simulated earthquake evacuation in a high fidelity virtual world developed from an open-city model, photogrammetry, etc. The participants make decisions in the virtual world while being influenced by numerous others.

Due to the rapid changes in the labor market, people need to constantly reshape their competencies, resulting in a tremendous need to reskill the workforce. Vocational training has traditionally been the task of educational institutions; however, today some companies also perform their own training. Overall success in establishing an individual's career depends on successful entry into the workforce, and in case of

textbook, blackboard, and chalk. Class 2 used augmented reality (FLARAS) and 3D visualization (Sketchup) and textbook. It was expected that, with the help of augmented reality, the students of Class 2 would perform better than Class 1. A better understanding of the content was achieved, as they would have better visualization of spatial objects. Consequently, better performance was achieved in the exercises and problem questions presented.

The use of virtual reality (VR) in the educational sector has increased considerably in the last decade, especially for its direct application in the development of virtual laboratories (VL) that, since the appearance of COVID-19, are being more demanded by universities. Therefore, knowing the opinion of students and professors about VR is essential for VR-based applications to be designed in an appropriate way and to be efficient at an educational level. In this sense, the results of this study, which analyzes the opinion of 420 engineering students and 44 engineering professors, can help future professors or software programmers in general to design VR-based educational resources in an appropriate way and in particular to better design their VLs.

This chapter presents the results of a systematic review that investigated the use of mixed reality (MR) technology to assist social competence learning in mainstream education. Social competence represents our ability to interact with others and, therefore, is a key determinant for many of the possibilities that are presented to us across the lifespan. In today's digital world, MR technology has been widely used in special and inclusive education for social competence training purposes but has not yet been generally applied to mainstream education. This systematic review bridges this research gap. Findings support (1) the potential for MR technology as a medium for social competence learning activities and (2) how the MR approach can contribute to a universally designed (UD) learning environment.

Preface

Extended Reality (XR) enhances the reality users experience, whether by blending the virtual and real worlds together or by creating a fully immersive digital experience that seems to the user as authentic as the real world. XR represents a continuum, with a set of less demanding technologies in one side of the continuum, and others, more advanced and with greater computational power, on the other extreme. Those latter technologies generally require specific hardware, while the first mentioned rely on average computational capabilities, such the one of the smartphones. Nevertheless, the interfaces are constantly evolving, and it's expected XR transformation, in completely new ways, in future. But the continuum line is becoming blurred, like the boundary between the real world and the digital world, as the different XR technologies – from Virtual Reality (VR) to Augmented Reality (AR), with Mixed Reality (MR) in the between – become more and more integrated. As XR evolves, the various technologies that sit under the XR continuum will become more and more linked, and users will be able to seamlessly move from one technology to another, using a blending of XR technologies.

The ability to create more immersive digital experiences or enhance the experience of the real world around is going to transform many organizations and industries. It will provide organizations with new ways to connect and engage with their collaborators and improve the clients' relationship. It will bring opportunities to improve organization processes, including training, education and hiring. In short, XR will turn information into experiences with the potential to dramatically change business processes. For now, XR is mostly used to create immersive experiences in industry, military, art, disaster management, marketing, education, among others. But in the future, it could extend to all aspects of life – to the point where each person could potentially transform the real world around her into something personalized, using special glasses, headsets, or maybe even contact lenses and implants. Industries such as aviation, automobile, and healthcare, among others, are exploring innovative approaches in the use of XR for operations' support. Some examples of how this is being done include the use of XR tools by medical professionals to diagnosis diseases in healthcare centres, or the functionality made available to a combat pilot of having flight data superimposed in their line of sight from the respective helmet. There are also many uses for AR in gaming industry and social networks, as are the examples of success mobile games or the use of philtres on Instagram or Snapchat. Some retailers make available AR apps that allow customers, before buying a product, to see how it will fit in their homes by laying virtual versions of the product, onto a specific room. The travel and tourism industry enhances travellers' experiences with AR technology by giving people more information about the streets, monuments, sights, and attractions, and even the menu of restaurants the visitors walk by when taking a tour.

Increasingly, people's experience of the world will take place in this blurred area between the real world and the digital one. If nowadays people invest their time on social media, shaping their online avatar, it's clear that the borderline between the virtual and the real world has already become indistinct. XR will accelerate this phenomenon. XR will going to change society and transform organizations, we hope, for the better. The chapters in this book will show, how it's already happening.

XR is implemented through a bundle that includes various peripherals for receiving user's proprioceptive sensation and skin feedback, such as display devices, motion and position detection devices, presentation devices, etc., to synergistically potentiate the features and technical characteristics of the system. XR systems have rapidly evolved integrating mobile and dedicated wearable technologies to enable users to experience immersive XR. Hence, the evolution of mobile technologies (smartphones, tablets, etc.) had impact XR evolution in terms of mobile intelligence and performance. In the same way, the diversity of functionalities offered by Head-Mounted Displays (HMDs) devices available played a significant role in XR technology development.

Virtual Reality, on the most advanced technological side of XR spectrum, offers an experience that is fully immersive, since the user effectively exit from the real world and enters a computer-simulated environment – typically using a special headset or glasses. VR offers a far more immersive experience than AR but, in order to accomplish that, it requires more technology and infrastructure (e.g., a VR headset), usually a standalone HMD that can be unplugged from other devices. For a best VR experience, the current technological sate currently still needs elaborate equipment, such as headsets, controllers, and speakers. While AR is grounded in the real world, VR generates a 3D, 360-degree digital experience. The VR headsets available include the Microsoft HoloLens, Oculus Rift, GearVR, HTC Vive, and the Google Cardboard viewer (for transformation of a smartphone into a VR device). A VR headset is, basically, a gear composed by a set of one or two small screens for the eyes; speakers and headphones for amplifying the sound and create an encompassing experience; the head- and eye-tracking technology which endorse the requirement of following the user's movements, using approaches, such as, laser points and infrared

LED lights within a headset, sensors within a mobile device, or special cameras and sensors installed in the compartment to detect movement.

Augmented Reality, the less technological intensive edge of the XR spectrum, mixes the real world and the digital world by superimposing digital items or data onto the real world. So, while VR creates a digitally simulated environment, AR is very much rooted in the real world. And unlike VR, AR doesn't require specialist equipment – a simple smartphone with a camera will suffice. Whether it's using specially designed glasses or a simple smartphone, AR involves the projection of digital items – such as charts, data, animation, or pictures – onto the real world, so that the digital content being overlaid looks like it is part of the physical world. Because the digital element is superimposed onto reality, the user is still very much in touch with the real world in front of them. Due to the AR projection, the real world becomes enhanced. AR devices include smartphones, tablets, smart lenses, and AR glasses. AR apps are created by developers using development environments, such as, ARKit, ARCore, or Unity. Head-up displays, which project information onto a windshield, are another example of AR deployment. The technology is now available in ships, cars and trucks that begin to use head-up displays as a safety feature, to help reduce driver distraction. These displays project real-time information such as georeferenced information or vehicle performance data either directly onto the vehicle's windshield or onto a film added to its windshield. The aim is to keep the driver's eyes in front and in the centre so that they can see the information they need immediately without obstructing the view of the road ahead. AR system uses a live camera feed to add digital content on top of the real-world elements. The camera feed collects information from the physical world, so that, in a next step, suitable digital can be rendered in the right spot, on top of the real world. This is updated in real time as the camera feed changes.

Mixed reality, the least mature of the three XR technologies, sits somewhere in between VR and AR to create a hybrid reality, where digital and real-life objects can interact with each other. With MR, the users, for example, can move or manipulate virtual elements as if they were right in front of them. Contrariwise to the AR - where the user is not able to interact with the objects or information being overlayed - MR takes this functionality to a new level by combining elements from VR and AR. Hence, MR blends components of the digital world and real world in real time, to an extent that the users can interact with the digital elements as if they were real objects. This creates a more immersive experience than the one attained through simple AR. For example, instead of seeing a projection of a digital object on top of the real world (as it happens in AR), MR would allow a user to make several operations upon a digital object using the user's hands, such as, move, rotate, transpose, expand, and shrink. With MR, on contrary of what would happen in a VR experience, the real world is not fully block out. Rather, the user can experience a virtual environment and the real world at the same time. MR requires a dedicated MR headset and additional processing power than VR or AR. MR may also require the use of controllers and motion tracking technology, such as gloves that track the users' hands movements to capture the interaction with digital objects. Currently, the HoloLens is the main MR headset on the market, and it comprises holographic lenses, a depth camera, a variety of sensors, plus speakers. With the HoloLens, the users can look for their real surrounding environment looking through the headset. Moreover, they can also see holograms perfectly integrated on the real world and, using specific gestures or hand controllers, they can interact with these 3D images as if they were physical objects.

XR technologies have been integrated into formal educational activities on different stages (early childhood education, primary education, secondary education, or higher education) aiming to create more attractive learning experiences, such as, presence, interactivity, or even deep immersion. XR has shown promising effects on learners' cognition, behavioural skills, and positive emotions such as the learning pleasure, and potential for enhancing the learning and teaching process by focusing on aspects such as the learning contents, the design elements, and learning theories. Other positive impacts claimed, upon the use of XR in education and training field, seem to be: (i) students' favourable attitudes towards XR; (ii) XR contributes for increasing motivation towards learning; (iii) XR favours the creation of a constructivist and realistic learning context; (iv) XR favours an active teaching environment; (v) XR arouses a high degree of satisfaction and positive attitudes in students; (vi) XR improves learning outcomes and long-term memory; (vii) XR can be adapted to different student profiles; and (ix) XR contributes for students' better communication, social interaction, and autonomy.

The theoretical foundation of incorporating XR in the learning process is grounded in several approaches: experiential learning, situated learning, active learning, and the multimedia learning theory. Experiential learning allows students to gain a deeper and more direct understanding of what they are learning through their participation in learning processes developed in a real context. Situated learning, on the other hand, involves learning in situations where knowledge exists and can be used and applied. Active learning means that learners actively participate in meaningful learning activities and reflect about their learning process. Multimedia learning theory put emphasis on the presentation of text and related graphic illustrations to improve learners' cognitive process. An extension of the multimedia learning theory includes emotional designs that motivate learners to make a cognitive effort to understand the material presented. There is no doubt that the ability of XR to combine multiple media content (video, audio, images, text), providing an interactive and amenable educational environment that supports experiential and contextual learning, allows learners to search for more information for better understandability, thereby promoting active learning.

The learning outcomes assessed in research works differ, but usually include the measurement of students' knowledge, creativity, affinities, critical thinking, etc. Hence, XR-assisted learning processes promote on students another level of thinking skills with impact in their motivation and emotions. Additionally, a multisensory XR environment can enhance empathy by allowing learners to experience various contextual circumstances from a baseline perspective. As previously mentioned, there is collected evidence of academic achievement and perceptions improvement among students using XR technology.

Researchers and practitioners have also found negative effects of XR-assisted learning. Compared to the traditional pen-and-paper learning method, XR games did not necessarily improve learning performance or social interaction. Furthermore, learners sometimes claim feel nauseous and dizzy when using some XR devices such as HMDs. Besides, these devices do not seem yet to be physically suited for a learning process of long and continuous duration. Some issues found with negative impact on XR dissemination, for educational purposes, are the low level of teachers' training, the scarcity of available XR devices, the lack of institutional support for educational experiments, and technical and accessibility problems when operating the XR tools. From a technical point of view, institutions need to count on XR costs, complexity of development, limited accessibility to content, unfamiliar features and functionality, and systems' maintainability.

This edited book, with 11 chapters, contains an international perspective from authors of different geographical locations and research centres. While the book is a comprehensive overview, and the research presented provides insights about specific topics, each chapter also raises additional questions that deserve further scrutiny and exploration.

ORGANIZATION OF THE BOOK

In Chapter 1, "XR Journalism Lab: An Innovative Space for Research and Training in Immersive Journalism", Gertrudix, Rubio-Tamayo, Wuebben, and Sanchez-Acedo argue that Extended Reality (XR) has great possibilities for the development and dissemination of multimedia content. One of the areas where XR can have a significant impact is in the field of journalism within information and communication sciences. In the chapter, they determine the features of current XR media, including virtual reality and augmented reality and their application in the teaching of journalism. The review shows that XR technology can serve to capture reality, simulate it, and recreate fictional scenarios. From 360° video to volumetric video, from artificial intelligence to deep learning, XR is reshaping how rigorous communication research is conducted and how scientific results are crafted for public audiences. Therefore, from the analysis of these available technologies and their potential evolution, the chapter establishes the key features of a learning laboratory for immersive journalism. The chapter concludes by showing how XR can open new space for journalism teaching and research.

In Chapter 2, "Virtual Reality for Teacher Training: An Experiential Approach to Classroom Conflict Management", Cárdenas, Alvarez, Manero, Romero-Hernández, discuss the use of Virtual Reality (VR) in the training of Preservice Secondary Education teachers in Spain as an integral part of their learning process. The authors propose some premises from which to design a training program to improve preservice teachers' communicative competence and their ability to manage conflict impacting the classroom climate. First, the chapter explains the experiential and experimental potential of a Virtual Learning Environment (VLE), its ability to create personalized virtual worlds, as well as the possibility to generate insightful instant feedback and feedforward. Finally, an example of a prototype scenario designed on this conceptual basis is provided. Furthermore, the chapter presents an overview of an educational proposal to implement this experiential immersive opportunity for preservice teachers to interact and manage disruptive situations in a safe and reliable environment conducive to the development of key communicative competences and strategies to turn conflict into a learning opportunity.

In Chapter 3, "Bringing the Metaverse to Higher Education: Engaging University Students in Virtual Worlds", Burnett, Harvey, and Kay provide a case study on the use of a virtual world as the predominant mechanism for interacting with university students. In Autumn semester 2020, 49 engineering students partook in weekly seminars with teachers and each other on a fantastical virtual teaching island, known as Nottopia. The majority of students accessed the virtual world on desktop computers, although four routinely used their own VR headsets. Survey data indicated that the student experience was extremely positive and motivation to learn was very high. Interviews, together with video observations, established that five themes dictated the positive outcome, namely: the design of the space; the nature of the integral content; the prevailing group dynamics; the role of avatars; and the magical interactions possible. These themes are realised in an initial design framework.

In Chapter 4, "An Immersive Virtual Reality Training Environment for CBRN Procedures", De Lorenzis, Pratticò, Cultrera, Migliorini, and Lamberti stated that first responders are exposed to numerous hazards and must be well prepared to act under dangerous conditions. This is especially true for operators working in the domain of CBRN (Chemical, Biological, Radiological, Nuclear), who need high-quality training to avoid fatal errors and ensure the success of operations. However,

CBRN practice sessions can reproduce only approximated, low-fidelity versions of real scenarios, whereas highly detailed simulations should be preferred. To address this issue, they developed a prototype of an immersive Virtual Reality (VR) training platform in cooperation with CBRN experts from the Italian Air Force. The devised platform is an improved version of an existing tool and offers a digital training ground where operators can learn CBRN procedures and test their abilities in a realistic virtual environment without facing the risks normally associated with real hazardous scenarios.

In Chapter 5, "Toward Evacuation Training in Metaverse: Transforming Normal Time Into Emergency Time", Mitsuhara, and Shishibori claim that traditional evacuation training is ineffective as it does not simulate decision making against tough disaster situations. Therefore, evacuation training should be significantly enhanced to offer realistic simulated evacuation experiences, entailing decision making. A promising approach to the enhancement is to introduce Virtual Reality (VR) into evacuation training, and there have been numerous VR-based evacuation training systems. The authors launched the project Evacuation Training in Metaverse (ETM) considering the recent surge of interest in the Metaverse as a VR extension. The ETM system is being developed based on the design principle: gathering numerous participants, pursuing high fidelity, and simulating a sudden earthquake. The ETM system transforms normal time to emergency time by creating a sudden earthquake, allowing participants to experience simulated earthquake evacuation in a high-fidelity virtual world developed from an open-city model, photogrammetry, etc. The participants make decisions in the virtual world while being influenced by numerous others.

In Chapter 6, "Case Experiences With Immigrants on Workforce Training Using Virtual Reality", Kauppinen, and Drake assert that due to the rapid changes in the labour market, people need to constantly reshape their competencies, resulting in a tremendous need to reskill the workforce. Vocational training has traditionally been the task of educational institutions; however, today some companies also perform their own training. Overall success in establishing an individual's career depends on successful entry into the workforce, and, in case of immigrants, entering the workforce is even more demanding. The key question is how educational institutions and companies can cooperate in this area. Immersive environments like Virtual Reality (VR) offer one type of solution. They are increasingly being used in workforce training and changing landscapes in educational institutions and companies. Using case examples, the chapter illustrates how several companies have jointly developed vocational materials with educational institutions and immigrants. The experiences are discussed, and examples of VR training tasks implemented and connecting them to relevant competencies are presented.

In Chapter 7, "Coordinated Control of a Collaborative 6R Robotic Arm With a Virtual Twin and Augmented Reality for Engineering Education", Islas, Orta, and Martell-Chavez describe the direct and inverse kinematics mathematical framework, the development procedure and data communications interface for the implementation of an Augmented Reality (AR) version of a six degrees of freedom (6-DOF) cobot (collaborative robot) under the Unity platform. The kinematic equations for the inverse kinematic control of the Techman® cobot are presented. The procedure to achieve communication between the virtual robot and the physical robot is described, this is, the communication link from the TM5-900 robot with the application in Unity. A safe environment was created to manipulate the collaborative robot and to avoid collisions to validate the applicability of the AR functionality. The virtual twin with its enhanced visualization based on AR can also run-on mobile devices either locally or remotely accessed. The developed platform has diverse potential applications and is particularly suitable for engineering education and training in robotics.

In Chapter 8, "Teaching Spatial Geometry Through 3D Visualization and Augmented Reality", Iwano, Pereira, and Scherer target Geometry, a branch of Mathematics that helps us to work with distances, volumes, and areas of the real world. But Spatial Geometry presents an unusual obstacle: How to understand the elements of a three-dimensional object whether they are normally presented in a two-dimensional form? The study was conducted with two classes in the 2nd year of high school in a public school. Class1 with traditional resources: textbook, blackboard, and chalk. In the Class2, was used Augmented Reality (FLARAS) and 3D visualization (Sketchup), and textbook. It was expected that, with the help of Augmented Reality, the students of Class2 would perform better than Class1. A better understanding of the content was achieved, as they would have better visualization of spatial objects. Consequently, better performance was achieved in the exercises and problem questions presented.

In Chapter 9, "Virtualization of Laboratories: Student and Professor Opinions", Vergara, Fernández-Arias, Extremera, and Antón-Sancho stated that the use of Virtual Reality (VR) in the educational sector has increased considerably in the last decade, especially for its direct application in the development of virtual laboratories (VL) that, since the appearance of COVID-19, are being more demanded by universities. Therefore, knowing the opinion of students and professors about VR is essential for VR-based applications to be designed in an appropriate way and to be efficient at an educational level. In this sense, the results of this study, which analyzes the opinion of 420 engineering students and 44 engineering professors, can help future professors or software programmers, in general to design VR-based educational resources in an appropriate way, and to better design their VLs.

In Chapter 10, "The Importance of Social Competence for 21st Century Citizens: The Use of Mixed Reality for Social Competence Learning in Mainstream

Education", Wang, Quirke, and McGuckin present the results of a systematic review that investigated the use of mixed reality (MR) technology to assist social competence learning in mainstream education. Social competence represents our ability to interact with others and, therefore, is a key determinant for many of the possibilities that are presented to us across the lifespan. In today's digital world, MR technology has been widely used in special and inclusive education for social competence training purposes but has not yet been generally applied to mainstream education. This systematic review bridges this research gap. Findings support (i) the potential for MR technology as a medium for social competence learning activities, and (ii) how the MR approach can contribute to a Universally Designed (UD) learning environment.

In Chapter 11, "The New Trends and Applications in E-Learning Environments and E-Technologies", Alfaro, Rivera, Luna-Urquizo, Elisa, Zuñiga-Cueva, and Urquizo-Abril consider the importance of the available e-Technologies to support teaching and learning in e-Learning systems as increasingly evident to educators and system developers. The chapter reviews some of the e-Technologies and e-Learning systems that are used to support the individual requirements of teachers, allowing them to provide the best opportunities to students, considering that in the current situation, in which educational systems have new immediate claims, derived in part from the COVID-19 pandemic, motivated face-to-face educational practices to give way to remote activities mediated by technological resources. The new contemporary trends in e-Learning and e-Technologies development and applications utilize a wide range of available technologies, which are framed in Web and Virtual Reality environments among other emerging technologies; therefore, the decision to use a particular technology must be based on solid research and evidence. The chapter reviews many of these e-Technologies and provides information on their use, opportunities and trends in development and applications.

We hope you find the chapters in this edited book both interesting and useful.

Anacleto Correia
Naval Academy, Portugal

Vitor Viegas
Naval Academy, Portugal

Chapter 1
XR Journalism Lab:
An Innovative Space for Research and Training in Immersive Journalism

Manuel Gertrudix
University Rey Juan Carlos, Spain

José Luis Rubio-Tamayo
University Rey Juan Carlos, Spain

Daniel Wuebben
University Rey Juan Carlos, Spain

Alberto Sanchez-Acedo
University Rey Juan Carlos, Spain

ABSTRACT

Extended reality (XR) has great possibilities for the development and dissemination of multimedia content. One of the areas where extended reality can have a significant impact is in the field of journalism within information and communication sciences. In this chapter, the authors determine the features of current XR media, including virtual reality and augmented reality and their application in the teaching of journalism. This review shows that XR technology can serve to capture reality, simulate it, and recreate fictional scenarios. From 360° video to volumetric video, from artificial intelligence to deep learning, the extended reality is reshaping how rigorous communication research is conducted and how scientific results are crafted for public audiences. Therefore, from the analysis of these available technologies and their potential evolution, this chapter establishes the key features of a learning laboratory for immersive journalism. The authors conclude by showing how XR can open new space for journalism teaching and research.

DOI: 10.4018/978-1-6684-3398-0.ch001

INTRODUCTION

In recent years, extended reality (XR) technologies and media have revolutionized the design and dissemination of interactive and immersive content for journalism and for education. This chapter reviews some of these new developments and then proposes a novel curriculum for training journalists and communication professionals in the creation of transmedia stories, immersive experiences, and interactive storytelling using XR tools (Bösch et al., 2018). The proposed actions will be carried out at the new XR Journalism Lab, which will support the master's degree program in Journalistic Investigation, New Narratives, Data, Fact-checking and Transparency offered by the University of Rey Juan Carlos (Spain) in collaboration with the Maldita.es, a non-profit foundation fighting against misinformation. The lab will support creative content development and experimental training from analytical perspectives. It will also promote professional transformation, critical analysis of professional practices, and the use of XR to facilitate the transfer of new knowledge. Together, scholars and students will design and test new audio-visual and multimedia products for investigative and data journalism based on XR environments (virtual, augmented, and mixed).

The methodological proposal includes a comprehensive process for applying the principles of educational action research (Lewin, 1946; Adelman, 1993) and active learning models (Goyette and Lessard, 1988) to XR. It is, in short, a process of learning by experimenting with formats drawn from XR technologies, applying them to research projects, and evaluating their application in real professional contexts. The rest of this chapter proposes the complete didactic process, beginning with an overview of the basic principles of XR in recent journalism practice followed by a review of current techniques and technologies often used. We then describe the challenges and opportunities for using XR to disseminate scientific findings. Our proposal for the XR Lab includes a table that describes and analyses the different genres of XR journalism. In our conclusion, we review the interventions and propose further lines of research.

Background and General Principles of XR

To contextualize our methodological proposal, we begin with a review of XR features based on what has been recently deployed in the field of journalism. This review helps to establish a state of the art for XR which can then be developed in the educational context.

Many recent XR laboratories are specialized in journalism innovation such as Google News Lab, the Brown Institute for Media Innovation, the Online News Association, the Knight Foundation, and the JoVRnalism Project. Each of these institutions explore the possibilities for XR combined with other technologies such as edge computing and artificial intelligence. The latest Reuters Institute report highlights the outstanding potential of immersive technologies such as virtual reality (VR) and augmented reality (AR) and forecasts that these technologies, in combination with other developments such as 5G, will have significant impact on communication platforms in the coming years (Newman, 2021). Immersive audio-visual, focused on journalism, has generated rapid interest from different media of international scope such as the BBC, the New York Times or The Guardian, or national media such as RTVE (Sora, 2017, p.6). In the following example from the New York Times, 3D photogrammetry is used to reconstruct one of New York's neighborhoods. The following link shows the final immersive product: [https://bit.ly/nyt-3d]. In the case of RTVE, a 360º video is shown in which you can see the different cities of Spain empty due to Covid-19: [https://bit.ly/rtve-3d].

For our purposes, the various features presented by XR technologies might be consolidated into three key characteristics: immersion, narrative flexibility, and active selection or curation of information:

- **First**: XR offers the opportunities for immersion. Immersion journalism has been defined as the use of technologies such as "360-degree video, virtual reality, augmented reality, cinematic reality, and mixed reality in journalistic storytelling" (Uskali, et al., 2021, 2). XR technologies allow users to experience in the first person (De la Peña et al., 2010, 291) and enhance the feeling of "being there" and experiencing a situation firsthand (Maschio 2017). These opportunities for immersion reveal a powerful way to connect with diverse audiences, as pointed out by Alex Wallace, GM of News, Entertainment and Studios at Verizon Media (Carron, 2019). However, according to Nonny de la Peña (Parker, 2015) more immersive formats are a necessity to attract young audiences. Immersive technologies still require experimental models for its full implementation and adaptation by both the media and users (Tejedor-Calvo et al., 2020, 10). There is also a need to understand the potential impacts of such immersive technologies, it is also necessary to study XR alongside other aspects like the psychological impact of its narratives (Benítez et al., 2019) and analyze the features of this technology (Rubio-Tamayo, 2019).
- **Second**: XR technologies offer powerful digital tools to register the physical world, as well as create and generate fictional worlds and scenarios (Kaputsos, 2020). Through XR, audiences can remain passive recipients or to choose more active roles through selecting certain viewpoints within the virtual environment and which particular voices, sounds, or backgrounds will be displayed (Marconi & Nakagawa, 2017). As communicators and journalists specializing in education and science communication, we see XR as a useful

tool for building narratives that convey complex concepts and recreating situations and landscapes.

- **Thirdly**: For journalists, XR opens the possibilities to combine techniques, procedures, and approaches to the representation of information (Kangasniemi, 2021). In recent decades, new technologies have brought both quantitative and qualitative advances in the field of communication. In this context, both extended reality technologies and other information and communication technologies have offered notable advances in the representation of information, as well as in the way in which users interact with information through different devices. Transformations in the way information is communicated and transmitted are carried out through an evolutionary process and the implementation of continuous and often exponential updates and improvements, in which it is necessary to train new journalists from universities.

Virtual reality, which is among the most representative of the technologies that make up XR, has also become a medium with its own particularities and features, both in terms of narrative and representation. A detailed study of the educational and narrative context in which this methodological proposal will be carried out implies knowing the state of the art of the technology itself, the medium, its scale of representation and of the degree of implementation in specific products or solutions for specific purposes on the market. The challenges of teaching immersive journalism (Uskali & Ikonen, 2021).

While helpful to establish these three general principles of XR based on recent developments, these principles must remain flexible as they are constantly under pressure. On the one side, online information and content increases continuously at an exponential rate. The stream of new data content seems to never cease. On the other, new virtual environments, such as the metaverse and augmented reality, are changing where and how publics engage with information. Therefore, XR has an increasingly relevant role in the development and curation of data as well as the dissemination of scientific information.

CURRENT DISCOURSE AND EMERGING TECHNOLOGIES

Numerous studies have been carried out in recent years on experimentation with new products, formats and narratives based on the use of immersive systems, with diverse applications in communication and journalism. While many address a conceptual framework for the use of immersive technologies in the field of journalistic communication, others adjust to contemporaneous technological improvements and optimizations.

Theories and User Perceptions

While not using the title XR, the scholarly discussions of virtual reality (VR) could be said to have begun in the 1990s, with Biocca's analysis of VR as a potential means of communication (1992) and Chesher's (1994) argument for VR as tool for discourse development. These studies established the expressive potential virtual reality to adjust narrative and interaction. They paved the way for further considerations of how contemporaneous technologies shape the public's reception of journalistic content. For example, de la Peña et al. (2010) examined Head-Mounted Displays (or virtual reality helmets) would place special emphasis on the experience from the point of view of the first person. Similarly, Vázquez Herrero and López García (2017) describe the way in which virtual reality is producing a change in the consumption of news by users.

Shin and Biocca (2018), meanwhile, focus on aspects related to the way in which users interact with immersive stories, considering the integration of areas of knowledge such as user experience, establishing factors such as behavioural, affective, and cognitive factors as primary determinants of the experience. Baía-Reis and Coelho (2018) also explore this dimension, trying to define a framework in which the main concepts, possible use cases, limits, or opportunities of immersive journalism are addressed. One controlled study suggested that, compared to 2D videos, immersive videos of awe-inspiring events: "increased the sense of engagement, the sense of physical space, and the perception of vastness, each of which increased self-reported awe" (Chirico et al. 2017, p. 5). The potential for 360° to thrill viewers and audiences is further supported by research by van Damme et al. (2019), who find that interactive 360° journalism, including interactive videos that can be viewed on a laptop, increases the viewers' sense of presence and leads to higher levels of enjoyment. While Nielsen and Sheets (2021) also study of user perception in a virtual reality medium, Paíno-Ambrosio and Rodríguez-Fidalgo (2021) propose the development of a new communicative model because of the emergence of experiences in the context of immersive journalism and that can be applied to different genres such as the documentary (Paíno-Ambrosio & Rodríguez-Fidalgo, 2020).

Technologies and Edited Environments

As XR technologies are constantly evolving and changing, there are two main focuses, also, of those technologies, that may be relevant in the area of XR journalism. One of them is the 360 video, which is a useful tool for film and has been approached by authors such as Sundar et al. (2017), Mabrook & Singer (2019), Bujic & Jamari (2020) and Lopezosa et al. (2021). 360 cameras, which enable, on the one hand, a wider view of the event and, on the other, a greater degree of proximity of the spectator to the event itself - increasing this degree of reality. And, of course, video 360 is also a relevant tool for dissemination of information, as well as news and journalistic content, and this should be taken into count (Sánchez-Acedo & Gertrudix, 2020).

Another important technological development in recent years has been the use of volumetric video. By surrounding a subject with small cameras to record from multiple angles, a three-dimensional simulation space can be created. The result is a certain degree of realism, and the use of volumetric video is a constant in the field of XR journalism research, as reflected in studies such as Huang et al. (2018), Schwarz et al. (2018), Schreer et al. (2019), Zerman et al. (2020), Han et al. (2020), and Zhang et al. (2021), and Moynihan et al. (2021).

Although volumetric video technology is not as developed and it is necessary to find the increase in the degree of reality in the news, as well as the need to further develop this technology for the genre of the news itself. Thus, the complexity of capturing volumetric video means that this type of technology is currently only possible in studios, laboratories, or film sets. However, the very concept of the development of an extended reality laboratory in the field of communication is one of the elements that makes it possible to contextualize the uses and applications of this type of technology.

Yet XR extends beyond 360 and volumetric video technologies. Pavlik (2020) explains how extended reality is accompanied using other devices—such as drones—which allow us to film and record the world and reality from different angles, increasing the approximation to reality. Pavlik (2020) also uses drone technology as another dimension in which content can be viewed (thus adding aerial vision). Each of these new and cutting-edge media technologies engender optimism and it appears we are on the cusp of a "new information frontier" (Toursel & Useille, 2019). However, scholars continue to call for the development of a consistent narrative grammar for XR (Stubbs, 2018; Laws, 2019). In short, there is a further need for clarification and best practices.

CHALLENGES AND OPPORTUNITIES FOR TRAINING IN IMMERSIVE JOURNALISM

As we have discussed, the training of future journalists requires innovation in teaching methodologies, technologies, and environments. The challenges of immersive journalism are not necessarily distinct from those faced by other communication disciplines, whether science of humanities, non-fiction or fiction. Communication technologies are evolving quickly, which implicitly entails new ways of accessing, manipulating, recording, and representing information. For our purposes, it's important to recognize that a journalism curriculum based on XR technologies forces us to conceptualise our relationship to information. How do we confirm that information accessible and accurate in environments as vast, fluctuating, and contested as XR? In what follows we present the challenges XR technologies pose and some of the opportunities for increasingly the transparency and fidelity of journalistic practice.

The state of technology and the level of interaction and immersion seems to determine the way in which information is recorded, processed, and represented. In this sense, one of the core principles of journalism is developing a maximum degree of correspondence between observed facts and phenomena and the resulting reportage or content. Therefore, to address the issue of disinformation and fake news, the XR Lab also proposes incorporating the traceability of information as a key variable of the journalistic practice. This variable is one of the features that will also make it possible for the format of the content to be adjusted, bearing in mind that each advance in the means of recording (in this case, 360 cameras, drones, volumetric video, etc.) has the possibility of increasing the degree of fidelity of the recording itself and creating a great correspondence between the media content and the observed facts.

One of these aspects to be considered, moreover, in the shaping of the laboratory, is the application of rigorous standards for information literacy. This process goes beyond mere fact-checking. It is an overall process of information gathering and verification based on explicit and declared methodologies that would allow their replication. It is also, in the context of increasingly advanced technologies, the challenge of recording reality with a greater degree of precision and fidelity. Before such a recording can take place, the journalist should practice systematic observation, measurement, and experimentation like the scientific method carried out by our colleagues in other kinds of laboratories.

Being also an account of concrete events in each context (in many cases mainly related to social issues), journalism must meticulously analyze the procedure of drawing general conclusions about a given event, always considering the existing support from scientific disciplines and areas of knowledge, which are constantly evolving. But journalism can, and one of its functions is, to record a specific event or a series of events within the same context, with the information recording tools available. On the other hand, the set of events and their potential repercussions for society and its evolution can also be approached through other disciplines, such as history, geopolitics, sociology, etc., to deepen the knowledge of the context in which the events take place. Journalism, in fact, just as it has to apply the scientific method in its ways of recording events, has to collaborate closely with the scientific disciplines related to the area in which the event takes place. Journalism must therefore be a science, working closely with other disciplines of science, and guaranteeing, within this application of the scientific method, freedom of the press, freedom of expression, the right to information, but also the right to privacy, honour, and the dignity of individuals, among many other issues in which journalistic ethics (Kool, 2016) and scientific ethics must contribute to continue developing frameworks for improving practices (journalistic, communicative, scientific).

What does this have to do with immersive journalism and extended reality? Precisely because of the multidimensional nature of extended reality, we find ourselves in a context in which these procedural models of recording, organizing and representing information need to be structured and perfected, trying, in addition to improving the experience, to establish a dividing line between the phenomena that are represented in the extended space, which corresponds to the recording of real events, on the one hand, from simulation (or reconstruction, as there is no direct recording in many cases) and fiction (essential to distinguish these phenomena from reality, but also to create content that is used for purposes such as entertainment, and in which the user is fully aware of this fictionalisation of -potentially real- events). Narrative fiction, although a powerful tool for generating content (also in reality widespread) is not, as journalistic practices clearly state, an element to be articulated in this field. However, the study of the fictional narrative itself within the journalistic field will help in the understanding of the narrative in the account of real and verifiable phenomena, since knowledge of the nature of fiction also helps in the understanding of the mechanisms of generation and dissemination of information, including the processes of information verification. In other words, knowledge of the nature of fictional narrative is precisely what is needed to ensure that fiction is not an element that is part of the realm of journalism.

PROPOSAL FOR AN IMMERSIVE JOURNALISM INNOVATION LABORATORY

The University of Rey Juan Carlos University (Spain) has been a pioneer in the development of undergraduate and postgraduate training in investigative journalism and data journalism. In 2012, they offered the first postgraduate specialization in this field, and in 2021 they begin a new master's degree in Journalistic Investigation, New Narratives, Data, Fact-checking, and Transparency.

The university has also contributed to innovative journalism research, including two major international projects related to media literacy and information literacy. For example, the CRESCEnt project (2018-2021) was a cross-sector initiative that created and analyzed "strategic communication concerning security, prevention, and counteraction of criminal acts" (CRESCEnt Project, 2021). The project results included a Massive Open Online Course, titled, "Strategic Communication to Counter Security Threats," in which participants gained a practical understanding of how to identify and counteract fake news. A separate project, DOMINOES (Digital cOMpetences INformatiOn EcoSystem) further reinforces the need for digital resilience in this new media ecosystem. Therefore, with a history of innovation in the field of journalism, active international research projects, and a group of scholars who analyze and create immersive communication products, the URJC is well suited to creating spaces where innovative journalism formats and narrative models can be developed, investigated, and disseminated to diverse groups of stakeholders.

The idea of using extended reality for training it's not new and has been approached since decades ago. In fact, one of the first applications for virtual reality was simulation (Psotka, 1995), and one of the main research lines of the technology has been, from their origins and, especially, in the last decades from the 90s, their simulative power for applications in education (Andolsek, 1995). The idea of a XR Lab is nowadays extended to the main domains of education, as their simulative power and the interaction with the information has dramatically evolved. Those approaches have been focused by many authors, by depicting the features that a lab based on extended reality technologies must integrate (Hurkmans & Rajagopal, 2020, Palmas & Klinker, 2020, Alnagrat et al., 2021, Zwoliński et al. 2022).

The following establishes the principles for the implementation of an XR Journalism Laboratory which will apply creative methodologies to immersive journalistic formats and narratives. The proposed genres or prototypes can be then transferred to the postgraduate classroom, where journalism students will use these heuristics to generate journalistic stories that will eventually be shaped into master's thesis projects. Eventually, the XR Journalism lab will help host and publish these projects, which will then serve as resources for new applications by readers can be evaluated. Finally, this will allow a joint evaluation of the creative and technical team of the laboratory with journalism students and media professionals to analyze the results and incorporate improvements in successive prototypes.

As outlined in the previous section, advanced recording devices and new media platforms make it possible today to generate, share, and access precise and critical information. However, this information is susceptible, and the reality it helps construct, to be manipulated. The study of verification processes implies a study of the layers of information implied by the extended reality content and the means of dissemination in which this complex structure of information is articulated. In short, verification processes must take place at all levels.

We are also faced with the very structure offered by journalistic genres, and how the format related to the structure of these genres should be approached within the complexity of the extended reality medium. The holistic approach of this chapter tries to establish this by exploring the processes of journalistic content production.

Figure 1. Experimentation process of data representation in a virtual reality environment generated with Babia XR. Source: González-Barahona, Villaverde, Lumbreras, Rubio-Tamayo, Romero-Luis, Carbonell-Alcocer, Sánchez-Acedo, Gertrudix (2022).
Data source: Open Data Euskadi (2022).

Thus, for example, starting from the most direct genre of information with the narration of facts, which corresponds to the news, this can only be produced from direct recording methods, which can be visual or auditory. As has been outlined in the previous sections, immersive technologies within the field of extended reality make it possible to increase this level of recording.

As for the other journalistic genres, two of them are directly derived from the news genre, namely the chronicle and the report. The chronicle incorporates interpretative elements, which may be related to the atmosphere or the narrator's point of view. To complete an effective chronicle, it is necessary to analyze the applied ecosystem of extended reality. The same applies to reportage, where events are structured through a narrative in time to understand the overall context of a phenomenon. From the recorded fragments, which are the news, as narrative units, a context is generated as a story that enables a more holistic understanding of the phenomenon. The proposed XR Journalism Lab can contribute to establishing, as far as possible, the parameters by which the narratives operate to tell the story of the events and to communicate them to the viewer or user. For example, exploring the possibilities of generating new ways of representing and visualizing data in immersive environments (see Figure 1).

The Table 1 shows how the different journalistic genres will be approached and some of the contexts in which extended reality technologies are dramatically evolving.

Table 1. List of journalistic genres and means of expression in extended reality. To approach journalism education in a laboratory, each journalistic genre must be analyzed according to its idiosyncrasies and try to develop structures adaptive to the new medium of extended reality.

Genre	Application Contexts
News	· Recording methods must be as accurate as possible. · Content must be produced in situ, with a direct source of information. · XR: The incorporation of volumetric video and 360° cameras should be as accurate as possible. · 360° cameras: Recording on site and as the event unfolds. No supplementary audio elements, such as music, can be added, although a narration can be included to narrate the events, as a form of augmented information. · Volumetric video: With current technology, volumetric video recording systems only allow for studio or on-set recording, so it would not be a useful component for recording most news stories. · XR broadcasting: Broadcasting with XR technologies (virtual reality, augmented reality) needs to have a transparent recording process and to be verifiable at different levels of reporting. Augmented information can be included, but it must be equally traceable and verifiable.
Chronicle	· The news sources providing the source content for the chronicle must be traceable and verifiable. · As it is a first-person account, the narrative must be structured to convey that view or position (first-person experience) to the user or viewer. In this case, the 360° video helps to reinforce this phenomenon. · XR: The complexity of the narrative can be structured with extended reality technologies and narrative techniques adapted to the medium. · 360° cameras: While this is primarily a means of recording the news, the results of a chronicle can also be disseminated through 360 videos. It is essential not to confuse 360° cameras as a means of recording (news) and the 360-video format as a means of dissemination (chronicles and storytelling with video content viewed through a device such as an HMD). It is important to structure models to generate narratives based on 360° video formats. · Volumetric video: It can serve as a tool for the author of the chronicle (narrated in the first person) to film him/herself with this technology, recounting the events that took place. The requirements of first being present at the scene of the events and narrating them in the first person must be met, always with an informative basis for the news item. This technology and this format make it possible for the narrator/journalist to articulate events as a participant in the story and as a narrator to the viewer.
Reporting	· The principles of reportage are based on the creation of a contextual story from a succession of news stories. · The basis of reportage is the news, and the gathering of the information that makes up the news must be, as for all news, a verifiable process. · A story is added to the set of facts (news), which is made up of the set of recorded facts. · XR: The digital media in which the report is represented, as in the case of extended reality, are the repository of this set of facts that are structured in a narrative adapted to the medium (XR). Its basis must be the facts (the news), although it can have a specific context and setting. The adaptation of this format to extended reality can include other phenomena, such as augmented information, increasing the degree of data shown to the user. All the addition of layers of information must be aimed at increasing the level of correspondence with the real facts, trying to design strategies of information verification at all levels (micro and macro). · 360° cameras: As in the previous one, it serves as a means of recording events (in the form of news). The visualization in this format can be immersive or not. · Volumetric video: As in the previous case, the journalist has the possibility of using this tool to present and narrate the events, in an analogy with a simile related to the filming of the summary of the story in a context external to the events, such as a set (artificiality of the narrative scenario). It would be, for example, a simile to when the presenter of a program goes on set to present the report, except using this technology. In the case of being on the scene, it can be used to contextualize, although the technology, as mentioned above, is not as developed outside the set.
Interview	· In this case, a series of questions are asked to an interlocutor. · XR: The extended reality format allows for multiple possible scenarios for an interview, and different layers of information. The linearity of the narrative - sequence of questions and answers - makes the construction of the medium relatively simple and raises the need for the use of media within this category of media (XR). · 360° cameras: Its use can serve to "contextualize" the interview in a given environment. To choose a scenario, or a series of scenarios, related to the subject matter or content of the interview. The possibilities of 360 video make it possible to use different approaches and to add environmental elements related to the context while making sure that they do not distract from the main purpose. · Volumetric video: It may be of interest to film interviews in volumetric video, as this increases the degree of realism and empathy of the user with the interviewee, without affecting the content of the interview. Depending on the interviewee's area of specialization (culture, science, politics), it may be possible to include the interviewee, in 3D, in a specific setting (museum, laboratory, etc.), which can also, unlike 360 videos, be interactive.
Data Journalism / Infographics	· Data journalism and infographic journalism involve the collection of data and its representation for the user's understanding. The modes of data representation, in the form of graphs, maps, etc., must be analyzed to optimize data representation. · XR: The development of a journalistic laboratory in the extended reality environment is a quantitative step in the representation of data to users. The process of representing information at this level of abstraction (data, information) differs from the representation on 2D screens. An immersive journalism lab should study these differences, incorporating factors related to user experience in the field of virtual reality, and interaction design. The level of representation and its possibilities acquire, in the context of extended reality, an exponential increase in narrative possibilities, but also an added difficulty in a scenario where there is a long way to go in terms of development. · 360° cameras: The recording process with 360° cameras can be used to create scenarios that can set the context of the data at an immersive level. It is recommended that the scenario has a narrative or conceptual relationship with the data (for example, if we are talking about science, a laboratory). However, it is not essential, although the narratives structured in the setting must be aimed at the highest possible degree of understanding by the user of the information contained in the data. · Volumetric video: Volumetric video can be used not only to generate avatars to explain, for example, the data (or its context) in the immersive environment but also to create representational elements of the data itself. It can be combined with objects created in 3D with programs such as Blender

continued on following page

Table 1. Continued

Genre	Application Contexts
Simulation and Reconstruction of Events	· Simulation occurs when we do not have direct recorded information about a specific event that we want to recreate. · It is important to have verification of the information represented and to contrast this information, trying to obtain as much information as possible, that cannot be obtained by direct means, by indirect means. · There is a level of conceptualization and abstraction that is unavoidable because it has not been possible to record the event by direct recording means, such as photographs, video, or sound recording. This level of conceptualization must be determined in the representation, indicating the impossibility of obtaining the information by direct means of recording. · It is related to facts and events, not conceptual information (data), which needs to be represented for a given reason. · XR: Extended reality technologies represent a qualitative and quantitative leap in terms of representation. These technologies add the variables of potential interaction with the content, on the one hand, and potential immersion in the medium, on the other, increasing the level of potential realism of the events represented. However, in such a context, they have to be subordinated to the representation, with the highest possible degree of information about the event, of the information. Immersive journalism and extended reality laboratories must consider this series of factors, as well as that of abstraction and fictitious representation. · 360° cameras: In the absence of direct means of recording (cameras, sound, etc.), the method of reconstruction and simulation is used. However, the 360-video medium can be used to represent reconstructed events, using digital technologies and motion graphics, and trying to explain the conceptualized elements and those for which they exist in a certain degree of abstraction. Immersive and extended reality journalism labs need to investigate these models of representation. · Volumetric video: In this case, it can serve for the recreation of an event, as previously explained, with filmed three-dimensional avatars. In fact, in this case, a high level of precision of the concept (not of the event itself) can be obtained. This level of precision of the concept would be of interest to explain certain generic phenomena that cannot yet be recorded by direct means, even less with volumetric video technology, but a lot of information is available indirectly. The most specific case, for example, would be the reconstruction of homicide, an event that, in many cases, cannot be recorded directly, but for which, due to advances in forensic science and the seriousness of the event, a lot of information exists. On the other hand, one of the most important factors is the victim's right to privacy and dignity, which can never be shown directly. And an immersive journalism laboratory must always prioritize these factors of the integrity of those affected and develop work methodologies that go in that direction. On the other hand, it is vitally important, in this field of simulation/reconstruction, to differentiate the event from the concept of the fact.

Source: the authors.

On the other hand, it is of vital importance to establish the parameters that a journalistic laboratory must analyze to design activities aimed at informing society with the highest possible degree of transparency, based on the verification of information and the highest degree of potential registration. That said, the right to information is one of the fundamental rights in democratic societies, although the right to honor, privacy, and dignity of people, especially those who have been victims of a tragic event, must always be considered. But protection must be extended to broader society.

Extended reality technologies draw a new framework in which many disciplines, related to communication sciences are dramatically changing. Nowadays, we only may draw and standardize models based on how we think this technology is going to change how we interact with information. Nevertheless, new applications and needs are also emerging in this framework, and extended reality is a very useful tool (and we need to analyze in which ways) to access the real world and know more about it, in one way, and to better communicate and show it to the people, disseminating knowledge. Communication sciences, arts, engineering, science, design, etc., must collaborate in this process of improving the ways to access knowledge and represent and disseminate it.

FUTURE RESEARCH DIRECTIONS

This chapter lays the foundations for the study and development of methodological strategies in the field of journalism in a context of XR technologies and practices. XR is a medium with a high degree of complexity, almost unlimited possibilities of representation, and, as has been explained, it is important to propose specific cases that adapt to the way audiences interact with reality and information gathering.

The methodological proposals do not differ, to a large extent, from those that have already been established for the analysis and development of content based on the medium of extended reality, which includes virtual reality and augmented reality. However, in this case, we seek a process of adaptation to the lines of work of the journalistic profession, considering these factors related to the right to information, as well as the right to privacy, honor, and dignity.

CONCLUSION

The conclusions allow, in the first place, to offer a set of recommendations on the application of XR in the teaching of journalism, based on this case study applied to a master's degree in the University Rey Juan Carlos in Spain. Second, it allows us to have a taxonomy for educational experiences in journalism, focusing on the potential of their learning features such as the transmission of information, representation of abstract ideas such as data, reconstructing happened facts (with different levels of accuracy or abstraction), simulating actions in immersive environments or facilitate the empathy with information, by its potential to drawn experiences close to our concept of reality.

Extended reality technologies offer, therefore, a new scenario where these concepts must be applied, but in which we find ourselves with a higher level of layers of information and immersiveness, as well as potential sources of information that constitute the units of the story. This is why the study and analysis of all these factors, in a constantly evolving technological ecosystem, represent a challenge of analysis from the communication sciences, the design of training strategies for future journalists (and also for citizens as a whole), and from the technological approach and close work with disciplines related to information and communication technologies, which today represent an increase in immersiveness and interactivity and an unprecedented scenario in which numerous layers of information are superimposed.

The information era is a period of ever-increasing possibilities for recording and disseminating information, which is why there is a need to develop more and more methodologies and strategies that enable us to manage the knowledge generated by it, in a context in which extended reality technologies are projected as the main agent for accessing and distributing data, information, and knowledge.

ACKNOWLEDGMENT

This research was co-funded by Erasmus+ Programme of the European Union [grant number RO01-KA220-HED-000031158 - Digital cOMpetences INformatiOn EcoSystem Project]; the University Rey Juan Carlos (Spain) [grant number 2021/00008/023 – Research group Ciberimaginario]; and the European Commission [grant number 754382 - Daniel Wuebben has a Marie Curie fellowship under the H2020 Got Energy Talent MSCA-COFUND]. Teaching innovation has been applied by the Teaching Innovation Group in Communication, Digital Technologies and Open Education GID-COMTEDEA (URJC)

The European Commission's support for the production of this publication does not constitute an endorsement of the contents, which reflect the views only of the authors, and the Commission cannot be held responsible for any use which may be made of the information contained therein.

REFERENCES

Adelman, C. (1993). Kurt Lewin and the origins of action research. *Educational Action Research, 1*(1), 7–24. doi:10.1080/0965079930010102

Alnagrat, A. J. A., Ismail, R. C., & Idrus, S. Z. S. (2021, May). Extended Reality (XR) in Virtual Laboratories: A Review of Challenges and Future Training Directions. In *Journal of Physics: Conference Series* (Vol. 1874, No. 1, p. 012031). IOP Publishing.

Andolsek, D. L. (1995). Virtual reality in education and training. *International Journal of Instructional Media, 22*(2), 145–155. https://www.learntechlib.org/p/85408/

Baía Reis, A., & Coelho, A. F. V. C. C. (2018). Virtual Reality and Journalism: A gateway to conceptualizing immersive journalism. *Digital Journalism, 6*(8), 1090-1100.

Benítez de Gracia, M. J., Herrera Damas, S., & Benítez de Gracia, E. (2019). Analysis of the immersive social content feature in the Spanish news media. *Revista Latina de Comunicación Social, 74*, 1655-1679.

Biocca, F. (1992). Virtual reality technology: A tutorial. *Journal of Communication, 42*(4), 23–72. doi:10.1111/j.1460-2466.1992.tb00811.x

Bösch, M., Gensch, S., & Rath-Wiggins, L. (2018). Immersive Journalism: How Virtual Reality Impacts Investigative Storytelling. In Digital Investigative Journalism (pp. 103-111). Palgrave Macmillan.

Bujic, M., & Hamari, J. (2020, January). Satisfaction and willingness to consume immersive journalism: experiment of differences between VR, 360 video, and article. In *Proceedings of the 23rd International Conference on Academic Mindtrek* (pp. 120-125). Academic Press.

Carron, L. (2019, March 19). *Yahoo News announces innovative XR partner program and world's first XR aggregator for users*. Verizon News Center. https://vz.to/3vS5Md7

Chesher, C. (1994). Colonizing virtual reality: Construction of the discourse of virtual reality. *Cultronix*, *1*(1), 1–27.

Chirico, A., Cipresso, P., Yaden, D. B., Biassoni, F., Riva, G., & Gaggioli, A. (2017). Effectiveness of immersive videos in inducing awe: An experimental study. *Scientific Reports*, *7*(1), 1–11. doi:10.103841598-017-01242-0 PMID:28450730

CRESCEnt Project. (2021). *Mind the Gap in media coverage and strategic communication in case of security threats*. Erasmus+ 2018-1-RO01-KA202-049449. https://crescentproject.eu

De-la-Peña, N., Weil, P., Llobera, J., Giannopoulos, E., Pomés, A., Spaniang, B., Friedman, D., Sánchez-Vives, M. V., & Slater, M. (2010). Immersive journalism: Immersive virtual reality for the first-person experience of news. *Presence (Cambridge, Mass.)*, *19*(4), 291–301. doi:10.1162/PRES_a_00005

Goyette, G., & Lessard, H. M. (1988). *La investigación-acción. Funciones, fundamentos e instrumentación*. Alertes.

Han, B., Liu, Y., & Qian, F. (2020, April). ViVo: Visibility-aware mobile volumetric video streaming. In *Proceedings of the 26th Annual International Conference on Mobile Computing and Networking* (pp. 1-13). Academic Press.

Huang, Z., Li, T., Chen, W., Zhao, Y., Xing, J., LeGendre, C., & Li, H. (2018). Deep volumetric video from very sparse multi-view performance capture. In *Proceedings of the European Conference on Computer Vision* (pp. 336–354). ECCV. doi:10.1007/978-3-030-01270-0_21

Hurkmans, B., & Rajagopal, K. (2020). The use of extended reality technologies for learning in industry. *EdMedia+ Innovate Learning*, 900-903. https://www.learntechlib.org/p/217460/

Kangasniemi, J. (2021, August 3) *What we can learn from the best examples of immersive journalism.* Reuters Institute Research. https://bit.ly/3ybXD54

Kaputsos, S. (2020, March 25). *Hacking Reality.* MIT Media Lab. https://bit.ly/3kLclbj

Kool, H. (2016). The ethics of immersive journalism: A rhetorical analysis of news storytelling with virtual reality technology. *Intersect: The Stanford Journal of Science, Technology, and Society, 9*(3).

Laws, A. L. S. (2019). *Conceptualising immersive journalism.* Routledge.

Lewin, K. (1946). Action research and minority problems. *The Journal of Social Issues, 2*(4), 34–46. doi:10.1111/j.1540-4560.1946.tb02295.x

Lopezosa, C., Codina, L., Fernández-Planells, A., & Freixa, P. (2021). Journalistic innovation: How new formats of digital journalism are perceived in the academic literature. *Journalism*. Advance online publication. doi:10.1177/14648849211033434

Mabrook, R., & Singer, J. B. (2019). Virtual reality, 360 video, and journalism studies: Conceptual approaches to immersive technologies. *Journalism Studies, 20*(14), 2096–2112. doi:10.1080/1461670X.2019.1568203

Marconi, F., & Nakagawa, T. (2017). *Report: How virtual reality will impact journalism.* Associated Press. https://bit.ly/3s9NnGp

Maschio, T. (2017, July 28). *Storyliving: An Ethnographic Study of How Audiences Experience VR and What That Means for Journalists.* Retrieved December 12, 2017, from https://newslab.withgoogle.com/assets/docs/ storyliving-a-study-of-vr-in-journalism.pdf

Moynihan, M., Ruano, S., & Smolic, A. (2021). Autonomous tracking for volumetric video sequences. In *Proceedings of the IEEE/CVF Winter Conference on Applications of Computer Vision* (pp. 1660-1669). https://bit.ly/3ym431E

Newman, N. (2021). *Journalism, media, and technology trends and predictions 2021.* Reuters Institute. https://bit.ly/3FcwrV1

Nielsen, S. L., & Sheets, P. (2021). Virtual hype meets reality: Users' perception of immersive journalism. *Journalism, 22*(10), 2637–2653. doi:10.1177/1464884919869399

Paino Ambrosio, A., & Rodríguez Fidalgo, M. I. (2021). Proposal for a new communicative model in immersive journalism. *Journalism, 22*(10), 2600–2617. doi:10.1177/1464884919869710

Palmas, F., & Klinker, G. (2020, July). Defining Extended Reality Training: A Long-Term Definition for All Industries. In *2020 IEEE 20th International Conference on Advanced Learning Technologies (ICALT)* (pp. 322-324). IEEE.

Parker, J. (2015). 'You become a witness'—Nonny de la Peña's immersive journalism. *Ochre*. https://bit.ly/3FtmYZU

Pavlik, J. V. (2020). Drones, augmented reality and virtual reality journalism: Mapping their role in immersive news content. *Media and Communication*, *8*(3), 137–146. doi:10.17645/mac.v8i3.3031

Psotka, J. (1995). Immersive training systems: Virtual reality and education and training. *Instructional Science*, *23*(5), 405–431. doi:10.1007/BF00896880

Rodríguez-Fidalgo, M. I., & Paino-Ambrosio, A. (2020). Use of virtual reality and 360° video as narrative resources in the documentary genre: Towards a new immersive social documentary? *Catalan Journal of Communication & Cultural Studies*, *12*(2), 239-253.

Rubio-Tamayo, J. L. (2019). Realidad extendida, interactividad y entornos inmersivos 3d: Revisión de la literatura y proyecciones. *Actas Icono 14*, *1*(1), 396-415. https://bit.ly/3skNPSi

Sánchez-Acedo, A., & Gertrudix, M. (2020). Comunicar la ciencia con vídeos 360. In M. Gertrudix & M. Rajas (Eds.), *Comunicar la ciencia. Guía para una comunicación eficiente y responsable de la investigación e innovación científica*. Gedisa.

Schreer, O., Feldmann, I., Renault, S., Zepp, M., Worchel, M., Eisert, P., & Kauff, P. (2019, September). Capture and 3D video processing of volumetric video. In *2019 IEEE International conference on image processing (ICIP)* (pp. 4310-4314). IEEE. https://bit.ly/3LIf5SD

Schwarz, S., Hannuksela, M. M., Fakour-Sevom, V., & Sheikhi-Pour, N. (2018, June). 2D video coding of volumetric video data. In *2018 Picture Coding Symposium (PCS)* (pp. 61-65). IEEE.

Sora, C. (2017). Una inmersión en el audiovisual VR y 360. *Serie DigiDoc-EPI*, 1. https://bit.ly/3LV0S4R

Stubbs, B. (2018). Virtual reality journalism: Ethics, grammar and the state of play. *Australian Journalism Review*, *40*(1), 81–90. https://bit.ly/3P494Sh

Sundar, S. S., Kang, J., & Oprean, D. (2017). Being there in the midst of the story: How immersive journalism affects our perceptions and cognitions. *Cyberpsychology, Behavior, and Social Networking*, *20*(11), 672–682. doi:10.1089/cyber.2017.0271 PMID:29125787

Tejedor-Calvo, S., Romero-Rodríguez, L. M., Moncada-Moncada, A. J., & Alencar-Dornelles, M. (2020). Journalism that tells the future: Possibilities and journalistic scenarios for augmented reality. *El Profesional de la Información*, *29*(6), e290602. doi:10.3145/epi.2020.nov.02

Toursel, A., & Philippe, U. (2019). Immersive Journalism, a "New Frontier" of Information Experience? *Brazilian Journalism Research, 15*(2), 336-357.

URJC. (2022). *Master in Journalistic Investigation, New Narratives, Data, Fact-checking and Transparency*. https://mastermaldita.es

Uskali, T., Gynnild, A., Jones, S., & Sirkkunen, E. (2021). *Immersive Journalism as Storytelling: Ethics, Production, and Design*. Taylor & Francis. doi:10.4324/9780429437748

Uskali, T., & Ikonen, P. (2021). Teaching immersive journalism. In *Immersive Journalism as Storytelling. Ethics, Production, and Design* (pp. 163–175). Routledge. doi:10.4324/9780429437748-18

Van Damme, K., All, A., De Marez, L., & Van Leuven, S. (2019). 360 video journalism: Experimental study on the effect of immersion on news experience and distant suffering. *Journalism Studies*, *20*(14), 2053–2076. doi:10.1080/1461670X.2018.1561208

Vázquez-Herrero, J., & López-García, X. (2017, April). Immersive journalism through mobile devices: How virtual reality apps are changing news consumption. In *World Conference on Information Systems and Technologies* (pp. 3–12). Springer. doi:10.1007/978-3-319-56541-5_1

Zerman, E., Ozcinar, C., Gao, P., & Smolic, A. (2020, May). *Textured mesh vs coloured point cloud: A subjective study for volumetric video compression. In 2020 Twelfth International Conference on Quality of Multimedia Experience (QoMEX)*. IEEE.

Zhang, A., Wang, C., Han, B., & Qian, F. (2021, February). Efficient volumetric video streaming through super resolution. In *Proceedings of the 22nd International Workshop on Mobile Computing Systems and Applications* (pp. 106-111). Academic Press.

Zwoliński, G., Kamińska, D., Laska-Leśniewicz, A., Haamer, R. E., Vairinhos, M., Raposo, R., Urem, F., & Reisinho, P. (2022). Extended Reality in Education and Training: Case Studies in Management Education. *Electronics (Basel), 11*(3), 336. doi:10.3390/electronics11030336

ADDITIONAL READING

Hertzfeld, L. (2020, April 7). *A Guide to AR/XR in Journalism*. Yahoo News. https://bit.ly/3KXB9ay

Jones, S. (2017). Disrupting the narrative: Immersive journalism in virtual reality. *Journal of Media Practice, 18*(2-3), 171–185. doi:10.1080/14682753.2017.1374677

Kishore, S., Navarro, X., Dominguez, E., De La Peña, N., & Slater, M. (2018). Beaming into the news: A system for and case study of tele-immersive journalism. *IEEE Computer Graphics and Applications, 38*(2), 89–101. doi:10.1109/MCG.2017.2801407 PMID:29672258

Rodríguez, N. L. (2018). Immersive journalism design within a transmedia space. *Exploring transmedia journalism in the digital age*, 67-82.

Rubio Tamayo, J. L., Barro Hernández, M., & Gómez Gómez, H. (2018). Visualización de Datos con Herramientas Interactivas y de Realidad Virtual. Revisión del Estado Actual y Propuesta de Modelo. *Revista ICONO 14. Revista Científica De Comunicación Y Tecnologías Emergentes, 16*(2), 40-65.

Shin, D., & Biocca, F. (2018). Exploring immersive experience in journalism. *New Media & Society, 20*(8), 2800–2823. doi:10.1177/1461444817733133

Toursel, A., & Philippe, U. (2019). Immersive journalism, a "new frontier" of information experience? *Brazilian Journalism Research, 15*(2), 336.

KEY TERMS AND DEFINITIONS

Augmented Information: Journalism, in the medium of XR, may represent information in many layers, taking always into account the origin of the information: the facts. Nevertheless, XR technologies give us the possibility to expand the information in a specific environment, as augmented reality works. This augmented information may be represented over the real world (so called augmented reality) or in other formats, such as a 360 (immersive or not) video. This layer of information will help to complement the information received by the user.

Extended Reality: The ensemble of digital technologies which represent different levels of reality, from real-physical world to virtual reality. Digital media combines different levels and layers of information.

Extended Reality Lab: Media Lab which focus their research on extended reality technologies, in many approaches. They may focus their research on the development of new technologies (software, devices, etc.), in one hand, but it has also many other approaches, such as the application of the technologies in fields such as sciences, communication science, art, design, architecture, and others. Other approaches are to develop case uses and improve user experiences, as well as integrate content developed under narrative structures to improve the experience.

Immersive Infographics: It consists of the creation of infographics in immersive environments, mainly of an interactive nature. The approach to data visualisation must be carried out in a completely different way to how they are visualised on 2D screens. There are different variables that will influence this, such as the user's point of view (their position in space with respect to the elements to be represented), the nature of the data to be represented, and the need to represent it in an immersive and interactive environment. The construct of the experience will also have a narrative associated with it, always bearing in mind the highest possible degree of objectivity of the data.

Immersive Journalism: Journalism applying extended reality technologies, specifically virtual reality, to improve the degree of digital information received by the user. The main senses for increasing the immersivity are sight and hearing, but not only. They may be many senses involved to increase the degree of immersive experience in user.

Immersive Media: Media which are developed to be consumed in devices such as HMD (head-mounted displays) and providing an immersive experience, essentially through the senses of sight and hearing. Other senses are also involved, and it's relevant the body position, which contributes to determine the feeling of presence, and, thus, the immersive experience. Other senses may be also involved in the feeling of immersiveness, but further research is necessary to determine which role are playing.

Volumetric Video: It consists of capturing a sequence of images or film footage of a person or other element of the physical world to recreate it in a 3D environment with digital technologies. There are different 3D capture technologies, such as scanners or cameras with multiple lenses. What is important is the fact that the movement and actions are captured and reproduced in that digital 3D space. Sometimes components such as chroma keys are used.

Chapter 2
Virtual Reality for Teacher Training:
An Experiential Approach to Classroom Conflict Management

Miriela M. Cárdenas
Universitat Autònoma de Barcelona, Spain

Borja Manero
University Complutense of Madrid, Spain

Ibis M. Alvarez
https://orcid.org/0000-0002-3250-3214
Universitat Autònoma de Barcelona, Spain

Alejandro Romero-Hernández
University Complutense of Madrid, Spain

ABSTRACT

This chapter discusses the use of virtual reality (VR) in the training of preservice secondary education teachers in Spain as an integral part of their learning process. The authors propose some premises from which to design a training program to improve preservice teachers' communicative competence and their ability to manage conflict impacting the classroom climate. First, it explains the experiential and experimental potential of a virtual learning environment (VLE), its ability to create personalized virtual worlds, as well as the possibility to generate insightful instant feedback and feedforward. Finally, an example of a prototype scenario designed on this conceptual basis is provided. Furthermore, the chapter presents an overview of an educational proposal to implement this experiential immersive opportunity for preservice teachers to interact and manage disruptive situations in a safe and reliable environment conducive to the development of key communicative competences and strategies to turn conflict into a learning opportunity.

DOI: 10.4018/978-1-6684-3398-0.ch002

INTRODUCTION

Learning to manage the daily conflicts that affect the classroom climate in Secondary education is imperative in the initial teacher training. Historically speaking teacher training for Secondary education has been a neglected field and vaguely studied in comparison, for example, to Primary education according to the OECD Teaching and Learning International Survey (TALIS) conducted in 2018 (Schleicher, 2020). This survey shows that Spain, for instance, is well below the average for teachers who refer to having received training regarding the management of students' conflicting behavior and classroom climate. Less than half of Spanish teachers (40%) reported that they felt prepared to control a class. On the other hand, the study reveals that Spanish teachers excelled in their responses to maintaining order in class.

In fact, the teacher's ability to stimulate and motivate students to develop responsible learning is identified among the key factors for the development of a positive climate. As Everston & Poole (2008) reminds us, despite the best-laid plans, student misbehavior will occur. Reactions to this misbehavior require careful planning to ensure a teacher's responses are productive. A teacher who motivates and contributes to a good classroom climate is one who makes the goals of the program and its expectations evident, knows his students, and instills in them the value of work and effort; at the same time, he values them and gives them formative and timely feedback (Winstone et al, 2017).

Therefore, providing teachers with a set of fundamental instruments and competencies to ensure and produce a good classroom climate should be an integral part of any initial or continuing professional development program. However, despite the undoubted importance of this topic, according to recent reports, in general, future teachers are dissatisfied with the theoretical nature of this training and consider the practical training received to be deficient (Hamit & Yildirim, 2020; Sarceda-Gorgoso et al., 2020). Consequently, teachers face the classroom without having the fundamental pedagogical and communicative skills to manage not only the learning process but also the interpersonal relationships within the institutional context to ensure and promote a positive classroom climate.

Certainly, teachers must build communication competency, "develop[ing] a diverse pool of communication strategies and tactics to draw from" and be able to choose among them to fit the people involved as well as the context (Hocker & Wilmot, 2014). The lack of training in classroom management, as well as the development of communicative competences, could potentially be resolved through the introduction of an initial training program with virtual reality (VR) to enhance preservice teachers' communicative skills and increase their ability to respond to frequently arisen conflicts in Secondary classrooms.

Exploiting the experiential, experimental, and scientific component that accompanies this technology (VR), could allow teachers to put into practice these competences in a safe and exciting environment. Several studies argue the need for training teachers to face this challenge in learning contexts that allow experimentation and reflection on practical performance (Clarà et al., 2019; Sorensen, 2014).

Against this background, this chapter presents a VR system specifically designed by a group of developers and educational psychologists to address this need. The authors witnessed its potential to build, model, and develop the necessary communicative competence needed to manage conflict in a Secondary School classroom as a valuable alternative for preservice teacher training within a safe environment. We set out to demonstrate how implementing a VR training proposal could contribute to developing preservice teachers' key communicative competences to manage classroom climate while providing accurate information on which emotions are positively or negatively involved in classroom conflict management.

Along with this chapter we, first, describe and highlight the characteristics of the classroom climate to explain the complexity of managing disruptive behaviors as well as the importance of identifying the affective and attitudinal factors that motivate teachers' current strategies while managing classroom climate. We also cite research that supports the premise of conflict management as a learning opportunity and the desirability of experiential learning and critical reflection. Next, we address the distinctive features of virtual learning environments to enable the creation of an optimal environment for teachers' education. Finally, we present the VR system we have developed for this purpose and advance a training proposal to implement it.

BACKGROUND

The Classroom Management

Classroom management can be defined as any of the actions that teachers conduct to use instructional time effectively and maintain students' attention and, through this, create an environment that facilitates both academic and socioemotional development (Doyle, 2006). Thus, classroom climate determines the quality of the learning process, conflicts undermine interpersonal relationships and can lead to disruptive events that could dramatically affect teaching and learning conditions.

Teachers often tend to have difficulty keeping track of everything that is going on in the classroom and, especially, noticing and responding when students cause disruptions. The complexity of the classroom environment is one factor that may contribute to this. Following Doyle (2006), classroom climate management is a complex issue for at least three reasons. First, because it depends on the quality of collaboration between teachers and students. Second, because it involves a wide range of circumstances and events that occur simultaneously, immediately and very often, unpredictably. Finally, classroom management involves the regulation of emotional and attitudinal aspects to face disruptive and/or conflictive events that hinder the development of the teaching activity.

We believe that exploring the affective attitudinal aspects underlying classroom conflict presents opportunities for teachers to learn how to manage it productively, but this is not enough. Successful classroom management also involves cognitive dimensions such as comprehension and interpretation, skills needed to recognize when and how to act in the presence of conflict events in the classroom. In this regard, teachers require training to recognize the affective cues triggering various reactive and ineffective automatic response patterns, and to become initiative-taking in implementing strategies to reduce the impact of said triggers, thereby increasing their sense of efficacy (Alvarez et al., 2022).

Tackling Conflict as a Learning Opportunity

A widely held conception describes conflict as "an expressed struggle between at least two interdependent parties who perceive incompatible goals, scarce resources, and interference by others in the achievement of goals (Hocker & Wilmot, 2014, p.13)". Giving greater weight to affective-motivational variables, conflict has also been described as a subjective experience: "To recognize that we are in conflict is to acknowledge that we have been triggered emotionally (Jones, 2000, p. 91)."

Conflict, at its core, is about how people perceive each other and the situation. That is, conflict occurs because individuals have different ideas about how things "should be," reflecting their own values, beliefs, and attitudes (Janke & Dumlao, 2019). Because conflict emerges due to natural and inherent differences among individuals, conflict itself is very normal. Many educational guidance specialists and advisers, to promote change, argue conflict is needed to transform individuals or circumstances for something new to develop. If one approaches conflict as a problem to be solved or an opportunity to persuade, more constructive choices are likely than if one views conflict as something to be feared (Dumlao, 2018).

Considering that conflict is unrelated to the communicative context in which they arise, several studies claim that adopting an emotional perspective, based on empathy, allows teachers to react more appropriately to disruptive behaviors (Keller & Becker, 2020; Mcgrath & Van Bergen, 2019). In contrast, coping strategies based on domination (repeated verbal reprimands or imposition of sanctions) or avoidance (delaying discussion or intentionally ignoring confrontation) appear less effective for classroom climate management (Chang & Taxer, 2020; Martinez et al., 2020).

Typically, during class interactions, conflict situations occur that require teachers' communicative competence to manage them effectively. The use of expressive, spontaneous, safe, and influential language is preferred over other courses of action (Terroni, 2009). The range of interventions a teacher prepares includes such mild responses as moving closer to the student, making eye contact, or giving a knowing glance, using a corrective consequence, or even ignoring the behavior if it self-corrects (Everston & Poole, 2008).

According to Doyle (2006), the key to a teacher's success in management appears to be his or her (a) understanding of the configuration of events in a classroom, and (b) skill in monitoring and guiding activities considering this information (p.116). Thus, the effectiveness of classroom conflict management cannot be defined solely by stereotypical behavior patterns as traditional teacher education often suggests. Successful classroom management also involves aspects of the affective-attitudinal dimension that allow us to recognize when and how to act to face conflictive events in immediate circumstances.

The process of emotion elicitation and regulation that emerges during the assessment of the conflict situation shapes the quality of teacher-student relationships (Frenzel et al., 2021) and becomes a decisive factor in classroom conflict management. According to Lauermann and Butler (2021), teachers' emotions convey important social messages with possible implications for students' beliefs, which can impact classroom climate management, in the short and long term.

As Ekman (1985) and Damásio (1999) have reliably demonstrated, the behavioral element of emotion is projected in the forms of expression of subjective emotional experience (facial expressions, vocal characteristics, gestures, and body postures) that we communicate intentionally or involuntarily. Considering this primary condition, during interactions with students, when conflicting events occur, some physiological changes and verbal and nonverbal emotional expressions will occur that will be consciously perceived by teachers and observed by their students. For both, these signals trigger certain modes of action (Keller & Becker, 2020; Sutton, 2004).

On the other hand, given that emotions are considered inseparable from the educational context in which they emerge, paying attention to explanations of significant emotional experiences after they have occurred can help teachers identify and characterize emotionally relevant "courses of action" developed in the classroom for classroom climate management. Therefore, the proposed VR system includes features to recognize and capture attitudinal and emotional aspects of the teacher-student interaction during disruptive situations. This is the most innovative aspect of our proposal, as little research is found to identify underlying emotions during the communicative situation in the classroom. Literature mostly refers to the result of conflict and its poor management in the classroom.

Conflict Management Strategies From the Emotional Perspective

Some studies show that engaging in emotional perspective-taking allows teachers to react appropriately to disruptive behavior (Barr, 2011; Evertson & Weinstein, 2006). Likewise, teachers who expressed close relationships with disruptive students also described emotional perspective-taking, empathy, and emotion regulation (Mcgrath & van Bergen, 2019). These characteristics are likely to be particularly helpful when forming relationships with disruptive students by guiding effective classroom management and supporting a positive classroom climate (Jennings & Greenberg, 2009).

The complexity of a Secondary classroom is difficult to simulate in a practice scenario in which the future teacher could experiment, without undergoing the challenges and tensions that may happen. In this sense, it seems interesting to explore whether an immersive VR training could be a useful tool, offering a Virtual Learning Environments (VLE) that simulate everyday classroom situations that, together with the opportunity for experimentation, provide information on which factors intervene (positively or negatively) in classroom conflict management, within a safe environment.

Managing conflicts constructively can help teachers and students build successful short-term and long-term relationships. Considering the above-identified opportunities, a VRLE could be an ideal resource for teachers to learn how to manage classroom conflicts that affect the classroom climate.

In summary, identifying the role emotions play seems necessary to better understand the nature of conflict as well as the need for a more immersive approach to classroom management training. The complexity of emotional processing, including the components of emotional expression through verbal behaviors, the transparency of emotional states that are projected in nonverbal language (facial expressions, vocal qualities, and body posture), and the appraisal of emotional experiences driven by emotional arousal, presages the decisions teachers make to manage classroom conflict.

We understand that providing preservice teachers with access to a VRLE could be a starting point to identify said factors and better prepare them to face a Secondary classroom.

VR Salient Features for Teacher Training

A virtual reality learning environment is presented to users in such a way that they accept it as a real environment, within which they can navigate and interact with objects or other avatars in the same way they would experience real life (Ke et al., 2020).

An important feature of VR is that it allows users to immerse themselves in the event or situation and examine it from different perspectives. From a technological point of view, the term immersion means the "degree to which computer screens are capable of providing an illusion of inclusive, extensive, immersive, and vivid reality (Slater & Wilbur, 1997, p. 3) ". More specifically, this includes the degree of exclusion of physical reality, the range of sensory modalities, the breadth of the surrounding environment, as well as the resolution and accuracy of technological attributes (Mütterlein, 2018, cited by Radianti et al., 2020).

Immersion is considered from a psychological perspective as a psychological state in which the user perceives isolation of the senses from the real world (Witmer and Singer, 1998). Paradoxically, however, immersive VR has been often evaluated in terms of presence, which can be defined as the sense of being there or naturalness (Bianchi-Berthouze, et al. 2007). The core focus of immersive technologies is indeed on capturing the user's senses in the most complete way (Freina & Ott, 2015), generating a feeling of presence where the mediation of technology disappears. This effect would help immersive VR in allowing users to experience situations and learning outcomes that are challenging to access in real life (Lau & Lee, 2015; Mulders et al., 2020). In this way, immersion and a sense of reality can promote interest and encourage participation and promote experiential, dynamic, self-organized, and self-directed learning that is informally structured, diverse, and vibrant, facilitating specific and contextualized experiential learning while increasing student motivation and engagement (Sheridan, 2000).

As shown by recent experimental studies (e.g., Chi-Yuan, 2022; Ke et. al., 2020), providing an immersive environment can promote student engagement and motivation, make them active learners, and increase creativity, to a greater extent than when using other technologies such as videos.

Video-based intervention are commonly used in teacher training programmes providing an opportunity of post-action reflection (e.g., Fadda & Sullivan, 2013; Kleinknecht & Gröschner, 2016). Although a video-based teaching method is simpler to implement, as no additional equipment or preparation time is needed, and it could offer more content; a VLE-based teaching method offers the same video case studies advantages but within an immersive learning experience allowing participants the capability of agency when facing simultaneous, immediate, and unpredictable events in the classroom, providing immediate feedback on learner's concerns, and making it more attractive to them. Furthermore, it not only increases the comprehensiveness of the immersive simulation, and true engagement but also provides positive effects on learning (Seufert et al. 2022). Effective user feedback allows errors and false assumptions to be corrected as doubts or challenges arise (Chi-Yuan, 2022). For example, one could simulate a situation in which, having driven the teacher to anger, the teacher is taught to practice strategies other than dominance or avoidance. This is especially important for pre-service teachers who are rarely exposed to real or simulated situations before starting to teach a real class (except for in mandatory internships). The study, explained in this chapter, aims to empirically contribute to advocating the use of VR in preservice teacher training.

In addition, the creation of a VLE allows us to incorporate increasingly complex and challenging situations for the teacher that will somehow jeopardize their safety and physical integrity within the program, but not in real life (Dalgarno & Lee, 2010). The functional interactivity or similarity of a simulation is framed by: (1) the extent to which the simulated environment recognizes the existence of the user and reacts to it in an analogous way to the operating environment of the real world does, and (2) the interaction and social presence of multiple users in the simulated environment.

Another aspect to highlight of VLE is its configurability, i.e., which allows the recreation of a multitude of high presence and realistic teaching scenarios and the inclusion of different tools and artifacts within them. This opens a wide range of possibilities, for example, the recreation of educational environments for the training of future teachers (e.g., Chi-Yuan, 2022). Researchers can define and control the characteristics of the environment, such as classroom size, layout, student characteristics, or the number and types of disruptive behaviors. The potential "danger" of the conflicting communicative situation in the classroom, represented in VR, can be brought to its fullest expression, prompting the teacher-in-training to use his or her intuition, put survival skills into practice, and draw on his or her conceptual knowledge, while rehearsing different alternative responses.

Nonetheless, the biggest contribution of VR is that it allows users to embody learning experiences in such a way that it produces intense and real emotional sensations (Stavroulia, et al., 2019). This feature helps teachers feel they are learning within a real environment, from an ecological learning perspective ('knowing how to learn') (Barnett & Jackson, 2019) that enhances and fosters the transfer of knowledge, professional skills, and learner empowerment in self-determining their own lifelong learning pathways (Sangrà et al. 2019).

Since VR allows for the opportunity to be immersed in a VLE that recreates real-life events and situations, we have considered it appropriate as a tool to digitalize and transform the current learning environment of our preservice teachers, allowing us to do things differently and closing the gap between analog and digital learning to provide a comprehensive educational experience bringing coherence and authenticity to their professional development, in tune with today's digitalized society dimension. The use of virtual simulations is increasingly seen as an opportunity to provide pre-service teachers with unique opportunities to experience examples of classroom life in a controlled and structured manner (McGarr, 2021).

It should be cautioned, however, that VR use is associated with several adverse effects, such as dizziness, headache, and nausea; this is not surprising, as in VR there is often an inconsistency between the information received by the body and the eyes (Roettl and Terlutter, 2018). For example, some VR scenes have inconsistent focal distances among all objects. As a result, continuous accommodation without changing eye vergence is needed; the disruption between eye vergence and accommodation may cause visual inconvenience. There are numerous potential causes of visual discomfort when viewing stereo displays. These include discomfort due to the eyewear needed to separate the two eyes' images, ghosting or crosstalk between the two images, misalignment of the images, inappropriate head orientation, vergence–accommodation conflict, visibility of flicker or motion artifacts, and visual-vestibular conflicts (Kooi & Toet,2004, cited by Vienne et al., 2014)

Recent VR devices have been developed for full immersion, with more realistic settings to facilitate an enhanced user experience, in addition to the development of innovative modern technology. However, the more complex and realistic settings may cause adverse effects, including dizziness (Watanabe & Ujike, 2008). Therefore, although innovative technologies can counteract these effects (Radianti et al., 2020), it is necessary to evaluate these aspects in usability tests. It is also necessary to warn users of these effects and to be attentive to possible manifestations during experiments to avoid discomfort.

During our pilot experience, few participants presented motion sickness and dizziness. We saw it happened on participants wearing prescription glasses and going immediately back to their mobile devices despite our suggestions in this regard. They also reported they felt these symptoms for at least ten minutes after the experience during the pilot exit interview.

Didascalia Virtual-Classroom

This proposal is part of a larger project in which the system Didascalia Virtual-ClassRoom (hereinafter Didascalia VC), was designed and validated (Alonso et al. 2021; Bocos-Corredor et al. 2020). The project has been funded by the Spanish Ministry of Science, Innovation, and Universities [Didascalia, RTI2018-096401-A-].

As previously mentioned, it is our intention to facilitate an experiential opportunity and provide feedback to preservice teachers on the impact of emotions and communicative skills involved in coping with classroom conflict modeled in Didascalia VC to enable future teachers to learn to effectively manage disruptive situations in an engaging and safe environment, before facing the challenging reality in the Secondary classroom.

Methodological Design

Based on mixed-method research (Creswell, 2002), the study analyses both quantitative and qualitative data to explain how an immersive VR training could help improve preservice teachers' communicative competence.

The research is contextualized on the module Psycho-pedagogical and Social Training of the master's degree in Teaching in Secondary school at Spanish universities. Intentionally, to guarantee diversity in the research population, former master's students will also be included in our participants' pool, currently enrolled students belonging to different disciplines (Sciences, Languages, and Social Sciences).

As this research is part of a developing educational program, such as the master's degree in Secondary Teacher Education in Spain, the present study adopts the principles of the European framework for Responsible Research and Innovation (RRI), involving stakeholders in its development (Carrier and Gartzlaff, 2020). It is an approach that anticipates and evaluates the potential implications of educational innovations with the purpose of fostering more effective, inclusive, and sustainable designs, implementation, and impact.

As part of the research, a pilot test and iterative validations were conducted. 162 preservice teachers took part in the validation of the training proposal described below. Most of them women (109, 67.3%), average age 27.3. Thirty-four percent (55 participants) reported teaching experience between one and five years. In addition, four teachers, implicated in the design and development of the practice in their respective class groups, validated and assessed the tool (Borja et al. 2022). Research participation was voluntary, and an informed consent was signed before interacting with the VR tool.

Our intention was to involve an even number of males and females in the testing sample, special attention to preservice teachers' gender and disciplines was and will be considered in future iterations.

The System Features

Didascalia VC is a reactive immersive virtual reality environment (IVRE) that allows trainee teachers to experience, record, and reflect on affective and attitudinal issues critical for effective conflict management in the Secondary classroom. The system Didascalia VC transports future teachers into a Secondary classroom by providing a context in which a conflict has occurred that requires their intervention (e.g., two students have been fighting for the entire previous week).

During the experience, the system collects different information from the user: where he is looking, his position in the classroom, his tone of voice, and the words he says. Based on these parameters - an aggressive tone of voice with offensive words, in close proximity to a student - the system adjusts the behavior of the virtual students. Each scenario begins with a context screen with background information about the incident. During the experimental situation, trainee teachers ("players") can choose different strategies to manage the simulated conflict (compete, collaborate, accommodate, compromise, and avoid).

VLE Design

Didascalia VC is programmed to prioritize user immersion in virtual reality. During its creation, we focused on creating an environment that was as close to a high school classroom as possible.

Previously, 1583 critical incident reports were analyzed to design the content of the virtual classroom scenarios; 468 were taken from Secondary schools in Madrid and 1115 in Barcelona (Masó, 2022). These incident reports were extracted from the last two academic years. The results of this study allowed for the creation of three virtual scenarios that simulate disruptive classroom behaviors, potentially escalating into conflicts frequently encountered in Secondary schools. These are (1) Overt academic disinterest (e.g., getting up without permission, not working in class, falling asleep), (2) Disruptions among classmates (e.g., chatting, or distracting classmates, confrontations between classmates in a workgroup), and (3) Disruptions affecting the teacher-student relationship (e.g., talking to the teacher inappropriately, challenging authority, among others). In addition, different actions that teachers usually implement to manage these conflicts, with greater or lesser success were identified.

As a result, Didascalia VC recreates three real-life Secondary school classroom scenarios offering teachers context to solve the potentially conflicting situations. Each scenario begins with the description of an initial conflict, in which the teacher had to make a choice. As shown in the algorithm presented in Figure 1, conceived for the second scenario design, every situation is described in the form of a flowchart. Depending on the action taken by the "player" (preservice teacher), the user can follow different paths, each one with positive or negative consequences for the class. Afterward, feedback is provided to the players on their performance.

To illustrate the procedure followed for the scenario design, we focus on the situation simulated in the second scenario: two students sit together, ignoring their teacher's prior prohibition. The Unity 3D software used to develop the Didascalia VC system includes functionalities that allow monitoring whether the player is within a specific range of the VLE students. Figure 2 showed the adapted pathway considering our software capabilities (the player features that it can detect). Thus, the scheme followed for the technological design of the second scenario was "Detect

Figure 1. Scenario proposed by Bocos-Corredor et al. (2020).

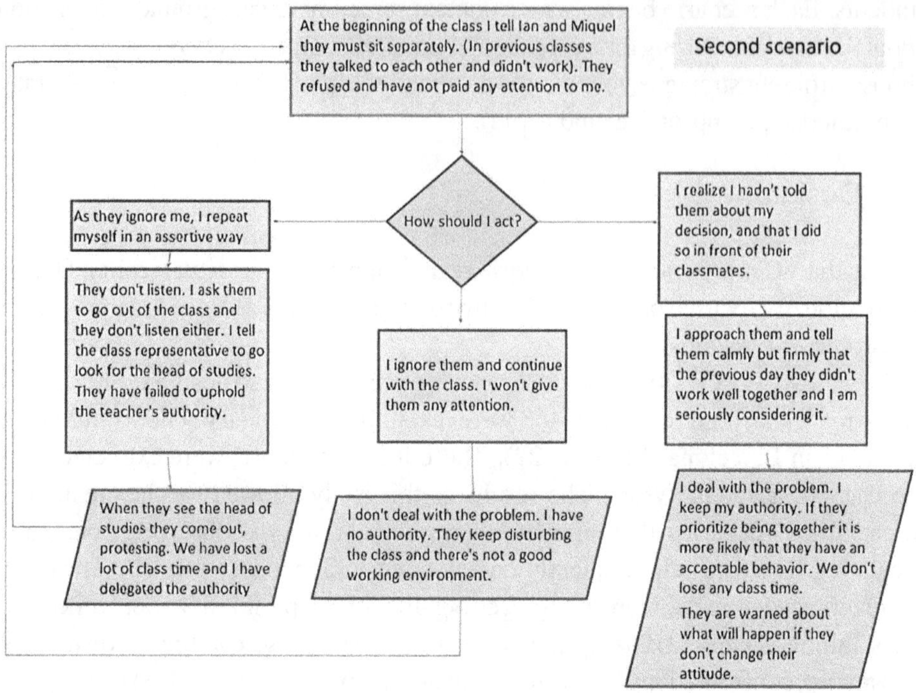

that the teacher approaches the students" and "uses appropriate words and tone of voice for assertive coping" (most appropriate path).

It is important to highlight that when designing the setting, a standard Spanish Secondary school classroom was taken as a reference. Its main components are desks, chairs, a blackboard, and a platform for the teacher with a lectern. To achieve this, an asset pack from the Unity Asset Store named "Classroom," which included all the necessary elements was used. Thirty seats were added to the VLE classroom, the maximum number of students allowed per classroom according to Spanish law as shown in Figure 3 (Ministry of Education, 2010). Another weighty decision for this scenario design was to place the teacher on a platform, higher than the students, a common feature in classrooms allowing the teacher to see and be seen by all the students. Initially, the teacher is facing the students, as the scenarios require him/her to be able to observe their behavior.

Next, models of students using *Adobe Fuse* were created. This program allowed the creation of 3D objects in a fast and straightforward manner, customizing their aspect and characteristics. Apart from that, each student was given a label with a name to help the player address them. Labels are important for the teachers-students

Figure 2. Scenario adapted by Bocos-Corredor et al. (2020).

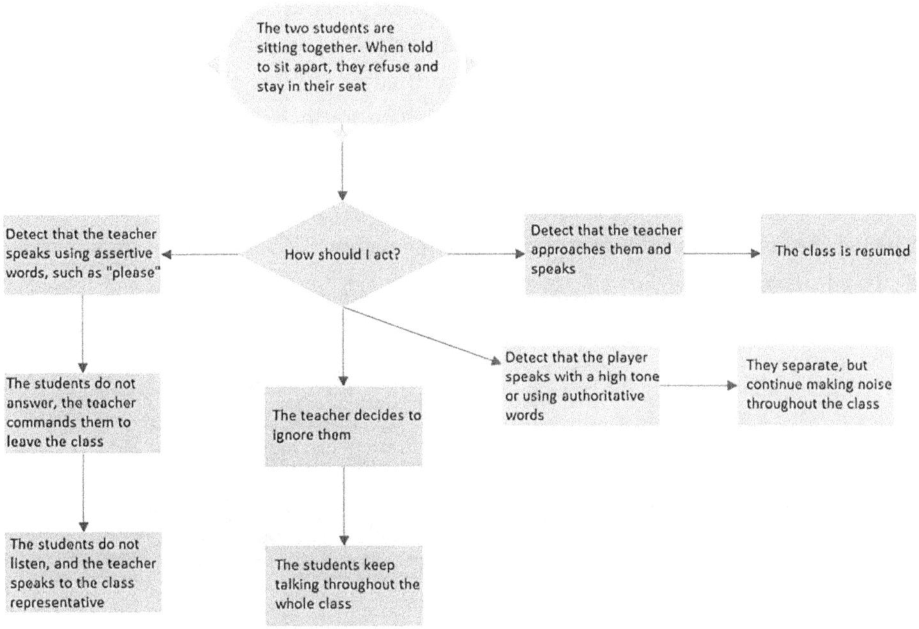

communication; since students can benefit from perceiving instructors know their names (Cant et al., 2022).

Despite having thirty seats, only a total of eight students are present in the VLE classroom. We considered this number of students to be high enough to successfully achieve the learning purpose in each scenario, but low enough not to be overwhelming for the teacher. Four students are boys, and four are girls, since according to the

Figure 3. Simulated Secondary school classroom.

Spanish Ministry of Education, 51% of all Secondary school students are male, and 49% are female (Ministry of Education, 2020). All of them were Caucasian, the most common ethnicity present in most European schools (see figure 4). After creating the students, Adobe Mixamo was used for animation. In this manner, we were able to represent common students' disruptive behaviors in the classroom accurately, such as their sitting, cheering, laughing, or getting distracted.

Figure 4. Students from the preservice teacher's view.

Pre-service teachers enter the virtual classroom equipped with virtual glasses (Oculus) and two controllers. The external trainer (the teacher or an advisor) controls the virtual students in the VR classroom through use of a desktop computer. Meanwhile, other students observe, on the computer screen, the actions taken by their partner to manage the virtual classroom (a practical example is shown in figure 5).

Figure 5. A group of student teachers during the VR experience (photo courtesy of participants). On the right, screenshot, the "player's" view.

A detailed explanation of the architecture and features of this system can be found in Bocos-Corredor et al. (2020), which was later adapted by Alonso et al. (2021). In the adapted version, the device ClassroomVR-MotionCapture (CVR-MC) was introduced. Based on this application, several extensions with new functionalities were developed, as shown below:

- Tone of voice analysis: changes are detected during key moments of the simulation.
- Analysis of proxemia between interlocutors: distance between interlocutors (student and teacher) is analyzed and will determine the simulation response.
- Keyword detection in conflict management: keywords are classified to determine the response to the simulation and relate them to the user´s emotions.
- Possibility of choosing the execution platform: CVR-MC allows you to choose your preferred execution platform: a virtual reality environment or a desktop environment (PC).
- Analysis of the user´s body expression to establish the predominant emotion: the Perception Neuron and EmoPose system (García-Magariño et al., 2019) captured and analyzed the teacher´s body expression to associate it with an emotion.
- Storage of the most relevant parameters of the simulation (e.g., voice tone, proxemia with students…).

A gameplay of the VLE prototype narrated in Spanish, with English captions, can be found https://youtu.be/3NPiaMzRSvE.

An Overview of an Educational Proposal to Implement Didascalia VC

The original idea of implementing this training proposal modality arises from a tangible need within the Official Master's Degree in Teacher Training for Secondary Education at the Autonomous University of Barcelona (UAB), for an experiential and experimental training component to develop key communicative competences in preservice teachers; not only to face the classroom for the first time but also to guarantee them a much-needed preparedness to manage classroom conflict and succeed in maintaining a suitable classroom climate.

Furthermore, the pilot training intended to demonstrate the value of technology in teaching communication' comprised of mutual feedback from both students and facilitators (teacher trainer). Early implementation, continued accessibility, enhancing realism, and technological improvements through the ClassroomVR-MotionCapture (CVR-MC) tool, were listed as key areas for program improvement, while increased situational sensitivity and conflict resolution training are recommended to further enhance students' communication skills (Alonso et al. 2021).

Near the training proposal implementation within the master's degree in Secondary Teacher Education an extensive study of the emotional states associated with different conflict management strategies in the classroom was conducted (Alvarez et al. 2022). New technical features were added to the design, such as the possibility of using a suit to capture the user's nonverbal communication while testing the product and learning its functionality (Alonso et al. 2021). This newly added feature will make capturing a set of emotional and attitudinal variables (expressions, gestures, and postures) possible. The inputs received will feed an analysis system in charge of delivering feedback to the players during the VR experience. Among these emotional and attitudinal factors, the following aspects were highlighted:

- Gaze direction (see which object you are looking at)
- Whether the person is speaking or not and the tone of voice used (if intense/overbearing, calm/persuasive).
- Words or phrases (please, thank you, shut up, punished, etc.).
- Body language (positions of hands, feet, head, arms, elbows, torso, etc.).
- Position in relation to objects (whether the preservice teacher is facing the students, or has turned their back to them, or is standing to the side).
- User's balance point (If you have all the weight resting on one of the feet or spread evenly between the two).

Considering that VR systems currently present serious usability problems, such as conceptual disorientation, inability to manipulate objects, and inadequacy of content or presentation, among others, mentioned in the introduction, finally, user testing was performed, following the Technology Acceptance Model (TAM) (Davis, 1989). As noted by Sanders (2010), usability testing should be mandatory before deploying any e-learning content, as it allows developers, trainers, and end-users (in this case, educators) to understand how players interact with the system and identify usability issues.

The main result we have obtained is that Didascalia-VC, as confirmed by users, could be especially useful in teacher training, as it would allow teachers to improve their competence in solving complex situations in the classroom. Participants highlighted the importance of the system's immersive and its realism. Moreover, all participants recognized that the tool is a perfect complement to be introduced in the training of pre-service teachers (Manero et al., in press).

The Training Proposal Step by Step

The training proposal for preservice teachers includes practical considerations in different areas to guarantee a successful pilot test implementation such as methodology, diagnosis of current praxis, curriculum, group size, evaluation strategies, student support, activities calendar, and practicum characteristics within the master's degree to allocate the workshop at a pivotal moment in the preservice teacher's instruction.

The classroom experience (workshop) will last two hours, divided into four stages:

1. **Stage 1**: Introduction. In this stage, the structure, objective, and framework supporting the experience will be presented. Time will be given to clarify doubts and address suggestions before signing the informed consent form. Participants will then be asked to complete the self-efficacy classroom management Questionnaire.
2. **Stage 2**: Analysis of classroom conflicts. After watching "classroom" videos, participants will be asked to discuss the conflict management process. Subsequently, the experience will be conducted in the VLE (one participant per group, 15 minutes, approximately). The rest of the team members will be able to witness the experience, through the computer screen, while the participant interacts with the VR device.
3. **Stage 3**: Focus group discussion. After experiencing the VRLE, each team will comment and reflect on the practice gathered in a focus group format. The team members will receive a script with questions to reflect on key issues to guide the discussion.
4. **Stage 4**: Evaluation and closure. In the following class, the results of the self-efficacy questionnaire will be commented on and different strategies for classroom management will be discussed, providing theoretical references.

This practical activity helps preservice teachers build their teaching identity as they acquire knowledge, and professional skills, and develop a self-image awareness in which personal and professional perspectives interact, creating an individual image of who they are as a teacher (Graus et al., 2022).

The opportunity of successive trials with various response options increased the safety benefit of the VLE by building confidence in the participants' ability to respond to the challenges the environment presents. During the experience, as teachers move up a level and resolve conflict situations, we expect to observe the communicative competence consolidation as a skill, to manage various conflict situations arising properly and effectively in the simulated Secondary school classroom.

In turn, since the VLE training provides immediate feedback through the adjustment of all its elements and algorithms, preservice teachers could reflect and review their performance individually or in peer groups. This tweaking tool capability enhances the skill tested promoting the development of new skills and offering more efficient results since teachers' errors and false assumptions can be corrected right when the doubt or challenge arises (Dann, 2019; Winstone et al., 2017).

In all, the implementation of this training provides substantial tangible benefits. First, via the possibility of an immersive experience close to a real-life classroom environment, eliminating the risk and anxiety associated with conflict and classroom management. Second, it fosters discussion, after-action reflection, and collaborative solutions teachers often point to as "challenging cases to manage in the classroom." Finally, it strengthens preservice teachers' ability to identify critical incidents and act from a mindful perspective bringing awareness to topics such as self-efficacy and conflict management styles.

FINAL REFLECTIONS AND PERSPECTIVES

After evaluating not only the benefits, but also other reference programs experiences which satisfactorily implement this technology in the initial and continuous professional teacher development courses, we recommend VR as an effective resource to include within the preservice Secondary education teachers' training curriculum.

The methodology proposed for its implementation requires further trials, in upcoming academic years and in other universities, to continue incorporating the voices of teachers, students, and managers of Spanish universities where the master's degree in Secondary Teacher Education is taught. Likewise, it would be advisable that this VR tool, with the improvements suggested by the participants in the pilot test, could be developed to iterate the training experience as part of a training module that would take into account some knowledge prior to the practice of preservice teachers in training and, subsequently, be linked to the teaching practices in different educational centers offering them a more holistic perspective and in accordance with the learning ecology approach (Sangrà et al., 2019).

In summary, Didascalia VC recreates challenging, formative virtual scenarios, but above all, it reminds users of experiences and situations lived. We see value in the experiential and experimental potential in which VR immerses the teacher and its ability to create challenging and personalized virtual worlds. This way preservice teachers face challenging, motivating, and suggestive situations supported by post-action reflections, immediate feedback, and prospective feedforward aiming to enhance their conflict management communicative competence.

This immersive initial experience merges both praxis and theory otherwise absent in today's Official master's degree. It is a 10-minute experience low in cost and high in value to develop and self-fed through Preservice Teachers' practicum observations which will keep the VLE current and synchronized with the day-to-day situations.

Additionally, Didascalia VC's capability to capture nonverbal emotional expressions permits to further evaluate preservice teachers' outcomes after their training immersion for the purpose of analyzing how emotions could positively or negatively impact teachers' performance and classroom conflict management. It could also be implemented within the subject of pedagogy to train preservice teachers to successfully implement pedagogical strategies and improve cognitive outcomes in the classroom.

The experiential approach to learning is useful not only to manage conflicting situations in the classroom but also to train both preservice and seasoned teachers to successfully cope with special needs students in the classroom. Thus, this training modality could be a potent tool to prepare them to be more inclusive and employ appropriate strategies.

In view of the diversity of disruptive situations in the classroom, it is deemed necessary to include new situations to continue to present fresh and relevant scenarios to train teachers to achieve professional readiness not only for the first day at work as a preservice teacher but also to assist in-service teachers.

We recommend the use of preservice teachers' practicum observations to feed relevant cases to VLE scenarios and understand the nature of the communicative situation beyond what is reported by in-service teachers in disciplinary reports. We also propose to use Didascalia VC for the training and development of other necessary skills such as the management of students with specific educational needs and cultural diversity, for which there is currently no intentional and specific training that promotes the professional training of in-service teachers.

ACKNOWLEDGMENT

This project has been funded by the Ministry of Science, Innovation and Universities of Spain (Didascalia, RTI2018-096401-A-I00). The researchers would like to thank the teachers and teachers-in-training who voluntarily participated in this study.

REFERENCES

Alonso, S., López, D., Puente, A., Romero, A., Álvarez, I. M., & Manero, B. (2021). Evaluation of a motion capture and virtual reality classroom for Secondary school teacher training. In *Proceedings of the 29th International Conference on Computers in Education*. Asia-Pacific Society for Computers in Education. https://icce2021.apsce.net/proceedings/volume1/

Alvarez, I. M., González-Parera, M., & Manero, B. (2022). The role of emotions in classroom conflict management. Case studies geared towards improving teacher training. *Frontiers in Psychology*, *13*, 818431. Advance online publication. doi:10.3389/fpsyg.2022.818431 PMID:35369238

Barnett, R., & Jackson, N. (Eds.). (2019). *Ecologies for learning and practice: Emerging ideas, sightings, and possibilities*. Routledge. doi:10.4324/9781351020268

Barr, J. J. (2011). The relationship between teachers' empathy and perceptions of school culture. *Educational Studies*, *37*(3), 365–369. doi:10.1080/03055698.2010.506342

Bianchi-Berthouze, N., Kim, W. W., & Patel, D. (2007). Does body movement engage you more in digital game play? and why? In A. C. R. Paiva, R. Prada, & R. W. Picard (Eds.), *International conference on affective computing and intelligent interaction* (pp. 102–113). Berlin: Springer.

Bocos-Corredor, M., Diaz-Nieto, A., Lopez-Garcia, A., Romero-Hernandez, A., Alvarez, I. M., & Manero, B. (2020). A VR game to improve communication skills in Secondary -school teachers. In *Proceedings of EDULEARN20. 12th International Conference on Education and New Learning Technologies* (pp. 8701–8710). IATED Academy.

Cant, R., Cooper, S., & Ryan, C. (2022, March 8). Using virtual simulation to teach evidence-based practice in nursing curricula: A rapid review. *Worldviews on Evidence-Based Nursing*. Advance online publication. doi:10.1111/wvn.12572 PMID:35261156

Carrier, M., & Gartzlaff, M. (2020). Responsible research and innovation: Hopes and fears in the scientific community in Europe. *Journal of Responsible Innovation*, *7*(2), 149–169. doi:10.1080/23299460.2019.1692571

Chang, M.-L., & Taxer, J. (2020). Teacher emotion regulation strategies in response to classroom misbehaviour. *Teachers and Teaching*, *27*(5), 353–369. doi:10.1080/13540602.2020.1740198

Chi-Yuan, Ch. (2022). Immersive virtual reality to train preservice teachers in managing students' challenging behaviours: A pilot study. *British Journal of Educational Technology*, *53*(4), 998–1024. Advance online publication. doi:10.1111/bjet.13181

Clarà, M., Mauri, T., Colombiana, R., & Onrubia, J. (2019). Supporting collaborative reflection in teacher education: A case study. *European Journal of Teacher Education*, *42*(2), 175–191. doi:10.1080/02619768.2019.1576626

Creswell, J. W. (2002). *Educational research: Planning conducting and evaluating quantitative and qualitative research*. Pearson.

Dalgarno, B., & Lee, M. J. (2010). What are the learning affordances of 3-D virtual environments? *British Journal of Educational Technology, 41*(1), 10–32. doi:10.1111/j.1467-8535.2009.01038.x

Damásio, A. (1999). *The feeling of what happens: body and emotion in the making of consciousness*. Harcourt Brace & Company.

Dann, R. (2019). Feedback as a relational concept in the classroom. *Curriculum Journal, 30*(4), 352–374. doi:10.1080/09585176.2019.1636839

Davis, F. D. (1989). Perceived usefulness, perceived ease of use, and user acceptance of information technology. *Management Information Systems Quarterly, 13*(3), 319–340. doi:10.2307/249008

Doyle, W. (2006). Ecological approaches to classroom management. In C. M. Evertson & C. S. Weinstein (Eds.), Handbook of classroom management: Research, practice, and contemporary issues (pp. 97-125). Mahwah, NJ: Erlbaum.

Dumlao, R. (2018). *A guide to collaborative communication for service-learning and community engagement partners*. Stylus Publishing, LLC.

Ekman, R. (1985). *Telling Lies*. Berkley Books.

Evertson, C., & Poole, I. (2008). Proactive classroom management. In T. Good (Ed.), 21st century education: A reference handbook (pp. I-131-I-140). Thousand Oaks, CA: SAGE Publications, Inc. doi:10.4135/9781412964012.n14

Evertson, M., & Weinstein, C. S. (Eds.). (2006). *Handbook of classroom management: Research, practice, and contemporary issues*. Erlbaum.

Fadda, P., & Sullivan, P. (2013). Using interactive video to develop preservice teachers' classroom awareness. *Contemporary Issues in Technology & Teacher Education, 13*(2), 156–174.

Freina, L., & Ott, M. (2015, April). A literature review on immersive virtual reality in education: state of the art and perspectives. In The international scientific conference eLearning and software for education (Vol. 1, No. 133, pp. 10-1007). Academic Press.

Frenzel, A. C., Daniels, L., & Burić, I. (2021). Teacher emotions in the classroom and their implications for students. *Educationnels Psychologist, 56*(4), 250–264. doi:10.1080/00461520.2021.1985501

García-Magariño, I., Cerezo, E., Plaza, I., & Chittaro, L. (2019). A mobile application to report and detect 3D body emotional poses. *Expert Systems with Applications*, *122*, 207–216. doi:10.1016/j.eswa.2019.01.021

Graus, M., van de Broek, A., Hennissen, P., & Schils, T. (2022). Disentangling aspects of teacher identity learning from reflective blogs: The development of a category system. *Teaching and Teacher Education*, *111*, 103624. Advance online publication. doi:10.1016/j.tate.2021.103624

Hamit, O., & Yildirim, R. (2020). Teacher perspectives on classroom management. *International Journal of Contemporary Educational Research*, *7*(1), 99–113. doi:10.33200/ijcer.645818

Hocker, J., & Wilmot, W. W. (2014). *Interpersonal conflict* (9th ed.). McGraw-Hill.

Janke, E., & Dumlao, R. J. (2019). Developing Communication Repertoires to Address Conflict in Community Engagement Work. *Journal of Higher Education Outreach & Engagement*, *23*, 35–56. https://eric.ed.gov/?id=EJ1212501

Jennings, P. A., & Greenberg, M. T. (2009). The prosocial classroom: Teacher social and emotional competence in relation to student and classroom outcomes. *Review of Educational Research*, *79*(1), 491–525. doi:10.3102/0034654308325693

Jones, T. S. (2000). Emotional communication in conflict: Essence and impact. In W. Eadie & P. Nelson (Eds.), *The language of conflict and resolution* (pp. 81–104). Sage. doi:10.4135/9781452205496.n6

Ke, F., Pachman, M., & Dai, Z. (2020). Investigating educational affordances of virtual reality for simulation-based teaching training with graduate teaching assistants. *Journal of Computing in Higher Education*, *32*(3), 607–627. doi:10.100712528-020-09249-9

Keller, M. M., & Becker, E. S. (2020). Teachers' emotions and emotional authenticity: Do they matter to students' emotional responses in the classroom? *Teachers and Teaching*, *27*(5), 404–422. doi:10.1080/13540602.2020.1834380

Kleinknecht, M., & Gröschner, A. (2016). Fostering preservice teachers' noticing with structured video feedback: Results of an online- and video-based intervention study. *Teaching and Teacher Education*, *59*, 45–46. doi:10.1016/j.tate.2016.05.020

Lau, K. W., & Lee, P. Y. (2015). The use of virtual reality for creating unusual environmental stimulation to motivate students to explore creative ideas. *Interactive Learning Environments*, *23*(1), 3–18. doi:10.1080/10494820.2012.745426

Lauermann, F., & Butler, R. (2021). The elusive links between teachers' teaching-related emotions, motivations, and self-regulation and students' educational outcomes. *Educational Psychologist*, *56*(4), 243–249. doi:10.1080/00461520.2021.1991800

Lee, E. A. L., & Wong, K. W. (2014). Learning with desktop virtual reality: Low spatial ability learners are more positively affected. *Computers & Education*, *79*, 49–58. doi:10.1016/j.compedu.2014.07.010

Manero, B., Alvarez, I. M., Romero, A., & Cárdenas, M. (2022). Adopting an immersive virtual reality system to enhance Pre-service teachers' communicative competence. *Proceedings. IEEE 22nd International Conference on Advanced Learning Technologies ICALT 2022.*

Martínez, M. B., Chacón, J. C., Díaz-Aguado, M. J., Martín, J., & Martínez, R. (2020). Disruptive behavior in compulsory Secondary education classrooms: A multi-informant analysis of the perception of teachers and students. *Pulso. Review of Education*, *43*, 15–34. https://revistas.cardenalcisneros.es/index.php/PULSO/article/view/380

Masó, I. (2022). Los conflictos en el aula de secundaria y las competencias comunicativas del profesorado [Conflict in the Secondary school classroom and teachers' communication skills]. In J.A. Marín, J.C. de la Cruz, S. Pozo, & G. Gómez (Eds.), Investigación e innovación educativa frente a los retos para el desarrollo sostenible (pp. 1383-1398). Andalucía: Dylinson. sl.

McGarr, O. (2021). The use of virtual simulations in teacher education to develop pre-service teachers' behaviour and classroom management skills: Implications for reflective practice. *Journal of Education for Teaching*, *47*(2), 274–286. doi:10.1080/02607476.2020.1733398

McGrath, K. F., & Van Bergen, P. (2019). Attributions and emotional competence: Why some teachers experience close relationships with disruptive students (and others don't). *Teachers and Teaching*, *25*(3), 334–357. doi:10.1080/13540602.2019.1569511

Ministry of Education. (2010). *Royal Decree 132/2010, of February 12, 2010, which establishes the minimum requirements for the centers that teach the second cycle of early childhood education, Primary education and Secondary education.* Available at https://www.boe.es/buscar/pdf/2010/BOE-A-2010-4132-consolidado.pdf

Ministry of Education and Vocational Training. (2020). *Facts and figures - School year 19/20.* https://sede.educacion.gob.es/publiventa/datos-y-cifras-curso-escolar-20192020/ensenanza-estadisticas/23109

Mulders, M., Buchner, J., & Kerres, M. (2020). A Framework for the Use of Immersive Virtual Reality in Learning Environments. *International Journal of Emerging Technologies in Learning, 15*(24), 208–224. doi:10.3991/ijet.v15i24.16615

Radianti, J., Majchrzak, T. A., Fromm, J., & Wohlgenannt, I. (2020). A systematic review of immersive virtual reality applications for higher education: Design elements, lessons learned, and research agenda. *Computers & Education, 147*, 103778. Advance online publication. doi:10.1016/j.compedu.2019.103778

Roettl, J., & Truter, R. (2018). The same video game in 2D, 3D or virtual reality – How does technology impact game evaluation and brand placements? *PLoS One, 13*(7), e0200724. Advance online publication. doi:10.1371/journal.pone.0200724 PMID:30028839

Sandars, J. (2010). The importance of usability testing to allow e-learning to reach its potential for medical education. *Education for Primary Care, 21*(1), 6–8. doi:10.1080/14739879.2010.11493869 PMID:20202315

Sangrá, A., Raffaghelli, J. E., & Guitert-Catasús, M. (2019). Learning ecologies through a lens: Ontological, methodological and applicative issues. A systematic review of the literature. *British Journal of Educational Technology, 50*(4), 1619–1638. doi:10.1111/bjet.12795

Sarcedo-Gorgoso, M. C., Santos-González, M. C., & Rego-Agraso, L. (2020). Las competencias docentes en la formación del profesorado de educación secundaria. *Profesorado. Revista de Currículum y Formación de Profesorado, 24*(3), 401–421. doi:10.30827/profesorado.v24i3.8260

Schleicher, A. (2020). *Teaching and Learning International Survey. TALIS 2018. Insights and Interpretations*. OCDE. https://www.oecd.org/education/talis/

Seufert, C., Oberdörfer, S., Roth, A., Grafe, S., Lugrin, J. L., & Latoschik, M. E. (2022). Classroom management competency enhancement for student teachers using a fully immersive virtual classroom. *Computers & Education, 179*, 104410. doi:10.1016/j.compedu.2021.104410

Sheridan, T. B. (2000). Interaction, imagination and immersion some research needs. *Proceedings of the ACM symposium on Virtual reality software and technology*, 1–7. 10.1145/502390.502392

Slater, M., & Wilbur, S. (1997). A framework for immersive virtual environments (FIVE): Speculations on the role of presence in virtual environments. *Presence (Cambridge, Mass.), 6*(6), 603–616. doi:10.1162/pres.1997.6.6.603

Sorensen, P. (2014). Collaboration, dialogue and expansive learning: The use of paired and multiple placements in the school practicum. *Teaching and Teacher Education, 44*, 128–137. doi:10.1016/j.tate.2014.08.010

Stavroulia, K., Christofi, M., Baka, E., Michael-Grigoriou, D., Magnenat-Thalmann, N., & Lanitis, A. (2019). Assessing the emotional impact of virtual reality-based teacher training. *The International Journal of Information and Learning Technology, 36*(3), 192–217. doi:10.1108/IJILT-11-2018-0127

Sutton, R. E. (2004). Emotional regulation goals and strategies of teachers. *Social Psychology of Education, 7*(4), 379–398. doi:10.100711218-004-4229-y

Terroni, N. N. (2009). La comunicación y la asertividad del discurso durante las interacciones grupales presenciales y por computadora [Communication and discourse assertiveness during face-to-face and computer-based group interactions]. *Psico-USF, 14*(1), 35–46. doi:10.1590/S1413-82712009000100005

Vienne, C., Sorin, L., Blondé, L., Huynh-Thu, Q., & Mamassian, P. (2014). Effect of the accommodation-vergence conflict on vergence eye movements. *Vision Research, 100*, 124–133. doi:10.1016/j.visres.2014.04.017 PMID:24835799

Watanabe, H., & Ujike, H. (2008). The activity of ISO/study group on "image safety" and three biological effect. *Proceedings of the 2nd International Symposium on Universal Communication, ISUC 2008*, 210–214. 10.1109/ISUC.2008.11

Winstone, N. E., Nash, R. A., Parker, M. P., & Rowntree, J. (2017). Supporting learners' agentic engagement with feedback: A systematic review and a taxonomy of recipience processes. *Educational Psychologist, 52*(1), 17–37. doi:10.1080/00461520.2016.1207538

ADDITIONAL READING

Chen, C.-Y. (2022, July). Immersive virtual reality to train preservice teachers in managing students' challenging behaviours: A pilot study. *British Journal of Educational Technology, 53*(4), 998–1024. Advance online publication. doi:10.1111/bjet.13181

Coskun, A., & Cagiltay, K. (2021). Investigation of classroom management skills by using eye-tracking technology. *Education and Information Technologies, 26*(3), 2501–2522. doi:10.100710639-020-10368-0

Gandolfi, E., Kosko, K. W., & Ferdig, R. E. (2021). Situating presence within extended reality for teacher training: Validation of the extended Reality Presence Scale (XRPS) in preservice teacher use of immersive 360 video. *British Journal of Educational Technology*, *52*(2), 824–841. doi:10.1111/bjet.13058

Lee, M., & van Vlack, S. (2018). Teachers' emotional labour, discrete emotions, and classroom management self-efficacy. *Educational Psychology*, *38*(5), 669–686. doi:10.1080/01443410.2017.1399199

Loulou, M. S., Garner, P. W., & Hamada, H. (2021). Teachers' emotional expressiveness and classroom management practices: Associations with young students' social-emotional and behavioral competence. *Psychology in the Schools*. Advance online publication. doi:10.1002/pits.22631

Luo, Z. (2021). Using eye-tracking technology to identify learning styles: Behaviour patterns and identification accuracy. *Education and Information Technologies*, *26*(4), 4457–4485. doi:10.100710639-021-10468-5

Noroozi, P.-D., Pijeira-Díaz, H. J., Sobocinski, M., Dindar, M., Järvelä, S., & Kirschner, P. A. (2020). Multimodal data indicators for capturing cognitive, motivational, and emotional learning processes: A systematic literature review. *Education and Information Technologies*, *25*(6), 5499–5547. doi:10.100710639-020-10229-w

Özen, H., & Yıldırım, R. (2020). Teacher perspectives on classroom management. *International Journal of Contemporary Educational Research*, *7*(1), 99–113. doi:10.33200/ijcer.645818

Pekrun. (2021). Teachers need more than knowledge: Why motivation, emotion, and self-regulation are indispensable. *Educational Psychologist, 56*(4), 312–322. doi:10.1080/00461520.2021.1991356

Ye, X., Liu, P., Lee, X., Zhang, Y., & Chiu, C. (2021). Classroom misbehaviour management: An SVVR-based training system for preservice teachers. *Interactive Learning Environments*, *29*(1), 112–129. doi:10.1080/10494820.2019.1579235

KEY TERMS AND DEFINITIONS

Academic Emotions: A set of emotions that are experienced by students and teachers in learning or teaching situations.

Attitude: A mental and neural state of readiness, organized through experience, exerting a directive or dynamic influence upon the individual's response to all objects and situations with which it is related.

Classroom Management: Actions teachers take to use instructional time effectively to maintain students' attention and, through this, create an environment that facilitates both academic and social-emotional development.

Conflict: A particular type of communication as an expressed contradiction that blocks communicative processes.

Emotional Activation: Tendency towards action experienced when facing conflicts could be caused by an incongruence with expectations or by the occurrence of an unforeseen event.

Learning Ecology: The learner self-directs her activity, cultivating relationships and using, producing, and sharing resources, interacting in an organised way with their context - their social, physical, and virtual environment to achieve a specific learning goal.

Virtual Learning Environment (VLE): An environment rich in meanings where subjects and technological objects interact, enhancing knowledge construction. VLE includes a variety of tools, documents, and artifacts that enable learning.

Chapter 3
Bringing the Metaverse to Higher Education:
Engaging University Students in Virtual Worlds

Gary E. Burnett
University of Nottingham, UK

Catherine Harvey
University of Nottingham, UK

Rebekah Kay
University of Nottingham, UK

ABSTRACT

This chapter provides a case study on the use of a virtual world as the predominant mechanism for interacting with university students. In the Autumn Semester 2020, 49 engineering students partook in weekly seminars with teachers and each other on a fantastical virtual teaching island, known as Nottopia. The majority of students accessed the virtual world on desktop computers, although four routinely used their own VR headsets. Survey data indicated that the student experience was extremely positive and motivation to learn was very high. Interviews, together with video observations, established that five themes dictated the positive outcome, namely the design of the space, the nature of the integral content, the prevailing group dynamics, the role of avatars, and the magical interactions possible. These themes are realised in an initial design framework.

DOI: 10.4018/978-1-6684-3398-0.ch003

INTRODUCTION

Higher Education teaching practice is in significant flux as staff reflect on the experiences of teaching and learning during the Covid-19 pandemic. As noted in a recent white paper (Manifesto, 2020), Universities face many challenges in understanding and responding to rapidly evolving student expectations when considering the relative merits of traditional campus-based versus online learning strategies. Moreover, there is widespread recognition that students' online learning experiences have not always been positive during the pandemic (Neves & Hewitt, 2021) – affected to a degree by the extensive appropriation of work/corporate platforms (such as 2D video conferencing software) into the predominately younger-person-focused Higher Education context.

In contrast, the pandemic has accelerated thinking regarding the use of Extended Reality (XR) for universities, expressed clearly in the Immersive Learning Network's 2021 report on the opportunities, barriers and catalysts to XR in the education domain (Lee et al., 2021). In their report they note that XR technologies have undergone massive developmental changes since early 2020 and now provide a level of maturity enabling practitioners to significantly enhance the student learning experience. Moreover, they emphasise the considerable potential of XR to enhance students' social learning experiences, as noted (p. 37):

Mixed reality environments will become integral parts of our students' learning and working experience—a world where we learn and work alongside virtual humans, digital avatars, and personal assistants.

This chapter provides an empirical study on the specific use of XR in a HE context. In particular, the Covid-19 pandemic created a unique opportunity to quantify and qualify the social experiences of Engineering students who only interacted with the teachers and each other within a virtual world. For the autumn/fall semester 2020 face-to-face teaching at the University of Nottingham where the study took place was severely restricted – and most interaction with students was conducted online. For the level 4 module (taken by final year undergraduate and postgraduate taught students), 'MMME4084 - Simulation, Virtual Reality and Advanced Human-Machine Interface', a decision was made to undertake *all* forms of teaching using the social VR platform Mozilla Hubs – the module convenors and the students never met face-to-face during the semester.

Specifically, the overall aim of this research was to understand the impact of a virtual world on University students' learning experiences. In terms of objectives, data needed to be collected and analysed for questionnaire/ interview (subjective) and behavioural (objective) responses throughout the teaching activities. Recommendations could then be made on the implications of the findings for Higher Education practice.

This chapter includes a review of background literature on the use of XR in the Higher Education sector, followed by a description of the study methodology utilised in our work. The chapter then outlines some key quantitative results, predominately focussing on survey data collected. The main bulk of the chapter discusses some central themes emerging from qualitative analysis of interviews and behavioural observations. The final section of the chapter sets out five fundamental guidelines for practitioners that have emerged from our study, together with four future work recommendations.

BACKGROUND

Extended Reality (XR) is a broad term encompassing many related concepts, such as Virtual Reality (VR), Augmented Reality (AR), Augmented Virtuality (AV) and Mixed Reality (MR) (Palmas & Klinker, 2018). The focus for this chapter is VR, which in itself has many competing definitions within the literature. As noted by Jerald (2016), these can be more technology-focused and related to the concept of immersion, or more people-focused and linked to presence ('being there'). In educational contexts, it is critical to consider VR in human-centred terms – and many authors have argued that it is human perception that is critical to a "VR" experience, rather than technological capabilities (see for example Häfner et al., 2013; Radianti et al., 2020).

A central component of VR will be the virtual world/environment itself. In this respect, a useful and comprehensive perspective is given by Girvan (2018, p. 1099) – who describes virtual worlds as:

Shared, simulated spaces which are inhabited and shaped by their inhabitants who are represented as avatars. These avatars mediate our experience of this space as we move, interact with objects and interact with others, with whom we construct a shared understanding of the world at that time.

In essence, virtual worlds are persistent spaces that can be accessed by multiple people (represented as avatars) interacting with each other and the environment itself. Moreover, the people have agency over the virtual world itself, i.e. they can change the environment, e.g. by adding 2D/3D content. Avatars are the static/animated figures that allow humans to interact within digital environments (Nowak & Fox, 2018). As such, they represent a ''tangible'' embodiment of an individual's personal identity when online. Moreover, they are usually highly customizable, and can be extremely fluid based on context. Authors have noted the increasing importance of avatars in Higher Education, as more teaching is conducted virtually, drawing upon gaming conventions (Freeman & Maloney, 2020). However, it is also recognized that little is known about how students make use of avatars and the subsequent impact on learning (Bombari et al., 2015).

Previous research regarding the use of VR in Higher Education has focused largely on the teaching of hard skills (e.g., procedural/practical knowledge), drawing on well-established benefits of VR in training – that is, the ability to carry out multiple exercises with immediate and easily accessible feedback (Lawson & Burnett, 2015). Considerably less work has considered students' acquisition of soft (e.g., group work/communication) skills via VR – although, it is apparent that work in this area has accelerated in recent years as a result of both hardware and software advancements (e.g. Kuznetcova & Glassman, 2020). Most recently, virtual worlds have emerged as a genuine alternative to campus-based spaces, and are seen as increasingly important to embed within University teaching – especially given the predicted rise in so-called Metaverse technologies in working contexts - as noted by Lee et al. (2021, p.44):

The workforce of the future will find it difficult to imagine how employees functioned in our era without extensive opportunities to improve their skills through immersive and mixed reality environments.

From an empirical viewpoint, studies have shown that VR can significantly enhance motivation and learning by providing environments that promote discovery, include natural group interactions, and allow students to experience worlds/objects from new/unique perspectives (Radianti et al., 2020; Won et al., 2020). Relatively little attention is given to the theoretical foundations that underpin such benefits, although some authors have noted that the educational use of VR is consistent with cognitive and social constructivism as well as experiential perspectives on learning (Radianti et al., 2020; Huang et al., 2010).

Despite such progress, there are two fundamental limitations related to the existing studies in this area. Firstly, previous work typically exposes students to an experience where they undertake one/few session/s in VR (i.e., in the minutes-hours timeframe). Such a focus fails to consider the impact of using VR over an extended period as an integral part of a course/module or even a programme (i.e., a regular experience over several weeks/months). Secondly, studies usually focus on measures related to knowledge and skill acquisition and retention. Whilst this is undoubtedly important, this focus neglects the role of social encounters for learning (Radianti et al., 2020) – a research gap that will be addressed in the current chapter.

METHODOLOGY

Participants

Forty-nine undergraduate and postgraduate students were enrolled on the module from different programmes within Engineering at the University of Nottingham, where the study was undertaken in the UK. They were split into the following four groups of roughly equal size for the purposes of the seminars: MEng Mechanical Engineering, BEng Engineering (Aerospace, Mechanical), MEng Product Design, and MSc Human Factors and Ergonomics.

Virtual World

A virtual world was created for use within the Mozilla Hubs social VR platform. Hubs was chosen over other platforms primarily because of two underlying factors:

- **Accessibility** - it could be accessed through the browser (i.e., no downloads/ installs) on desktop computers, tablets and phones, as well as Head Mounted Displays (HMDs). This was important given that access to HMDs was limited (only four students in the cohort routinely used them) and that some people will inevitably feel discomfort/sickness symptoms with immersive displays (Chang et al., 2020).
- **Customizability** - it was possible for both the teacher and the students to easily modify the world to suit educational goals. For instance, using Mozilla's editing software (Spoke) the convenors were able to adapt a pre-existing fantastical building which had a convenient gathering space for discussions with all students, together with two break-out rooms for more focused activities. Moreover, both the teachers and students could readily bring 3D objects into the world.

A decision was made to place the virtual building within the context of a lake - as this is a prominent landmark in all of the University's three campuses in the UK, China and Malaysia. Moreover, pictures of the UK campus were placed on walls throughout the building. Subsequently, the overall environment was branded as 'Nottopia' – see Figure 1.

Activities

The primary content for the module was delivered via pre-recorded lectures (each 20-30 minutes long) given primarily by the module convenor and released weekly

Figure 1. Image of Nottopia, the virtual world used in teaching.

to students (i.e., asynchronous engagement). These were all given by the convenor (in avatar form using an HMD) from within different areas of Nottopia utilising PowerPoint slides and numerous accompanying props (e.g., pens, videos, pointers). An example lecture can be viewed online[1]. The reason for recording these lectures in immersive VR was partly to increase student motivation to watch them, but primarily as it allowed the teacher to explain VR concepts more easily to the students.

For practical engagement with the lecture content, a series of seminar sessions were organised each week (i.e., synchronous engagement). Students were allocated to one of four slots (each lasting 30 minutes and optional) – so that 10-14 students attended a session for each of the 11 weeks of the semester. Seminar sessions were deliberately designed by the module convenor to exploit the capabilities of a virtual environment for education – based largely on previous studies, e.g., Hafner at al., 2013; Vergara et al., 2019. Examples of seminar activities included:

- **Treasure hunts** – where students in small groups had to find and label particular objects within Nottopia linked to a problem under discussion
- **Show and tells** – where students brought in 2D/3D content and discussed its significance to the week's topic
- **'Meet the expert' discussions**. – involving world experts who 'sat' by a fireside and responded to questions from the audience who essentially had 'front-row' seats
- **Design workshops** – highly interactive sessions in which students working in teams had to import 2D/3D objects to help design some new technology, such as an autonomous car

- **Virtual field trips** – 'away-day' events where students and the teachers would use a portal in Nottopia to visit a different virtual world, usually linked to existing real-world spaces, such as Stonehenge, a Fireworks show, etc.

An excerpt from a seminar can be viewed online[2].

Data Capture

To investigate students' experiences, a mixed method approach was taken, including a questionnaire released to all students, a series of interviews with a sample of students, and observations of the students in real-time via video recording of sessions. Attendance figures for the seminars were also recorded. This combination of subjective and objective data collection methods is typical to this area of research (Won et al., 2020; Jaligama & Liarokapis, 2011) and here aimed to provide an overall understanding of student experience within the virtual world.

Questionnaire: Many questions were repurposed from studies investigating similar themes, such as those within Picciano (2002) and Yen and Tu (2008) – considering issues of motivation, communication, collaboration and social interactions. Bespoke questions pertaining to overall experience, avatars, and technical difficulties were also included. Open questions allowed students the chance to directly express their opinions – e.g., related to how the experience compared with other forms of online learning, what they liked most/least about the experience and how it could be improved.

Interviews: In-depth one-on-one semi-structured interviews with six students were carried out, including one student who routinely utilised an HMD. All students were invited for the interview via the module online message board – and the first six volunteers were subsequently approached. Interviews lasted 15-20 minutes and focused upon broad themes associated with the experience of VR in this context, such as how the use of Nottopia compared with other forms of teaching they had encountered I their education (online and face-to-face), their primary likes/dislikes for the virtual world and how their experiences could be improved for the future.

Observations: Based on Open Broadcaster Software (OBS) screen recordings, a total of 18 recorded hours of observational data were collected from the seminars. Approximately three-quarters of videos were taken from the point of view of the module convenor within the session, however some sessions were recorded by way of a fixed camera in one area of the virtual environment. The students' behaviour was analysed and coded from a qualitative perspective, with a general view to understanding how students interacted with each other and the space, as well as gathering instances of social interaction, communication, and collaboration, or a lack thereof, within the sessions. The use and selection of avatars was also noted.

RESULTS FOR QUANTITATIVE DATA

In relation to attendance, the number of students who engaged with the seminars never dropped below 90% (44 of the 49 students) and reached 100% on occasion – despite it being an optional activity.

For the survey, 28 out of 49 students filled in the questionnaire, giving a 57% response rate. All students believed Nottopia was, on the whole, a positive experience. Moreover, 93% (26 out of 28 students) felt that virtual worlds such as Nottopia represented the future of how Universities could teach students. Figures 2-5 show survey results for three specific questions related to motivation, engagement with peers, and engagement with teaching staff. In essence, these graphs highlight the positivity in which students viewed their overall experiences in relation to traditional (face-to-face) classroom teaching.

Figure 2. Number of students responding to question concerning motivation to participate when learning within a virtual world.

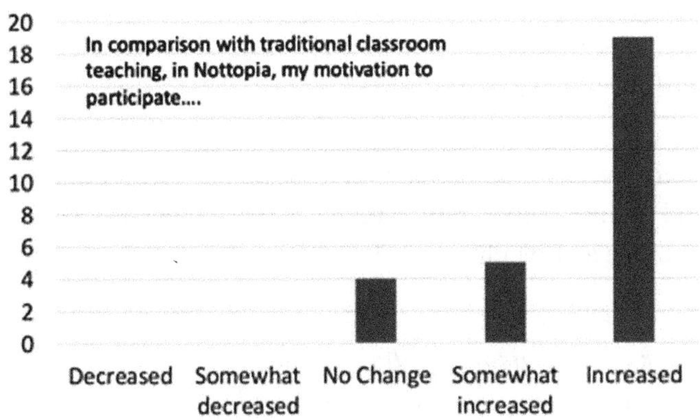

DISCUSSION AND THEMES

A theme-based analysis was conducted by the authors utilizing the various qualitative data generated by the open-ended questionnaire responses, the interviews and the behavioural observations. Five themes were apparent from this analysis: virtual world; content; group dynamics; avatars; and magical interactions. These themes are discussed below, with quotes from students (either from open-ended questionnaires or interview transcripts) to emphasise specific points.

Figure 5 provides an initial structure to the five themes, and, as such serves as a useful framework for considering the different socially oriented factors that will

Figure 3. Number of students responding to question concerning interaction with other students when learning within a virtual world.

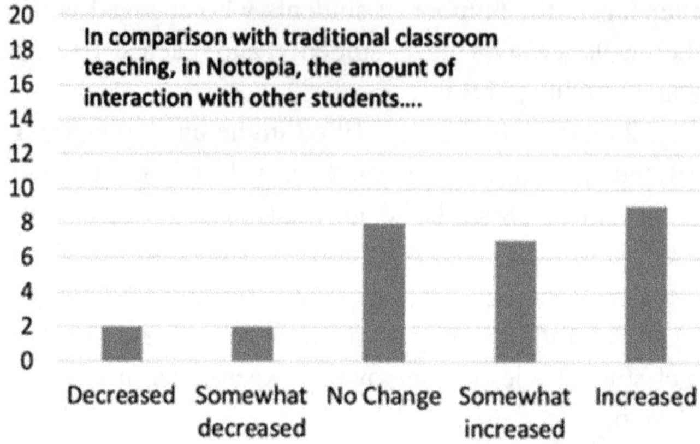

influence the student experience within VR. It is intended that practitioners reflect on each of the themes in turn when planning to use VR as an integral part of their teaching.

Virtual World

The Nottopia environment was deliberately designed to be both functional *and* fantastical – and did not seek to replicate the physical campus (although there was an attempt to include a university-style building). The fantastical elements (island,

Figure 4. Number of students responding to question concerning interaction with teaching staff when learning within a virtual world.

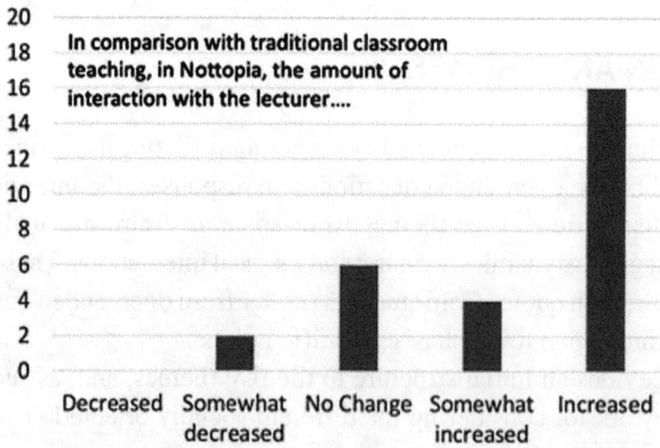

Figure 5. A framework for considering the impact of VR on the student experience within university teaching.

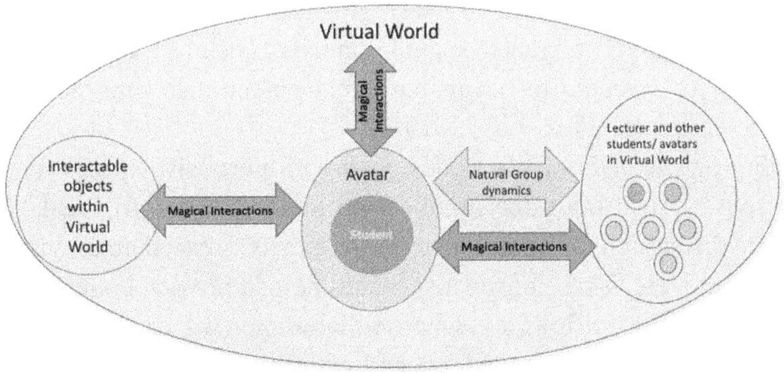

skyline, aquarium, etc.) were deemed important in the development of the world prior to the module commencing – particularly to provide some form of escapism during the pandemic.

Furthermore, the virtual environment design was inspired by prior work by Batey et al. (2021) highlighting the importance of nature in encouraging well-being and creativity. In this respect, students in their feedback picked up on the calming nature of the Nottopia experience, partly influenced by characteristics of the virtual environment itself (such as the lake, sunny skies etc.):

I liked the general calmness of the environment and the lecturers.

Relaxed atmosphere, virtual setting allowed for unique teaching method, very different to anything else experienced so far in Nottingham.

With respect to functional characteristics of Nottopia, there was a conscious attempt to support the constructivist method of learning, as it allowed learners to enter an 'authentic environment' that might otherwise be unavailable to them (Scavarelli et al., 2020). In the midst of a pandemic where students were universally working from home and unable to access typical University facilities, this was especially pertinent.

Nottopia resembled a university environment, which was nice considering we were all at home and couldn't see each other.

The virtual environment also facilitated 'situated learning'- enabling learners to 'be capable of collaborating and solving problems in different contexts and situations' (Pérez-Sanagustín et al., 2015). Authors have noted that VR facilitates the use of highly-contextual environments to support situated learning experiences (Dawley & Dede, 2014), simulating realistic and safe spaces for learners to perform specific tasks (Huang et al., 2010). Memory is also highly dependent on environment (Smith, 1979), and so using VR to create 'spatial contexts', such as a university building where learning is *expected* to occur, has great potential in improving students' knowledge retention (Krokos et al., 2019).

Reflecting on this, Nottopia was designed with purposive spaces for different learning activities, such as a gathering/meet-up area (see Figure 6), break-out rooms where student discussion took place, a 'meet the expert' area where discussions with experts were held, etc. These purposive spaces helped provide context for student learning, and created specific spaces where collaboration was expected, thus helping to promote interaction between students and with the teaching staff.

Figure 6. Gathering space in Nottopia used in teaching activities.

There was no attempt to make the environment student-owned, but this happened organically during the running of the module. For instance, it became apparent following interviews and incidental observation by teaching staff that enrolled students were visiting Nottopia outside of the seminar period to show friends and family the environment, and also to personalize the space (e.g., by adding selfies to a picture board or including objects associated with the physical University campus). As noted by Natale et al. (2020), VR provides a unique opportunity for educators to work with students in the creation of spaces that can feel personal and encourage a sense of togetherness. In particular, memorabilia such as group photos taken within the virtual environment can represent 'traces of social activity' – providing semi-permanent evidence of shared experiences and heightened motivation to engage (Ackerman & Starr, 1995).

Figure 7. Students interacting with vehicle during design workshop activity.

Content

It is not just the physical environment itself that is important to a student experience of VR – it is also the objects present within it. It has been noted that one of the most significant benefits of a virtual environment for use in learning is the 'enhanced spatial knowledge representation, which facilitates learning spatially about environments and/or objects' (Dalgarno & Lee, 2010). This latter point is especially pertinent for Engineering students, as it allows students to load any array of objects in 3D, such as vehicles, engines etc., into the environment and view, investigate and manipulate them from a multitude of perspectives, essentially providing considerable situated context in learning, as noted by students:

This form of teaching will be important where looking at something is quite important to the subject.

Creative medium, I could add videos and 3D objects into the space which was cool.

This capability is also of considerable value for teachers who can easily add objects to support learning objectives - many of which could be extremely difficult/ impossible to incorporate into real-world classes. As an example, Figure 7 shows students within/outside an autonomous vehicle, which was added to the virtual environment for a design workshop related to interfaces for future transport scenarios.

Nevertheless, on occasion, students brought in themselves overly complex 3D models or other media (Gifs, videos) which them impacted on the overall performance of the virtual world. This observation highlights the importance of educating students as to what can/cannot be uploaded to the virtual world (linked to file sizes, number of polygons, texture sizes, and so on) and potentially limiting students' powers for specific learning activities.

Group Dynamics

A significant benefit of utilising social VR platforms such as Mozilla Hubs for teaching is that students could utilise the spatial audio capabilities to move in and out of different conversations in a natural and efficient fashion. This was in stark contrast to the other forms of online video conferencing-based modes of teaching the students were using at that time.

In their comments, students noted these issues – raising the value of being able to move freely around the environment - but also contrasting the experience with traditional classroom teaching:

... moving around the space made it more engaging and less passive.

You could more physically see people who were present rather than a flat 2D box on a screen with their initials.

Nottopia.....allowed for easy and informative interactions which didn't feel as awkward as they probably would do in a real-life classroom.

Observations of the videos revealed a number of interesting behaviours from students that either confirmed or challenged social norms for a university group-based teaching experience. For instance, students generally maintained personal space conventions (also noted by Williamson et al., 2021) which included 'waiting at a distance' behaviour when arriving early for a session (see Figure 8). Nevertheless, on occasion it was apparent that students were willing to break such rules to compensate for certain technical limitations of VR, e.g., when joining the lecturer on stage to see an image on a slide more clearly.

Students also exhibited a range of positive social behaviours within the virtual world, such as helping others when they were experiencing difficulties, e.g., when pinning objects or moving text boxes, or explaining when a fellow student had to temporarily leave the space. Moreover, they adopted a range of non-verbal adaptive strategies to express themselves socially in the environment – e.g., writing on a wall to explain a problem with their microphone, or using their mouse to move their avatar to indicate yes/no gestures.

For education practitioners, the important implication here is to encourage such natural group dynamics, for instance, by providing appropriate cues in the world

Figure 8. Students conforming to social norms by 'waiting at a distance' in the virtual world.

(e.g., obvious places to 'stand', 'sit', 'gather', 'view', etc.). It will also be critical to experiment with sound drop-off parameters, so participants can have private conversations (e.g., for breakout sessions) whilst still being conscious of discussions occurring elsewhere in the world.

Avatars

The ability to utilise avatars as a visual/physical representation of self (personal identity) was critical to the success of the VR experience – and perhaps the most significant issue. Three sub-themes emerged from the qualitative data.

Presence

Being represented by an avatar within a virtual environment has been shown to increase feelings of 'co-presence' or 'social presence' (Nowak & Biocca, 2003), an aspect of presence that implies the feeling of 'being there, in the same virtual space, together with virtual humans' (Bombari et al., 2015). It can also enhance the feeling of co-location (Nowak & Biocca, 2003) - all issues picked up by students within the interviews:

It comes back to the presence of actually feeling like you're there... and [in Nottopia] it feels like you are with people, whereas in a Teams meeting or something it doesn't have that.

In the present era, these issues took on an increased significance and students particularly valued the sense of being together (also observed by Radianti et al.,

2020) – that was enabled by the use of avatars (as well as being within a virtual environment):

Being able to be with people [in Nottopia] almost like physically in the real world was a huge help through the pandemic…moments of randomly saying "sorry" when you virtually bump into someone… small details like that made me feel like I was living in the normal world.

Social Anxiety

Based on the interviews, it was apparent that the use of avatars reduced social discomfort in communications due to the increased anonymity they afforded for students. In particular, this led to an increased inclination for them to collaborate and actively engage in seminar sessions – potentially even more so than for traditional face-to-face classes.

You could talk to one person next to you without being the centre of attention.

I engaged with students I wouldn't normally have engaged with when sat in a seminar in person as people group with who they know and only work with them. I've had a more diverse range of opinions than I would have normally received from my usual group of peers.

I didn't feel quite as self-conscious... people were seeing my avatar, not me.

Personalization

Avatar choice and customisation provided considerable opportunities for students to represent elements of their personal identity and was particularly valued.

The lack of using a video camera to show yourself was different, instead having an avatar was fun and allowed people to have a bit more freedom.

Novel form of interaction and I like customizing an avatar.

It was observed that students utilised a wide range of avatars (see Figure 9) – representing aspects of their true-self, ideal-self, ought-self and/or value-self (Nowak & Fox, 2020). From interviews, it was also apparent though that some students purposely aimed not to represent elements of their self in their avatar, either through a random choice or a decision to conceal aspects of their identity or even to explore alternative identities (so-called identity tourism) (Nowak & Fox, 2020).

Figure 9. Examples of avatars used by students within the virtual world.

Magical Interactions

VR affords many magical or super-human possibilities (defying gravity, passing through physical objects, teleportation, etc.) and multiple students responded within the questionnaire and the interviews noticing the gamification of their experiences.

Nottopia felt more like a game than a lecture, and as such I was more willing to engage in the session(s).

I particularly liked the fun things we added.

It was novel and fun compared to Teams and [I was] more likely to stay engaged.

With respect to the 'magical' aspects present, it has been noted that Human-Computer Interaction (HCI) often fails to acknowledge the complexity of the concept and its roots in the social and philosophical anthropology disciplines (Gladden, 2019). Moreover, there is a basic assumption that 'magical' means a positive experience ('amazing, enjoyable, effortless', etc.) even though there may be negative ramifications of employing magic. Whilst the students clearly appreciated the superhuman abilities afforded to them by VR, this was not always optimum in this educational context. For instance, within Nottopia it became apparent during the early sessions that the abilities to fly and create needed to be curtailed, at least initially, to allow students to remain focused on the class activity. Such powers were then introduced, where relevant, in later seminars.

Similarly, gamification is commonly referred to as a key motivational advantage of VR (Dalgarno & Lee, 2010) but is also noted as difficult to define (Deterding et al., 2011). Nevertheless, there is at least some agreement that three elements are generally present in a 'game': Challenge, Fantasy, and Curiosity (Malone, 1981). To varying degrees all elements were present within the student experience in the module. Challenge was provided through teaching design, as an academic or class challenge was set by the lecturer at the beginning of each session. Fantasy was certainly embedded within Nottopia due to its setting – a familiar but fantastical environment of a University-esque building located in the middle of a lake – as well as through the ability to design/select non-human avatars. Lastly, curiosity was cultivated due to the novelty of the experience – through the magical interactions that could take place such as the ability to fly or manifest objects at will within the environment. Moreover, the customisation capabilities of Hubs empowered the lecturers to theme Nottopia throughout the semester – for example, including scary objects and noises for Halloween or festive scenes approaching the Christmas holidays.

It was quite difficult to get bored. The Nottopia sessions always kept up the excitement with new things every time. It never got repetitive!

This mix of the challenging, curious, and fantastical elements within the virtual environment created an engaging, playful, creative atmosphere which was also evident in the students' behaviour. For instance: students on occasion chose funny and outlandish avatars with the intention of creating humour; groups of students creatively repurposed learning materials in Nottopia for humorous effect; students used learning materials playfully, such as taking a vehicle model created by the lecturer for a drive.

As noted earlier (Figure 2) students also overwhelmingly reported within the questionnaire that their motivation to participate in class increased. Thus, the magical/gamification aspects of VR appeared to greatly increase motivation and engagement, as has also been found within other studies in educational contexts (Dalgarno & Lee, 2010).

CONCLUSION

This study sought to understand how students interact within a virtual world in seminar-based activities across a whole semester. It was apparent that the virtual

Figure 10. Students and teacher present in virtual world and in real world able to interact via a mixed-reality window.

world (including the space, interactions and use of avatars) could facilitate considerable social interaction between students and teachers, as well as providing an overwhelmingly positive overall student experience. Through a theme-based analysis of questionnaire responses, interviews, and behavioural observations, it is suggested that the benefits of VR are due to the fundamental characteristics of the environment itself, the 3D nature of the objects within it, the ease of social-based communications and the many magical interactions possible through gamification.

At an overall level, it is highly recommended that Higher Education institutions should seriously consider the use of virtual worlds across multiple modules/courses and programmes. Based on the cumulative learning from our teaching in VR for the last two years, it is possible to articulate five high-level recommendations for those interested in the use of VR for providing engaging experiences for their students:

1. Design a virtual world to be 'fit for purpose' – that is, created predominately with the teaching activities and learning outcomes in mind.
2. Incorporate 3D objects and media into the world suitable for use in specific teaching activities, but not overly complex.
3. Exploit the spatial audio characteristics of VR by using teaching activities that require discussion and frequent avatar movement.
4. Employ avatar creation interfaces with the flexibility and usability for students to easily design personalised representations.
5. Utilise the magical interaction possibilities of VR in an appropriate fashion, to enhance student motivation, whilst avoiding potential negative impacts, such as distraction.

Whilst the goals of the present study were quite broad, it is clear that a number of more specific research areas are now emerging – and these will be investigated with future cohorts of the module. Four topics are given here.

1. In the 2020 running of the module only a handful of students used HMDs, and they were clearly expert users. In the future, it will be important to consider the student's widespread use of HMDs to understand how students make use of this hardware, the role of immersion in the student/teacher experience and the potential negative issues of sickness.
2. Blended learning will be increasingly important in the Higher Education sector, where face-to-face and online experiences are offered (Stone & Glover, 2021). This is notoriously difficult to achieve with synchronous teaching – but could be attained with students present in real spaces and virtual spaces interacting with each other through mixed-reality windows (Schnädelbach et al., 2006). In this respect, a rudimentary version of this was trialled recently at the University of Nottingham (see Figure 10).
3. Avatars are clearly critical to students' interactions within virtual worlds, and some initial understanding of their use in Nottopia is described above – yet our data collection did not focus on the myriad of questions particular to how the specific choice of avatars could impact on social behaviours between students and teachers (both positive and negative), addressing issues such as identity, anonymity, distraction and so forth (Nowak & Fox, 2020).
4. The design concept of Nottopia naturally encouraged some degree of community building for our students, as noted above – evidenced by students visiting the space outside of teaching times and personalising the world to some extent. Nevertheless, this was not universal behaviour and was limited in scope. Consequently, our assessments are presently being re-designed to be more 'authentic' to the virtual world experience (inspired by Lee at., 2021) – specifically, by requiring students in groups to design their own virtual worlds that can be accessed via portals from Nottopia.

The intention is for this module to continue to be run this way for future years, regardless of the status of the pandemic. It is apparent in recent publications (e.g. Han et al., 2022) that other institutions worldwide have used the catalyst of Covid-19 to experiment with social VR during the last two years and have had a largely positive response from students. It is interesting to observe that such teaching is typically undertaken in modules that concern VR to some extent, where the argument to use VR is undoubtedly stronger than for courses without such content. Nevertheless, the on-going data collected in virtual worlds such as Nottopia and elsewhere will considerably help in our understanding of how VR worlds should be developed for teaching more widely.

In summary, the module provides a unique testbed for investigating how University students can interact with lecturers and fellow students within VR – and will continue to challenge the prevailing models of learning for Higher Education.

ACKNOWLEDGMENT

We would like to thank our students who continue to be willing partners in our quest to understand the impacts of XR technology on the University learning experience. We also thank colleagues in the Faculty of Engineering at the University of Nottingham who support us in our novel teaching approaches and provided ethics clearance for the data collection undertaken within the module.

REFERENCES

Ackerman, M. S., & Starr, B. (1995, December). Social activity indicators: interface components for CSCW systems. *Proceedings of the 8th annual ACM symposium*, 159–168. 10.1145/215585.215969

Batey, M., Hughes, D. J., Crick, L., & Toader, A. (2021). Designing creative spaces: An experimental examination of the effect of a nature poster on divergent thinking. *Ergonomics*, *64*(1), 139–146. doi:10.1080/00140139.2020.1811398 PMID:32819209

Bombari, D., Schmid Mast, M., Canadas, E., & Bachmann, M. (2015). Studying social interactions through immersive virtual environment technology: Virtues and challenges. *Frontiers in Psychology*, *6*, 6. doi:10.3389/fpsyg.2015.00869 PMID:26157414

Chang, E., Kim, H. T., & Yoo, B. (2020). Virtual Reality Sickness: A Review of Causes and Measurements. *International Journal of Human-Computer Interaction*, *36*(7), 1658–1682. doi:10.1080/10447318.2020.1778351

Dalgarno, B., & Lee, M. J. W. (2010). What are the learning affordances of 3-D virtual environments? *British Journal of Educational Technology*, *41*(1), 10–32. doi:10.1111/j.1467-8535.2009.01038.x

Dawley, L., & Dede, C. (2014). Situated Learning in Virtual Worlds and Immersive Simulations. In J. M. Spector, M. D. Merrill, J. Elen, & M. J. Bishop (Eds.), *Handbook of Research on Educational Communications and Technology* (pp. 723–734). Springer. doi:10.1007/978-1-4614-3185-5_58

Deterding, S., Dixon, D., Khaled, R., & Nacke, L. (2011, September). From game design elements to gamefulness: defining 'gamification. *MindTrek'11: Proceedings of the 15th International Academic MindTrek conference: Envisioning Future Media Environments*, 9-15.

Freeman, G., & Maloney, D. (2020). Body, Avatar, and Me: The Presentation and Perception of Self in Social Virtual Reality. *Proceedings of the ACM on Human-Computer Interaction, 4.*

Girvan, C. (2018). What is a virtual world? Definition and classification. *Educational Technology Research and Development*, *6*(5), 1087–1100. doi:10.100711423-018-9577-y

Gladden, M. E. (2019). Novel forms of "magical" human-computer interaction within the cyber-physical smart workplace: Implications for usability and user experience. *International Journal of Research Studies in Management*, *8*(1), 25–48. doi:10.5861/ijrsm.2019.4001

Häfner, P., Häfner, V., & Ovtcharova, J. (2013). Teaching Methodology for Virtual Reality Practical Course in Engineering Education. *Procedia Computer Science*, *25*, 251–269. doi:10.1016/j.procs.2013.11.031

Han, E., Miller, M. R., Ram, N., Nowak, K. L., & Bailenson, J. N. (2022, May 26-30). Understanding Group Behavior in Virtual Reality: A Large-Scale, Longitudinal Study in the Metaverse. *72nd Annual International Communication Association Conference.*

Huang, H. M., Rauch, U., & Liaw, S.-S. (2010). Investigating learners' attitudes toward virtual reality learning environments: Based on a constructivist approach. *Computers & Education*, *55*(3), 1171–1182. doi:10.1016/j.compedu.2010.05.014

Jaligama, V., & Liarokapis, F. (2011). An Online Virtual Learning Environment for Higher Education. *Third International Conference on Games and Virtual Worlds for Serious Applications*, 207–214. 10.1109/VS-GAMES.2011.44

Jerald., J. (2016). *The VR Book: Human-Centred Design for Virtual Reality*. ACM Books.

Krokos, E., Plaisant, C., & Varshney, A. (2019). Virtual memory palaces: Immersion aids recall. *Virtual Reality (Waltham Cross)*, *23*(1), 1–15. doi:10.100710055-018-0346-3

Kuznetcova, I., & Glassman, M. (2020). Rethinking the use of multi-user virtual environments in education. *Technology, Pedagogy and Education*, *29*(8), 1–17. do i:10.1080/1475939X.2020.1768141

Lawson, G., & Burnett, G. E. (2015). Simulation and Digital Human Modelling. In J. Wilson & S. Sharples (Eds.), *Evaluation of Human Work* (4th ed., pp. 201–220). CRC Press.

Lee, M. J. W., Georgieva, M., Alexander, B., Craig, E., & Richter, J. (2021). *State of XR & Immersive Learning Outlook Report 2021*. Immersive Learning Research Network.

Malone, T. W. (1981). Toward a Theory of Intrinsically Motivating Instruction. *Cognitive Science*, *5*(4), 333–369. doi:10.120715516709cog0504_2

Manifesto. (2020). *Digital estates within Higher Education – A white paper.* Manifesto. https://pages.manifesto.co.uk/higher-education-guide

Natale, A. F. D., Repetta, C., Rova, G., & Villani, D. (2020). Immersive virtual reality in K-12 and higher education: A 10-year systematic review of empirical research. *British Journal of Educational Technology*, *51*(6), 2003–2033. doi:10.1111/bjet.13030

Neves, J., & Hewitt, R. (2021). *Student Academic Experience Survey 2021*. Higher Education Policy Institute. https://www.hepi.ac.uk/2021/06/24/the-student-academic-experience-survey-2021/

Nowak, K. L., & Biocca, F. (2003). The Effect of the Agency and Anthropomorphism on Users' Sense of Telepresence, Copresence, and Social Presence in Virtual Environments. *Presence (Cambridge, Mass.)*, *12*(5), 481–494. doi:10.1162/105474603322761289

Nowak, K. L., & Fox, J. (2018). Avatars and computer-mediated communication: A review of the definitions, uses, and effects of digital representations. *Review of Communication Research*, *6*, 30–53. doi:10.12840/issn.2255-4165.2018.06.01.015

Palmas, F., & Klinker, G. (2020, July). Defining Extended Reality Training: A Long-Term Definition for All Industries. *Proceedings of the 2020 IEEE 20th International Conference on Advanced Learning Technologies (ICALT)*, 322–324. 10.1109/ICALT49669.2020.00103

Pérez-Sanagustín, M., Muñoz-Merino, P. J., Alario-Hoyos, C., Soldani, X., & Delgado Kloos, C. (2015). Lessons learned from the design of situated learning environments to support collaborative knowledge construction. *Computers & Education*, *87*, 70–82. doi:10.1016/j.compedu.2015.03.019

Picciano, A. G. (2002). Beyond Student Perceptions: Issues of Interaction, Presence, and Performance in an Online Course. *Journal of Asynchronous Learning Networks*, *6*(1).

Radianti, R., Majchrzak, T. A., Fromm, J., & Wohlgenannt, I. (2020). A systematic review of immersive virtual reality applications for higher education: Design elements, lessons learned, and research agenda. *Computers & Education*, *147*, 147. doi:10.1016/j.compedu.2019.103778

Scavarelli, A., Arya, A., & Teather, R. J. (2020). Virtual reality and augmented reality in social learning spaces: A literature review. *Virtual Reality (Waltham Cross)*, *25*(1), 257–277. doi:10.100710055-020-00444-8

Schnädelbach, H., Penn, A., Steadman, P., Benford, S., Koleva, B., & Rodden, T. (2006, November). Moving office: inhabiting a dynamic building. In *Proceedings of the 2006 20th anniversary conference on Computer supported cooperative work* (pp. 313-322). 10.1145/1180875.1180924

Smith, S. M. (1979). Remembering in and out of context. *Journal of Experimental Psychology. Human Learning and Memory*, *5*(5), 460–471. doi:10.1037/0278-7393.5.5.460

Stone, R., & Glover, I. (2021). *Adapting HE teaching for an online environment: A practical guide*. Sage Publications Ltd.

van der Land, S., Schouten, A. P., Feldberg, F., van den Hooff, B., & Huysman, M. (2013). Lost in space? Cognitive fit and cognitive load in 3D virtual environments. *Computers in Human Behavior*, *29*(3), 1054–1064. doi:10.1016/j.chb.2012.09.006

Vergara, D., Extremera, J., & Dávila, L. (2019). Meaningful Learning Through Virtual Reality Learning Environments: Case Study in Materials Engineering. *Applied Sciences (Basel, Switzerland)*, *9*(21), 4625. doi:10.3390/app9214625

Williamson, J. R., Li, J., Vinayagamoorthy, V., Shamma, D. A., & Cesar, P. (2021, May). Proxemics and Social Interactions in an Instrumented Virtual Reality Workshop. *CHI '21*.

Won, A. S., Bailey, J. O., & Yi, S. (2020, June). Learning about Virtual Worlds in Virtual Worlds: How Remote Learning in a Pandemic Can Inform Future Teaching. *6th International Conference of the Immersive Learning Research Network (iLRN)*, 377–380. 10.23919/iLRN47897.2020.9155201

Yen, C. J., & Tu, C. H. (2008). Online Social Presence: A Study of Score Validity of the Computer-Mediated Communication Questionnaire. *Quarterly Review of Distance Learning*, *9*(3), 297–310.

ADDITIONAL READING

Bailenson, J. (2018). *Experience on demand. What virtual reality is, how it works, and what it can do*. W. W. Norton & Company.

Stefaniak, J. E., Conklin, S., Oyarzun, B., & Reese, R. M. (2021). *A Practitioner's Guide to Instructional Design in Higher Education*. EdTech Books. https://edtechbooks.org/id_highered

KEY TERMS AND DEFINITIONS

Avatar: A digital representation of a specific person, in this case within a virtual world.

Higher Education: Learning that occurs, usually at university establishments and for students aged 18 and above.

Immersion: The objective degree to which Virtual Reality technologies engage a person's senses.

Metaverse: Shared virtual spaces that individuals can access in avatar form via a range of different computing and communications technologies.

Nottopia: A specific virtual world used at the University of Nottingham for teaching students.

Presence: The subjective experience of immersion, such that a person might believe they are somewhere different to where they are.

Qualitative Research: A form of research that involves the collection and analysis of non-numerical data, such as images, videos, words, etc.

Quantitative Research: A form of research that involves the collection and analysis of numerical data, such as time, errors, ratings on scales, etc.

Social VR Platforms: Specific (usually web-based) technologies that enable people in avatar form to interact within a virtual world.

ENDNOTES

1 https://www.youtube.com/watch?v=zn2NVkK6IQI

2 https://www.youtube.com/watch?v=puktO2g-Wpc

Chapter 4
An Immersive Virtual Reality Training Environment for CBRN Procedures

Federico De Lorenzis
Politecnico di Torino, Italy

Massimo Migliorini
LINKS Foundation, Italy

Filippo Gabriele Pratticò
https://orcid.org/0000-0001-7606-8552
Politecnico di Torino, Italy

Fabrizio Lamberti
https://orcid.org/0000-0001-7703-1372
Politecnico di Torino, Italy

Matteo Cultrera
Politecnico di Torino, Italy

ABSTRACT

First responders are exposed to numerous hazards and must be well prepared to act under dangerous conditions. This is especially true for operators working in the domain of CBRN (chemical, biological, radiological, nuclear), who need high-quality training to avoid fatal errors and ensure the success of operations. However, CBRN practice sessions can reproduce only approximated, low-fidelity versions of real scenarios, whereas highly detailed simulations should be preferred. To address this issue, the authors developed a prototype of an immersive virtual reality (VR) training platform in cooperation with CBRN experts from the Italian Air Force. The devised platform is an improved version of an existing tool and offers a digital training ground where operators can learn CBRN procedures and test their abilities in a realistic virtual environment without facing the risks normally associated with real hazardous scenarios.

DOI: 10.4018/978-1-6684-3398-0.ch004

INTRODUCTION

The CBRN (Chemical, Biological, Radiological and Nuclear) is a domain that encompasses procedures and practices required to deal with events associated with a wide range of risks, mainly caused by the deployment of mass-destruction weapons (NATO, 2018). These events differ from generic hazards since they are usually designed with malicious intents. The term refers the four risks that are considered by these procedures:

- **Chemical:** indicates an explosion of a chemical weapon with toxic properties, such as Chlorine or Hydrogen cyanide. These weapons act with four different agent types, i.e., choking agents, blistering agents, blood agents, and nerve agents. This type of risk can spread over wide areas and is heavily inñuenced by the wind direction.
- **Biological:** it is due to an attack performed using biological vectors, such as bacteria, viruses, or insects.
- **Radiological:** it is caused by the use of a so-called "dirty bomb", which can irradiate alpha and beta particles. This weapon combines explosive and radioactive material but is different than the atomic bomb since the explosion is smaller, and most of the risk comes from the radiological exposure rather than from the explosion itself.
- **Nuclear:** it is associated with an attack performed with a nuclear weapon, such as a ðssion bomb. This attack produces massive damage to both the population and the environment.

Since the situations requesting the intervention of CBRN teams are often dangerous for all the involved actors, it is essential that operators correctly follow every step of the mandated response procedures defined by CBRN protocols. Training CBRN operators' capacity to deal with these procedures represents a major challenge, since practical exercises usually involve instrumentations and vehicles with high maintenance costs, as well as the simultaneous participation of many subjects coming from different geographic areas. Moreover, to avoid severe risks for the trainees' safety, the fidelity of the simulated scenarios could show inconsistencies and be too restrictive to achieve efficient training.

In order to cope with these problems, it is necessary to create alternative tools that can offer training experiences with a high level of realism, while minimizing the risks for the trainees. This outcome can be obtained by leveraging Virtual Reality (VR) technologies to create training experiences that can offer a series of advantages with respect to real trials:

- **Safety:** using VR, it is possible to train a subject to engage in situations that he or she could not face safely in real life. For instance, it is possible to simulate a collapsing building without any risk.
- **Cost:** training in a VR environment is less expensive than real-life training experiences. For instance, it is possible to train a subject to pilot a plane without using real aircrafts, thus lowering signiðcantly the associated costs.
- **Realism:** even though VR is still not comparable, in terms of realism, with a real exercise, it enables the simulation of various situations that subjects could hardly face in real life. An explosion, for instance, could be witnessed from a close distance in a VR environment.
- **Repeatability:** a VR simulation can be easily repeated multiple times, thus letting a subject to master the considered procedure with a trial-and-error approach, without the need to organize a real exercise every time.

In this paper we present an extended version of an experimental VR platform designed to train CBRN operators on a NATO procedure named RECCE. The RECCE procedure is a reconnaissance operation performed during the ðrst approach to a possible contaminated area. The RECCE team is formed by four members that carry out an initial assessment of the area in order to ðnd the source of risk. In particular, the team must perform various measures using different tools in the risk area, ðnd the correct risk source and delimit it. Finally, each operator must be decontaminated to remove any possible residual contaminating agent. During the entire procedure, which can require several hours to be completed, the operators must wear the proper Personal Protective Equipment (PPE). The four operators are assigned different tasks, depending on the role:

- **Dirty Man 1**: the first of the two operators who are assigned the Dirty Man role is tasked to check for contamination. He or she is equipped with a set of probes and is the first operator to approach the area of the accident to find a non-contaminated place from where to start the operations. Afterwards, he or she must make preliminary measurements and delimit the area where there is the risk of contamination. This Dirty Man is the first operator to leave the vehicle used to approach the area, and the first in the line when making the measurements; therefore, he or she is the first operator to be exposed to possible dangers.
- **Dirty Man 2**: this operator follows the Dirty Man 1 during the check of all the potential hotspots (the places where the accident occurred and could be contaminated). He or she makes preliminary measurements together with the Dirty Man 1 and collects all the data during the procedure.

- **Clean Man:** this operator should not be contaminated during the operations; thus, he or she does not leave the vehicle during the ðrst approach until the Dirty Man 1 identifies a safe, non-contaminated area. The Clean man is tasked to create a safe area where the other operators can return and be decontaminated after the measurement procedure.
- **Team Leader:** the main goal of this operator is to follow the Dirty Man 1 and Dirty Man 2 and coordinate the operations. He or she is equipped with a radio that can be used to communicate with the team and the Command Center.

The devised immersive VR application, developed in the context of a collaboration between Politecnico di Torino, Fondazione LINKS and Terzo Stormo – Aeronautica Militare, Villafranca di Verona, offers a configurable experience in which one or multiple users can impersonate the various roles in a CBRN team and complete the RECCE procedure while interacting in a scenario that simulates in detail a real incident, precisely, a drone explosion that causes a leakage of radiological material in the Villafranca di Verona airport. The user is able to witness the explosion and must operate accordingly. All the actions performed will be then evaluated and a ðnal report will be provided to the user for assessment. This chapter is a follow-up to the work in Lamberti et al. (2021), where the authors described a previous version of the application that was developed and tested with CBRN operators. The feedback collected by the authors was used to restructure and extend the application, as described in the following sections. The main goal was to further enhance the realism of the simulation, in order to create a training experience that could be possibly integrated in the official CBRN training of the Italian Air Force.

BACKGROUND

With VR it is possible to create a completely simulated experience in which the user can explore a computer-generated environment and interact with digital objects to complete various tasks. This technology has been widely used in the entertainment sector (video games and movies), but it is now spreading also in other fields like, in particular, education (both in formal and non-formal contexts). In this context, mainly due to its flexibility and its ability to create highly detailed simulations of real scenarios, VR is increasingly adopted for the development of training tools. The value of VR Training Systems (VRTSs), which are VR applications developed for educational purposes, has been proved, already: as a matter of example, it is a frequent practice to use flight simulators to train pilots, improving their confidence during flight without exposing them to dangerous situations (Rantanen & Talleur, 2005). Today, the use of this technology for training is well-established, especially in procedural training contexts where it has been demonstrated that VRTS are more effective than printed (Buttussi and Chittaro, 2021) and video based (Lovreglio et al., 2021) training materials.

VRTSs have been adopted in various fields, like medicine (e.g., in Kaluschke et al., 2018, presenting a simulator for hip replacement surgeries), industry (e.g., in Pérez et al., 2019, and in Pratticò & Lamberti, 2021, showing training systems tailored to industrial robots), maintenance (e.g., in García et al., 2015, focusing on the training of operators working on electric power lines), etc. However, the field in which the use of VR has been particularly prolific is that of VRTSs for first responders (the category of users the RECCE procedure refers to). In facts, due to their characteristics (limited costs, limited exposition to risks, repeatability, etc.), VRTSs are particularly suitable to prepare operators whose life is often in danger, like, e.g., CBRN operators or first responders acting in case of hydrogeological disasters (Pratticò et al., 2021).

By analyzing the literature, it is possible to find many examples of VR applications simulating procedures for disaster management (such as the RECCE procedure), e.g., in case of fires or evacuations: for instance, Calandra et al. (2021) presented a multi-role, multi-user VR application where one or more users can train in the best practices to adopt in case of tunnel fires. Experiencing the same situation impersonating different roles allowed the users to get a broader overview of the considered case study, whereas the possibility to share a simulation with other users enhanced the realism of the experience, and in particular of the interactions. Another example can be found in Sharma et al. (2014), where a multi-role, multi-user application was designed to train users in crowd management during emergencies; the application was used to train multiple subjects at the same time in a safe, immersive environment while collecting data to evaluate their behavior. Finally, in De Lorenzis et al. (2022), an application that builds on the two mentioned studies is presented; it consists of a configurable, multi-role and multi-user application targeted to first responders and focused on risk management in case of hydrogeological disasters, and the overall quality of the simulation is enhanced using Inverse Kinematics (IK) to create more realistic Non-Playable Characters (NPCs) the users can interact with.

Moving to training experiences for first responders in civil-military training, Mossel et al. (2015) proposed a review of applications for CBRN training, concluding that, at that time, no available systems could satisfy the needs of the relevant stakeholders. In particular, focusing on the RECCE procedure, the authors highlighted that the future applications should offer large environments in which the users can walk freely to perform dismounted CBRN operations (e.g., taking measurements or performing the decontamination), use virtually simulated equipment and interact with other users. In recent years, Maciejewski et al. (2020) proposed a study on the use of a CAVE virtual environment to train CBRN operators, outlining the potential of VR in this context. However, the study was limited to a conceptual analysis, and no application was actually developed to support the conclusions; moreover, the authors focused on the CAVE technology and did not consider solutions characterized by a higher level of immersion such as Head-Mounted Displays (HMDs). Finally, Schönauer et al. (2020) presented a multi-user application for RECCE operations where physical objects were integrated using Augmented Virtuality, although, based on the few details provided, the developed tool seemed closer to a testbed for the developed technology than a concrete VRTS.

Despite the diffusion of VRTSs witnessed also by the above review, there is no standard approach yet for the creation of new systems, since every application is very context-dependent and requires specific design choices or technologies. Some reviews of the state of the art give an overview of the existing literature, but reported results are quite difficult to generalize due to the task-dependent nature of VRTSs. Nevertheless, it is possible to extrapolate some guidelines regarding different aspects of a VR simulation, like the best approach for creating a guiding system (according to Feng et al., 2018, it should provide the user with step-by-step instructions) or the most appropriate technology to use depending on the nature of the interactions the user has to perform in the virtual environment. In particular, the literature suggests that VRTSs in general and, especially, those that require the user to move and interact with multiple virtual objects (like in the experience described in this paper) can benefit more from high levels of immersion (Gisler et al., 2020 and Berkman and Akan, 2019). Thus, HMDs and other immersive technologies (like VR gloves, locomotion treadmills, etc.) are to be preferred to more traditional hardware like, e.g., desktop displays and 2D interfaces (mouse and keyboard, joystick, etc.), as reported by Cummings & Bailenson (2016).

THE VR APPLICATION

The application presented in this paper was designed with the advice of CBRN experts from Terzo Stormo – Aeronautica Militare, Villafranca di Verona to consistently reproduce the considered training procedure, with a particular focus on the behavior of the NPCs and the probes used during the operations. The platform is an improved version of the tool described in Lamberti et al. (2021). The new version was developed as an immersive VR application using the Unity Game Engine and the SteamVR framework. The 3D assets were generated using Blender (for the creation of the scenarios and the probes) and image-editing software (for the textures). Most of the logic and algorithms controlling the virtual 3D objects were rewritten in the C# programming language using the Visual Studio IDE.

The final implementation consists of a configurable experience that can be used by a single user (single-player mode) or four simultaneous users (multi-player mode) to learn the steps of the simulated CBRN procedure. The application was designed to be experienced using an HMD (HTC Vive or Oculus Rift/Quest, in both cases connected to a PC) to have a stereoscopic view of the virtual environment, and the associated hand controllers to interact with the virtual objects. The details of the application will be provided in the following sections.

Scenario

The entire location of the Villafranca di Verona airport was rebuilt in the VR environment. The area comprehends a part of the airport (Figure 1) where the users can freely move to perform the procedure, together with some buildings that define the context and the boundaries of the simulation but are not interactable. This place was chosen because it is the location in which the RECCE team of Terzo Stormo – Aeronautica Militare perform real exercises and simulations of CBRN operations.

Particular attention was dedicated to the modeling of the buildings and the concrete floor, which was made using a Physically Based Rendering (PBS) material to give the users the same feeling as standing in a real airport. This choice was driven by the fact that, as stated in Zibrek & McDonnell (2019), the sense of social presence and place illusion are improved in realistic environments.

Simulation

Similar to the original platform, the extended simulation models a situation in which a drone, transporting a bomb containing chemical or radiological material, explodes in the Villafranca di Verona airport. In the simulation, the users can witness the entire explosion and then operate accordingly after a brief introduction in which the Command Center dispatches the RECCE team to the area of the accident. The specific types of interactions and the actions that can be performed by the users vary based on the risk and the role taken; in brief, the users can choose from which direction approach the accident area (based on the wind direction); find a non-contaminated area where it is possible to park the vehicle and set up a working area; set up the working area where the Clean Man will wait for the other operators to finish their tasks; measure, signal and delimit the hotspot location choosing between four different places; decontaminate the rest of the team or be decontaminated; leave the area and receive an evaluation of the work done. In the final implementation, the simulation is split into five different scenes, which are detailed below.

Figure 1. View of the airport where the VR experience takes place.

- **Main Menu Scene:** In this scene, the user can select the parameters of the simulation by means of a diegetic menu which is displayed on the screen of a tablet that can be found in the scene. In particular, it is possible to choose the mode (single-player or multi-player), the procedure (at present, just the RECCE), the role (either Clean Man, Dirty Man 1, and Dirty Man 2, or Team Leader in multi-player mode), and whether to activate a guidance system (the Virtual Instructor or a list of objectives) offering hints about the chosen procedure.
- **Video Scene:** The main purpose of this scene is to allow the user to witness the explosion and to be introduced to the overall context of the simulation. The user is not allowed to move but can see the drone attack and understand the reason behind the RECCE team intervention. At the end, he or she can hear a radio transmission about the explosion before being moved automatically to the next scene. This scene is witnessed independently from the role selected, since all the roles should be aware of what happened and know why the team must intervene.
- **Wind Scene:** In this scene, the user is inside the vehicle with all the other components of the team. He or she holds a map and can choose the direction from which to approach the airport. The wind direction can be seen on a screen in the vehicle and allows him or her to make the correct decision. In Figure 2 it is possible to see the interior of the vehicle and the screen.
- **Vehicle Check Scene:** In this scene, the user must check for possible contamination outside the vehicle and in the location where the working area will be built. The user is outside the vehicle and can use different probes in order to check if the location is safe. After checking the vehicle, he or she

must notify if it is safe to operate, and then proceed to check the working area. This scene is experienced only by the Dirty Man 1 or the Dirty Man 2, since the Clean Man should stay inside the vehicle during this phase in order not to be contaminated if the location is not clean.

- **RECCE Scene:** This is the main scene of the simulation and the overall experience changes signiðcantly based on the role played by the user. If he or she acts as the Dirty Man 1 or the Dirty Man 2, the ðrst objective is to ðnd the correct hotspot. In order to do so, he or she should reach its position in the formation. The approach is carried out in a straight line towards the closest hotspot. In this phase, the user can hear all the orders coming from the Team Leader and should act accordingly. Once the correct formation is complete, it is possible to move towards the hotspots. When one of the possible hotspots is reached, the user should perform a measure using one of the probes. If the correct hotspot is found, the user should place a pole (called signaling pole) to highlight it. After placing the pole, he or she can choose among three different signaling triangles, one for a radiological risk, one for a chemical risk, and one for a biological risk. He or she should place the correct triangle on the signaling pole in order to identify the correct risk, and then write the correct information on the triangle, using a pen. All the tools used by the operator can be stored in an inventory system. It is worth to point out that the other roles that help the user in the simulation could ðnd and signal the correct hotspot; in this case, they will automatically place a signaling pole with the correct triangle, but the user should write the correct information on the triangle anyway. Once these actions are completed, the user should retrieve other poles and triangles from the Clean Man and delimit the area around the hotspot. To delimit the area, he or she should place at least six poles around the hotspot, then place the correct triangles on them and write the correct information on each triangle. The user should then place a tape around all the poles except the signaling one to delimit the hazardous area. Afterwards, the user can return to the working area to be decontaminated and terminate the scene. If the user impersonates the Clean Man, he or she is initially tasked to build the working area. After that, he or she should take some objects from a crate nearby and place them on the ground to organize all the tools necessary for the procedure. Then, the user should pass the poles and the correct triangles (that can be found in the crate) to the other operators or the other users that needs to perform the delimitation of the area. Finally, he or she is tasked to decontaminate all the other operators before leaving the scene.

The complete workflow of the simulation is described in Figure 3.

Figure 2. Vehicle interior during the Wind Scene. The user is holding a map that he or she can use to choose the approach direction. To guide this choice, the wind direction is displayed on a screen.

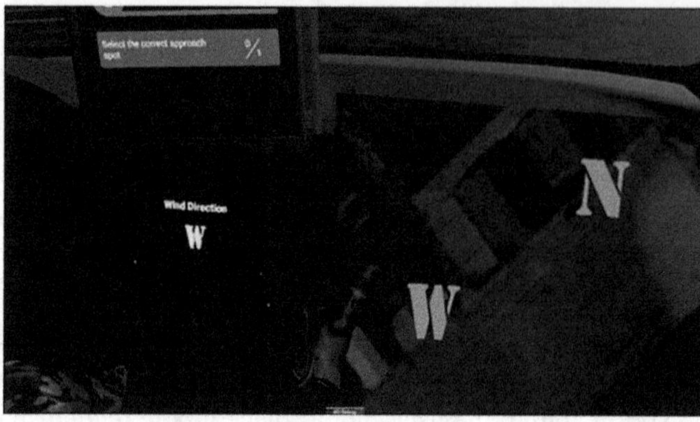

Interactions

All the VR interactions were managed using the new SteamVR framework (2.0 version), which was absent when the previous version of the platform was created. Due to this choice, it was possible to leverage the SteamVR Hand System to add two fully animated hand models and improve the overall realism of the experience (although controllers were still used as an input system and hand tracking was not considered yet). Thanks to the possibilities offered by this system, it was possible to grab each 3D object in the scene in a unique way, meaning that the hand models assume different poses depending on the grabbed object, as shown in Figure 4.

Moving to the 3D tools in the scene, the user is required to use alpha or beta-gamma probes (when impersonating one of the Dirty Man roles) to identify the contaminated area and the type of particles in the scene, together with an ANPDR device (a multipurpose radiation detection system) that shows real-time radiation measurements. The alpha probe is an instrument that detects the presence of alpha particles, which are non-volatile and are typically concentrated near the hotspot, whereas the beta-gamma probe is an instrument signaling the presence of beta particles. All the probes react in real-time to the presence of harmful material and show real-time radiation measurements that change depending on the distance from, and the quantity of, the said material. Regardless of the type of material, a user impersonating the Clean Man is required to use a dispenser (called PSDS) of decontaminating liquid in combination with the proper probe (beta-gamma probe in presence of radiological material, chemical agent field detector in presence of chemical material) to decontaminate the other operators and check for residual

Figure 3. Flowchart of the simulation.

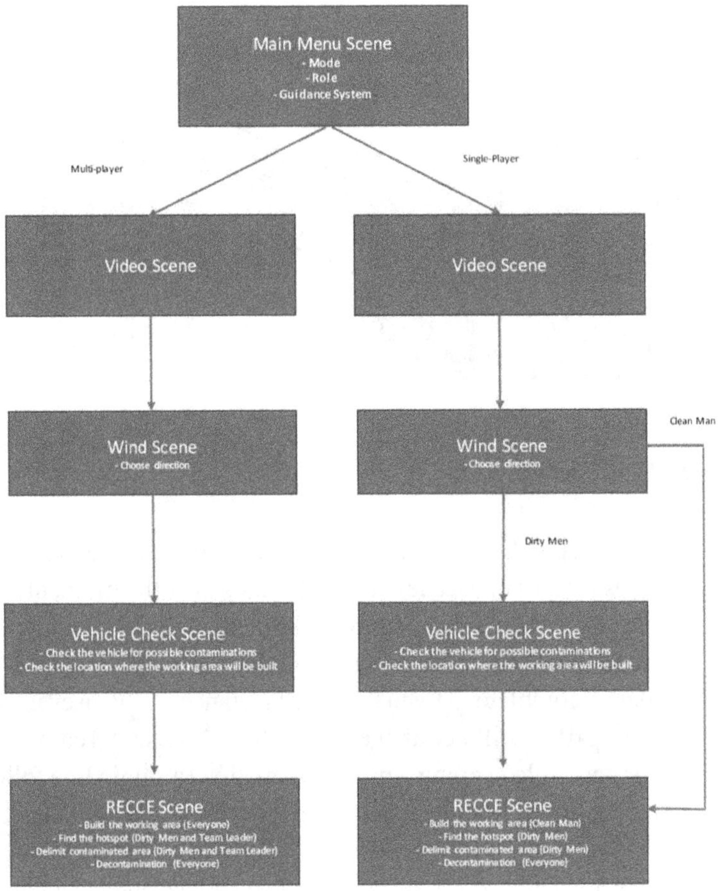

particles. Besides specific probes, the users are provided with a series of tools required to complete the procedure, i.e., poles and tape to delimit the contaminated area, as well as signs and pen to write down the information collected using the probes.

Given the high number of instruments used, a new inventory system was added in order to simplify the management of the different tools (probes, poles, triangles, pen, etc.). The functioning of the inventory, that the user can activate by using one of the buttons on the controllers, is based on a series of sockets where it is possible to place or retrieve one or more 3D objects, as illustrated in Figure 5.

Figure 4. View of three different hand poses while grabbing three different objects (namely, a signaling pole, a beta-gamma probe, and a pen).

Non-Playable Characters

In the single-player mode, the user can play, as said, either the Clean Man or one of the Dirty Man roles (the Team Leader cannot be chosen at the moment). The other three roles are nevertheless represented in the scene by NPCs, which are an active part of the procedure: depending on the chosen role, the user is required to interact with them in order to complete a given task. For instance, if the user impersonates the Dirty Man, two NPCs will act as the other Dirty Man and Team Leader, and will follow him or her while keeping a proper formation (a single line following the Dirty Man in presence of radiological material); the third NPC will take the role of

Figure 5. View of the inventory system. The spheres are the sockets where the user can place the tools used during the simulation.

the Clean Man and will guide the user during the decontamination procedure. The Finite-State Machines (FSMs) controlling the NPCs in the previous version of the application were restructured and rebuilt: in particular, the newly designed NPCs are characterized by new animations and new, more realistic interactions to enhance the fidelity of the simulation and improve the users' experience.

Since many actions are based on the position of speciðc limbs or characters, it was necessary to introduce a mechanism to guarantee the proper positioning of the NPCs and ensure the correct functioning of the simulation (e.g., during the decontamination of an NPC). For this reason, an IK module was implemented to control the NPCs animations. A custom C# script was created, called IkManager, to manage nine control points (Look Target, Left Foot, Right Foot, Left Knee, Right Knee, LeftHand, Right Hand, Left Elbow, Right Elbow) distributed on the NPCs avatars. This script is tasked to ðnd all the points and then ensure that all the limbs follow those points, overriding (partially or completely) the Unity system that normally controls characters animation. Since the IK module was developed to manage only a subset of the animations, or only parts of the body during a specific animation, additional parameters were introduced to control the influence of the IK module. Moreover, by using this module it was possible to control the NPCs and make them reach specific objects in the simulations, set as targets, to achieve realistic animations for actions like grabbing an object, placing a pole, and so on.

In the following, the role of each control point is detailed.

- **Look Target:** This point controls the view direction of the NPC. It can also inñuence the torso and make the character rotate around the waist. It can be used to look at the objects that must be grabbed.
- **Left Hand:** This point controls the position and rotation of the left hand and can be used to change the animation of the NPC (the level of influence is controlled by a parameter). It can be used during the grab action but is crucial during the decontamination phase to correctly position the hands.
- **Right Hand:** This point controls the position and rotation of the right hand and can be used to change the animation of the NPC (the level of influence is controlled by a parameter). It can be used during the grab action but is crucial during the decontamination phase to correctly position the hands.
- **Left Elbow:** This point controls the pivot point of the left elbow rotation and was introduced to improve the realism of the animation.
- **Right Elbow:** This point controls the pivot point of the right elbow rotation and was introduced to improve the realism of the animation.
- **Left Knee:** This point acts as pivot for the left leg.
- **Right Knee:** This point acts as pivot for the right leg.
- **Left Foot:** This point controls the target to be reached by the left foot.

- **Right Foot:** This point controls the target to be reached by the right foot.

Multi-Player

The multi-player mode originally created using the high-level API of UNet was redesigned using the new Mirror asset. The final module is a server-authoritative architecture in which the server handles the synchronization of all the data in order to keep a consistent state among the clients. This aspect is relevant for the physics of the simulation and, in particular, for the evaluation of the users' actions, since discrepancies could lead to inconsistencies between the evaluations of the different users and, therefore, of the entire team. In the multi-player mode, four users impersonate the four roles required by the RECCE procedure and cooperate to complete the tasks. In this mode, all the possible interactions of the single-player mode are present; furthermore, the synchronization between the participants, along with teamwork, become a central part of the simulation: each user must actively talk with the others (the communication is implemented via Voice over Internet Protocol, VoIP) to exchange information, and therefore, understand how to proceed with the operations. In this mode, the Team Leader is tasked to coordinate the other operators, but he or she can also take part in the delimitation of the contaminated area. At the end of the simulation, he or she is evaluated considering the overall performance of the team.

Guiding Tool

To provide the user with the possibility to control the simulation and receive hints on the procedure, a guiding tool was added in the form of a virtual tablet device that the user can interact with, as shown in Figure 6. With this device, the user can perform various actions, such as skip a phase, set simulation parameters, or read the hints provided by the application. This tool provides two guiding modes that can be chosen in the Main Menu Scene:

- **Virtual Instructor:** In this mode, the tablet acts as a text visualizer, showing several types of hints depending on the phase of the simulation. These hints are hardcoded into a dictionary and updated on the tablet screen when the simulation reaches a new state. In Figure 7 it is possible to see how the hints are presented to the user. If the user selects this mode, the tablet is always present in the inventory, and can be used every time help is needed.
- **Objectives:** In this mode, the tablet does not show hints, but a series of objectives that the user should complete in order to proceed in the simulation, as illustrated in Figure 8. These objectives are updated every time the user

achieves one of them, even partially, and guide the user in a less obvious way. If the user completes all the possible objectives of the phase, he or she can proceed to the next one.

Figure 6. View of the tablet that can be used to manage the simulation.

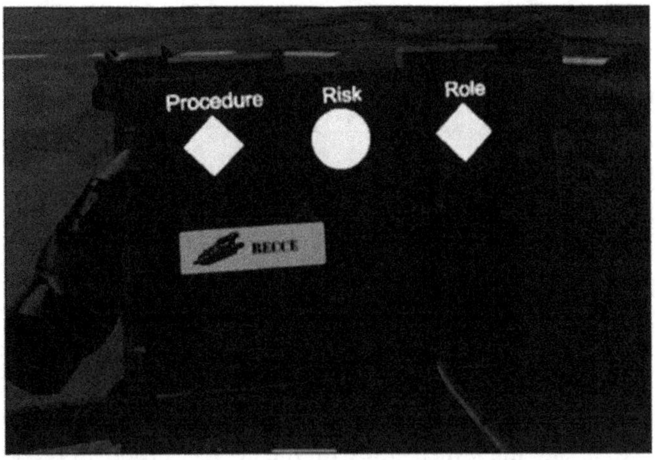

Evaluation Logic

A new evaluation module was added to the platform to assess the user's behavior during the simulation and provide a ðnal score according to his or her actions during all the phases. In particular, to improve over the previous version of the platform, some of the evaluation criteria were redefined. When the simulation is over, a summative report is shown on the tablet screen. The same report is also saved on the computer, to allow an instructor to evaluate the performance of the team and do some debrieðng outside of the simulation. In the single-player mode, the evaluation criteria depend on the chosen role. In particular, the evaluation criteria for the Dirty Man roles are the following:

- **Check Vehicle:** The user is evaluated while checking the vehicle for possible contamination. In this phase, he or she must check all the four tires, the four car doors, the hood, and the bumper. The user receives a score based on the number of zones checked with the right probe.
- **Check Working Area:** The user must check, with the correct probe, the zone in which the working area will be built.

Figure 7. View of the tablet used as a Virtual Instructor, providing simple step-by-step instructions regarding the procedure.

- **Hotspot Found:** The user receives a point if he or she is able to find the correct hotspot. He or she must measure with the correct probe all the hotspots until the correct one is found.
- **Signaling Pole Distance:** The user must place the signaling pole at the correct distance from the correct hotspot.

Figure 8. View of the tablet used to display the objectives of the procedure.

- **Signaling Pole Triangle:** The user must place the correct triangle on the pole, depending on the risk. If the correct triangle is selected, he or she receives a point, zero otherwise.
- **Signaling Pole Information:** The user must write the correct information on the hotspot triangle. Every time the user writes the correct piece of information on the triangle, he or she receives a point.
- **Poles Distance:** The user must place at least six poles around the hotspot to delimit the contaminated area. Each pole must be placed in non-contaminated spot, at the correct distance from the others.
- **Poles Triangles:** The user must place the correct triangles on all the poles delimiting the contaminated area.
- **Poles Writings:** The user must write the correct information on each pole.
- **Deco Limbs:** The user, during the last phase of the simulation, must go through the decontamination process. He or she can reach the Clean Man and decontaminate each limb. A point is assigned for each decontaminated limb (left hand, right hand, left foot and right foot).
- **Deco Order:** The user must decontaminate his or her limbs in a ðxed order. He or she must start with the right hand, then decontaminate the left hand, and then the right foot and the left foot. If he or she performs the decontamination in the correct order, a point is assigned
- **Check Limbs:** After the decontamination process, the user must be checked for residual contamination. He or she gets a point for each limb showed to the Clean Man.

If the user takes the role of the Clean Man, the evaluation criteria are the following:

- **Working Area:** The user should build the working area, placing every object onto protective sheets to avoid contamination; in addition, the user is tasked to place two special poles, with the entry and exit signs on them, to signal the entry and exit of the area. He or she gets a point for each object placed correctly.
- **Triangles:** The user can fetch the triangles from a crate and pass them to the other operators. If the correct triangles are chosen, he or she gets a point.
- **Deco:** During the decontamination process, the user must decontaminate all the other operators. After this process, he or she should also decontaminate the ground underneath them. He or she gets a point for each decontaminated operator.
- **Check:** After the decontamination process, the user must check the other operators and the ground for residual contamination. He or she gets a point for each check.

In the multi-player mode, the evaluation module keeps track of the actions of each user and produces a report that considers both individual and cooperative actions. Each user is responsible for a part of the procedure but can potentially interact with the other operators and invalidate certain actions correctly performed by them. To handle that, at the end of the simulation the module produces a report that contains a section regarding the individual actions (e.g., the decontamination, which can be performed only by the Clean Man) and a section regarding the cooperative actions (e.g., the delimitation of the contaminated area, which can be potentially performed by every user). A wrong cooperative action is evaluated negatively for each user but using the collected data it is possible to identify the specific users that made the error.

Collected data are saved in the application folder (as .csv and .json files) and can be later used to perform additional processing or to assess the users' knowledge of the taught procedure. Furthermore, all the objects' positions and rotations are recorded, and can be imported in Unity and used to replay the whole experience; in the future, they could also be used to program (train) the NPCs movements in order to further improve the realism of the simulation.

Testing

The application has not undergone complete testing yet, but the preliminary open feedback collected by CBRN operators and instructors was positive, as it showed an overall appreciation for the new features integrated in the extended version. In particular, it was noted that the newly integrated features represent an improvement over the previous version, and the platform was praised for its high graphics quality and the realism of the interactions.

FUTURE RESEARCH DIRECTIONS

For the follow-up of this work, the addition of a dedicated training mode (e.g., with a voice-over that guides the users through the procedure and visual cues, such as highlights, that can direct the users in the VR environment) could improve the efficacy of the devised VRTS, potentially making it a stand-alone tool that can be used in substitution of the traditional exercises.

Future development lines include the extension of the simulation to consider new scenarios, risks (biological and nuclear), sources of risk (e.g., the explosion of a helicopter instead of the drone attack), procedures (e.g., the SIBCRA procedure or the Aircraft Decon) and tools, as well as the integration of other VR technologies (e.g., to further enhance the fidelity in multi-player mode and the interaction with the virtual environment). A further possibility could be the implementation of the

Team Leader role in single-player mode, with its own interface to command and direct the other NPCs in the execution of the procedure.

Validation

Another development envisioned for this work is the organization of coordinated training sessions in VR and real exercises aimed to collect more extensive feedback to be exploited for validating and further developing the platform, thus paving the way to the creation of a standard training tool for CBRN operators.

In particular, a comparison between a traditional CBRN training experience, a training session based on the devised VRTS, and a mixed approach that combines traditional and VR training should be held in order to evaluate the effectiveness of the developed application and investigate its potential as a complementary tool or as a substitute for real exercises. To conduct this type of study, it would be necessary to collect data by leveraging widely used and consolidated questionnaires available in the literature, like the VRUSE (Kalawsky, 1999) or the SUS (Brooke, 1996) to evaluate the overall usability of the VRTS, the IMMS (Keller, 2010) to compare the motivation at learning associated with the three experiences, and the AttrakDiff (Hassenzahl, 2008) to determine the attractiveness, the hedonic quality stimulation and other characteristics of the training. Finally, to conclude the study, the knowledge gain and knowledge retention associated with the three approaches should be investigated and compared by organizing trial sessions (with practical activities and exercises) before the experiences, after the experiences, and after several weeks, thus determining which of three approaches is/are best suitable to train CBRN operators.

Machine Learning and NPCs

A possible research direction to enhance the realism of the devised application could consist in the use of Machine Learning (ML) techniques to improve the behavior of the NPCs and boost the believability of the whole experience. As said, currently the NPCs behavior is controlled by FSMs, thus the interactions with the user are scripted (e.g., they are activated by specific commands performed by the user or start when the user reaches a specific position).

By leveraging tools like the Unity ML-Agents Toolkit it would be possible to implement the NPCs using Reinforcement Learning (RL). This approach is based on a reward/penalty mechanism, which makes an NPC be rewarded if it executes a correct action, penalized otherwise. It is particularly interesting since it does not require human training data (it is the environment itself that rewards the agent for the correct actions). However, a possible drawback of this solution is tied to the complexity of designing an appropriate reward/penalty system, since a flawed design could lead to the development of NPCs with superhuman and/or non-realistic behavior.

An alternative could consist in the use of Imitation Learning (IL): by leveraging the human actions recorded by the devised application, it may be possible to train the NPCs to reproduce them. This approach avoids the problem of superhuman/non-realistic behaviors since the NPCs would learn directly from real human actions. A drawback of this solution is the time needed to train the NPCs and achieve realistic results, since the system requires multiple recordings. In order to overcome this limitation, it could be possible to adopt a hybrid solution in which the RL and IL techniques are combined, as proposed by Harmer et al. (2018): NPCs use RL during the simulation, accessing the training input only in situations where RL fails to determine the behavior. This approach requires less recordings, hence it could be used in situations in which there are not enough human demonstrations to perform the complete IL training.

CONCLUSION

In this paper, an application supporting the training of CBRN operators using immersive VR is presented. The system was designed with the support of members of Terzo Stormo – Aeronautica Militare and developed to overcome the economic, organizational, and safety-related issues associated with real-life CBRN exercises. This work extends an existing platform, which was redesigned and rebuilt based on the feedback collected during the NATO event Toxic Trip 2019 in order to create a training experience that could be integrated in real CBRN training. This new version focuses on the realism of the VR simulation, which was improved in terms of graphics quality and interaction fidelity. The new platform provides a configurable simulation where one or four users can experience the RECCE procedure in presence of a radiological risk. The users can play the role of one of the four operators that compose the RECCE team, perform all the steps of the procedure (using the hints provided by the system, if necessary) and receive an evaluation report that assesses their overall performance.

The platform was preliminarily tested with the participation of CBRN operators, and early results highlighted the realism of the simulation and its potential as a training tool, confirming the premises of this study, despite its present limitations regarding currently available features and technologies used in the prototype implementation. The open feedback collected during the early testing showed an overall appreciation of the devised solution, although further investigations will be needed to validate the system and evaluate its potential as a training tool. In particular, a formal testing session should be organized using a rigorous protocol that leverages questionnaires already used in the literature to evaluate the knowledge gain associated with the training experience (thus, the training efficiency of the platform), the motivation at learning, the usability, and the overall quality of the devised application w.r.t. the traditional CBRN training.

ACKNOWLEDGMENT

This work was developed in the context of the collaboration between Politecnico di Torino, Fondazione LINKS, and Terzo Stormo – Aeronautica Militare, Villafranca di Verona. Activities have been partly supported by the VR@POLITO initiative. The authors want to acknowledge the support provided by Stefano Cimaroli, Davide Preziusi, and Giuseppe Imperatrice from Terzo Stormo – Aeronautica Militare, Villafranca di Verona in the design and validation phases.

REFERENCES

Berkman, M. I., & Akan, E. (2019). *Presence and Immersion in Virtual Reality*. Springer International Publishing. doi:10.1007/978-3-319-08234-9_162-1

Brooke, J. (1996). SUS: A 'quick and dirty' usability scale. *Usability Evaluation in Industry, 189*.

Buttussi, F., & Chittaro, L. (2021). A comparison of procedural safety training in three conditions: Virtual reality headset, smartphone, and printed materials. *IEEE Transactions on Learning Technologies*, *14*(1), 1–15. doi:10.1109/TLT.2020.3033766

Calandra, D., Prattico, F. G., Migliorini, M., Verda, V., & Lamberti, F. (2021). A Multi-role, Multi-user, Multi-technology Virtual Reality-based Road Tunnel Fire Simulator for Training Purposes. In *Proceedings of the 16th International Joint Conference on Computer Vision, Imaging and Computer Graphics Theory and Applications – GRAPP* (pp. 96–105). SciTePress.

Cummings, J. J., & Bailenson, J. N. (2016). How immersive is enough? A meta-analysis of the effect of immersive technology on user presence. *Media Psychology*, *19*(2), 272–309. doi:10.1080/15213269.2015.1015740

De Lorenzis, F., Prattico, F. G., & Lamberti, F. (2022). Hcp–vr: Training first responders through a virtual reality application for hydrogeological risk management. *HUCAPP*, *2022*, 273–280.

Feng, Z., González, V. A., Amor, R., Lovreglio, R., & Cabrera-Guerrero, G. (2018). Immersive virtual reality serious games for evacuation training and research: A systematic literature review. *Computers & Education*, *127*, 252–266.

García, A. A., Bobadilla, I. G., Arroyo-Figueroa, G., Pérez-Ramírez, M., & Román, J. (2015). Virtual reality training system for maintenance and operation of high-voltage overhead power lines. *Virtual Reality (Waltham Cross)*, *20*(1), 27–40. doi:10.100710055-015-0280-6

Gisler, J., Hift, C., Kunz, A., & Holzwarth, V. (2020). Designing virtual training environments: Does immersion increase task performance? In *2020 International Conference on Cyberworlds (CW)* (pp. 125–128). 10.1109/CW49994.2020.00026

Harmer, J., Gisslén, L., del Val, J., Holst, H., Bergdahl, J., Olsson, T., Sjoo, K., & Nordin, M. (2018). Imitation learning with concurrent actions in 3d games. In *2018 IEEE Conference on Computational Intelligence and Games (CIG)*. IEEE. 10.1109/CIG.2018.8490398

Hassenzahl, M., Koller, F., & Burmester, M. (2008). Der user experience (UX) auf der spur: Zum einsatz von. In H. Brau, S. Diefenbach, M. Hassenzahl, F. Koller, M. Peissner, & K. Rose (Eds.), *Tagungsband UP08* (pp. 78–82). Fraunhofer Verlag. www.attrakdiff.de

Kalawsky, R. S. (1999). VRUSE – A computerised diagnostic tool: For usability evaluation of virtual/synthetic environment systems. *Applied Ergonomics*, *30*(1), 11–25. doi:10.1016/S0003-6870(98)00047-7 PMID:10098813

Kaluschke, M., Weller, R., Zachmann, G., Pelliccia, L., Lorenz, M., Killmant, P., Knopp, S., & Hatze, J. P. G. (2018). Hips - a virtual reality hip prosthesis implantation simulator. In *2018 IEEE Conference on Virtual Reality and 3D User Interfaces (VR)* (pp. 591–592). IEEE.

Keller, J. (2010). *Motivational Design for Learning and Performance: The ARCS Model Approach.* Academic Press.

Lamberti, F., De Lorenzis, F., Pratticò, F. G., & Migliorini, M. (2021). An immersive virtual reality platform for training CBRN operators. In *Proceedings of 2021 IEEE 45th Annual Computers, Software, and Applications Conference (COMPSAC)* (pp. 133–137). 10.1109/COMPSAC51774.2021.00030

Lovreglio, R., Duan, X., Rahouti, A., Phipps, R., & Nilsson, D. (2021). Comparing the effectiveness of fire extinguisher virtual reality and video training. *Virtual Reality (Waltham Cross)*, *25*(1), 133–145. doi:10.100710055-020-00447-5

Maciejewski, P., Gawlik-Kobylińska, M., Lebiedź, J., Ostant, W., & Aydın, D. (2020). To Survive in a CBRN Hostile Environment: Application of CAVE Automatic Virtual Environments in First Responder Training. In *Proceedings of the 3rd International Conference on Applications of Intelligent Systems (APPIS 2020)*. Association for Computing Machinery. 10.1145/3378184.3378212

Mossel, A., Peer, A., Goellner, J., & Kaufmann, H. (2015). Towards an immersive virtual reality training system for CBRN disaster preparedness. *5th International Defense and Homeland Security Simulation Workshop, DHSS 2015*, 23 – 32.

NATO. (2018). *Commander's guide on medical support to chemical, biological, radiological, and nuclear (cbrn) defensive operations*. https://www.coemed.org/files/stanags/03_AMEDP/AMedP-7.6_EDA_V1_E_2873.pdf

Pérez, L., Diez, E., Usamentiaga, R., & García, D. F. (2019). Industrial robot control and operator training using virtual reality interfaces. *Computers in Industry*, *109*, 114–120. doi:10.1016/j.compind.2019.05.001

Pratticò, F. G., De Lorenzis, F., Calandra, D., Cannavò, A., & Lamberti, F. (2021). Exploring simulation-based virtual reality as a mock-up tool to support the design of first responders training. *Applied Sciences (Basel, Switzerland)*, *11*(16), 1–13. doi:10.3390/app11167527

Pratticò, F. G., & Lamberti, F. (2021). Towards the adoption of virtual reality training systems for the self-tuition of industrial robot operators: A case study at kuka. *Computers in Industry*, *129*, 129. doi:10.1016/j.compind.2021.103446

Rantanen, E. M., & Talleur, D. A. (2005). Incremental transfer and cost effectiveness of groundbased flight trainers in university aviation programs. *Proceedings of the Human Factors and Ergonomics Society Annual Meeting*, *49*(7), 764–768. doi:10.1177/154193120504900705

Schönauer, C., Bösch, C., Wechdorn, T., Göllner, J., Peer, A., Mossel, A., & Kaufmann, H. (2020). Physical object interaction in first responder mixed reality training. *Proceedings of SPIE - The International Society for Optical Engineering*, *11426*. 10.1117/12.2557396

Sharma, S., Jerripothula, S., Mackey, S., & Soumare, O. (2014). Immersive virtual reality environment of a subway evacuation on a cloud for disaster preparedness and response training. In *2014 IEEE Symposium on Computational Intelligence for Human-like Intelligence* (pp. 1–6). 10.1109/CIHLI.2014.7013380

Zibrek, K., & McDonnell, R. (2019). Social presence and place illusion are affected by photorealism in embodied VR. In *MIG '19* (pp. 1–7). Motion, Interaction and Games. doi:10.1145/3359566.3360064

KEY TERMS AND DEFINITIONS

Alpha Particles: Particles that may be found in a location in case of radiological attack.

Beta Particles: Particles that may be found in a location in case of radiological attack. They are heavier than the alpha particles and they spread onto a wider area.

CBRN: Chemical, Biological, Radiological, Nuclear. The term represents a set of procedures required to deal with events associated with a wide range of risks, mainly caused by the deployment of mass-destruction weapons.

Clean Man: One of the operators of the RECCE team. He or she is tasked to decontaminate the other operators at the end of the procedure.

Dirty Man: One of the operators of the RECCE team. He or she is tasked to find and delimit the contaminated area.

Immersion: The sensorial stimulation experienced in a simulation.

Presence: The sense of being there, where a simulation is set.

PSDS: Dispenser of decontaminating liquid, typically used by the Clean Man to decontaminate the other operators.

RECCE Team: A reconnaissance team tasked to find and delimit the contaminated area in case of a CBRN risk.

Team Leader: One of the operators of the RECCE team. He or she is tasked to manage the team and coordinate the operations.

VR: Virtual Reality.

VRTS: Virtual Reality Training System.

Chapter 5
Toward Evacuation Training in Metaverse:
Transforming Normal Time Into Emergency Time

Hiroyuki Mitsuhara
https://orcid.org/0000-0001-8230-3379
Tokushima University, Japan

Masami Shishibori
Tokushima University, Japan

ABSTRACT

Traditional evacuation training is ineffective as it does not simulate decision making against tough disaster situations. Therefore, evacuation training should be significantly enhanced to offer realistic simulated evacuation experiences, entailing decision making. A promising approach to the enhancement is to introduce virtual reality (VR) into evacuation training, and there have been numerous VR-based evacuation training systems. The authors launched the project Evacuation Training in Metaverse (ETM) considering the recent surge of interest in the metaverse as a VR extension. The ETM system is being developed based on the design principle: gathering numerous participants, pursuing high fidelity, and simulating a sudden earthquake. The ETM system transforms ordinary time to emergency time by creating a sudden earthquake, allowing participants to experience simulated earthquake evacuation in a high fidelity virtual world developed from an open-city model, photogrammetry, etc. The participants make decisions in the virtual world while being influenced by numerous others.

DOI: 10.4018/978-1-6684-3398-0.ch005

INTRODUCTION

Natural or artificial disasters threaten human beings of all ages. For example, the incidence of floods and typhoons (or hurricanes and cyclones) has recently increased, and damages have tended to become critical due to climate change (WMO, 2022). In terms of unpredictability, an earthquake is a very devastating disaster. A large earthquake can cause devastating damage and numerous casualties. For example, the 2011 Tōhoku earthquake and tsunami killed over 15,000 people (Kazama & Noda, 2012). In 2021, earthquakes with a magnitude of 7 or higher have occurred approximately 19 times worldwide (USGS, 2022). A large earthquake is never in someone else's affair. In this disaster-prone age, we must prepare to outlive disasters.

Disaster education is fundamental but influential disaster preparedness targeted at a wider range of people. Although there are different types of disaster education (e.g. watching a video and visiting a disaster museum), evacuation training is the most common disaster education regularly held in schools, businesses and communities. However, traditional evacuation training is insufficient to offer simulated evacuation experiences because participants (trainees) are urged to follow a predefined path to a specified safe location (e.g. shelter). In a real disaster, they may encounter challenging situations that require making decisions during evacuation. When the recommended route is inaccessible, for example, they will have to decide on another safe route as rapidly as feasible. Evacuation training entailing such a decision making is effective in terms of preparing against real disasters. Therefore, evacuation training should be significantly enhanced to offer realistic simulated evacuation experiences.

Disaster education can be enhanced using information and communication technology (ICT), and there have been numerous examples of ICT-based disaster education. For example, a web hazard map (Song, et al., 2022) and a map-based message-sharing tool (Uchida et al., 2021) were used for disaster education programmes in school. Regarding evacuation training, for example, the authors developed a location based mobile game application where participants evacuate to a shelter in the real world within a time limit while making decisions against disaster situations expressed (controlled) using a branching scenario (Mitsuhara et al., 2015). As other examples, mobile applications have been developed that visualise simulated approaching tsunamis on digital maps and allow participants to experience pseudo evacuation by sprinting in the real world toward a shelter while looking at the visualised tsunami (Yamori & Sugiyama, 2020) (Mitsuhara & Shishibori, 2022). These applications can be regarded as supplements to or enhancement of real-world evacuation training.

Real-world evacuation training entails challenges ensuring scenario variety and participant safety. Considering disaster unpredictability, evacuation training should be conducted in various situations that assume compound disasters (e.g. earthquake in heavy rain), different hours (e.g. early morning and midnight) and weathers (e.g. high temperature and strong wind). However, in numerous cases, real-world evacuation training is conducted during the day on a beautiful day based on a basic scenario (i.e. a single disaster). In addition, outdoor evacuation training is cancelled when severe weather (e.g. heavy rain and snowstorm) is forecast, and participants must pay close attention to avoid traffic accidents. Therefore, virtual-world evacuation training has been demanded, which can be conducted in various situations (assumptions) in a safe environment, and virtual reality (VR)-based evacuation training has been actively investigated, developed and practised based on the demand.

The authors prototyped simple VR evacuation simulators and conducted preliminary experiments (Mitsuhara et al., 2019; Mitsuhara et al., 2021) to establish a well-suited design for VR-based evacuation training. The experiments showed that even in VR, the situation where numerous participants simultaneously evacuate can make evacuation more difficult, i.e. more realistic, due to cognitive biases (e.g. normalcy bias and conformity bias) and interactions with others. Thus, VR-based evacuation training should simulate others' behaviour and provide more realistic simulated evacuation experiences. Based on this indication, the authors aim at VR-based evacuation training, which allows several participants to evacuate simultaneously while focusing on Metaverse, which can be regarded as a VR extension. Currently, the authors have specified the design principle of the ETM system and then implemented and tested parts of the ETM system in a work-in-progress project named 'Evacuation Training in Metaverse (ETM)'. The ETM project's research goal is to open up an application field of Metaverse and clarify how the ETM system can help several people prepare to outlive disasters.

The remainder of this chapter is organised as follows. The Background section offers a quick overview of VR-based evacuation training and some Metaverse topics. The section on VR Earthquake Simulator Prototype explains a simple VR earthquake simulator prototype that serves as the basis of the ETM system and reports on a preliminary experiment using the prototype. The Evacuation Training in Metaverse section introduces the ETM system's ideas in terms of the design principles (requirements), architecture and implementation (functions), demonstrating screenshots (e.g. virtual worlds) of the ETM system under development. The Future Research Direction section presents the remaining tasks of completing and evaluating the ETM system. This chapter is summarised in the Conclusion section.

BACKGROUND

Recently, VR and augmented reality (AR) have attracted a considerable amount of attention in disaster/emergency management (Zhu & Li, 2021) (Khanal et al., 2022) and simulation training (Li et al., 2022). This trend is no exception to evacuation training, and VR has already been popularised as an evacuation training platform. This section overviews VR-based evacuation training by introducing recent examples and presents the potential of Metaverse-based evacuation training to clarify the ETM project's current position.

Virtual Reality-Based Evacuation Training

VR has been actively applied to evacuation training to offer realistic simulated evacuation experiences in a three-dimensional (3D) virtual world because of advantages like high immersiveness, interactivity and safety. VR-based earthquake evacuation training system, for example, enhances survival skills (e.g. detecting potential danger) through a realistic simulation of earthquakes, environment and humans (Li et al., 2017). The behaviours of participants in VR-based evacuation training have been actively investigated. A VR simulator and field experiment (Feng et al., 2021), for example, revealed that exit choice behaviours during an evacuation are similar. It has been asserted by various experiments that VR-based fire evacuation training should prioritise behavioural realism (Arias et al., 2021). Furthermore, VR can be used to investigate factors causing undesirable evacuation behaviours in real disasters. For example, an influential factor investigation of indoor evacuation by a comparative experiment using a VR building fire simulator revealed that building spatial configurations (e.g. corridor width and evacuation signage) affects the retraction and selection of an evacuation route (Snopková et al., 2022). An investigation of participants' evacuation behaviours in the VR building fire simulator revealed that the participants' route choices were affected by their neighbours' behaviours (Fu et al., 2021). The authors developed a simple VR evacuation simulator (earthquake and fire) and discovered that participants with failed evacuations in the first session tended to have successful evacuations in the next (Mitsuhara et al., 2019).

Combining With Serious Game

VR can enhance training efficacy and training motivation when combined with a digital game. Numerous VR-based games focusing on evacuation training have been released. Regarding fire evacuation, for example, a VR-based serious game working on a web browser conveys not only smoke but also crowds as non-player characters (NPCs) using simulation techniques and visualises participant evacuation paths after the training (Yang et al., 2021). Another serious game working in a cave automatic virtual environment enhances teachers' fire preparedness skills (e.g. executing school evacuation protocol) by introducing not only gaming elements but also editable scenarios, fire propagation simulation and other elements to enhance training efficacy (Mystakidis et al., 2022). Another employs BIM (building information modelling) to simulate fire in an actual hospital model and trains staff to ensure patients' and visitors' safety during an emergency (Rahouti et al., 2021). A VR-based serious game for earthquake evacuation, for example, improves behavioural responses and evacuation preparedness by modelling an actual hospital, offering navigation to and interaction with waypoints and replaying for explaining the recommended behaviours (Feng et al., 2020a). Regarding another disaster evacuation, for example, a VR-based serious game focusing on aircraft emergency landing evacuation adopts an error-based learning approach and proposes ways to avoid errors in the evacuation by offering participants not only negative but also corrective feedback explaining the errors (Chittaro & Buttussi, 2022). A recent VR-based serious game allowed trainers to customise environmental, disaster, narrative and pedagogical settings for a wider use (Feng et al., 2020b).

Adopting Collaborative Virtual Reality

Collaborative VR that allows multiple users to simultaneously share a virtual world has been applied to emergency training, e.g. first response in a building fire (Molka-Danielsen et al., 2018) and rescue in a road tunnel fire (Calandra, et al., 2021), where each participant is assigned a particular role. Given that decision-making will be more challenging owing to uncertain situations caused by others (simultaneous participants), collaborative VR-based evacuation training can make evacuation training more realistic. In other words, it can simulate complex situations involving positive (e.g. cooperation and encouragement) and negative (e.g. conflict and panic) behaviour with or by others. Participants controlling 3D agents evacuate occasionally interacting with other participants and computer-controlled agents during bomb blasts and active shooter events, for example, a collaborative VR-based evacuation (emergency response) training system was developed (Sharma, 2020).

Virtual Reality to Metaverse

VR technologies and devices have advanced and spread worldwide. VR is being extended to Metaverse, which allows numerous users (avatars) to get immersed into a large 3D virtual world and synchronously interact with other users as daily or game-playing activities. *Second Life*, for example, has been a prominent service of Metaverse since its inception, and nowadays, new services (e.g. *Horizon Worlds* and *VRChat*) are gaining more users. Metaverse has attracted a considerable amount of attention in different domains while involving various agendas not only in technology but also in society, economy, security, privacy, etc. (Lee et al., 2021) (Park & Kim,

2022). The educational use of Metaverse is a promising domain, and there have been investigations, case studies and development projects for it. For example, the advantages and barriers to the successful educational use of *Second Life* in higher education were investigated (Warburton, 2009). Examples of the use of *Second Life* in medical and health education were examined focusing on pedagogical potential (Kamel Boulos et al., 2007). An investigation of university students' perceptions of Metaverse educational values suggested that perceptions can be significantly affected by their perceived usability and usefulness (Akour et al., 2022). An investigation of learning experiences in an academic conference held in Metaverse service revealed that participants who valued communication with others tended to enhance their learning experience as to an innovative mindset (Goda & Mitsuhara, 2021). A Metaverse-based collaborative learning platform was prototyped, which simulates classrooms and allows students to learn through e-Learning materials presented on a classroom panel and through communication with other students and/or virtual agents (Jovanović & Milosavljević, 2022). Metaverse-based education can gain the public's attention by emphasising its advantages, not only high usability and usefulness but also new learning experiences and high learning efficacy brought by immersiveness and multiuser interactions.

Collaborative VR-based evacuation training could be extended to include Metaverse-based training. In other words, Metaverse-based evacuation training can simulate more complex situations (or chaotic situations) and improve training efficacy while including numerous participants. Metaverse-based evacuation training is a relatively new direction that has received little attention.

VR EARTHQUAKE SIMULATOR PROTOTYPE

The authors sought to investigate how evacuation behaviour differed in the conditions of single and multiple participants before evaluating how Metaverse can be applied to evacuation training. Thus, the authors prototyped a simple VR earthquake simulator in which a large earthquake suddenly occurs and participants are forced to evacuate (Mitsuhara et al., 2021). In other words, the simulator makes simulated earthquake evacuation experiences more realistic by transforming normal time into emergency time in the 3D virtual world.

Overview

The simulator was designed and prototyped for a binocular opaque head-mounted display (HMD), *Oculus/Meta Quest 2*, and double-handed controllers, *Oculus Touch Hand Controllers*, using a *Unity3D* game engine. In the virtual world, participants

Figure 1. Prototyped VR earthquake simulator (left: after-shake situations, middle: floor map indicating fire locations, right: building exterior).

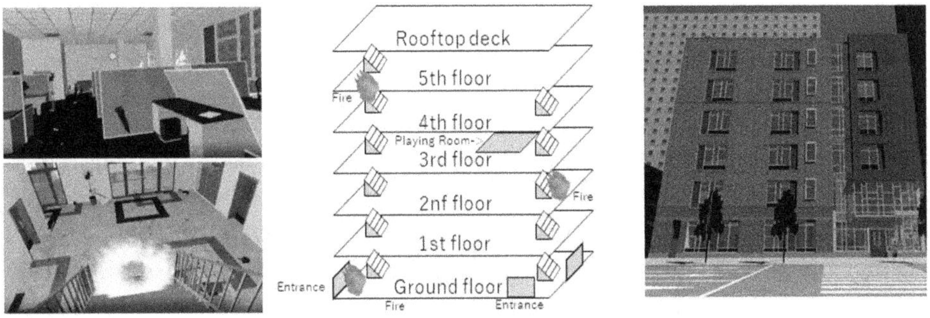

can walk down a street and enter a six-story office building with a rooftop deck in an urban area. The office building has three entrances on the ground floor, two stairways between each floor, one stairway between the fifth floor and rooftop deck and a playing room on the third floor where participants can play a simple game, which allows shooting a gun at static targets using controllers.

The large earthquake occurred suddenly while participants were playing the gun-shooting game. The following audio-visual effects are used to convey the earthquake realistically.

- **Step 1:** Sound an earthquake early warning.
- **Step 2:** Swing the HMD's screen and sound a roar for 15 s. Simultaneously shake objects (e.g. desktop items and chairs) and collapse some light objects, causing the objects to scatter on the floor.
- **Step 3:** Produce shake-caused fires with burning sounds at three locations: one entrance on the ground floor, one stairway on the second floor (to the third floor) and one stairway on the fourth floor (to the fifth floor).

After the shakes, the participants decide what to do. The simulator does not boost their decisions or hinder evacuation time. Participants are unharmed even when touching fire (e.g. decreasing moving speed by injury). Figure 1 presents screenshots of the simulator.

Preliminary Experiment

The authors conducted a preliminary experiment to observe how participants reacted to the simulator. This experiment focused on differences between one- and two-participant settings under the assumption that the presence or absence of an accompanier influences participant behaviour.

Settings

The participants were nine undergraduate students (aged 21 to 23, majoring in computer science and having once or no previous VR experience) who congregated after hearing that they could play a VR game. All participants never imagined that an earthquake would occur in the VR game. Participants were randomly divided into two groups and walked through the virtual world for a while wearing the HMD and holding the controllers.

- **Group A (*N* = *3*):** One participant entered the simulator with no accompanier. An earthquake early warning sounded after a participant was playing the game for a while, then several seconds later, shakes started.
- **Group B (*N* = *6*):** In each subgroup (B1, B2 and B3), two participants positioned within a conversing range entered the simulator simultaneously. An earthquake early warning sounded while two participants were playing the game together, and several seconds later, the shakes started.

The participants' simulator screens were video-recorded using the HMD's mirroring function. Furthermore, their utterances were also recorded during the experiment. After using the simulator, all participants were given a questionnaire.

Results

The authors used the (Student's) t-test, assuming a normal population and homoscedasticity, despite the sample size (the number of participants) being too small for statistical analysis.

- **Evaluation Time:** All participants attempted to evacuate immediately after the shakes stopped, and eight participants completed evacuation. One participant in B2 dropped out because of VR sickness, but another participant kept evacuating alone. The participants in B1 and B3 evacuated together. The recorded videos revealed that the evacuation times of three participants in Group A were 278, 241 and 204 s. The mean evacuation time was 241.0 s. The evacuation times of B1, B2 and B3, estimated at the time when both participants in B1 and B3 or one participant in B2 completed evacuation, were 334, 294 and 409 s, respectively, and the mean evacuation time was 345.6 s. The mean evacuation time in Group B was approximately 100 s slower than that in Group A. However, the t-test revealed no significant difference between the two groups ($p = 0.058$).

- **Utterance:** Group A participants did not utter anything except for 'Oh' and 'Oops' during evacuation. However, Group B participants uttered primarily when they had to make decisions (e.g. 'What do we do?' and 'Which is better to go?'). Occasionally, the participants uttered to mention the danger (e.g. 'Let's detour to avert fire'.). The participants in B3 uttered to synchronise evacuating pace (e.g. 'Please wait' and 'Come on this way').
- **Questionnaire:** Table 1 shows the mean values, standard deviations and p-values of the t-test of the participants' answers to 5-point Likert scale questions. For the participants' self-evaluation of evacuation (Q1), the mean values of Groups A and B were more than 4.0——one participant in B2 did not answer this question because of dropping out. For their sensed uneasiness (Q2), the mean value of Group A was 1.5 points higher than that of Group B, and the t- test revealed a considerable difference between the two groups at the 5% level. For their sensed urgency (Q3), the mean value of Group A was approximately 1 point higher than that of Group B, but the t-test revealed no significant difference. For their sensed confusion (Q4), the mean value of Group A was 1.5 points lower than Group B, and the t-test revealed a significant difference between the two groups at the 1% level. For their sensed scare (Q5), the mean value of Group A was approximately 1.7 points higher than that of Group B, and the t-test revealed a considerable difference between the two groups at the 5% level. For their sensed fun (Q6), the mean values of Groups A and B were more than 4.0.

Table 1. Questionnaire results.

Question	Group A Mean (SD)	Group B Mean (SD)	t-Test p-Value
Q1. Do you feel that you made a successful evacuation?	4.33 (0.57)	4.80 (0.44)	0.243
Q2. Did you feel uneasy during the evacuation?	4.33 (0.57)	2.83 (0.98)	0.047 *
Q3. Did you feel urgency during the evacuation?	4.33 (0.57)	3.30 (1.21)	0.227
Q4. Did you feel confused during the evacuation?	3.0 (0.0)	4.50 (0.54)	0.002 **
Q5. Did you feel scared during the evacuation?	4.0 (1.0)	2.33 (0.81)	0.030 *
Q6. Did you feel fun during the evacuation?	4.67 (0.57)	4.33 (0.51)	0.407

* $p < 0.05$, ** $p < 0.01$

Consideration

For the evacuation times, Group A participants completed the evacuation faster than Group B participants. The authors think the following evacuation behaviours contributed to this result:

- **Group A:** Participants, who had to make decisions on their own, tended to move fast. Two participants passed through the fire toward the entrance or rooftop deck. This observed behaviour could imply that these participants felt able to pass through the virtual fire believing that the virtual fire never causes harm or injury. The mean value of Q1 could imply that the virtual fire boosted the wrong successful experience. The mean values of Q2–Q5 showed that the participants experienced a certain degree of reality represented as negative emotions, but safety in the simulator could have boosted them to take dangerous behaviours that should be prevented during real disasters.
- **Group B:** The participants tended to pause to discuss evacuation routes and synchronise the evacuation pace by waiting for another participant (accompanier). The mean value of Q1 could imply that cooperative evacuation in the virtual world increases self-evaluation of evacuation. The simulator does not give (display) a time limit, and thus, the participants in both groups could evacuate without any concern for time. If given a time limit, the participants in Group B might not have undertaken cooperative evacuation behaviours (i.e. discussion and synchronisation) and instead have taken dangerous behaviours.

The mean values of Q2, Q3 and Q5 indicated that Group A participants experienced more uneasiness, urgency and scare than Group B participants. The authors believe that the high mean values of Group A resulted from evacuating alone, whereas the low mean values of Group B resulted from cooperative evacuation behaviours that can alleviate uneasiness, urgency and scare. The mean values of Q4 show that Group B participants experience more confusion than Group A participants. The discussion and synchronisation could have promoted the confusion though Group B participants did not state their evacuation policy or desire for self-determination during evacuation and, thus, had no explicit conflicts. Although the mean values of Q2–Q5 were overall high, the mean values of Q6 were positive in both groups. Fostering fun is expected to motivate people to regularly participate in VR-based evacuation training that entails negative elements (i.e. uneasiness, urgency, confusion and scare).

Through this experiment, the authors confirmed that differences existed between Group A (one participant) and Group B (two participants). In the one participant setting, participants tended to keep moving and consequently completed the evacuation faster. In the two-participant setting, participants tended to have discussion and synchronisation and consequently completed the evacuation slower. Furthermore, Group A participants tended to feel uneasiness, urgency and scare more than Group B participants. This finding could imply that the presence of an accompanier causes calm evacuation behaviour. However, Group B participants tended to experience confusion more than Group A participants. Confusion may be amplified when more participants evacuate simultaneously.

The experiment had limitations and thus was inadequate to show evacuation behaviours in different situations depending on the disaster and human factors. The biggest limitation of this study was that the participants were only a small group of university students (i.e. maximum of two simultaneous participants). It might be rare to evacuate alone or in twos in real disasters, and when numerous people simultaneously evacuate, situations may get more complicated and difficult. Therefore, as a prerequisite, the VR-based evacuation training should simulate evacuation by many people.

EVACUATION TRAINING IN METAVERSE

Metaverse can work as a more realistic evacuation training platform that involves numerous simultaneous participants if being recognised as an alternative world for everyday activities. Therefore, the authors thought that Metaverse is an excellent platform for evacuation training and launched the project Evacuation Training in Metaverse (ETM).

Currently, the authors aim at ETM focusing on earthquakes. The targeted participants are students, professors and clerks from Tokushima University, the university where the authors work; the university students are the dominant participants in the ETM. The university campus is located in Tokushima, a coastal city facing the Pacific Ocean in the western area of Japan. Tokushima is predicted to be hit by a major earthquake (magnitude 9) and a resulting tsunami. Thus, the authors are developing an ETM system that simulates a major earthquake and tsunami and requires the participants to determine a safe location on the university campus within a time limit (i.e. time to tsunami arrival).

Design Principle

The ETM system was designed as extension of the aforementioned earthquake simulator. In other words, the ETM system was designed for the Oculus devices and developed using Unity3D. The ETM system's design principle (requirements) is presented in Figure 2.

Figure 2. The ETM system's design principle.

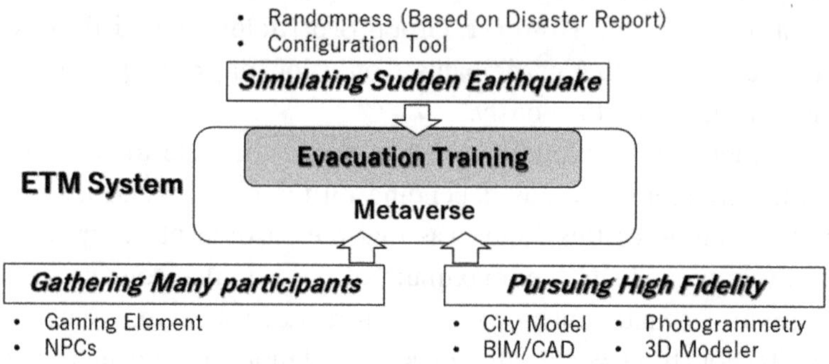

Gathering Many Participants

A prominent Metaverse service gathers numerous users and allows the users to simultaneously exist in the virtual world. If developed from scratch, the ETM system will face the first challenge of gathering users (participants). Especially, the ETM system aims to offer simulated earthquake evacuation experiences that entail decision making against difficult situations caused by numerous others. That is, the ETM system must gather numerous participants as the absolute requirement. In addition, Metaverse users may be uninterested in evacuation training and may hesitate to enter the virtual world where evacuation training is conducted. Therefore, the ETM system should have appealing features to gather numerous participants unconscious of evacuation training.

Pursuing High Fidelity

VR frequently aims for high fidelity to the real world, focusing on audio-visual effects (and physical phenomenon reproduction, if needed). Metaverse also aims for high fidelity in a comparatively large virtual world. However, the virtual world is not necessarily modelled from the real world. Considering that traditional evacuation training is conducted in the real world, the ETM system should simulate (3D model) a targeted evacuation training area while pursuing a high fidelity that focuses on audio-visual effects and geographical aspects. The participants can immerse themselves in a high-fidelity virtual world that is similar or identical to their living area, and their simulated evacuation experiences will become more realistic and thought-provoking.

Simulating Sudden Earthquake

In the real world, an earthquake suddenly occurs. If an earthquake early warning system is running, people can know the occurrence several seconds before shakes start, and some can immediately take appropriate precautions against the shakes (e.g. drop, cover and hold). However, some people may become panicked or dazed and then not evacuate properly even after the shakes stop. Participation in evacuation training can lead to taking appropriate precautions, but an evacuation training that notifies participants beforehand of settings such as start time (when shakes start), safe locations and damages cannot cause panic or daze. In other words, such an evacuation training cannot offer realistic simulated earthquake evacuation experiences entailing decision making against difficult situations. Therefore, the ETM system should simulate a sudden earthquake to generate difficult situations. Considering that the Metaverse's essence is to spend normal time (i.e. do daily activities) in a virtual world, the sudden earthquake will convert normal time into emergency time. Simulation of sudden earthquakes can bring higher efficacy in the use of a VR-based triage training where something salient happens suddenly and unexpectedly (van der Spek et al., 2013). This simulation might be thought most useful in ETM.

System Architecture

The ETM system adopts a client–server architecture. Figure 3 roughly shows the ETM system's architecture.

Client

The client is the Unity3D software that runs on the Oculus devices. A participant wearing the Oculus device connects to the synchronising server and enters a virtual world rendered in the client. Then, at a regular interval, the client sends the avatar's data (e.g. current position) to the synchronising server and receives all avatars' data from the synchronising server and renders the virtual world from the received data. Through this data exchange, the current virtual world (i.e. replicated and synchronised 3D objects) is shared among all simultaneous participants.

Synchronising Server

One of the two servers corresponds to *Photon Fusion*, a multiplayer game network engine on the cloud that allows simultaneous participants by synchronising the virtual world containing avatars and disaster situations. Immediately after receiving the data from clients, the synchronising server updates avatars in the virtual world and

Figure 3. System architecture.

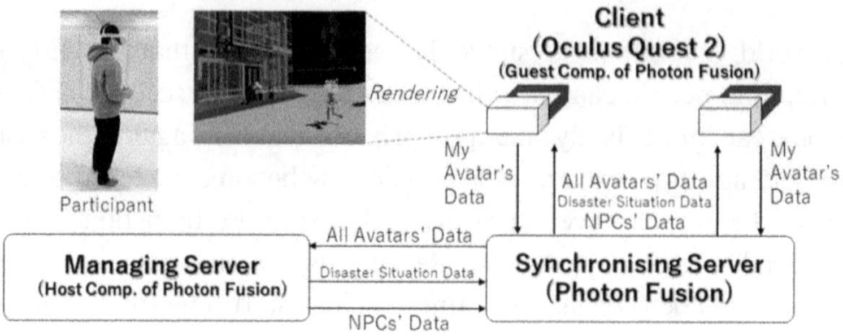

delivers the updated data to all clients and the managing server. If receiving a request to synchronise disaster situations from the managing server, the synchronising server delivers the disaster situation data (e.g. disaster type and location) to all clients.

Managing Server

Another server, where the Unity3D software serves as Photon Fusion's host computer, manages the training and records evacuation logs (e.g. avatar's movement trajectory) of all participants through the synchronising server. The managing server simulates a sudden earthquake and executes functions for gathering participants.

How to Have Many Participants

Metaverse allows users to communicate through voice chat, text chat and/or avatar's body actions. The ETM system develops the university campus virtual world (the evacuation training area) and thus should allow participants (i.e. university students, professors and clerks) to take, give and support classes as daily activities in addition to such basic communications. For example, professors will want to present and control a slideshow or video on a classroom panel. Furthermore, the ETM system should have an appealing feature for gathering numerous participants——the participants initially enter the ETM system, not while supposing that evacuation training may start.

Introducing the Gaming Element

Some Metaverse services have transformed into video game platforms. Considering that university students may like playing video games, the ETM system presents gaming as an appealing feature. In other words, to gather numerous participants, the ETM system does not manifest evacuation training but emphasises entertainment.

In terms of the balance or connectivity between gaming and training, it is crucial to carefully select a gaming element from different types of video games. If the ETM system presents a gaming element unrealistic for the context of 'university' (e.g. first-person battle shooting), participants may perceive an earthquake that occurs in the virtual world to be unrealistic as a gaming part and try dangerous evacuation behaviours. Therefore, the ETM system should present a gaming element that university students can possibly play on a university campus, for example, 'tag' and 'hide-and-seek' might be the candidates. However, it is unknown whether such a simple (or childlike) gaming element interests the participants and keeps their motivation to play for the long term. Introducing gamification (e.g. ranking and coupon) may also need to be considered.

Non-Player Characters

Supposing that several participants are not simultaneously present in the virtual world, the ETM system produces NPCs in the emergency time mode (i.e. when an earthquake occurs in the virtual world). Although NPCs can act like humans based on the AI technology, the ETM system aims at generating NPCs based on participants' evacuation logs (movement trajectory) recorded in the emergency time mode. This generation approach requires a certain amount of evacuation logs, but the generated NPCs act like humans by reproducing participants' behaviours (e.g. pausing and going back and forth). The client generates (renders) NPCs according to the following steps.

- **Step 1 (recording evacuation logs):** Every 0.05 s obtains a participant avatar's position (X, Y, Z coordinates and angle to Y) and sends the obtained position to the synchronising server. Through the synchronising server, the managing server receives and records the position together with the time stamp and participant ID. The recorded angle is used to animate the diagonally upward or downward movement of avatars.
- **Step 2 (generating NPCs):** After switching to the emergency time mode, receives NPCs' data from the managing server *via* the synchronising server every 0.05 s. The every-time received data of each NPC indicate the momentary (current) position in the corresponding participant avatar's movement trajectory recorded as the evacuation log.
- **Step 3 (generating NPCs):** Renders NPCs based on the received data. Only NPCs that exist inside a participant's field of view are rendered to reduce processing load while rendering.

Figure 4 presents screenshots of rendered NPCs in a sample virtual world. The authors investigated the frame rate (fps: frames per second) when one participant was viewing NPCs under the condition where NPCs increased by 20–100 every 5 s. Table 2 presents the measured frame rates' minimum and mean values. As the number of generated NPCs increased, the minimum and mean values decreased. For both values, there were differences of approximately 25 fps between 0 and 100 NPCs. Even when there were 100 NPCs, both values were more than 30 fps, and the authors did not visually notice significant latency. Therefore, the NPC generation is believed to work enough to compensate for an insufficient number of simultaneous participants in the emergency time mode and express challenging situations caused by many others.

Figure 4. NPCs rendered.

Table 2. Frame rates (per second) when rendering NPCs.

No. of NPCs	Minimum	Mean
0	59.8	61.4
20	50.9	53.5
40	44.9	49.8
60	41.4	44.2
80	35.8	40.7
100	34.3	35.8

Figure 5. A virtual world (Numazu City in the eastern area of Japan) built from the PLATEAU model.

How to Build a Virtual World

Building a virtual world is an indispensable crucial step in Metaverse development. The authors aim at building a large virtual world (evacuation training area) covering the university campus and surrounding areas. For this aim, the following approaches, which can be combined according to the circumstances, are promising.

Using City Model

It is difficult (time-consuming, burdensome and costly) to build a high fidelity, large virtual world from scratch. Especially when an evacuation training area is at the municipal level (i.e. covering a village, town or city), the difficulty level will significantly increase. To efficiently build such a virtual world, a city model based on precisely measured geographical data should be used.

The authors attempt to use open-city models provided by a Japanese national project called *PLATEAU*, which have been applied to various fields, such as disaster management, including evacuation training. For example, to realise VR-based fire evacuation training that covers the inside and outside areas of a high-rise building in Tokyo, a PLATEAU model is integrated seamlessly with the precise building model. The PLATEAU models are based on CityGML (City Geography Markup Language) consisting of data about geography, planimetric features (e.g. building and road) and building structure and texture (Façade pictures), and some models are provided as FBX (Filmbox) and/or OBJ (Wavefront Object) files. Unity3D occasionally needs to convert the models from CityGML to FBX or OBJ as it cannot directly load CityGML. Figure 5 presents screenshots of a virtual world built from a PLATEAU model.

Oculus Quest 2 is a lightweight, highly immersive HMD and is also available as a PC-connectable display. The ETM system attaches significance to its widespread and is supposed to use Oculus Quest 2 in the independence mode that does not require a PC. However, Oculus Quest 2 has a heavy processing load when visualising a virtual world based on a precise PLATEAU model with a huge amount of data. Thus, the authors optimise the visualisation along with the following steps.

- **Step 1:** Convert the building texture's image file format from TIFF (Tag Image File Format) to JPEG (Joint Photographic Experts Group). This is because TIFF has a low compression ratio and imposes more load in rendering (texture mapping) than JPEG with a high compression rate. This conversion can be done using a data-converting software (e.g. *FME Desktop*).
- **Step 2:** Reduce the polygons of 3D objects in the PLATEAU model. This reduction can be done using a 3D modeler (e.g. *Blender*) or Unity Assets (e.g. *Mesh Optimizer*).
- **Step 3:** Render only the 3D objects that exist inside a participant's field of view. This rendering can be done by activating Occlusion Culling in Unity3D.

Unfortunately, Tokushima is still not included in the PLATEAU models. As a preliminary test, the authors selected a PLATEAU model of a city similar to Tokushima (i.e. a city that is anticipated to hit a large earthquake and a resulting tsunami) and estimated the frame rate during a walk-through task under the two conditions: active or inactive optimisation. The results indicated that the optimisation could get approximately 60–90 fps, which are double to triple values than when inactive. Therefore, the optimisation is believed to be effective.

Using BIM/CAD

BIM (building information modelling) or CAD (computer aided design) software is suitable for building a small or medium high fidelity virtual world from 3D models with detailed structures. If BIM/CAD software outputs the models as major file formats, it is most convenient for Unity3D to load the output models (files). Figure 6 presents screenshots of a lecture building built from 3D models created using CAD software.

Using Photogrammetry

Photogrammetry is not a new 3D modelling technology but has recently gained a considerable amount of attention. This is because advanced smartphones or tablets (e.g. *iPhone 12 Pro*) equipped with a 3D-scanning sensor called 'LiDAR'

Figure 6. Virtual world built from CAD data (left: lecture building in the Tokushima University campus, right: classroom).

has enabled easy use of photogrammetry with a high visual reality and modelling accuracy. Photogrammetry can be applied to small, medium and large virtual worlds. To complete a large virtual world, however, numerous digital photos (or scanning data) are required for numerous spots, and the virtual world generated from the digital photos may need manual adjustment. Figure 7 presents the 3D model of Tokushima University campus that is generated by LiDAR-based photogrammetry and manually adjusted. When building a large virtual world *via* photogrammetry, the advantages (e.g. high visual reality) and disadvantages (e.g. time-consuming in manual adjustment) should be carefully investigated.

Figure 7. The virtual world is generated via LiDAR-based photogrammetry and manually adjusted (part of Tokushima University campus).

Using 3D Modeler

A 3D modeler (e.g. *Blender*) and/or Unity3D (e.g. terrain generator and assets) can be used to model a small or large virtual world from scratch. This approach may be time-consuming for a high fidelity virtual world compared with the aforementioned approaches.

How to Express Sudden Earthquake

It is easiest for expressing a sudden earthquake that the ETM system generates the earthquake at random timing. On the other hand, using an ETM system that generates the earthquake based on actual earthquake data (e.g. occurrence frequency) may be the best scientific and educational approach. Therefore, considering the two expression approaches, the ETM system attaches significance to scientific and educational viewpoints and generates the earthquake immediately after an actual large earthquake occurs somewhere in Japan. The Japan Meteorological Agency (JMA) delivers a disaster report as open data updated every minute. The earthquake-related items in the disaster report are occurrence time, intensity, magnitude, epicentre, possibility of a tsunami, etc. Loading the report at a regular interval, the ETM system starts to express a sudden earthquake (i.e. changes the mode from normal time to emergency time) when the report contains the items of a large earthquake with an intensity of 4 and higher. As the default expression, the ETM system sounds an earthquake early warning, shakes originally existing objects and collapses some light objects. In 2021, 54 earthquakes with an intensity of 4 and higher hit Japan (JMA, 2022). This frequency shows that average a sudden earthquake will happen in the ETM system every 7 days. This expression approach may be effective in making participants conscious of the possibility to be involved in an earthquake somewhere in Japan.

Some evacuation training practitioners will prefer to perform an evacuation training at a scheduled date not depending on randomness and configure disaster situations. Thus, the ETM system allows practitioners (administrators) to begin expressing a sudden earthquake at their arbitrary timing and offers an immersive configuration tool where the practitioners wearing the Oculus devices can set objects (e.g. fire, smoke, debris and injury) and safe locations in the virtual world. Figure 8 presents screenshots of the configuration tool where a practitioner is setting objects while pointing the position.

Evacuation Procedure

In the ETM system, when an earthquake occurs unexpectedly, users can decide whether to evacuate. In other words, in the emergency time mode, users who evacuate and those who do not evacuate may coexist.

Figure 8. Configuration tool.

1. **A user who was not driven to evacuate:** Will spend their normal time (e.g. talking with friends) under the disaster situation, watching others evacuating; the user is presumed not to be feeling an emergency.
2. **A user who decided to evacuate:** Will take appropriate precautions (e.g. hide under a sturdy table) against the shaking and then move to a safe location through passages with scattered objects, encountering various disaster situations (e.g. fire and debris), and occasionally communicate with others through voice chat; the user is presumed to be in an emergency. The user (i.e. a participant in evacuation training) must reach the safe location within a time limit that is not displayed on the screen. The ETM system indicates injury by painting the screen red or slowing down the moving speed if the participant engages in dangerous behaviour (e.g. touches fire).

When the time limit is exceeded, the ETM system displays a message for telling of failure in evacuation and tips for effective evacuation (e.g. 'You should get to a safe location on the third floor and above the buildings on this campus to outlive tsunami'.) to the participants who have not reached a safe location. After that, by deleting the disaster situations, the ETM system returns to the normal time mode from the emergency time mode. Figure 9 shows the evacuation procedure between the normal and emergency time modes.

FUTURE RESEARCH DIRECTIONS

ETM system should be developed as fast as possible based on the design principle. First, the virtual world (university campus and its surrounding areas) requires to be developed through the effective use of modelling technologies. Second, the mechanism for gathering numerous participants, i.e. a gaming element and NPCs,

Figure 9. Evacuation procedure.

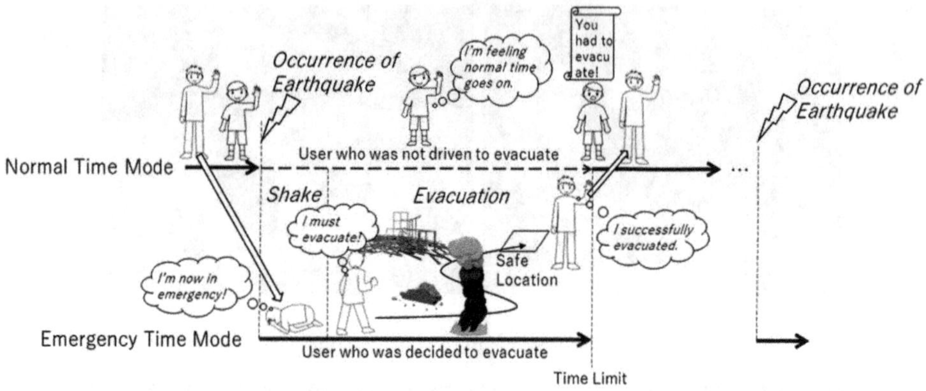

needs to be implemented. Third, transforming normal time to emergency time using the occurrence of a sudden earthquake needs to be implemented as the ETM system's feature is different from the existing VR-based evacuation training systems. As with other implementations, the functions for setting a time limit of evacuation and causing damages against participants who take dangerous behaviours are needed. In the future, the detailed efficacy of this transformation should be evaluated in addition to the ETM system's overall efficacy. Evaluation approaches for evacuation training have not been fully established yet. For the ETM system's multi-perspective evaluation, many data on participant evacuation behaviours should be gathered such as evacuation time, trajectory (distance), utterance and emotions.

Although Metaverse frequently investigates high fidelity by focusing on audio-visual effects (realities), the ETM system currently focuses on visual effects rather than audio effects. Probably, the visual effects positively affect immersiveness of the virtual world, but it should be explained whether evacuation training requires detailed visual effects. This is because participants may not focus on the virtual world's details but concentrate on evacuation. If this is true, the prioritisation of photogrammetry employment for building the virtual world might decline. On the other hand, if participants are affected by other participants through communications, the visual reality of avatars may affect participant evacuation behaviours. Currently, the ETM system adopts cartoon character-looking avatars. The use of such avatars may be unrealistic in the university campus' virtual world. For example, if a professor was expressed as an unrealistic avatar like a cute cartoon character, a student participant might not express the usual behaviour to the professor based on the superior–inferior relationship. One of the interesting topics to examine is whether avatars should be expressed realistically in the ETM system.

Although the ETM system enables practitioners to set objects in the virtual world, the objects are currently not controlled using a branching scenario. In other words, disaster situations are unchanged according to time passage, participant behaviours and environmental factors (e.g. temperature and wind) in the virtual world. For example, fire does not enlarge or diminish even as time passes. Therefore, the use of an ETM system that adopts a branching scenario that can express more variable disaster situations is another future direction.

CONCLUSION

This chapter explained the ongoing project of ETM. The ETM system is under development with the aim of gathering numerous participants, pursuing high fidelity and simulating a sudden earthquake. Metaverse use will continue to spread to the public while offering different valuable services. The ETM system is expected to become one of such services in terms of offering realistic simulated earthquake evacuation experiences. However, to date, there is still a long way to go to complete the ETM system. For example, building a high-fidelity virtual world may require more time than predicted. The authors continue to develop the ETM system, believing in its significance.

The occurrence of natural or artificial disasters, such as earthquakes, floods, typhoons, pandemics and war, transforms our everyday lives and brings death in the worst case. Participation in evacuation training is crucial for the preparedness to outlive disasters. The authors aim to apply the ETM system to any kind of disaster.

ACKNOWLEDGMENT

The authors thank I. Tanioka, K. Oe and T. Saito for their efforts in system implementation and experiment.

This work was supported by the Japan Society for the Promotion of Science Grants-in-Aid for Scientific Research [grant number 18H01054].

REFERENCES

Akour, I. A., Al-Maroof, R. S., Alfaisal, R., & Salloum, S. (2022). A conceptual framework for determining metaverse adoption in higher institutions of gulf area: An empirical study using hybrid SEM-ANN approach. *Computers and Education: Artificial Intelligence*, *3*, 100052. doi:10.1016/j.caeai.2022.100052

Arias, S., Wahlqvist, J., Nilsson, D., Ronchi, E., & Frantzich, H. (2021). Pursuing behavioral realism in virtual reality for fire evacuation research. *Fire and Materials, 45*(4), 462–472. doi:10.1002/fam.2922

Boulos, M. N. K., Hetherington, L., & Wheeler, S. (2007). Second life: An overview of the 9otential of 3-D virtual worlds in medical and health education. *Health Information and Libraries Journal, 24*(4), 233–245. doi:10.1111/j.1471-1842.2007.00733.x PMID:18005298

Calandra, D., Pratticò, F., Migliorini, M., Verda, V., & Lamberti, F. (2021). A multi-role, multi-user, multi-technology virtual reality-based road tunnel fire simulator for training purposes. In *Proceedings of the 16th International Joint Conference on Computer Vision, Imaging and Computer Graphics Theory and Applications* (vol. 1, pp. 96-105). 10.5220/0010319400960105

Chittaro, L., & Buttussi, F. (2022). Learning safety through public serious games: A study of "Prepare for Impact" on a very large, international sample of players. *IEEE Transactions on Visualization and Computer Graphics, 28*(3), 1573–1574. doi:10.1109/TVCG.2020.3022340 PMID:32894716

Feng, Y., Duives, D. C., & Hoogendoorn, S. P. (2021). Using virtual reality to study pedestrian exit choice behaviour during evacuations. *Safety Science, 137*, 105158. doi:10.1016/j.ssci.2021.105158

Feng, Z., González, V. A., Amor, R., Spearpoint, M., Thomas, J., Sacks, R., Lovreglio, R., & Cabrera-Guerrero, G. (2020a). An immersive virtual reality serious game to enhance earthquake behavioral responses and post-earthquake evacuation preparedness in buildings. *Advanced Engineering Informatics, 45*, 101118. doi:10.1016/j.aei.2020.101118

Feng, Z., González, V. A., Mutch, C., Amor, R., Rahouti, A., Baghouz, A., Li, N., & Cabrera-Guerrero, G. (2020b). Towards a customizable immersive virtual reality serious game for earthquake emergency training. *Advanced Engineering Informatics, 46*, 101134. doi:10.1016/j.aei.2020.101134

Fu, M., Liu, R., & Zhang, Y. (2021). Do people follow neighbors? An immersive virtual reality experimental study of social influence on individual risky decisions during evacuations. *Automation in Construction, 126*, 103644. doi:10.1016/j.autcon.2021.103644

Goda, Y., & Mitsuhara, H. (2021). Learning experiences in a full 3D conference: Relationships with 3D factors and innovative mindsets. In *Proceedings of 2021 IEEE International Conference on Engineering, Technology and Education* (pp.119-125). 10.1109/TALE52509.2021.9678846

Japan Meteorological Agency (JMA). (2022). https://www.jma.go.jp/jma/indexe.html

Jovanović, A., & Milosavljević, A. (2022). VoRtex metaverse platform for gamified collaborative learning. *Electronics (Basel)*, *11*(3), 317. doi:10.3390/electronics11030317

Kazama, M., & Noda, T. (2012). Damage statistics (Summary of the 2011 off the Pacific Coast of Tohoku Earthquake damage). *Soil and Foundation*, *52*(5), 780–792. doi:10.1016/j.sandf.2012.11.003

Khanal, S., Medasetti, U. S., Mashal, M., Savage, B., & Khadka, R. (2022). Virtual and augmented reality in the disaster management technology: A literature review of the past 11 years. *Frontiers in Virtual Reality*, *3*, 843195. doi:10.3389/frvir.2022.843195

Lee, L. H., Braud, T., Zhou, P., Wang, L., Xu, D., Lin, Z., Kumar, A., Bermejo, C., & Hui, P. (2021). *All one needs to know about metaverse: A complete survey on technological singularity, virtual ecosystem, and research agenda*. https://arxiv.org/abs/2110.05352

Li, C., Liang, W., Quigley, C., Zhao, Y., & Yu, L. F. (2017). Earthquake safety training through virtual drills. *IEEE Transactions on Visualization and Computer Graphics*, *23*(4), 1275–1284. doi:10.1109/TVCG.2017.2656958 PMID:28129163

Li, N., Sun, N., Cao, C., Hou, S., & Gong, Y. (2022). Review on visualization technology in simulation training system for major natural disasters. *Natural Hazards*, *112*(3), 1–32. doi:10.100711069-022-05277-z PMID:35308193

Mitsuhara, H., Inoue, T., Yamaguchi, K., Takechi, Y., Morimoto, M., Iwaka, K., Kozuki, Y., & Shishibori, M. (2015). Web-based system for designing game-based evacuation drills. *Procedia Computer Science*, *72*, 277–284. doi:10.1016/j.procs.2015.12.141

Mitsuhara, H., Tanimura, C., Nemoto, J., & Shishibori, M. (2019). Failure-enhanced evacuation training using a VR-based disaster simulator: A comparative experiment with simulated evacuees. *Procedia Computer Science*, *159*, 1670–1679. doi:10.1016/j.procs.2019.09.337

Mitsuhara, H., Tanioka, I., & Shishibori, M. (2021). Observing evacuation behaviours of surprised participants in virtual reality earthquake simulator. In *Proceedings of the 29th International Conference on Computers in Education* (*vol.* 2, pp. 576-582). Academic Press.

Mitsuhara, H., & Shishibori, M. (2022). Tsunami evacuation drill system focusing on mobile devices. *International Journal of Interactive Mobile Technologies*, *16*(6), 4–20. doi:10.3991/ijim.v16i06.23419

Molka-Danielsen, J., Prasolova-Forland, E., Fominykh, M., & Lamb, K. (2018) Use of a collaborative virtual reality simulation for multi-professional training in emergency management communications. In *Proceedings of the 2018 IEEE International Conference on Teaching, Assessment, Learning and Engineering* (pp. 408-415). 10.1109/TALE.2018.8615147

Mystakidis, S., Besharat, J., Papantzikos, G., Christopoulos, A., Stylios, C., Agorgianitis, S., & Tselentis, D. (2022). Design, development, and evaluation of a virtual reality serious game for school fire preparedness training. *Education Sciences*, *12*(4), 281. doi:10.3390/educsci12040281

Park, S. M., & Kim, Y. G. (2021). A metaverse: Taxonomy, components, applications, and open challenges. *IEEE Access: Practical Innovations, Open Solutions*, *10*, 4209–4251. doi:10.1109/ACCESS.2021.3140175

Rahouti, A., Lovreglio, R., Datoussaid, S., & Descamps, T. (2021). Prototyping and validating a non-immersive virtual reality serious game for healthcare fire safety training. *Fire Technology*, *57*(6), 3041–3078. doi:10.100710694-021-01098-x

Sharma, S. (2020). Improving emergency response training and decision making using a collaborative virtual reality environment for building evacuation. In C. Stephanidis, J. Y. C. Chen, & G. Fragomeni (Eds.), Lecture Notes in Computer Science: Vol. 12428. *HCI International 2020–Late Breaking Papers: Virtual and Augmented Reality* (pp. 213–224). Springer. doi:10.1007/978-3-030-59990-4_17

Song, J., Yamauchi, H., Oguchi, T., & Ogura, T. (2022). Application of web hazard maps to high school education for disaster risk reduction. *International Journal of Disaster Risk Reduction*, *72*, 102866. doi:10.1016/j.ijdrr.2022.102866

Snopková, D., Ugwitz, P., Stachoň, Z., Hladík, J., Juřík, V., Kvarda, O., & Kubíček, P. (2022). Retracing evacuation strategy: A virtual reality game-based investigation into the influence of building's spatial configuration in an emergency. *Spatial Cognition and Computation*, *22*(1-2), 30–50. doi:10.1080/13875868.2021.1913497

Uchida, O., Tajima, S., Kajita, Y., Utsu, K., Murakami, Y., & Yamada, S. (2021). Development and implementation of an ICT-based disaster prevention and mitigation education program for the young generation. *Information Systems Frontiers*, *23*(5), 1115–1125. doi:10.100710796-020-10082-9

United States Geological Survey (USGS). (2022). *The USGS Earthquake Hazards Program*. https://earthquake.usgs.gov/

van der Spek, E. D., van Oostendorp, H., & Meyer, Ch. (2013). Introducing surprising events can stimulate deep learning in a serious game. *British Journal of Educational Technology*, *44*(1), 156–169. doi:10.1111/j.1467-8535.2011.01282.x

Warburton, S. (2009). Second life in higher education: Assessing the potential for and the barriers to deploying virtual worlds in learning and teaching. *British Journal of Educational Technology*, *40*(3), 414–426. doi:10.1111/j.1467-8535.2009.00952.x

World Meteorological Organization (WMO). (2022). https://public.wmo.int/en

Yamori, K., & Sugiyama, T. (2020). Development and social implementation of smartphone app Nige-Tore for improving tsunami evacuation drills: Synergistic effects between commitment and contingency. *International Journal of Disaster Risk Science*, *11*(6), 751–761. doi:10.100713753-020-00319-1

Yang, Y., Xu, Z., Wu, Y., Wei, W., & Song, R. (2021). Virtual fire evacuation drills through a web-based serious game. *Applied Sciences (Basel, Switzerland)*, *11*(23), 11284. doi:10.3390/app112311284

Zhu, Y., & Li, N. (2021). Virtual and augmented reality technologies for emergency management in the built environments: A state-of-the-art review. *Journal of Safety Science and Resilience*, *2*(1), 1–10. doi:10.1016/j.jnlssr.2020.11.004

KEY TERMS AND DEFINITIONS

AR (Augmented Reality): Focusing on visual effects, it is a technique that superimposes a virtual world (computer graphics) onto the real world (a real-time vision captured by camera devices, including smartphones or tablets). AR is roughly divided into three categories: marker based, markerless and location based.

BIM (Building Information Modelling): It is a process that manages information of steps (parts) in a life cycle for building construction, and as a BIM model, the information (e.g. dimension, internal structure, material and functionality) can be shared uniformly among steps. BIM differs from CAD (Computer Aided Design) that basically supports 2D or 3D technical drawing.

CityGML: It is a standard format of city-scaled geospatial data available for visualisation, analysis and simulation and has the concept of LOD (Level of Detail) ranging from 1 to 4. For example, LOD1 contains a simple dimension data (box model) for buildings. LOD4 corresponds to a BIM model.

Metaverse: The term Metaverse (meta + universe) appeared in a cyberpunk novel in 1992 and was getting recognised as the concept or service of multiuser VR. Metaverse can be extended to AR that integrates real and virtual worlds by superimposing multiusers (avatars) in a virtual world onto the real world.

NPC (Non-Player Character): It is a term used especially in video games and indicates a computer-controlled character that players cannot operate. Many simultaneous NPCs are occasionally called a mob and introduced in disaster simulators as evacuee agents.

Oculus/Meta Quest 2: It is a binocular opaque head-mounted display (HMD) that is lightweight (approximately 500 g) and works on Android-based operating systems. Of the HMD products, Oculus Quest 2 is thought to be most popular owing to its good performance and reasonable price.

Photogrammetry: It is an image-processing technique for generating the 3D model or obtaining geometric properties of a target object from many digital photos (taken from many angles). A variety of photogrammetry software (e.g. *3DF Zephyr*) have been provided, and some advanced smartphones or tablets with a 3D-scanning sensor make photogrammetry easier.

PLATEAU: It is a Japanese project of creating and distributing open-city models led by the Ministry of Land, Infrastructure, Transport and Tourism (MLIT). PLATEAU models are based on CityGML 2.0. As of the end of 2021, the project has provided 3D models of 56 cities in Japan (e.g. Tokyo and Osaka) (https://www.mlit.go.jp/plateau/, in Japanese).

Unity3D: It is a cross-platform game engine involving an integrated development environment (IDE). Unity3D can make the development of VR software easier by providing 3D modelling, audio-visual effects, physics and collision calculations, etc.

VR (Virtual Reality): It provides simulated experiences in a virtual world while stimulating senses (especially vision and hearing). A VR where a user can get immersed in the virtual world by wearing an HMD is often called 'Immersive VR' (IVR). This chapter does not make a strict distinction between VR and IVR.

Chapter 6
Case Experiences With Immigrants on Workforce Training Using Virtual Reality

Raine Kauppinen
https://orcid.org/0000-0002-6420-4091
Haaga-Helia University of Applied Sciences, Finland

Merja Drake
https://orcid.org/0000-0003-1929-630X
Haaga-Helia University of Applied Sciences, Finland

ABSTRACT

Due to the rapid changes in the labor market, people need to constantly reshape their competencies, resulting in a tremendous need to reskill the workforce. Vocational training has traditionally been the task of educational institutions; however, today some companies also perform their own training. Overall success in establishing an individual's career depends on successful entry into the workforce, and in case of immigrants, entering the workforce is even more demanding. The key question is how educational institutions and companies can cooperate in this area. Immersive environments like virtual reality offer one type of solution. They are increasingly being used in workforce training and changing landscapes in educational institutions and companies. Using case examples, this chapter illustrates how several companies have jointly developed vocational materials with educational institutions and immigrants. The experiences are discussed, and examples of virtual reality training tasks implemented and connecting them to relevant competencies are presented.

DOI: 10.4018/978-1-6684-3398-0.ch006

INTRODUCTION

Nowadays, with the rapidly changing labor market and careers, people need to constantly to reshape their skills and competencies. The World Economy Forum (World Economy Forum, 2020) has calculated that new technology will be transforming over one billion jobs worldwide in the next decade, and there is a tremendous need to reskill the workforce. Traditionally, educational institutions were mainly responsible for conducting vocational training of the workforce. Currently, to a greater degree than before, companies such as Google, Apple, Hilton, and especially start-ups are training their own workforce. Thus, what is the role of higher education in the future? How could companies and educational institutions work in cooperation to reskill and train the workforce using emerging technologies?

Success in establishing an individual career depends on successful entry into the workforce after completing compulsory education. However, the direct transition from compulsory education into initial on-the-job training and to the workforce has become more difficult than ever before. In the case of immigrants, this is even more demanding (Eronen et al., 2014; OECD, 2018); for example, this is because of the diverse background of the immigrants. Although they often possess the skills and the competencies needed to be a part of the workforce, it is often difficult to recognize them due to the lack of formal degrees or diplomas.

New technologies and immersive learning environments such as extended reality (XR) including virtual reality (VR) may offer one type of a solution. VR can be particularly useful for training and recognizing the competencies of immigrants because instructions and the training material need not necessarily be only linguistic. Instead, training can be produced so that the correct modes of action are first demonstrated before being practiced. In addition, exercises can be safely repeated, and knowledge can be verified on a virtual world. The largest obstacles to using VR have been the cost and the required resources (Kavanagh et al., 2017). Decreasing the software and equipment costs may make more experiments possible, while some challenges might occur due to the rapidly changing technology (McGrath et al., 2018).

Thus, VR is one of the emerging technologies that is changing the training landscapes both in companies and in educational institutions. However, despite VR's potential, its full potential in workforce education and the process in which collaborating educational institutions and companies design, develop, and create VR-based training materials with the potential employees have not yet been researched to an adequate extent. This chapter, using case examples, discusses how educational institutions and companies in the health care, hospitality, and cleaning services have jointly and collaboratively developed, produced, and tested vocational training materials created using VR technology with immigrants.

The objective of this chapter is to help understand the potential of VR as a tool for vocational training, illustrate the potential with examples of the general types of VR training tasks that can be implemented, and present a model for connecting the necessary competencies to VR implementations used in training to evaluate learning and recognize competence. In addition, the experiences from the viewpoints of the educational institutions, companies, and immigrants are explored to provide insights on the feasibility of the approach. Based on the work done and on the experiences gained, future research directions are also discussed.

BACKGROUND

VR is increasingly being used in delivering learning and training material. VR has been particularly relevant in fields such as medicine, engineering, aviation, and safety training with suggested benefits of interaction, immersion, deep concentration, and real-life experiences (Dalgarno et al., 2002; Kulik et al., 2017; Melo et al., 2019; Wallach et al., 2011). Training situations can be either individual or collaborative, and participants learn by actively participating in the learning situation. The learning situation is an immersive experience without external distractions, and it can enhance interpersonal communication. VR also supports different types of learning styles.

Regarding immigrants, authors have previously performed research focusing on how to find how to recognize immigrants' competencies using VR to reduce language-related barriers to immigrants' employability (Drake, 2019; Kauppinen et al., 2021; Kauppinen & Drake, 2020b, 2020a). Based on this, it is important to understand how immigrants can participate in workforce training and what the role of educational institution is to foster personal growth and active citizenship of the immigrants. Furthermore, because the companies in different fields are the employers, a joint and collaborative effort is essential to provide usable training materials focusing on the relevant competencies.

As used in this chapter, competence is a combination of knowledge, skills, attitudes, and abilities required in the workplace and is a measure of skills and proven knowledge (Kauppinen et al., 2021). To develop and recognize competencies, the general approach is to use a learning taxonomy such as Bloom's original (Bloom et al., 1956) that has since been revised (Anderson et al., 2001). An alternative to Bloom's taxonomy, designed as a tool for practitioners and providing a more research-based alternative, is Marzano's new taxonomy (Marzano & Kendall, 2007) which focuses on cognitive abilities comprising three main systems: the self-system, the metacognitive system, and the cognitive system. These taxonomies are hierarchical systems in which one must master lower levels before proceeding to higher levels. In addition to hierarchical taxonomies, there are non-hierarchical taxonomies that broaden the understanding of the competences that are relevant for learning (Fink, 2003; Wiggins & McTighe, 2006) by highlighting the aspects of learning that are difficult to measure.

Using VR's potential as a tool for vocational training and creating usable training material requires associating the learning modeled by learning taxonomies and concrete competencies related to the specific job descriptions of companies. This can be achieved by joint collaboration. For example, universities of applied sciences in Finland mainly focus on conducting applied research because they cooperate closely with companies and different stakeholders in the region and innovate new services and products in cooperation. There are several relevant approaches to applied research in terms of the use of VR in workforce training, for example, research and innovation ecosystems and living labs.

Recently, the number of discussions on how to define research and innovation ecosystems and their meaning has been increasing. The importance of ecosystem in the field of the management of technology and innovation has been emphasized (Tsujimoto et al., 2018). Notably, the range of ecosystem concepts and definitions used is broad, and five different types of ecosystems have been identified: digital, complementary, supplier, business group, and global professional human network ecosystems. An ecosystem can be defined to be a historically self-organized or managerially designed multilayer social network. It consists of actors that have different attributes, decision principles, and beliefs. Furthermore, an ecosystem exits to provide a product, a service, or a system. (Tsujimoto et al., 2018).

An ecosystem brings competition value for the participating companies (Clarysse et al., 2014). When focusing on defining universities' research ecosystems (Pandey & Pattnaik, 2015), two different viewpoints can be identified: the stakeholder viewpoint and the process viewpoint. However, the innovation ecosystem is claimed to be the all-too-often ambiguously utilized concept across academia (Ritala & Almpanopoulou, 2017). Furthermore, it is stressed that appending "eco-" to "innovation systems" adds nothing of substance, that an innovation ecosystem is actually a faulty analogy of natural ecosystems, and that it leads to cognitive dissonance and potentially also to harmful policy choices (Oh et al., 2016).

The core concept of the living labs is to create novel products and new services, produce prototypes, and test prototypes with the help of a network. A living lab can be viewed from two viewpoints. First, it can be viewed as a platform which can be owned, for example, by a city, a company, or an educational institution and has a large external developer network. Second, it can be viewed as participation emphasizing the aims, activities such as development, co-creation, and iteration in the context of the living lab (Leminen et al., 2017; Pallot et al., 2011; Steen & van Bueren, 2017). As with the ecosystem, the key function of living labs is to add value for the participants.

Both the living lab and the ecosystem concept also include an idea of expanding the innovation and research network for non-business actors such as citizens, associations, and end-users. Similar to the five types of ecosystems mentioned earlier, five types of living labs have been defined (Ståhlbröst & Holst, 2021). These include research living labs that focus on the innovation process, corporate living labs that focus on innovations co-created with stakeholders, organizational living labs that focus on innovations of organization members, intermediary living labs that focus on various stakeholders innovating in the cooperation in a neutral area, and time-limited living labs that focus on a specific project and will close when the project ends. Living labs are useful in changing end-users roles from passive consumers to active prosumers and in innovating and involving citizens in developing solutions for everyday problems with educational institutions, companies, and other stakeholders (Ståhlbröst & Holst, 2021).

WORKFORCE TRAINING USING VR

Although VR is already being used in companies and education, there are several aspects in which its potential is not yet fully applied. First, VR could be more beneficial in tackling the challenge of the declining workforce and employing immigrants because it provides a safe and fast way of testing and training potential employees. Second, the current vocational virtual learning environments focus on certain fields, mainly excluding, for example, the service sector which provides an array of entry-level positions and possibilities for on-the-job training. Finally, workforce training and recognizing competencies could be more clearly connected to concrete tasks—implementable also in VR—in the workplace to the levels of a learning taxonomy providing good basis for evaluating competence and learning.

Declining Workforce and Employment of Immigrants

Especially young peoples´ success in establishing their individual career paths depends on successful entry into the workforce once they have completed their compulsory education. However, at the same time, it has become difficult to make a direct transition from compulsory education into initial on-the-job training and into the workforce. If young people stay outside education and outside working life, it has negative effects, which will last for around 5 to 7 years (Åslund & Rooth, 2007).

In case of immigrants or people of foreign background, making their own career path is even more demanding. For example, four of five immigrants living in Finland are of working age. However, the employment rate of working-age immigrants is considerably lower than that of the general population: 51.1% of people from foreign backgrounds aged 20 to 64 and 71.0% of people from Finnish backgrounds were employed. The difference between groups in the proportion of employed people in the total population was 19.9 percentage points (Pasila & Sutela, 2019; Statistics Finland, 2021).

One challenge is that the educational and professional backgrounds of immigrants and of people of foreign backgrounds are very diverse—from lawyers and professors to basic or even no formal education. According to a study conducted in 2019, 7% respondents were without an undergraduate degree and 23% were mere undergraduate graduates, while there were 25% secondary graduates and 45% tertiary graduates (Witting, 2019). Many of the immigrants also face language challenges. However, it is worth noticing that some of the immigrants speak better Finnish than English.

Nevertheless, immigrants are predicted to play a key role in maintaining an adequate level of the working-age population (OECD, 2018). This means that the existing competencies of immigrants need to be recognized and feasible ways of learning, such as multisensory and immersive materials and environments, need to be developed. Creating such environments jointly between educational institutions, employing companies, and immigrants is one solution to this problem, and a living-lab–based way of achieving it is discussed later in this chapter.

VR and Virtual Learning Environments

As stated earlier in this chapter, while VR has been employed as a learning environment, its use has been focused on certain fields such as engineering, aviation, and safety training. In other words, VR in learning is currently applied mainly in industrial environments and not so much, for example, in the service sector. Some applications in the service field do exist, such as completing different work stages (Nirhamo, 2019) in restaurant work. VR has also been applied to some extent in hospitality (Torrico et al., 2020) and tourism (Kim et al., 2020); however, it has broad application prospects in vocational learning in the service sector.

In the health care sector, especially medicine, VR has been used more extensively, for example, in assessing the food-related emotional responses of patients with eating disorders (Gorini et al., 2010) and in psychotherapy as an alternative to exposure (Wallach et al., 2011). Recently, VR has been used to assess the competence of emergency medicine students (McGrath et al., 2018). However, even in the more extensively covered fields, virtual learning environments rarely have a direct connection with the related curriculum and evaluation of learning.

However, an example on how this can be done has been illustrated. In the 90s, the training potential of VR in laparoscopy was identified (Ota et al., 1995), and the model was later further improved, providing evidence-based curriculum for laparoscopy students. The related tasks can be divided into three levels of difficulty:

easy, medium, and difficult (Aggarwal et al., 2006). The laparoscopy curriculum was developed even further when descriptions of three types of surgical skills measured (safety, technical skill, and dexterity) were created as tasks that were implemented in VR (Loukas et al., 2011).

The example in laparoscopy can and should be followed in other VR applications and virtual learning environments because it ties the implementation and the environment to the curricula. Furthermore, it helps in the evaluation of learning, workforce training in companies, as well as in competence recognition overall, as discussed next. In addition, later in this chapter, several VR learning environments for the service sector are presented as examples.

Workforce Training and Competence Recognition

Companies have a practical approach to workforce training, and, understandably, they are interested in having employees trained specifically for their environments. However, educational institutions providing formal degrees and related education aim to prepare their learners to be part of a workforce and to be able to work in any organization in a field. Work has been done in combining these viewpoints, for example European Skills, Competencies, and Occupations combines specific work roles and the necessary competencies and has input both from the educational institutions and from companies (European Commission, 2019).

From the viewpoint of recognizing competence and evaluating learning, the domains or basic types of educational objectives are well known in educational institutions and are taken from selected taxonomy such as Bloom's original (Bloom et al., 1956), mentioned earlier in this chapter. Typically, educational objectives are divided into three types: cognitive objectives involving mental processes such as memory recall and analysis; affective objectives involving interest, attitudes, and values; and psychomotor objectives involving motor skills.

Furthermore, motivation is the primary factor that determines whether a learner will complete a learning-related task and is highly predictive of engagement. In turn, engagement is a strong predictor of retention. More often, motivation and engagement are emphasized better in the non-hierarchical taxonomies (such as (Fink, 2003; Marzano & Kendall, 2007); however, they are less applied in educational institutions than the traditional hierarchical ones.

Because the taxonomy of learning objectives is a framework for classifying statements of what is expected or intended to be learned based on instructions, companies in a specific field are indeed a good source of the objectives. However, despite the work done, a gap exists in vocational workforce training between companies and educational institutions. In addition to the joint cooperation, this gap can be closed by having a method to explicitly connect the learning objectives of a relevant competence to a learning taxonomy and also to the related task where the competence is applied in the workplace. Later in this chapter, we present a model for this to provide a basis for evaluating the competence and learning usable for both companies and educational institutions. Notably, it uses tasks that can be implemented in VR.

SOLUTIONS AND RECOMMENDATIONS

The solutions and recommendations presented here are based on the work and results on a project called VR Fast Track, in which the issues related to vocational learning and workforce training were addressed by applying VR and working in collaboration with the relevant stakeholders. The solution for the joint collaboration in the project has characteristics of both a research and innovation ecosystem and a living lab. However, it is closest to an intermediary living lab because active involvement from different stakeholders is required in the different stages of the project which include ideation, planning, implementation, and evaluation. The stakeholders form a living lab network shown in Figure 1.

Figure 1. Living lab network of the VR Fast Track Project.

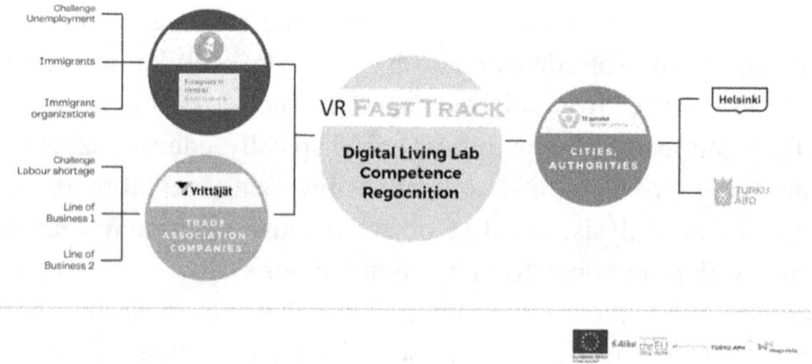

The stakeholders included immigrants and immigrant organizations (upper left in Figure 1), companies and related associations (lower left in Figure 1), and educational institutions (center in Figure 1) and authorities (right in Figure 1). The challenges were caused by immigrants (unemployment) and companies (labor shortage), whereas educational institutions provided coordination (living lab setting and network) and offered expertise (VR training and learning solutions) and authorities provided support (information and benefits for participating immigrants). The immigrant organizations and associations of companies were used to contact immigrants and companies, respectively, although immigrants and companies were also contacted directly by educational institutions.

VR Solutions for Workforce Training

The case examples of VR solutions presented here are for workforce training for the hospitality, health care, and cleaning sectors (see also Drake & Kauppinen, 2021). They were developed in the living lab network in Figure 1. The stakeholders involved are detailed in Table 1. The case examples are chosen from hospitality, health care, and cleaning services because these lines of business offer entry-level positions suitable for immigrants with low or no formal education and who face challenges in language skills. Furthermore, these lines of businesses suffer from labor shortage in Finland, while at the same time, the Finnish society as a whole is facing the challenge of inadequate employment of immigrants.

The number of immigrants involved in the case examples is over 100. They are from the cities of Helsinki and Turku and have been involved in groups from a couple of immigrants to around 20 at a time. Small groups have made it possible to achieve in-depth participation from each individual.

As seen in Table 1, four immigrant organizations, six companies, one association of companies, three educational institutions, and the authorities in two cities were also involved. The authorities were represented by skill centers and unemployment offices. Although the example cases and their stakeholders were from Finland and the target group of employees was immigrants, similar VR solutions can be applied in other countries and lines of business as well as for other relevant stakeholder and target groups. For this, general VR task types appearing in the solutions are summarized after the case examples.

Hospitality Case Example

The hospitality case example domain is restaurant work (see also Kauppinen et al., 2021). It is related to hygiene competence, which is an essential competence, since there are mandatory requirements that all employees working with food products must follow. Therefore, it is considered an important competence by the employers represented by the two restaurant company representatives as well as experts in restaurant work education, i.e., the vocational teachers from Stadin AO educational institution.

The VR solution for the restaurant work involves answering true or false questions presented in a multisensory manner (combination of text, voice, and visual) in the VR restaurant environment by pointing to the right answers. It is implemented

Table 1. Stakeholders of the case examples.

Case Example	Immigrants and Organizations	Companies and Associations	Educational Institutions	Authorities
Hospitality	• Immigrants interested and training in restaurant work (Helsinki) • African Care (Helsinki) • Finnish Refugees Council (Helsinki) • Association of Thai Women Network in Finland Council (Helsinki)	• One regional restaurant company (Helsinki) • One national restaurant company • Trade association (Helsinki)	• Haaga-Helia University of Applied Sciences (Helsinki) • Stadin AO (Helsinki)	• City of Helsinki (Skill center)
Health care	• Immigrants interested in health care (Turku) • Daisy Ladies (Turku)	• Two national health care companies	• Haaga-Helia University of Applied Sciences (Helsinki) • Turku University of Applied Sciences	• City of Turku (Skill center, unemployment office)
Cleaning service	• Immigrants interested and training in cleaning services (Helsinki and Turku) • Daisy Ladies (Turku)	• Two regional cleaning service company (Helsinki and Turku)	• Haaga-Helia University of Applied Sciences (Helsinki) • Turku University of Applied Sciences • Stadin AO (Helsinki)	• City of Helsinki (Skill center) • City of Turku (Skill center, unemployment office)

Figure 2. The VR solution for hospitality.

Figure 3. The assisted living VR solution for health care.

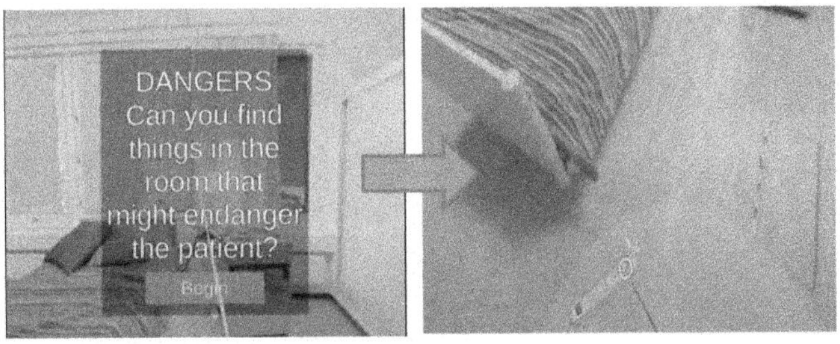

using the Unity game engine (Unity, n.d.) and illustrated in Figure 2 (a video is also available, see VR Fast Track Project, 2021b).

Finnish or English can be selected as the language, and there is a time limit for answering the questions. After the questions, the number of correct answers is shown. The questions are the similar to those in the official hygiene certificate test (Finnish Food Authority, 2020), which is administered as a pen-and-paper test under a controlled environment. A certificate is required for anyone working with food products; thus, the solution is used in learning about hygiene and in preparing the immigrants for official tests.

Based on the information obtained from using the VR solution and from the results of the official test, it can be said that the results correlate very well. This means that the solution can be used to both recognize the hygiene competence of an individual and, for example, if used before and after teaching hygiene, also to evaluate learning. For companies, this is a good way to evaluate if a person can be sent directly to the official certificate test or if additional training provided by the company or an educational institution is required.

Based on the feedback from immigrants, the immersion of the solution is surprisingly strong, even though the restaurant environment is cartoonlike. Immersion makes it possible to focus on answering the questions even under noisy environments. However, the disadvantage is that due to the strong immersion, some of the users experience symptoms similar to motion sickness.

Health Care Case Example

The health care case example is twofold because there were two national companies in the living lab network. Separate VR solutions were prepared with both companies; however, the same VR solution base could be used because the platform was implemented by educational institution. For one company, an assisted living related

Figure 4. VR solution for dispensing medication for health care.

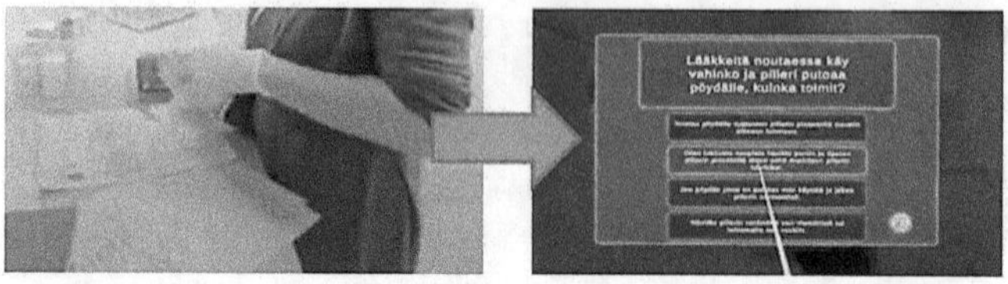

VR solution was developed. It is illustrated in Figure 3 (a video is also available, see VR Fast Track Project, 2021a).

In the assisted living VR solution, the goal is to look around of an apartment of an elderly person in an assisted living facility and point out indicators of areas related to the state of the person as well as the quality of living. Looking around can be done freely and pointing the correct items or similar features in the apartment can be done in a free order, although the solution is divided into the sections that are done one by one with different indicators to be identified.

Finnish or English can be selected as the language, and after all the sections, the number of correct answers by sections is shown. The indicators to be spotted can be positive or negative; however, the number of indicators to be found can be shown. Nevertheless, the solution is a bit more difficult than one would think at a glance, for example, because no additional information is given of the asked indicators. For example, in Figure 3, the section is about things that can endanger the patient, but no examples are given. Furthermore, the goal is shown only at the beginning of the section; thus, it must be remembered throughout the section.

This solution follows a checklist of the company on what things an employee visiting a person in an assisted living facility should focus on; thus, it serves both as training material as well as a way to recognize and evaluate competence in following practices in assisted living related work. Although it is done based on information obtained from one company, it is usable in similar companies and, for example, in training provided by an educational institution as well.

For other companies, a VR solution for medication dispersion was developed. It is illustrated in Figure 4 (a video is also available, see VR Fast Track Project, 2021d). In this solution, the goal is to answer multiple choice questions related to dispensing medication. Here, a video showing the correct procedure is provided so that the video advances for some time, after which a related question is asked. If the answer is incorrect, another choice can be selected. The feedback is immediate, and the video advances either after the correct answer is given or after two incorrect answers. At the end, when all of the video has been shown and all the questions have been answered, the breakdown of the results is shown.

Figure 5. The cleaning machine maintenance VR solution for cleaning services.

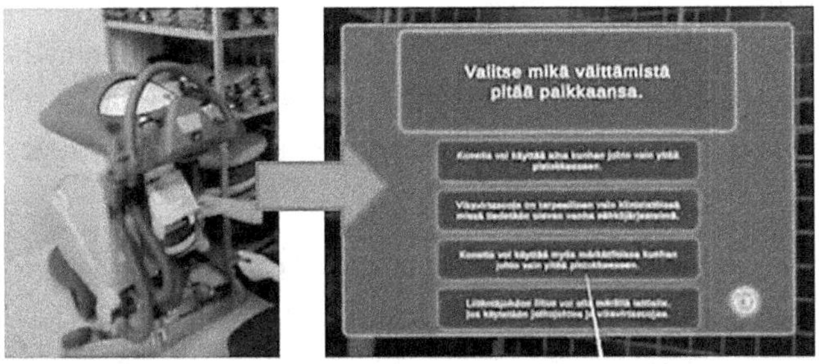

In this solution, currently only Finnish is available as a language. There is sound in the video; however, there is no talking, and the questions are not read out aloud. This means that the solutions are not as multisensory as the hospitality case example. For the company, this has not yet been an issue because they are planning to use the solution in on-the-job training for new employees and as a recap material for more experienced employees. This means that the users of the solution are, at least at first, already familiar with the procedure of dispensing medication. However, notably, dispensing medication is a critical task because there is no margin for error. As with the assisted living solution, although this solution is provided based on one company's input, it is usable in similar settings and in educational institutions. However, for better feasibility, English language and multisensory support should be added.

Both solutions are developed using 3DVista (3dVista, n.d.) and 360° videos; thus, they require less modeling than the hospitality solutions. However, they require physical real-life locations and real people. The solutions also illustrate an advancement of the living lab network because the same base could be used to develop solutions for different companies.

Cleaning Service Case Example

The VR solution for cleaning services involves the maintenance of a cleaning machine. It is illustrated in Figure 5 (a video is also available, see VR Fast Track Project, 2021c). The solution follows the ideas of health care solutions. It also has the same characteristics; thus, currently, only Finnish is available as a language, there is no talking, and the questions are not read aloud. However, because this solution is intended to be used with little or no experience in the maintenance of the cleaning machine, English language and multisensory support should be added.

The lack of narration was also mentioned in the feedback when the solution was tested with immigrants. The feedback contained other development ideas as well. Especially, it was hoped that the solution would include more content than that related to cleaning machines. For example, adding content related to the maintenance of the cleaning carriage as well as other cleaning equipment was suggested.

Table 2. General VR task types based on the case examples.

Task Type	Variations	Case Example
Answering questions	• True or false without video • Multiple choice with video	• Hospitality • Health care and cleaning
Spot the problems	• Free order	• Health care

This solution is used here as a further example of the benefits of the living lab network. In addition to being able to use the technical base of the VR solution in different cases, the living lab network could also use the same ideas over different lines of business. This shows that the task types are independent from the content such as learning objective or competence and can be seen as general VR task types applicable to multiple settings.

General VR Task Types

Based on the case examples, two basic types of general VR task types can be identified: answering questions and spotting problems. These have several variations. The questions can be true or false or multiple-choice questions, and they may include videos. Spotting the problems can be free or in a fixed order (although only free variation is included in the case examples). The general task types and their variations are summarized in Table 2.

Notably, these are not the only general VR task types but the ones that can be derived from the case examples. The general task types are useful, for example, in planning new VR solutions in the existing or new business areas. However, for feasible evaluation and recognition of competence, they need to be explicitly associated with the level in the taxonomy, the learning objectives, and the competences.

Evaluating and Recognizing Competence With VR

Evaluating and recognizing competence with VR requires identifying the relevant competences and learning objectivities with their level in the learning taxonomy and connecting them. Competencies have several levels and different levels have different learning objectivities. To reach a level of competence, the related learning objectives need to be met. The learning objectives for different levels also need to have concrete VR tasks that are used to evaluate whether the level has been reached. Next, these areas are explored using an example of hygiene competence from the previous hospitality case example (see also Kauppinen et al., 2021). After that, a model for competence recognition and evaluation constructed based on the case examples is presented.

Identifying Relevant Competencies

For workforce training, as illustrated by the case examples, the input for the relevant competencies is taken from companies. However, as also seen in the case examples, some of them may be required by authorities. Educational institutions also have the related expertise because they maintain curricula for vocational education. However, for example, the priorities of competencies may rapidly change and from company to company; thus, in the regional sense, local and locally operating national companies are a valuable source of the current and relevant competencies.

In this example, hygiene competence in restaurant work is used. This is because it is currently essential according to the companies in the living lab network and because it is also required by the food authorities. However, hygiene is an important topic as competencies in general; thus, the related learning objectives must be defined to be able to evaluate and recognize it.

Connecting Competencies and Learning Objectives

The learning objectives are statements of concrete things that a person must be able to do. These are often skills that are applied as part of the work; however, they can also be something that can be handled mentally, verbally, or in writing and relate to knowledge. Again, especially for the objectives that are part of the everyday practical work, companies of the line of business in question are a valuable source for the learning objectives. However, educational institutions are traditionally especially good in defining knowledge based on the learning objectives.

In this example, for the hygiene competence, a learning objective related to knowledge is what is required for passing the hygiene certificate test, namely being able to answer questions regarding hygiene based on the available guidelines and information. This corresponds to the hospitality case example. However, another related learning objective is being able to identify problems (indicators) in hygiene in the workplace. This can be compared to the assisted living solution in the health care case example.

Table 3. Hygiene in restaurant work as an example of evaluating and recognizing competence.

Competence	Learning Objectives	Taxonomy Levels	VR Task
Hygiene (Restaurant work)	• Spot the problems in hygiene in the workplace	• Knowledge	• Spot the problems in free order
	• Answer questions related to hygiene	• Comprehension	• Answer true / false questions, no video

Connecting Learning Objectives, Taxonomy Levels and VR Tasks

Different learning objectives and VR tasks match different levels in the learning taxonomy. Mapping these objectives requires the selection of a learning taxonomy used and based on its levels and analyzing the learning objectives and the VR tasks against it. Although some companies may have expertise in this, this is typically the key area of expertise for educational institutions.

In the example, Bloom's original taxonomy's (Bloom et al., 1956) cognitive part is applied. It has six levels: knowledge, comprehension, application, analysis, synthesis, and evaluation. Of the learning objectives defined, identifying problems (assuming they are straightforward) would be on the knowledge level and answering (often quite tricky) questions in the hygiene certification test would be on the comprehension level, as shown in Table 3.

In Table 3, suitable VR tasks have also been selected and associated with the learning objectives via taxonomy levels. Here, VR tasks are of general VR task types identified earlier (see Table 2). However, if there is no suitable existing VR task type, one should be designed. As can be seen, the example is partial and its full version would have the remaining four taxonomy levels, related learning objectives, and VR tasks. Based on the experiences gained from the living lab network, effort should focus on VR should be in the first two or three levels because they seem to provide good benefits, and the complexity of VR tasks and their implementation is likely to rise in the higher levels. Rising complexity also means the rise of necessary resources such as time spent in implementation; after the third level, the use of effort may overweigh the benefits.

A Model for Competence Recognition and Evaluation

Based on previous discussions and the work done in the living lab network, the model shown in Figure 6 can be presented for competence recognition and evaluation. The model shows the relationships between lines of businesses, competencies, learning objectives, taxonomy levels, learning taxonomies, VR tasks, and VR solutions. The

Figure 6. A model for competence recognition and evaluation.

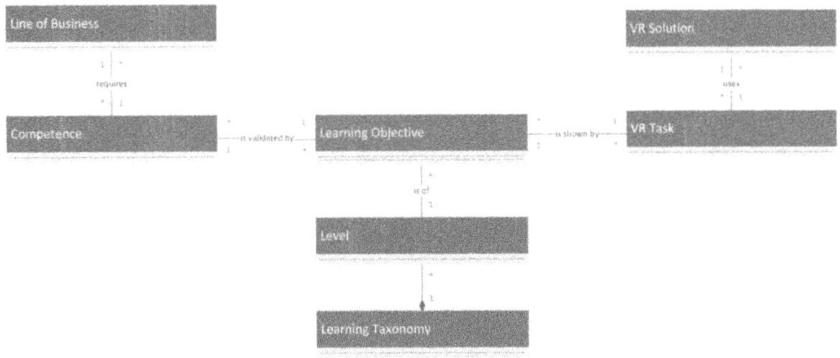

notation of the model follows the class diagram of UML (unified modeling language) (Object Management Group, 2021).

According to the model, a line of business requires several competencies, and the same competence may be required by several lines of businesses. A competence is validated by several learning objectives, and the same learning objectives can be used while validating several competencies. Each learning objective is of one level in a learning taxonomy, and the same level may be used for several learning objectives. Each learning taxonomy consists of several levels; however, the individual level is always a part of one taxonomy. Learning objectives are shown by several VR tasks, and one VR task can be used to show several learning objectives. Finally, VR solutions use several VR tasks, and the same VR task may be used in several VR solutions.

Notably, the model in Figure 6 is a metamodel. This means that the model has to always be applied (in UML language instantiated) for the specific cases having the actual line of business, competencies, learning objectives, learning taxonomy with its levels, VR tasks, and VR solution. The application of the model is similar to the result of the example shown in Table 3.

Recommendations

Based on the experiences and solutions, several recommendations for VR-based workforce training with immigrants can be presented. The recommendations are summarized in Table 4, and they are related to joint collaboration, developing VR solutions, and evaluating and recognizing competence with VR. They are applicable to other similar settings and target groups than the one covered in this chapter.

Overall, both joint collaboration, for example, using living lab approach as well as applying VR for workforce training can be recommended. However, to apply VR meaningfully in workforce training, joint collaboration is required

Table 4. Recommendations on VR-based workforce training with immigrants.

Area	Recommendations
Joint collaboration	• Educational institutions should coordinate • Educational institutions should be responsible for the platform • Several regions and companies should be involved
Developing VR solutions	• Iterative approach should be used • Testing should be performed often • Feedback should be collected and evaluated when testing
Evaluating and recognizing competence with VR	• High priority competencies should be identified with companies • Learning objectives should be practical • General VR tasks should be applied

because all stakeholders have important contributions. The recommendations for joint collaboration are about the roles as educational institutions seem to be in the best position to coordinate collaboration and are responsible for the development platform. This is because educational institutions are neutral parties, can facilitate cooperation, and also spread ideas freely via facilitation or platform. Furthermore, the gained experiences show that it is beneficial to have participants from several geographical regions as well as to have several companies involved even from the same lines of businesses.

Regarding the development of VR solutions, an iterative approach is another must. This goes well with the observation on benefits of testing often both with companies and immigrants. This way, valuable input can be obtained early, and VR solutions can be shaped based on that. Furthermore, when testing, feedback should be collected and evaluated in a systematic manner. This way, the trends and repeating issues can be found. Systematic data collection makes it possible to perform qualitative or quantitative research, which is an added benefit for higher education institutions.

Regarding evaluating and recognizing competencies with VR, the companies know the current priorities of competencies and are very good in stating practical learning objectives. Furthermore, even though educational institutions are very good in knowledge-based learning objectives, practicality should be the focus. For the fluent implementation of the VR solution, existing general VR task types should be prioritized because definition, planning, and implementations of new VR tasks is a time-consuming task. Of course, new VR tasks must be developed at times; however, this should always be evaluated thoroughly and only be done when necessary.

FUTURE RESEARCH DIRECTIONS

Overall, VR is still a relatively new technology, and it is likely that its use will increase in the future. However, the focus is moving on XR having other types of virtuality in addition to VR such as augmented reality. The application of XR in workforce training is therefore a viable future research direction.

Of the topics discussed in this chapter, there are several prominent future research directions. First, the living lab approach along with ecosystems is likely to be used more extensively if the future. This is because joint collaborative development will be increasingly important due to the rapid changes in society such as in the labor market. The resulting challenges can be resolved best by using agile and co-operative approaches such as living lab or ecosystems.

Because the examples in this chapter are individual cases, it is natural that they would provide ground for future research. Their content could be expanded further, and there are several development issues and ideas mentioned in the case descriptions. Work on these would make the implemented VR solutions more comprehensive and would improve their quality.

Finally, the presented model for competence recognition and evaluation is an initial one. It should be further studied and improved. The model is proven to be viable because it is applicable throughout the cases presented in this chapter. It also has novelty in explicitly connecting the VR tasks into the learning objectives and via them, to the relevant competencies.

CONCLUSION

In this chapter, workforce training using VR has been discussed and several case examples have been presented. The target group here was immigrants because they have specific challenges associated with entering the workforce, although they are considered an important part of the future workforce. In addition to the case examples, a living lab approach used, and the experiences gained have been covered. Furthermore, a model for competence recognition and evaluation has been presented.

Overall, the full potential of using VR in workforce training is yet to be discovered. In particular, additional efforts should be directed toward cooperation between companies, educational institutions, and end-users such as immigrants in the development of VR-based training content. This position can be justified by the fact that the labor needs of the companies vary, and the employee must have the current competencies suitable for the company. While creating training materials, different viewpoints are required. Professionals from educational institutions are familiar with the learning pedagogy, and the required competences will come from the companies. However, the learning is experienced and can be expressed only by the learner.

ACKNOWLEDGMENT

This research was supported by the European Social Fund.

REFERENCES

Aggarwal, R., Grantcharov, T., Moorthy, K., Hance, J., & Darzi, A. (2006). A competency-based virtual reality training curriculum for the acquisition of laparoscopic psychomotor skill. *American Journal of Surgery, 191*(1), 128–133. https://doi.org/10.1016/j.amjsurg.2005.10.014

Anderson, L., Peter, K., Airasian, D., Cruikshank, K., Mayer, R., Pintrich, P., Raths, J., & Wittrock, M. (2001). *Taxonomy for learning, teaching, and assessing: a revision of Bloom's taxonomy of educational objectives*. Addison Wesley Longman.

Åslund, O., & Rooth, D. (2007). Do When and Where Matter? Initial Labour Market Conditions and Immigrant Earnings. *Economic Journal (London), 117*(518), 422–448. https://doi.org/10.1111/j.1468-0297.2007.02024.x

Bloom, B., Engelhart, M., Furst, E., Hill, W., & Krathwohl, D. (1956). *Taxonomy of educational objectives. Book 1 Cognitive domain*. Longmans.

Clarysse, B., Wright, M., Bruneel, J., & Mahajan, A. (2014). Creating value in ecosystems: Crossing the chasm between knowledge and business ecosystems. *Research Policy, 43*(7), 1164–1176. https://doi.org/10.1016/j.respol.2014.04.014

Dalgarno, B., Hedberg, J., & Harper, B. (2002). The Contribution of 3D Environments To Conceptual Understanding. *19th Annual Conference of the Australasian Society for Computers in Learning in Tertiary Education (ASCILITE 2002), 1*, 149–158. http://ascilite.org.au/conferences/auckland02/proceedings/papers/051.pdf

Drake, M. (2019). Embedding virtual reality into competence recognition. *16th International Conference on Cognition and Exploratory Learning in Digital Age, CELDA 2019*, 465–467. doi:10.33965/celda2019_201911r064

Drake, M., & Kauppinen, R. (2021). *New Technology - A New Approach to Further Vocational Training?* doi:10.21125/iceri.2021.1811

DVista. (n.d.). *3DVista*. Retrieved November 29, 2021, from https://www.3dvista.com/

Eronen, A., Härmälä, V., Jauhiainen, S., Karikallio, H., Karinen, R., Kosunen, A., Laamanen, J.-P., & Lahtinen, M. (2014). *Maahanmuuttajien työllistyminen : taustatekijät, työnhaku ja työvoimapalvelut* [Labour Market of Immigrants in Finland]. Publications of Ministry of Economic Affairs and Employment. http://linda.linneanet.fi/F/?func=direct&doc_number=006622519&local_base=fin01%5Cnhttp://www.tem.fi/files/38664/TEMjul_6_2014_web_10022014.pdf

European Commission. (2019). *ESCO handbook* (2nd ed.). Directorate-General for Employment, Social Affairs and Inclusion.

Fink, L. D. (2003). *Creating significant learning experiences for EAL learners*. Jossey-Bass.

Finnish Food Authority. (2020). *Hygienie Passport*. https://www.ruokavirasto.fi/en/private-persons/hygiene-passport/

Gorini, A., Griez, E., Petrova, A., & Riva, G. (2010). Assessment of the emotional responses produced by exposure to real food, virtual food and photographs of food in patients affected by eating disorders. *Annals of General Psychiatry*, *9*(30). http://www.annals-general-psychiatry.com/content/9/1/30

Kauppinen, R., & Drake, M. (2020a). Recognizing competencies of immigrants for restaurant work using virtual reality. *ICERI2020 Proceedings*, 2707–2017. doi:10.21125/iceri.2020.0629

Kauppinen, R., & Drake, M. (2020b). Virtual reality in competence recognition for immigrants. *INTED2020 Proceedings, 1*(March), 5578–5582. doi:10.21125/inted.2020.1515

Kauppinen, R., Drake, M., Anttila, K., & Lindgren, E. (2021). Implementing Virtual Reality Based Competence Recognition. *2021 9th International Conference on Information and Education Technology (ICIET)*, 415–422. doi:10.1109/ICIET51873.2021.9419617

Kavanagh, S., Luxton-Reilly, A., Wuensche, B., & Plimmer, B. (2017). A Systematic Review of Virtual Reality in Education. *Themes in Science and Technology Education*, *10*(2), 85–119.

Kim, M. J., Lee, C. K., & Jung, T. (2020). Exploring Consumer Behavior in Virtual Reality Tourism Using an Extended Stimulus-Organism-Response Model. *Journal of Travel Research*, *59*(1), 69–89. https://doi.org/10.1177/0047287518818915

Kulik, A., Kunert, A., Beck, S., & Fröhlich, B. (2017). Collaborative Virtual Reality for Joint Learning Experiences. *12th International Conference on Computer Supported Collaborative Learning (CSCL 2017)*, 721–722.

Leminen, S., Rajahonka, M., & Westerlund, M. (2017). Towards Third-Generation Living Lab Networks in Cities. *Technology Innovation Management Review, 7*(11), 21–35. doi:10.22215/timreview/1118

Loukas, C., Nikiteas, N., Kanakis, M., & Georgiou, E. (2011). Deconstructing laparoscopic competence in a virtual reality simulation environment. *Surgery, 149*(6), 750–760. https://doi.org/10.1016/j.surg.2010.11.012

Marzano, R. J., & Kendall, J. S. (2007). *The New Taxonomy of Educational Objectives* (2nd ed.). Corwin Press.

McGrath, J. L., Taekman, J. M., Dev, P., Danforth, D. R., Mohan, D., Kman, N., Crichlow, A., & Bond, W. F. (2018). Using Virtual Reality Simulation Environments to Assess Competence for Emergency Medicine Learners. *Academic Emergency Medicine*, *25*(2), 186–195. https://doi.org/10.1111/acem.13308

Melo, M., Bentley, E., McAllister, K. S., & Cortez, J. (2019). Pedagogy of Productive Failure: Navigating the Challenges of Integrating VR into the Classroom. *Journal of Virtual Worlds Research*, *12*(1), 1–21. https://doi.org/10.4101/jvwr.v12i1.7318

Nirhamo, N. (2019). *XR Studio created virtual learning environment with Hololens for Perho Culinary, Tourism & Business College*. Softability.

Object Management Group. (2021). *Unified Modelling Language*. https://www.uml.org/

OECD. (2018). *Working Together: Skills and Labour Market Integration of Immigrants and their Children in Finland*. OECD. doi:10.1787/9789264305250-en

Oh, D.-S., Phillips, F., Park, S., & Lee, E. (2016). Innovation ecosystems: A critical examination. *Technovation*, *54*, 1–6. https://doi.org/10.1016/j.technovation.2016.02.004

Ota, D., Loftin, B., Saito, T., Lea, R., & Keller, J. (1995). Virtual reality in surgical education. *Computers in Biology and Medicine*, *25*(2), 127–137. https://doi.org/10.1016/0010-4825(94)00009-F

Pallot, M., Trousse, B., Senach, B., & Scapin, D. (2011). *Living Lab Research Landscape : From User Centred Design and User Experience towards User Cocreation. In First European Summer School 'Living Labs', Inria (ICT Usage Lab), Userlab, EsoceNet*. Universcience.

Pandey, S. C., & Pattnaik, P. N. (2015). University Research Ecosystem: A Conceptual Understanding. *Review of Economic and Business Studies*, *8*(1), 169–181. https://doi.org/10.1515/rebs-2016-0021

Pasila, A., & Sutela, H. (2019, April 12). *Ulkomaalaistaustaisten työllisyysaste eroaa rekisteri- ja haastattelupohjaisissa tilastoissa* [Employment rate of immigrants is different in statistics based on registers and interviews]. https://www.stat.fi/tietotrendit/blogit/2019/ulkomaalaistaustaisten-tyollisyysaste-eroaa-rekisteri-ja-haastattelupohjaisissa-tilastoissa/

Ritala, P., & Almpanopoulou, A. (2017). In defense of 'eco' in innovation ecosystem. *Technovation, 60–61*, 39–42. doi:10.1016/j.technovation.2017.01.004

Ståhlbröst, A., & Holst, M. (2021). *The Living Lab Methodology Handbook*. https://www.ltu.se/cms_fs/1.101555!/file/LivingLabsMethodologyBook_web.pdf

Statistics Finland. (2021). *Persons with foreign background*. https://www.stat.fi/tup/maahanmuutto/maahanmuuttajat-vaestossa/ulkomaalaistaustaiset_en.html

Steen, K., & van Bueren, E. (2017). The Defining Characteristics of Urban Living Labs. *Technology Innovation Management Review, 7*(7), 21–33. doi:10.22215/timreview/1088

Torrico, D. D., Han, Y., Sharma, C., Fuentes, S., Gonzalez Viejo, C., & Dunshea, F. R. (2020). Effects of Context and Virtual Reality Environments on the Wine Tasting Experience, Acceptability, and Emotional Responses of Consumers. *Foods*, *9*(2), 191. https://doi.org/10.3390/foods9020191

Tsujimoto, M., Kajikawa, Y., Tomita, J., & Matsumoto, Y. (2018). A review of the ecosystem concept—Towards coherent ecosystem design. *Technological Forecasting and Social Change*, *136*, 49–58. https://doi.org/10.1016/j.techfore.2017.06.032

Unity. (n.d.). *Unity*. Retrieved November 29, 2021, from https://unity.com/

VR Fast Track Project. (2021a). *Health Care VR Implementation (video)*. https://video.haaga-helia.fi/media/VR - Assisted Living/0_l1mgekua

VR Fast Track Project. (2021b). *Restaurant Work VR Implementation (video)*. https://video.haaga-helia.fi/media/VR - Restaurant Work/0_3hp1qcp1

VR Fast Track Project. (2021c). *VR implementation for cleaning (video)*. https://video.haaga-helia.fi/media/t/0_7wrayri7

VR Fast Track Project. (2021d). *VR implementation for medication dispension (video)*. https://video.haaga-helia.fi/media/t/0_ccy3580i

Wallach, H. S., Safir, M. P., Samana, R., Almog, I., & Horef, R. (2011). How can presence in psychotherapy employing VR be increased? Chapter for inclusion in: Systems in health care using agents and virtual reality. *Studies in Computational Intelligence, 337*(2009), 129–147. doi:10.1007/978-3-642-17824-5_7

Wiggins, G., & McTighe, J. (2006). *Understanding by design* (2nd ed.). Perason Education.

Witting, M. (2019, September 16). *Korkeasti koulutettuja ja vähän koulutettuja – ulkomaalaistaustaisten koulutuksesta tulossa tarkempaa tietoa* [Highly educated and less educated - additional information on the education level of immigrants coming up]. https://www.stat.fi/tietotrendit/blogit/2019/korkeasti-koulutettuja-ja-vahan-koulutettuja-ulkomaalaistaustaisten-koulutuksesta-tulossa-tarkempaa-tietoa/

World Economy Forum. (2020). *Jobs of Tomorrow: Mapping Opportunity in the New Economy*. Author.

ADDITIONAL READING

Chesbrough, H. (2003). *Open innovation: The new imperative for creating and profiting from technology*. Harward Business School Press.

De Witte, N. A., Adriaensen, I., Broeckx, L., Van Der Auwera, V., & Van Daele, T. (2021). Cross-cultural differences in user-centred research: An international living lab survey. *Health Informatics Journal, 27*(3). Advance online publication. doi:10.1177/14604582211038268 PMID:34424056

Kauppinen, R., Drake, M., Lindblad, J., & Ranta, J. (2021). From Worklife Competencies to Educational Virtual Reality Implementations. *ICIE*, T2022.

Oculus. (2020). *Oculus Quest*. https://www.oculus.com/quest/

Schluse, M., & Rossmann, J. (2016). From Simulation to Experimentable Digital Twins. *IEEE International Symposium on Systems Engineering*, 1–6.

Zheng, L., Xie, T., & Liu, G. (2019). Affordances of Virtual Reality for Collaborative Learning. *Proceedings - International Joint Conference on Information, Media and Engineering, ICIME 2018*, 6–10. 10.1109/ICIME.2018.00011

KEY TERMS AND DEFINITIONS

Competence: The ability to do something.

Ecosystem: Distributed and adaptive system that has ability to self-organize, scale and be sustainable.

Learning Objective: Statement that define an expected goal of a study unit.

Learning Taxonomy: A way of describing different aspects and levels of learning something.

Living Lab: A user centered innovation system.

Stakeholder: A person or organization with an interest to an issue or entity and ability to affect it.

Virtual Reality: The use of modeling and simulation to enable interaction in an artificial sensory environment.

Chapter 7
Coordinated Control of a Collaborative 6R Robotic Arm With a Virtual Twin and Augmented Reality for Engineering Education

Lorena Rodríguez Islas
https://orcid.org/0000-0002-3713-9896
Centro de Investigaciones en Óptica, Mexico

Fernando Martell-Chavez
https://orcid.org/0000-0002-2741-0689
Centro de Investigaciones en Óptica, Mexico

Carlos Alberto Paredes Orta
https://orcid.org/0000-0002-7235-1614
Centro de Investigaciones en Óptica, Mexico

ABSTRACT

This work describes the direct and inverse kinematics mathematical framework, the development procedure, and data communications interface for the implementation of an augmented reality version of a six degrees of freedom (6-DOF) cobot (collaborative robot) under the Unity platform. The kinematic equations for the inverse kinematic control of the Techman® cobot are presented. The procedure to achieve communication between the virtual robot and the physical robot is described, that is, the communication link from the TM5-900 robot with the application in Unity. A safe environment was created to manipulate the collaborative robot and to avoid collisions to validate the applicability of the augmented reality functionality. The virtual twin with its enhanced visualization based on augmented reality can also run-on mobile devices either locally or remotely accessed. The developed platform

DOI: 10.4018/978-1-6684-3398-0.ch007

has diverse potential applications and in particular is suitable for engineering education and training in robotics.

INTRODUCTION

Today's industries require greater speed and sophistication for decision making, this new era of Digital Transformation and Artificial Intelligence makes possible truly data-driven businesses. Emerging techniques such as Industrial Internet of Things (IIoT), Cyberphysical Systems CPS), Collaborative Robots, Virtual and Augmented Reality and those related with Artificial Intelligence (Big Data and Deep Learning) can create great leaps in efficiency, meaning and knowledge in companies and in society in general. In short, it represents a great opportunity for companies to respond to the challenges of competitiveness. In this sense, according to a survey conducted in 2018 by McKinsey & Company to companies about the adoption of Artificial Intelligence (Rao & Verweij, 2017), 47% of the 2,135 participants mention having incorporated it into some business process, which means a significant increase compared to a similar study carried out in 2017 where only 20% of participants reported using this type of technology. The majority of the participants (58%) indicated that less than 10% of digital investment is destined to the development of products that incorporate AI (Artificial Intelligence), but many of those surveyed (78%) are very confident that there will be an increase in investment in AI in the coming years.

The growing popularity of collaborative robots for process automation does not come exclusively from their capabilities, but is also due to the fact that it is a competitive product, which is why many companies are betting on its implementation, which is why it is essential to know how correctly handle a collaborative robot, since when you have one, it is dangerous to use it without prior training; Currently there is a diversity of simulators, however, the physical essence of the robot is lost. Another unfavourable aspect is that the physical robot cannot be used remotely, since it is necessary to use the indicated instruments, but these tools are expensive and therefore they are not available in most companies, which is why it is an excellent option to generate these tools virtually.

One of the main technological trends, highlighted in recent years by various consultants, is the creation of digital twins, a concept that is sometimes also referred to by its name in English: 'Digital twins'. That it is a virtual replica of a product in this case that of a collaborative robot (cobot), this medium-sized robotic arm is easy to program, fast to configure and, with fast amortization times, it simulates the behaviour of its counterpart physical, with the aim of monitoring it, analysing its reaction to certain situations and problems and thus improving its performance and efficiency. Likewise, it combines digital and operational data from industrial resources with a software, simulation and analysis platform to obtain information on present and future operations. The result is improved production, reduced costs, accelerated innovation, and ultimately a solution that is much more than a product – it is the result the industry demands. Therefore, the implementation of a digital twin is specified in a real system or object whose structure and the information it handles have a virtual copy where it is possible to experiment safely and in an innovative way and in real time through reality. increased, which is very beneficial for manufacturing processes and to improve performance, reduce downtime and speed up the development of new products.

This chapter presents an extension of a research work (Rodríguez et al., 2021), that is about how to manipulate the virtual twin of a 6 Degree of Freedom (DOF) collaborative robot (cobot) using a platform developed in Unity under the augmented reality technique and to present and discuss several possible applications. In practice a robot is a mechatronic system, for this application, it is necessary to consider that a robot is a virtual entity, that by its appearance and its movements reproduces that behaviour of a real one. The chapter is organized in the following sections: Introduction, background, methodology; Section "Robot direct and inverse kinematics" presents the procedure to deduct the direct and inverse kinematics; "Implementing robot kinematics in unity" section, describes the implementation in Unity; "Physical and virtual robot communication" section contains the detailed description of the various phases that were passed through to manage to manipulate the robot virtually. "Robot operation space" section explains how the robot work area was delimited in both unity and TMflow® and, conclusions section.

BACKGROUND

In industrial environments, multiple sensors are used to obtain information from the work environment, analyse it and process it. It is intended to use augmented reality, applied on devices tactile mobiles, as an element of sensorization. With the advancement of new technologies, it is possible to have very powerful and small mobile devices at your fingertips. With the power of the processors and using the sensors that are already integrated (cameras, GPS...) information can be computed quickly and appropriate actions can be taken. Augmented reality is a system on which many applications are currently being developed due to its simplicity and power. It allows a great interaction between user and environment. Therefore, it could be integrated into a work environment in order to reduce costs and make communication between user and robot more intuitive (Martínez, 2012). To achieve a clearer understanding of this chapter, will begin by recalling the terms of augmented reality, virtual twin and collaborative robot (cobot), since they are the main elements for the development of this work.

Augmented reality (AR) is a technology that integrates signals captured from the real world with signals generated by computers; it makes them correspond to build new coherent, complemented and enriched worlds, it makes objects of the real world and objects of the virtual world coexist in cyberspace (Heras & Villarreal, 2004). The AR implementation is generally based on some form of real-world anchor used for navigation and to provide information based on the information context to the user (Syberfeldt et al., 2017). AR is in continuous development in Virtual Reality Research. This increases a person's cognition, building a unitary structure in which, ultimately, the individual real and virtual elements cannot be differentiated (Blaga & Tamas, 2018, pp. 1-3).

There are different levels of AR according to their degree of complexity or fusion with reality. In the specific case of Industry 4.0, the concept of Augmented Industrial Reality (ARI) can be defined, which involves AR hardware and software, which make them ideal for factories in industrial environments (Caramés & Lamas, 2018). The digital twin, in its broadest definition, is understood as a virtual replica of a real product, service or system that allows experimentation with it through its sensors and mechanisms without taking risks when looking for solutions to a problem, which is an important tool in decision making (Hyre et al., 2022); it is the combination of a mathematical model and a computer program that represent the appearance and behavior of a real system (Kelly, 2013). The term was coined in 2012 by NASA (Investigate to Innovate, n.d), the digital twin is the model that results from integrating information from the different areas of engineering (mechanics, mechatronics, thermodynamics) in the virtual world (Qi et al., 2021).

A collaborative robot (cobot) is a robotic arm created to work alongside humans in a production chain, hence they are also known as collaborative robots. Thanks to technological advances, collaborative robots are capable today of taking industrial automation to new heights as they can deal with tasks inaccessible to industrial robots (Pelegrí, 2020). The continued development of cobots (collaborative robots) is due in large part to the security aspect (IAT, 2020). According to Universal Robots (Danish manufacturer of collaborative robotic arms), the term robot has been coined until 1921, by the Czech writer Capek, where the word comes from robot which means servitude (Ripipsa, 2020).

To achieve communication between the virtual robot and the physical one, the MODBUS TCP protocol was used, which is a communications protocol located at level 7 of the OSI Model, based on the master/slave architecture RTU (Remote Terminal Unit) or TCP/IP client/server (Transmission Control Protocol/Internet Protocol). This "version" of the protocol encapsulates the base frame of the Modbus protocol in the TCP/IP application layer, multiplexing inputs / outputs in a Host/

Server based on IP address and a destination port (Sockets). Modbus/TCP simply encapsulates a Modbus frame in a TCP segment (CUYO, 2016).

Using a cobot means that it can work together with humans on a production line, that is, it is a control system, which governs the robot's strength, which eliminates the risk in terms of safety with the operator, as well as efficient productivity in the production chain.

LITERATURE REVIEW

In recent years, due to the rapid advancement of technologies and rising labor costs, the use of robots with artificial intelligence algorithms in industrial automation to save costs and improve productivity has attracted much attention in various industrial sectors (Jing et al., 2018). Since the manipulation of parts carried out by a robot involves the spatial movement of its links, due to the variation of its joint variables, it is very important to know how the position and orientation of the end effector of the robot is represented to know with precision where in the workspace it will be placed.

For this it is necessary to study the representation and transformation of the typical movements of a manipulator robot (Granja Oramas, 2014, p. 19). It is important to notice that generally the analysis of kinematics is approached directly in order to calculate the position of the end point of the robot as a function of the joint values (angles) and inversely to calculate the value of the joint coordinates as a function of the final position; This procedure is important, since it allows the robot to be positioned at a point within its workspace volume. The solution of the inverse kinematics of an industrial robot can provide multiple configurations for a single position, since this arises from the solution of an equation that is not of the first order. This is how the system can have multiple solutions, being frequent the use of algorithms that allow approaching a numerical solution (Ramírez & Rubiano, 2018).

Similar research shows that efficient control systems can be designed for manipulators, as is the case with SCORBOT, thus, it is exposed by Muñoz (2015) in which he explains about the implementation of a PD + G setpoint controller for the second and third joint of the SCORBOT ER-4u robot. For which the dynamic parameters of the robot were calculated through laboratory measurements and calculations in a CAD model (Bonilla, 2020).

On the other hand, augmented reality can also be used for data visualization, as Leutert explains in (Herrmann & Schilling, 2013), who exposes Augmented Reality (AR), as a form of Mixed Reality that it is a technique that enhances the user's natural environment with additional useful virtual information to help him in his task.

It is important to give an overview of recent research and applications related to the topic of this chapter, which is why research and applications are presented below, where the efficiency of augmented reality in the industry is demonstrated.

In the Iberian Magazine of Information Systems and Technologies, that presents the need to implement systems with a high degree of automation in the oil and gas industry, which has grown dramatically in recent years, due to the fact that the extreme conditions that exist in each deposit make it difficult to carry out daily tasks such as maintenance or inspection of equipment. As a solution to this problem, teleoperation systems must be developed that provide high scalability using standardized messaging protocols. This research presents the development of a remote operation system that, through the use of the MQTT protocol to integrate the information of the industrial process, allows the operator to carry out inspection and remote maintenance tasks in the oil production centers of the company Petroamazonas EP in Ecuador. In addition, a virtual environment developed in Unity 3D is implemented, in order to obtain a high degree of transparency within the system and transmit the experience and skill of the operator to the slave robot (William et al., 2020).

According to Hongchao Fang, human-robot interaction problems, especially for industrial robots, have largely been limited to finding better ways to reconfigure or program the robots. In his article, a Robot Programming System based on Augmented Reality (RPAR-II) is proposed. A virtual robot, which is a replica of a real robot, is used in a real environment to perform and simulate the robot path planning process. The RPAR-II system supports users during the robot programming process, from task planning to execution. In this system, methodologies based on stereo vision were developed for the registration of virtual objects, as well as the position tracking of interactive devices. Practical issues related to the implementation of the system are discussed (Fang et al., 2009).

Another different scenario is the design and implementation of an augmented reality (AR) tool to help operators be in a hybrid, human and robotic collaborative industrial environment. The system aims to provide information related to production and the process, as well as to improve the immersion of operators in the security mechanisms, dictated by the collaborative workspace. The developed system has been integrated with a service-based station controller, which is responsible for orchestrating the flow of information to the operator, according to the execution status of the task. The tool has been applied to a case study in the automotive sector, which has resulted in a better integration of the operator with the assembly process (Makris et al., 2016).

METHODOLOGY

Robot Direct and Inverse Kinematics

Robot Overview

The main component with which this research will be carried out is the cobot TM5-900 (Figure 1), which is a collaborative robot with 6-DOF with the following main characteristics (IAS, 2020, p.8):

- 6-axis Collaborative Robot
- Reach: 900mm
- Payload: 4 kg
- Power supply: 100-240 VAC, 50-60Hz
- Safety: ISO10218-1 / ISO TS15066
- Includes: Controller (Control Box)
- 5MPx Embedded Vision System
- Typical speed: 1.4 m/s

With this cobot it is desired to develop an application to carry out visual inspection tasks in assembly lines, under the generation of its virtual twin, as well as the use of augmented reality focused on the manipulation analysis of the collaborative robot.

It is essential to propose the mathematical model for the direct and inverse kinematics of the manipulating cobot; since they are necessary to create your routes from your database; That is why the calculations and data gathered to obtain the direct and inverse kinematics are presented below.

The direct kinematics determines the position of the robot with respect to a reference coordinate system, knowing the values of the joints and the geometric parameters of the robot elements, while the inverse kinematics, having the location of the robot, determines which should be the configuration of the robot, that is, the joints and geometric parameters. The robot physical dimensions are depicted in Figure 2, considering the parameters defined in Table 1.

The Figure 3 is presented with the intention to give a more easily visualization of each degree of freedom of the cobot, as well as its rotations and all the essential elements to carry out the necessary algebra to obtain the direct and inverse kinematics.

To compute the kinematics, it is necessary to know both the measures and the ranges of angles that each degree of freedom is allowed, which is why these values are presented below (see Table 1).

At present there are different methods to solve the direct and inverse kinematics, but in this study the homogeneous transformation matrices were used, using the

Figure 1. TM5-900 collaborative robot with 6-DOF
(Omron, 2018, pp.35-67).

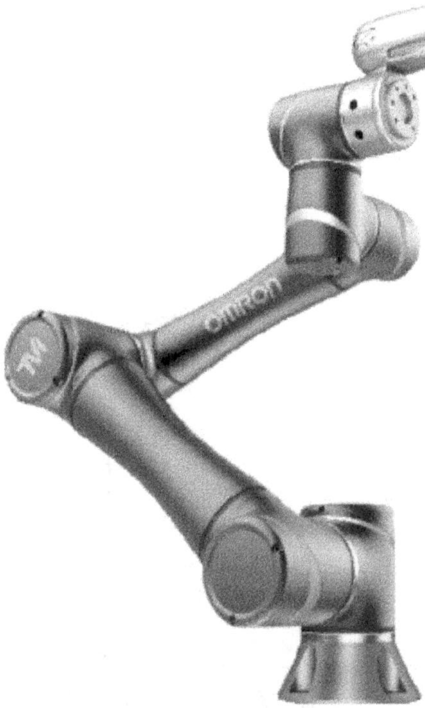

method of systematic representation of Denavit-Hartenberg. Although the kinematics of the robot can be solved geometrically, the proposed method offers the advantage of knowing both the final position of the manipulator and the position of each of its joints (Ramírez & Rubiano, 2018). Therefore, the next step to obtain the direct and inverse kinematics is the identification of a the Denavit-Hartenberg (DH) parameters, shown in Table 2.

Forward Kinematics

As it is well known, the solution to the problem of direct kinematics is to find the value of the final position of the cobot, this solution is a function of the joint values, that is, the translational or rotational value of the joints (Ramírez & Rubiano, 2018). The Denavit-Hartenberg representation is replaced in the homogeneous transformation matrix ${}^{i-1}A_i$, which is a 4x4 arrangement that contains information related to the position and orientation of the reference frame attached to the *i* link of the manipulator in relation to the system of connection reference *i*-1 (Ramírez & Rubiano, 2018). The general form of the transformation matrices is

Figure 2. Dimensions in millimetres of 6-DOF robot
(Tarré, 2019).

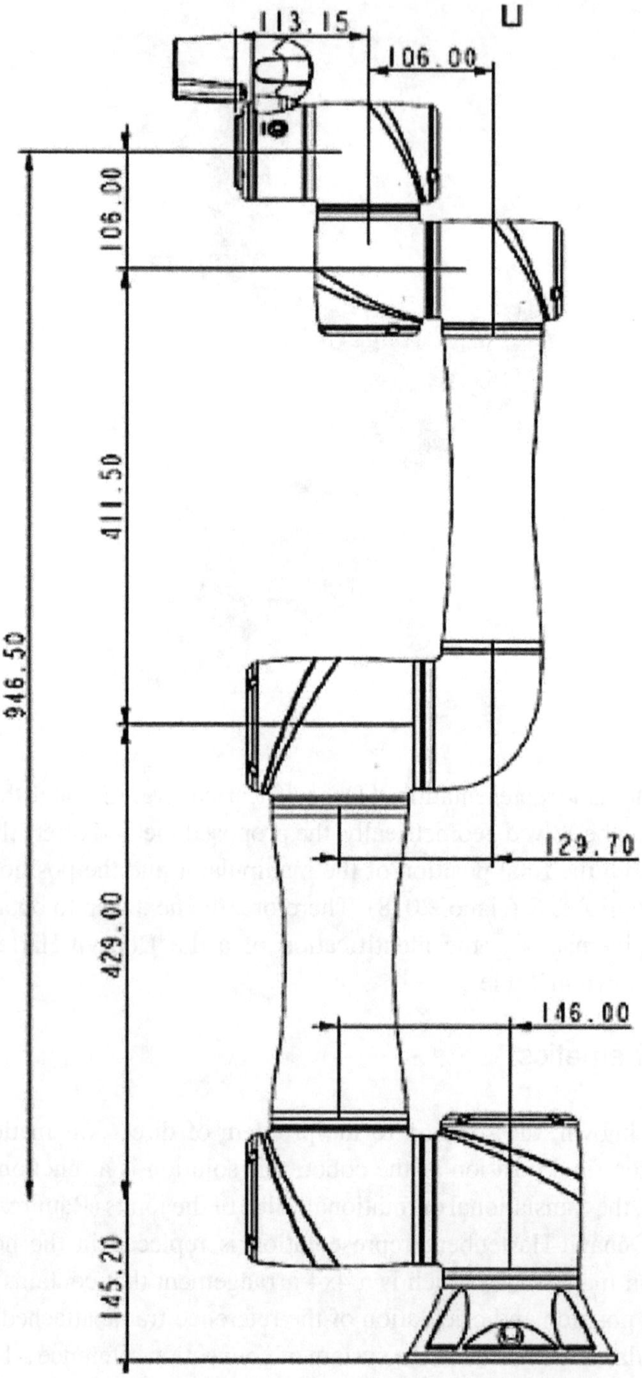

Figure 3. Kinematic robot structure with 6-DOF.

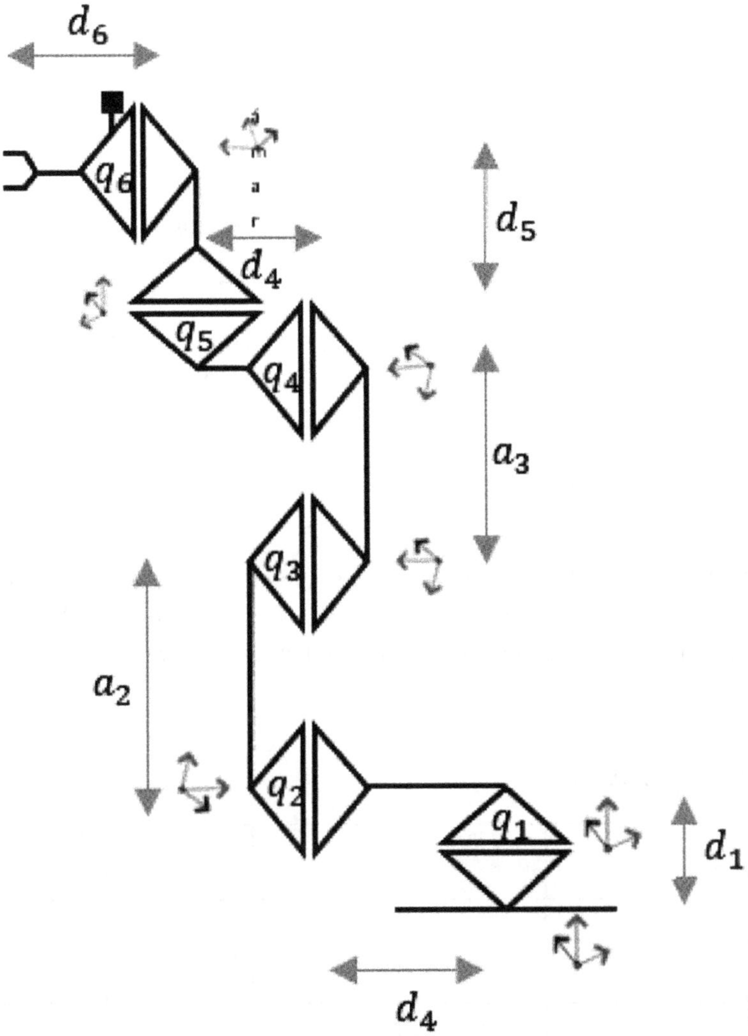

$$
{}^{i\text{-}1}T_i = \begin{bmatrix} \cos\theta_i & -\sin\theta_i \cos\alpha_i & \sin\theta_i \sin\alpha_i & \alpha_i \cos\theta_i \\ \sin\theta_i & \cos\theta_i \cos\alpha_i & -\cos\theta_i \sin\alpha_i & \alpha_i \sin\theta_i \\ 0 & \sin\alpha_i & \cos\alpha_i & d_i \\ 0 & 0 & 0 & 1 \end{bmatrix} \quad (1)
$$

Table 1. Degrees and distances of the cobot.

Degrees		Distances (mm)	
q_1	±270°	d_1	145.20
q_2	±180°	a_2	429
q_3	±155°	a_3	411.50
q_4	±180°	d_4	106
q_5	±180°	d_5	106
q_6	±270°	d_6	113.15

To calculate ${}^{i\text{-}1}A_i$, the Denavit-Hartenberg parameters must be defined, which are based exclusively on the geometric characteristics of each link and the coordinate systems in each one. The characteristics of the parameters are:

Table 2. DH Parameters.

i	α_i	a_i	d_i	θ_i	
1	$\frac{\text{À}}{2}$	0	d_1	θ_1	${}^{0}A_1$
2	0	a_2	0	θ_2	${}^{1}A_2$
3	0	a_3	0	θ_3	${}^{2}A_3$
4	$\frac{\text{À}}{2}$	0	d_4	θ_4	${}^{3}A_4$
5	$-\frac{\text{À}}{2}$	0	d_5	θ_5	${}^{4}A_5$
6	0	0	d_6	θ_6	${}^{5}A_6$

- θ_i rotation around the axis Z_{i-1}
- d_i translation along Z_{i-1} axis
- a_i translation along the X_i axis
- A_i rotation around the X_i axis (Ramírez & Rubiano, 2018).

Likewise, it is necessary to define the following variables:

- r_{kj} : Represent the rotational elements of transformation matrix.
- c_i : $\cos\theta_i$
- s_i : $\sin\theta_i$
- c_{ij} : $\cos(\theta_i + \theta_j)$
- s_{ij} : $\sin(\theta_i + \theta_j)$

$$ {}^{0}T_{6} = {}^{0}A_{1}\,{}^{1}A_{2}\,{}^{2}A_{3}\,{}^{3}A_{4}\,{}^{4}A_{5}\,{}^{5}A_{6} = \begin{bmatrix} r_{11} & r_{12} & r_{13} & p_x \\ r_{21} & r_{22} & r_{23} & p_y \\ r_{31} & r_{32} & r_{33} & p_z \\ 0 & 0 & 0 & 1 \end{bmatrix} \tag{2} $$

Replacing the values from Table 2, in equation (1), the following is calculated (Villalobos et al., 2021):

$$ r_{11} = c_1 c_{234} c_5 c_6 + c_6 s_1 s_5 - c_1 s_{234} s_6 \tag{3} $$

$$ r_{21} = c_{234} c_5 c_6 s_1 - c_1 c_6 s_5 - s_1 s_{234} s_6 \tag{4} $$

$$ r_{31} = c_5 c_6 s_{234} + c_{234} s_6 \tag{5} $$

$$ r_{12} = -c_1 c_{234} c_5 s_6 - s_1 s_5 s_6 - c_1 c_6 s_{234} \tag{6} $$

$$r_{22} = -c_{234}c_5s_1s_6 + c_1s_5s_6 - c_6s_1s_{234} \tag{7}$$

$$r_{32} = -c_5s_{234}s_6 + c_{234}c_6 \tag{8}$$

$$r_{13} = -c_1c_{234}s_5 + c_5s_1 \tag{9}$$

$$r_{23} = -c_{234}s_1s_5 - c_1c_5 \tag{10}$$

$$r_{33} = -s_{234}s_5 \tag{11}$$

The coordinates of the end point are:

$$p_x = -c_1c_{234}s_5d_6 + c_5s_1d_6 + c_1s_{234}d_5 + s_1d_4 + c_1c_{23}\alpha_3 + c_1c_2\alpha_2 \tag{12}$$

$$p_y = -c_{234}s_1s_5d_6 - c_1c_5d_6 + s_1s_{234}d_5 - c_1d_4 + c_{23}s_1\alpha_3 + c_2s_1\alpha_2 \tag{13}$$

$$p_z = -s_{234}s_5d_6 - c_{234}d_5 + s_{23}\alpha_3 + s_2\alpha_2 + d_1 \tag{14}$$

Inverse Kinematics

The inverse kinematics of a robot is a term used to denote the calculation of joint values (joint angles) of the manipulator, necessary to position a point in space referenced to the manipulator's global coordinate system (Ramírez & Rubiano, 2018).

1. As a first step, find q_1, q_2, q_3 such that the center of the wrist is located.
2. Later, with the variables calculated in the first step, evaluate R_0^3.
3. Finally, calculate the set of Euler angles corresponding to the rotation matrix.

The equations developed by applying the steps mentioned above are shown below. It is worth mentioning that *K*, *B*, *C* and *D*; are auxiliary variables to simplify the equations (Villalobos et al., 2021).

$$A_1 = p_x - d_6 r_{13} \tag{15}$$

$$B_1 = d_6 r_{23} - p_x \tag{16}$$

$$\theta_1 = a\tan 2(A_1, B_1) \pm a\tan 2\left(\sqrt{A_1^2 + B_1^2 - d_4^2}, d_4\right) \tag{17}$$

$$c_5 = s_1 r_{13} - c_1 r_{21} \tag{18}$$

$$s_5 = \sqrt{\left(s_1 r_{11} - c_1 r_{21}\right)^2 + \left(s_1 r_{12} - c_1 r_{22}\right)^2} \tag{19}$$

$$\theta_5 = \pm a\tan 2(s_5, c_5) \tag{20}$$

$$c_6 = \frac{s_1 r_{11} - c_1 r_{21}}{s_5} \tag{21}$$

$$s_6 = \frac{c_1 r_{22} - s_1 r_{12}}{s_5} \tag{22}$$

$$\theta_6 = a\tan 2(s_6, c_6) \tag{23}$$

$$A_{234} = c_5 c_6 \tag{24}$$

$$B_{234} = s_6 \tag{25}$$

$$C_{234} = c_1 r_{11} + s_1 r_{21} \tag{26}$$

$$D_{234} = r_{31} \tag{27}$$

$$\theta_{234} = a\tan 2(A_{234} D_{234} - B_{234} C_{234}, A_{234} C_{234} + B_{234} D_{234}) \tag{28}$$

$$K_S = p_z - d_1 + c_{234} d_5 + s_{234} s_5 d_6 \tag{29}$$

$$K_c = c_1 p_x + s_1 p_y - s_{234} d_5 + c_{234} s_5 d_6 \tag{30}$$

$$c_3 = \frac{K_s^2 + K_c^2 - \alpha_2^2 - \alpha_3^2}{2\alpha_2 \alpha_3} \tag{31}$$

$$s_3 = \sqrt{1 - c_3^2} \tag{32}$$

$$\theta_3 = \pm a\tan 2(s_3, c_3) \tag{33}$$

$$\theta_2 = a\tan 2(K_S, K_c) - a\tan 2(\alpha_3 s_3, \alpha_3 c_3 + \alpha_2) \tag{34}$$

Figure 4. Graph obtained using Matlab from cobot TM5-900.

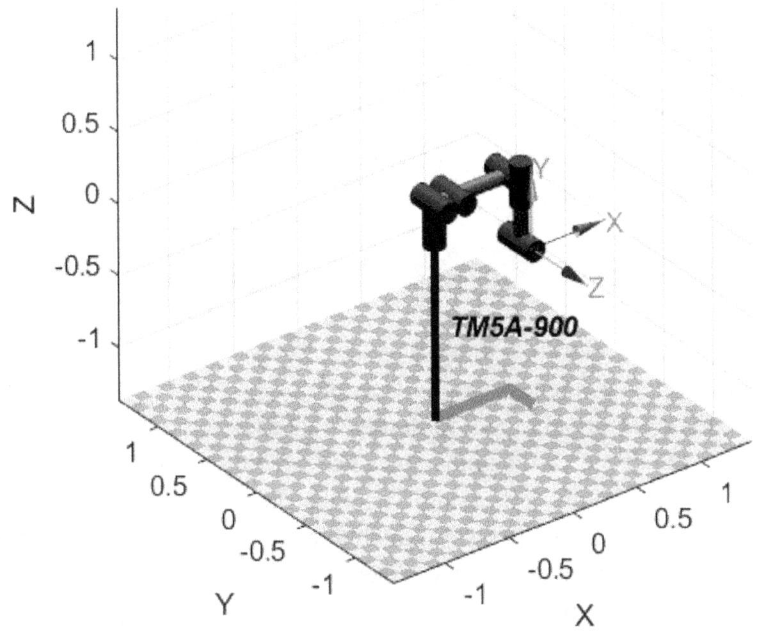

$$\theta_4 = \theta_{234} - \theta_2 - \theta_3 \tag{35}$$

To verify the methodology used and the equations calculated, the equations were implemented in the programming and numerical calculation platform MATLAB®, where the following graph was obtained, see Figure 4.

With this graph (Figure 4), it is validated that the equations developed are correct, since the kinematic configuration of the robot can be seen where the reference frames are described, as well as the reference frame of the final position of the end effector can be observed.

Implementing Robot Kinematics in Unity

In order to generate augmented reality with the cobot TM5-900 and achieve the desired movements and positions, the equations already calculated for forward and inverse kinematics were implemented using scripts in the Unity platform. Similarly, sliders were added by means of Unity with the Canvas tool and the realization of a

Figure 5. Control panel in Unity.

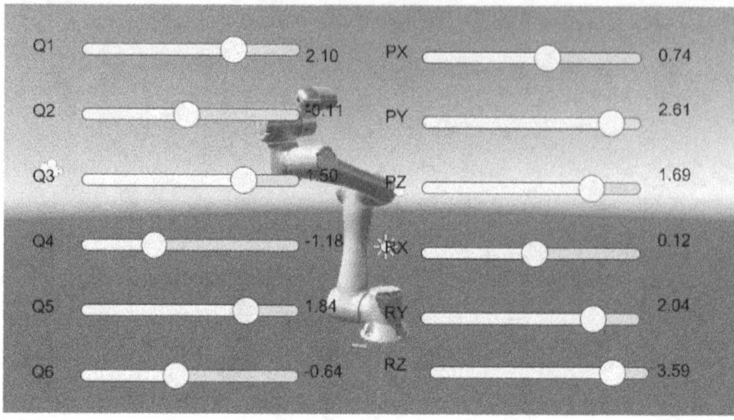

script for each correspondent degree of freedom of the cobot. In this way, the user can observe the operational ranges in degrees that exists in each joint of the cobot and thus be aware of the various movements allowed to perform on the cobot.

As can be seen in Figure 5, the control panel in Unity is made up of two columns, where on the left side are the forward kinematics sliders, and on the right column are the sliders that make up the inverse kinematics. In this way, the user only slides the degrees or end point that he wants the cobot to be positioned, to later visualize the movement of the cobot model in augmented reality in the selected position and in real time.

In order to create augmented reality, the necessary permissions to use Vuforia, which is an Augmented Reality (AR) application development platform (Vuforia, 2020), were configured and activated in Unity. For the augmented reality generation, a marker seen in Figure 6, provides the AR application itself with a trigger key on where to position the AR content. After performing all the pertinent tests by means of this marker, it is required to create the scenario where the robot will be positioned and thus omit the marker.

When executing the SDK (Software Development Kit) (Amin & Govilkar, 2019, pp. 1-2), and reading the marker, the virtual 6 DOF robot in AR will be reflected with a real size projection, together with all the characteristics that were developed and applied, see Figure 7, and thus achieving the different positions of the cobot through its virtual twin in augmented reality before applying them to the physical robot.

Figure 6. Marker used for augmented reality generation in Unity (Disney, n. d.).

Figure 7. Execution of application in Unity.

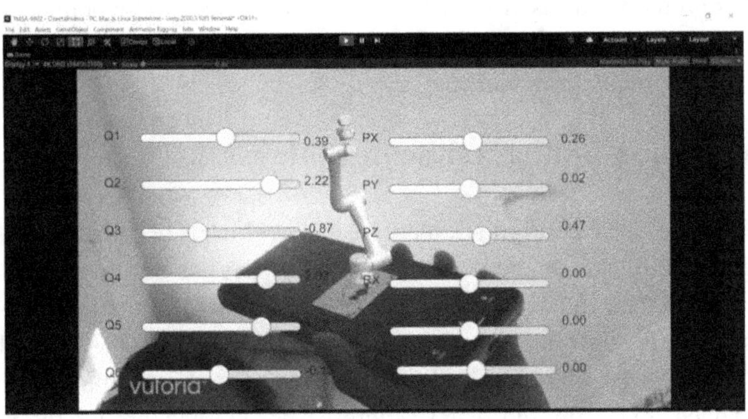

Physical and Virtual Robot Communication

To carry out remote manipulation of the physical robot through a mobile device, it is necessary to develop an application, which was carried out with Unity software.

In the same way, to be able to operate both the virtual and physical robot, it is essential to communicate with each other. For this, the open communication protocol called MODBUS was used (Figure 8), which is designed to allow industrial equipment such as Programmable Logic Controllers (PLCs), computers, drivers for motors and other types of physical input/output devices to communicate over a network (Ruiz et al., 2022).

Modbus/TCP basically encapsulates a MODBUS frame within a TCP frame in a simple way. In the present project, EasyModbus was used as a simulator, which allows

Figure 8. Communication scheme between physical and virtual robot.

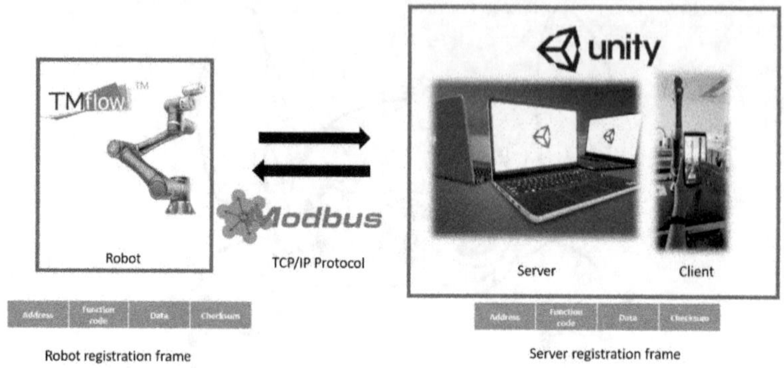

sending and receiving commands without complex programming, that is, only a few lines of code are needed to read or write data from or to a device (Easymodbustcp, 2022). This protocol was used via a client, with which tests were being carried out and the data produced by the robot was displayed. Modbus Server Simulator makes software development quick and easy.

Communication Configuration in TMflow®

Next, the Modbus TCP configuration is presented, which is responsible for reading the address coordinates of the robot. These addresses are required to be able to interpret the robot coordinates using TMflow®, which is a fully graphical, flowchart-based programming user interface for the TM5-900 robot. TMflow® has a block to structure the MODBUS devices. Within this interface the relevant parameters for the TCP device are configured. The IP address was obtained through the Windows Command Prompt (CMD), which is the one that will connect to the robot.

Once the configuration is complete, the location prior to the reading and writing of the device is added, that is, the input address corresponding to each joint of the robot is inserted, according to the list of addresses, as well as the type of variable of each degree of freedom, which corresponds to buoyant (Figure 9).

Later this configuration will be used to program the flow and read the position of the current coordinates of the robot. For this it is necessary to create variables to store the value of the coordinates in the registry. It is worth mentioning that Big-endian is the high byte stored in the lowest memory address, so it is necessary to select this option when adding the variable of each joint.

The variables "var_Joint#", of type float, obtain the value of the coordinates of the robot in its respective direction of each degree of freedom. So, to insert the new variables and the variables obtained by Modbus, as well as verify if the value of each

Figure 9. MODBUS input address configuration.

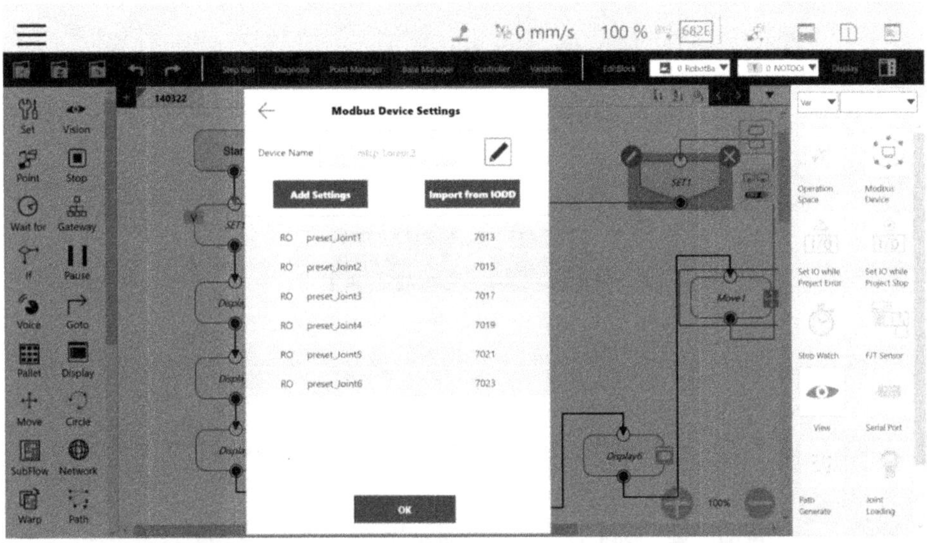

coordinate obtained in the Modbus address is correct, it is necessary to perform the following edition, see Figure 10.

To achieve this configuration, it is necessary to select the MODBUS protocol, as well as the local device that is being used, and thus finish with the selection of the variables created previously for the 6-DOF. Within TMflow®, there is a node called "Connection" whose objective is to perform the network configuration. In order for the robot to communicate with external devices over the network, this module is edited with the IP address of the local device.

Programming in TMflow®

Next, the block diagram (Figure 11) that was developed in TMflow® is presented, to achieve communication with Unity, as well as show the values obtained, the block called "SET1" was configured, which is responsible for establishing the I/O states and change the type and value of variables. When this node is traversed, all node parameters change to the set result.

In the "move" node, the six-axis angles J1~J6 were set to determine the robot's moving distance and angle, and then perform relative movement from the current position. The function of the "Display" node is to display the specified variable or string on the screen according to the format specified by the users. In this case it is used to show the value obtained by the serial port, the robot parameters and the execution results.

Figure 10. Variable obtained from the SET node to obtain the Modbus value.

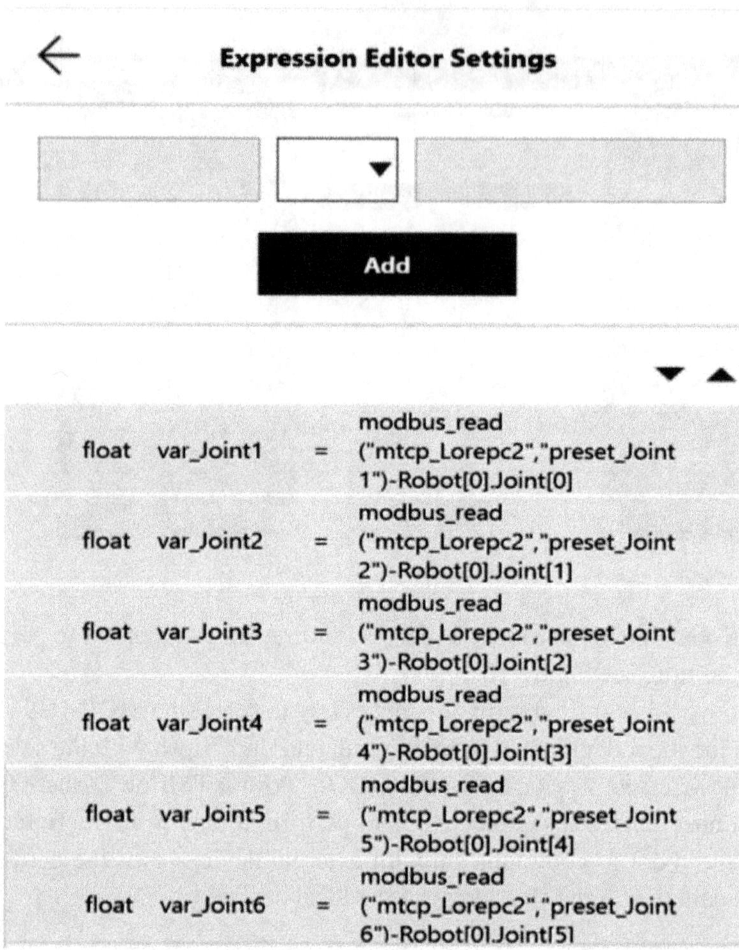

Finally, the obtained value is displayed on the screen using the "Display" node and the "Go To" node is used to continuously update the value.

Communication Configuration in Unity

The virtual model of the TM5-900 robot was made in Unity, which is why it is necessary to achieve communication with this software through the MOTBUS communication protocol. To achieve this, the EasyModbus library was added to the "Assets" folder, in the same way within the script, said library was called. Next, a byte converter was developed within the same script, since the robot sends and receives data in Big endian format, that is, the highest (most significant) byte is

Figure 11. Block diagram in TMflow®.

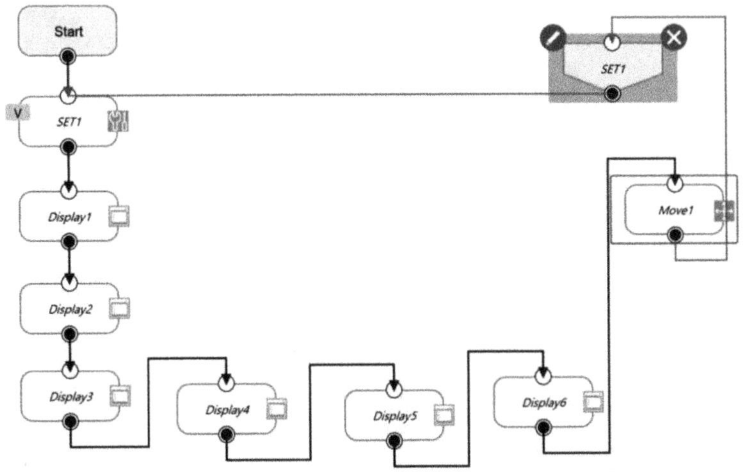

stored in the lowest address (Eulermat, 2022). In order to achieve this conversion from bytes to big endian, it was necessary to convert them to hexadecimal and then to floats, since Unity receives the data in float numbers, see Figure 12.

Figure 12. Data Conversion.

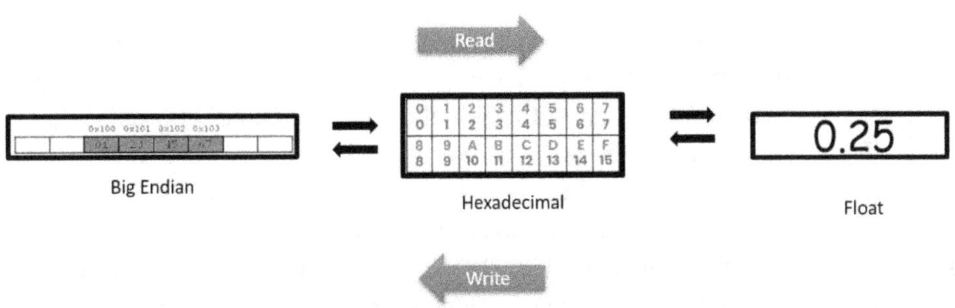

Subsequently, code was developed and added to a script with the aim of being able to write and read in the robot, that is, send the points of each degree of freedom that the user chooses in the application to the real robot, as well as send routines and read the current position of the physical robot.

Figure 13. Modbus TCP Server running.

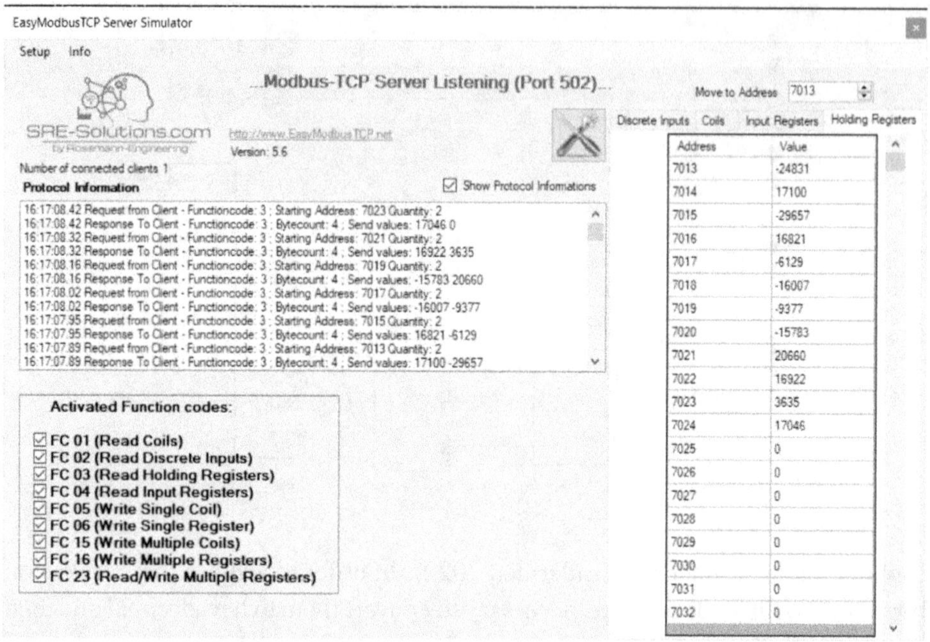

Execution of Reading and Writing in Virtual and Physical Robot

Once the parameters were configured for reading and writing in both Unity and TMflow®, their respective tests were carried out and, in this way, their correct operation was verified. When running EasyModbus Client, the connection is displayed on the IP address as well as the port that corresponds to the physical robot, and a correct server connection is verified, as are the bytes you are writing.

The Figure 13 shows the EasyModbus TCP server window running correctly, and it is in the "Holding Registers" tab where the data being written in each degree of freedom is observed according to the address that corresponds to it according to the Robot TM table in the Modbus address list.

In the Figure 14 shown below, the application interface is observed in the window where the position of the robot is established in each degree of freedom, in the same way that the "Controller" module is shown, which provides users with direct robot control from motion control, I/O control and FreeBot configuration. Motion control includes three tabs: Joint, Base and Tool, which correspond respectively to "move according to joint angle setting", "move according to robot base or current base" and "move according to the tool coordinate.

Figure 14. Verification of written data with the "Controller" module.

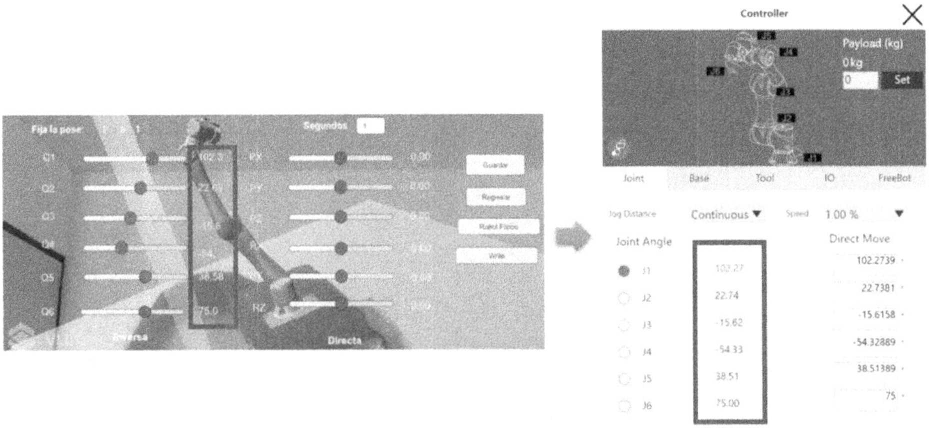

With the "Controller" module it was verified that the degrees established in each degree of freedom in Unity have been correctly written in the physical robot (Figure 15).

The Figure 16 shows evidence that the degrees established in the physical robot have been successfully read in the application made in Unity, since the angles established in each joint coincide.

In this way, the correspondence of the position of both the physical and virtual robots was confirmed. It is worth mentioning that, when executing the program, within the Unity console, it is possible to analyse all the byte conversions that are being executed in real time.

Robot Operation Space

In the laboratory where the TM5-900 robot is installed, it is necessary to limit the movements of each joint, since the workspace is limited by the table where the robot is located, as well as by the electronic components that are around it. around. The workspace of a robot is defined as the set of points that can be reached by its end-effector. The limits that need to be set must be configured in both Unity and TMflow®. For TMflow®, there is a module in which these points are determined with the physical robot, that is, this page provides the configuration of the space, the middle is the virtual robot interface and the right side is the controller interface.

The "Add or Modify Layout" page can be accessed by clicking the button to add a new layout or to reset features after selecting layout features. On this page, a plane is created by setting three points. The setting order of the three points can be random, and the virtual interface of the robot will display the corresponding-colored

Figure 15. Writing data to physical robot from Unity.

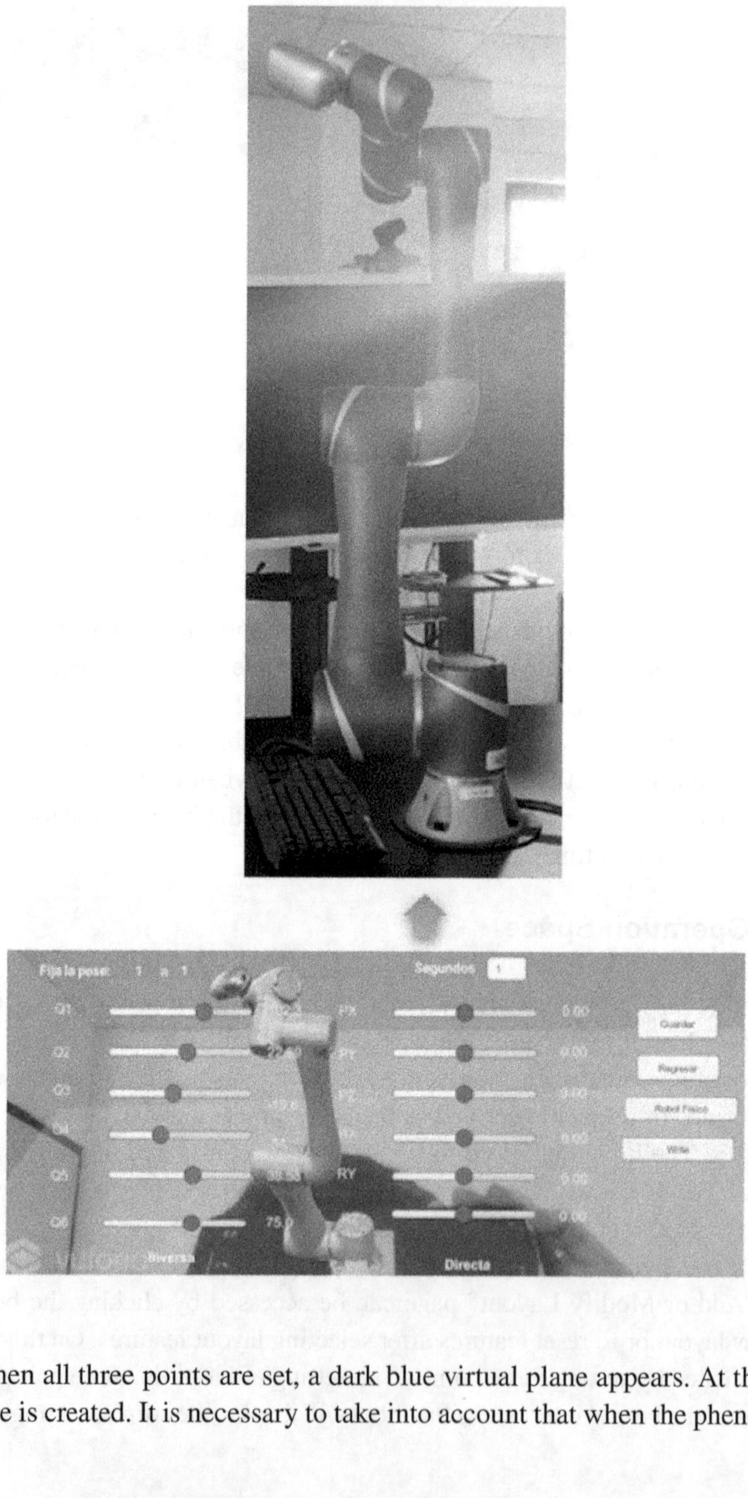

ball. When all three points are set, a dark blue virtual plane appears. At this time, the plane is created. It is necessary to take into account that when the phenomenon

Figure 16. Verification of data read with the "Controller" module.

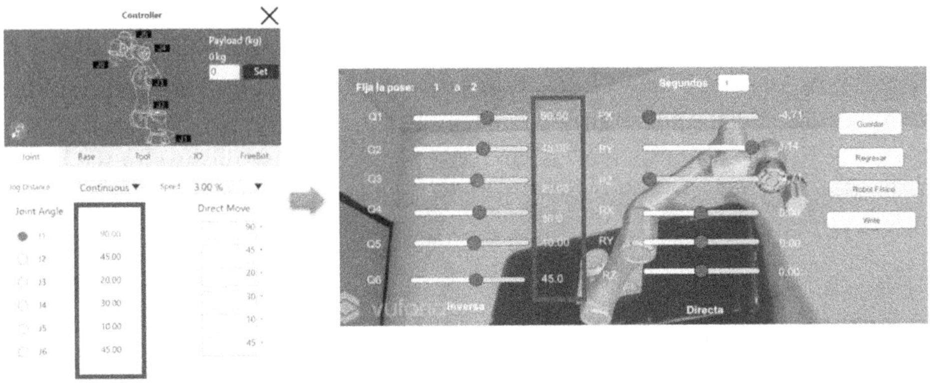

of common point or collinearity occurs, the virtual plane cannot be created. After the operation space creation is complete, you can identify objects on the 3D screen as shown in Figure 17. The entire sphere is the maximum range of robot mobility, the reduced space is green, the maximum speed space is red, and the stop space is the space removed from the robot's mobility range (Techman robot INC., 2022).

Figure 17. Workspace established in TMflow®.

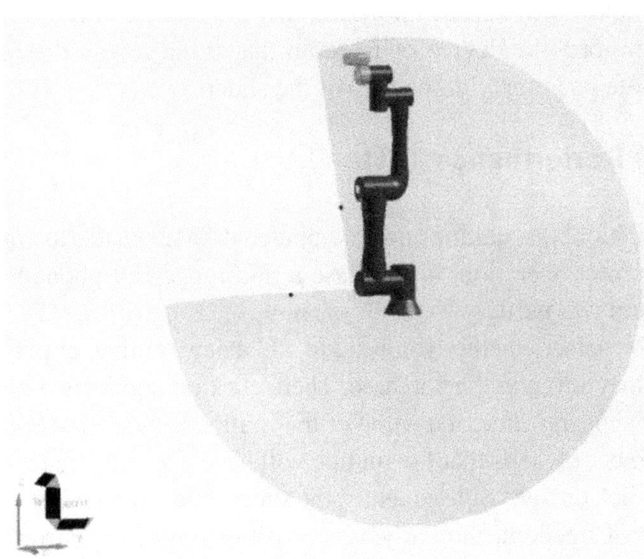

To delimit the planes in Unity, a plane was created both in the "X" axis, and in the "Y" axis. The position of the physical robot was taken into account to be able to reference both planes. The "X" axis corresponds to the table where the physical robot is positioned and the "Y" axis limits the movements of the robot to prevent it from encountering the electronic components that are physically located around the robot. The Figure 18 shows the "X" and "Y" planes duly established for the Unity application, and thus avoid any accident with the physical robot from the simulation.

Figure 18. Limits set in Unity.

If the user exceeds one of its limits, that is, either the "X" or "Y" plane, a notification window will appear informing that the robot's work limits have been exceeded; Therefore, the degree of freedom that is exceeding the limit must be returned to a safe position with the help of the slider.

Application Performance Tests

Once the application was running on the computer, it was exported to a mobile device to verify its correct operation, in this case a mid-range cell phone with Android operating system was used.

In which you select whether you want to add a new routine, or play some other routine previously saved in the database. Then, click on "Add new routine", in this way the menu appears where the name of the routine is written in the text box, as well as the number of steps that the routine will have. Once the requested data has been entered, click on save. Subsequently, the sliders slide to select the desired angle in each degree of freedom. Similarly, it is possible to read the current position of the physical robot instead of using the sliders, by clicking on "Physical Robot". Finally, in the Figure 19 you can see how the execution environment of the robot is displayed in a real way, that is, in the real environment only the marker is displayed, and through the application the view of the virtual robot is obtained.

Figure 19. Visualization of the real environment when executing the application.

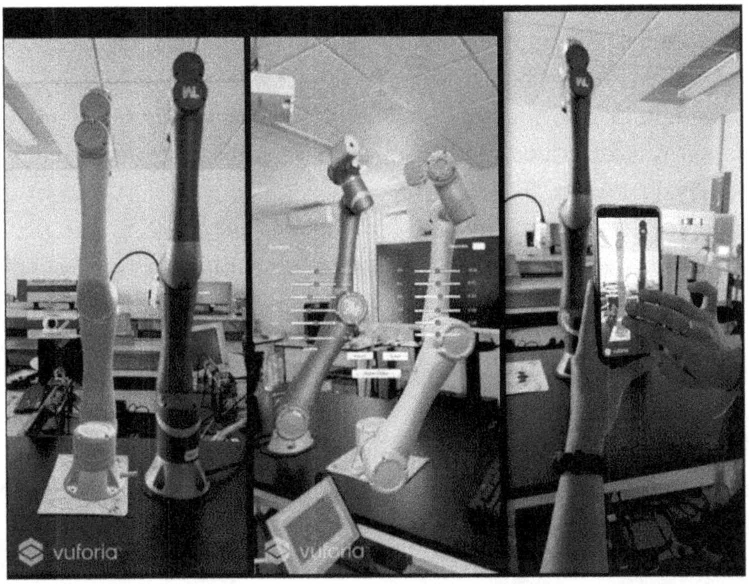

DISCUSSION OF RESULTS AND POSSIBLE APPLICATIONS

The developed system that incorporates augmented reality into a digital twin represents an advance system for robot programming teaching and validation and other possible applications, such as remote online programming. Augmented reality benefits the validation of robot programs by providing to the user a 3D visual tool for an easier detection of collisions and to ensure the workspace, in this way, the validated robot programs can be reused as long as the workspace is kept and this helps to reduce the programming time. Augmented reality also allows a safer environment for remote online programming while the users can remotely design and test robot programs. The virtual twin with its enhanced visualisation base on augmented reality can also run-on mobile devices either locally or remotely accessed. For all the previously commented functionality the develop platform is suitable for engineering education and training in robotics.

To be able to operate both the virtual and physical robot, it is essential to communicate with each other. For this, the open communication protocol called MODBUS was used. The process that was developed to achieve communication between the virtual robot and the physical robot was completely described, this is, the communication link from the user interface of the TM5-900 robot with Unity application. A safe environment was created to manipulate the collaborative robot and to avoid collisions, in other words, the workspace limits for the cobot were established both in Unity and TMflow®, the operation of these limits is shown and how the user can interact with them, as well as the correct operation of this communication in both software, just like in the mobile app. Once the parameters were configured for reading and writing in both Unity and TMflow®, their respective tests were carried out and, in this way, their correct operation was verified. The procedure for its verification was described in the section "Execution of reading and writing in virtual and physical robot."

Regarding the communication between the physical and virtual robot, it can be concluded that the purpose of being able to interact with the virtual robot on a real scale through an application generated through Unity was fulfilled, and thus have a remote control of the techman® of 6-DOF, as well as seeing it in a fully graphical way and then running the saved routines through a database. In relation to the limitation of the cobot's workspace, the purpose was fulfilled, and tests were carried out to validate its correct operation, which is to prevent the robot from colliding, that is, not exceeding the established work limits. and thus, prevent possible collisions with objects that are in their real environment.

With these activities completed and working correctly, the result is a full-scale virtual robot, which can be manipulated remotely from the mobile application and graphically see the movements of the robot that the user wants to generate, and at the same time make it work in real time. a safe workspace. This will avoid accidents both with the user (human risks) and with the physical robot, since the routine generated by the user can be seen and reproduced from different perspectives and clearly seen when the robot collides.

In summary, to generate a virtual twin of a collaborative robot with 6-DOF using augmented reality as an interface, to achieve its manipulation and be able to teach the capabilities of the cobot and be able to generate routines of the techman® robot. The developed system that incorporates augmented reality into a digital twin represents an advance system for robot programming teaching and validation and other possible applications, such as remote online programming. Another possible application is to design an assembly line with more than two robots and get the robots to work together. Augmented reality benefits the validation of robot programs by providing to the user a 3D visual tool for an easier detection of collisions and to ensure the workspace, in this way, the validated robot programs can be reused as long as the workspace is kept and this helps to reduce the programming time.

CONCLUSION

This chapter explains the methodology to calculate the direct and inverse kinematics of a 6-DOF Cobot. The goal is to correctly execute the positions that are required for each joint of the robot, and thus move it to the final position accurately and optimally. For the calculation of the direct and inverse kinematics, homogeneous transformation matrices were used, as well as the Denavit-Hartenberg parameters. Direct and inverse kinematic equations were code in Unity and embedded into the virtual 3D representation of a 6-DOF cobot and reproduced in an augmented reality scaled version. The direct and inverse kinematic control of the robot was achieved. The presented forward and inverse kinematic solution is validated and applied to a virtual robot and its augmented reality representation. The developed application was validated and verified for its intended use, that is for educational and distance learning of cobots.

The proposed technique can also be extended. Another possible application is to design an assembly line with more than two robots and get the robots to work together, i.e., collaboratively with more than one digital twin to visualize the workspace and routines. graphically. On the other hand, developing an application with which, from the mobile device interface, the different elements that appear in the robot's work area can be identified. It is worth mentioning that by implementing the previous simulation of the cobots in the third dimension of the assembly line, the robot can be controlled in its work area and the elements that may appear in it, that is, the robot can be automatically moved to the position of the object and carry out the desired handling operation on it, considering the possible obstacles that may appear, detecting possible collisions and notifying the movement in said case. Future work is to adapt the developed system for industrial applications such as executing tasks without operational risks in the inspection processes of assembly lines. Virtual and augmented reality robot could be used to seek for possible collision and to generate obstacles that can interact with the robot, in this way different manufacturing scenarios could be simulated to achieve safe, effective, and efficient positioning.

ACKNOWLEDGMENT

This engineering research work was possible using the infrastructure of the Centro de Investigaciones en Óptica (CIO) virtual laboratories and with the postgraduate scholarship of CONACYT.

REFERENCES

Amin, D., & Govilkar, S. (2015). Comparative study of augmented reality SDKs. *International Journal on Computational Science & Applications*, *5*(1), 11–26. doi:10.5121/ijcsa.2015.5102

Blaga, A., & Tamas, L. (2018). Augmented reality for digital manufacturing. *2018 26th Mediterranean Conference on Control and Automation (MED)*, 173-178.

Bonilla, V. P. (2020). *Design of industrial robot control systems based on industry 4.0* [Diseño de sistemas de control industrial de robots basados en industria 4.0]. Universidad técnica de ambato. https://repositorio.uta.edu.ec/bitstream/123456789/31221/1/t1698id.pdf

Disney. (n. d.). Stitch [Imagen]. ClipArtMag. https://clipartmag.com/download-clipart-image#stitch-drawing-ohana-36.jpg

Easymodbus, T. C. P. (2022). *Communication library and professional tools for industrial communication*. Easymodbustcp. http://easymodbustcp.net/en/

Fang, H., Khim, S., & Nee, A. (2009). *Robot Programming Using Augmented Reality*. IEEE Conference Publication. https://ieeexplore.ieee.org/document/5279717

Granja Oramas, M. V. (2014). *Modeling and analysis of the direct and inverse kinematics of the Stanford manipulator of six degrees of freedom* [Modelación y análisis de la cinemática directa e inversa del manipulador Stanford de seis grados de libertad]. Repositorio Digital Institucional de la Escuela Politécnica Nacional. https://bibdigital.epn.edu.ec/handle/15000/8693

Heras, L., & Villarreal, B. (2004). *Augmented reality: a technology waiting for users* [La realidad aumentada: una tecnología en espera de usuarios]. https://www.revista.unam.mx/vol.8/num6/art48/jun_art48.pdf

Herrmann, L. & Schilling. (2013). A spatial augmented reality system for intuitive display of robotic data. *Int. Conf. Human-Robot Interact*. doi: 10.1109/HRI.2013.6483560

Hyre, A., Harris, G., Osho, J., Pantelidakis, M., Mykoniatis, K., & Liu, J. (2022). Digital Twins: Representation, Replication, Reality, and Relational (4Rs). *Manufacturing Letters*, *31*, 20–23.

IAT. (2020). *Augmented reality. What is it? Features and types* [Realidad aumentada. ¿Qué es? Características y tipos]. IAT. https://iat.es/tecnologias/realidad-aumentada/#:~:text=La%20realidad%20aumentada%20es%20aquella,ofreciendo%20as%C3%AD%20una%20realidad%20transformada

Jing, W., Goh, C. F., Rajaraman, M., Gao, F., Park, S., Liu, Y., & Shimada, K. (2018). *A Computational Framework for Automatic Online Path Generation of Robotic Inspection Tasks via Coverage Planning and Reinforcement Learning*. IEEE Xplore. https://ieeexplore.ieee.org/stamp/stamp.jsp?arnumber=8476296

Kelly, A. (2013). *Mobile robotics: mathematics, models, and methods*. Cambridge University Press.

Makris, S., Karagiannis, P., Koukas, S., & Matthaiakis, A. (2016). Augmented reality system for operator support in human–robot collaborative assembly. *CIRP Annals*. https://www.sciencedirect.com/science/article/abs/pii/S0007850616300385

Martínez, J. (2012). *Integration of augmented reality by vision in applications for an industrial robot* [Integración de realidad aumentada por visión en aplicaciones para un robot industrial] (1st ed.). Universidad Politécnica de Valencia. https://riunet.upv.es/bitstream/handle/10251/18013/Tesina.pdf?sequence=1

Muñoz, P., & Moctezuma. (2015). PD+G set-Point Controller for the Second and Third Joint of a ER-4u Scorbot Robot. In *Int. Conf. Mechatronics, Electron. Automot. Eng*. ICMEAE. doi:10.1109/ICMEAE.2014.36

Pelegrí, J. (2020). *What are the differences between a cobot and an industrial robot?* [¿Cuáles son las diferencias entre un cobot y un robot industrial?]. https://blog.universal-robots.com/es/cobots-vs-robots-industriales

Qi, Q., Tao, F., Hu, T., Anwer, N., Liu, A., Wei, Y., & Nee, A. Y. (2021). Enabling technologies and tools for digital twin. *Journal of Manufacturing Systems*, *58*, 3–21.

Ramírez, J., & Rubiano, A. (2018). *Mathematical modeling of the direct and inverse kinematics of a manipulative robot of three degrees of freedom* [Modelamiento matemático de la cinemática directa e inversa de un robot manipulador de tres grados de libertad]. Ingeniería Solidaria. https://revistas.ucc.edu.co/index.php/in/article/download/47/48/

Rao, D., & Verweij, G. (2017). *Sizing the prize What's the real value of AI for your business and how can you capitalise?* PWC.

Ripipsa. (2020). *History of Collaborative Robot* [Historia de los Robots Colaborativos]. Ripipsa Cobots. https://ripipsacobots.com/historia-robots-colaborativos/

Rodríguez, L., Paredes, C., & Martell, F. (2021). *Forward and Inverse Kinematics Control of a Collaborative 6-DOF Robot for an Augmented Reality Educational System.* https://ieeexplore.ieee.org/document/9590903

Syberfeldt, A., Danielsson, O., & Gustavsson, P. (2017). *Augmented reality smart glasses in the smart factory: Product evaluation guidelines and review of available products*. IEEE.

TarréR. (2019). *UPC*. https://upcommons.upc.edu/bi tstream/handle/2117/174167/Samper_Marc_memoria_TFG%20%282%29.pdf?sequence=1&isAllowed=y

Universidad Nacional de Cuyo. (2016). *Industrial application of ethernet networks* [Aplicación industrial de redes ethernet]. https://sistemamid.com/panel/uploads/biblioteca/2017-08-03_04-22-46141559.pdf

Villalobos, J., Sanchez, I. Y., & Martell, F. (2021). Statistical comparison of Denavit-Hartenberg based inverse kinematic solutions of the UR5 robotic manipulator. *2021 International Conference on Electrical, Computer, Communications and Mechatronics Engineering (ICECCME)*. doi:10.1109/iceccme52200.2021.9591104

Vuforia. (2020). *Market-Leading Enterprise AR-PTC*. https://www.ptc.com/en/products/augmented-reality/vuforia

William, M., García, C., Naranjo, J., Ortiz, A., & García, M. (2020). *Tele-operation system for Mobile Robots in the Oil and Gas industry* [Sistema de Tele-operación para Robots Móviles en la industria del Petróleo y Gas]. Revista Ibérica de Sistemas e Tecnologias de Información. https://www.researchgate.net/profile/Jose-E-Naranjo-2/publication/341522855_Sistema_de_Tele-operacion_para_Robots_Moviles_en_la_industria_del_Petroleo_y_Gas/links/5fc46ee0458515b7978932fb/Sistema-de-Tele-operacion-para-Robots-Moviles-en-la-industria-del-Petroleo-y-Gas.pdf

ADDITIONAL READING

Blanco, O., Fernandez-Carames, T. M., Fraga-Lamas, P., & Vilar-Montesinos, M. A. (2018). A practical evaluation of commercial industrial augmented reality systems in an industry 4.0 shipyard. *IEEE Access: Practical Innovations, Open Solutions*, *6*, 8201–8218. doi:10.1109/ACCESS.2018.2802699

CepymeNews R. (2020). *Consequences of unadjusted production* [Consecuencias de una producción no ajustada]. CepymeNews. https://cepymenews.es/consecuencias-de-una-produccion-no-ajustada

Chen, Q., Zhu, S., & Zhang, X. (2015). Improved Inverse Kinematics Algorithm Using Screw Theory for a Six-DOF Robot Manipulator. *International Journal of Advanced Robotic Systems*, *12*(10), 140. doi:10.5772/60834

Company, O. (2018). Collaborative Robot Hardware Installation Manual. *EU:7M Robot*, 35-67. https://assets.omron.eu/downloads/manual/en/v2/i623_collaborative robots_hardware_installation_manual_en.pdf

Grassmann, R., Modes, V., & Burgner-Kahrs, J. (2018). Learning the Forward and Inverse Kinematics of a 6-DOF Concentric Tube Continuum Robot in SE(3). *2018 IEEE/RSJ International Conference on Intelligent Robots and Systems (IROS)*. 10.1109/IROS.2018.8594451

Investigate to Innovate. (n.d.). *ITI*. https://www.iti.es/proyectosidi/proyecto-gemelos-digitales-industria-4-0/

Maly, I., Sedlacek, D., & Leitao, P. (2016). Augmented reality experiments with industrial robot in industry 4.0 environment. *2016 IEEE 14th International Conference on Industrial Informatics (INDIN)*. 10.1109/INDIN.2016.7819154

Mourtzis, D., Zogopoulos, V., & Vlachou, E. (2017). Augmented Reality Application to Support Remote Maintenance as a Service in the Robotics Industry. *Procedia CIRP*, *63*, 46–51. doi:10.1016/j.procir.2017.03.154

Olaya, A., López, A., & Moreno, F. (2004). Implementation of a MODBUS/TCP Network [Implementación de una Red MODBUS/TCP]. *Ingeniería y Competitividad*, *6*(2), 35–44.

Ong, S., Yew, A., Thanigaivel, N., & Nee, A. (2020). Augmented reality-assisted robot programming system for industrial applications. *Robotics and Computer-integrated Manufacturing*, *61*, 101820. doi:10.1016/j.rcim.2019.101820

Organización de Computadoras. (2022). *Eulermat*. http://euler.mat.uson.mx/~havillam/ca/Slides/08-Organization.pdf

Pace, F., Manuri, F., Sanna, A., & Fornaro, C. (2020). A systematic review of Augmented Reality interfaces for collaborative industrial robots. *Computers & Industrial Engineering*, *149*, 106806. doi:10.1016/j.cie.2020.106806

Propuesta Técnico-Comercial. (2020). *Techman IAS User Manual* [Manual de Usuario Techman IAS]. IAS Automation.

KEY TERMS AND DEFINITIONS

Cobot: Cobot that can work safely alongside workers, eliminating the need for cages or security fences. This gives even small and medium manufacturers the ability to automate your facilities without having to invest in cost-prohibitive technologies or a total refurbishment of manufacturing plants.

Database: It is called a database, or also a data bank, to a set of information belonging to the same context, ordered in a systematic way for its later recovery, analysis and/or transmission. There are many forms of databases today, ranging from a library to the vast user data sets of a telecommunications company.

Degrees of Freedom: When speaking of the degrees of freedom, it refers to the movement of the pieces in a three-dimensional space, such as the translation in the three perpendicular axes (forward, backward, left, right, up, and down), the rotation in cylindrical pieces or the combination of previous movements.

Script: In simple terms, a programming script is a text document where instructions or orders are placed that will later be executed by an intelligent device.

TCP: The TCP protocol (Transmission Control Protocol) is one of the fundamental protocols on the Internet, it allows applications to communicate with guarantees regardless of the lower layers of the TCP/IP model.

Unity: Unity is a development engine for the creation of video games that offers a multitude of functionalities for developers, which has also been used in virtual reality, in Architecture and Design projects and also in the edition and preview of miniseries.

User Interface: Refers to the interface with which people interact with machines. It is the interface that allows you to use a computer to place an order in an online store or to access an app through a smartphone. To do this, it has the control elements of an interface, which are visible to the user or through which they can perform some action. This ranges from simple text-based command lines to more complex graphical user interfaces.

Virtual Robot: Virtual robotics is based on the use of virtual environments for robot programming. That is, it is not necessary to have the physical robot or the development kit to experiment. The programming of virtual robots is especially useful for educational work and for learning about robotics by the little ones. They suppose a safe environment in which to practice, experiment and acquire concepts that will later be applicable to a real environment.

Vuforia: Vuforia is an SDK that allows building applications based on Augmented Reality; An application developed with Vuforia uses the device's screen as a "magic lens" where elements from the real world are intertwined with virtual elements (such as letters, images, etc.).

Workspace: The working area of a robot is the spatial volume that the end of the robot can reach. The workspace of a robot is defined as the set of points that can be reached by its end-effector.

Chapter 8
Teaching Spatial Geometry Through 3D Visualization and Augmented Reality

Thiciany Matsudo Iwano
Paraiba State University, Brazil

Dayvson Duarte Pereira
Paraiba State University, Brazil

Daniel Scherer
Paraiba State University, Brazil

ABSTRACT

Geometry is a branch of mathematics that helps us to work with distances, volumes, and areas of the real world. But spatial geometry presents an unusual obstacle: how to understand the elements of a three-dimensional object when they are normally presented in a two-dimensional form. The study was conducted with two classes in the 2nd year of high school in a public school. Class 1 used traditional resources: textbook, blackboard, and chalk. Class 2 used augmented reality (FLARAS) and 3D visualization (Sketchup) and textbook. It was expected that, with the help of augmented reality, the students of Class 2 would perform better than Class 1. A better understanding of the content was achieved, as they would have better visualization of spatial objects. Consequently, better performance was achieved in the exercises and problem questions presented.

DOI: 10.4018/978-1-6684-3398-0.ch008

Figure 1. Regular tetrahedron.

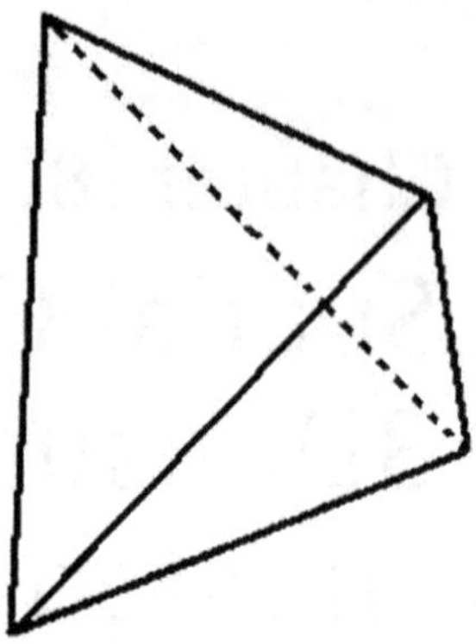

INTRODUCTION

In this chapter, an experience of using Augmented Reality and 3D Visualization to teach Spatial Geometry content will be discussed. This work was carried out in part on the premises of the State University of Paraba (UEPB) and with direct support from the Educational Informatics Research Group (NIEP). The discussion starts with the presentation of the background covering related works and the concepts of augmented reality and 3D visualization. After that, there is a presentation of the methodology used in the study, followed by the presentation of the experiments conducted. Then there are discussions about what was identified as solutions and problems. After that, there is a presentation some limitations of work and future directions, ending with the conclusions.

Geometry is a branch of Mathematics that is linked to human life. From civil construction to the children delimiting a field to play soccer, we can observe the presence of figures, relationships, and geometric associations. According to (Brito, 2014) as a response to human needs, whether for land demarcation or for the development of tools and housing construction that geometric knowledge was developing.

For example, if a student cannot associate Figure 1 with its three-dimensional shape, he will have difficulties in identifying elements and relating the properties of this solid to the structures studied in plane geometry. The difficulty also exists in a traditional class, based on blackboard and chalk. For the teacher to draw three-dimensional elements on the two-dimensional blackboard, there are obstacles, such as:

- The loss of information due to the lack of the third dimension.
- The teacher's unwillingness to design these structures.

Many teachers are faced with these dilemmas in the teaching of Spatial Geometry but are not always familiar with three-dimensional visualization applications or with the use of concrete material to facilitate the understanding and assimilation of concepts by the student.

Figure 2. Spatial geometry with straw concrete material.

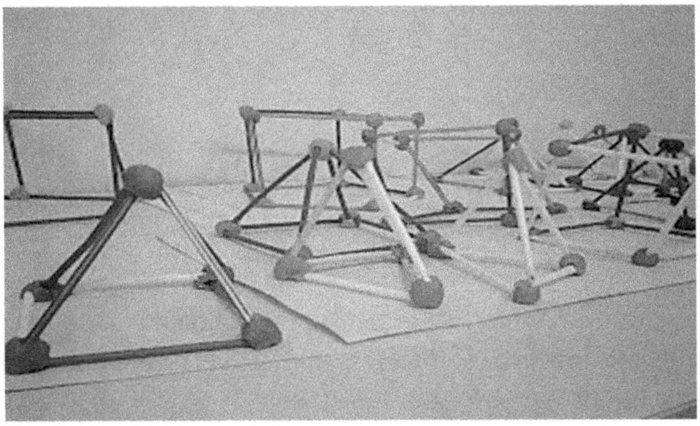

Concrete material for teaching Spatial Geometry is quite common and ranges from the construction of solids by the students themselves (Fanelli, 2013) to the use of commercial materials (Moraes, 2014). The use of applications for viewing in three dimensions, seeks to incorporate innovative technologies, such as computers, tablets, or smartphones (Pereira, 2014). For the teaching of spatial geometry, there are several methodologies to help teaching and learning, among which we can mention:

- **Blackboard (and chalk):** most used by teachers. Its use in the teaching of Spatial Geometry requires considerable skill in drawing on the part of the teacher. The observation of the three-dimensional object depends on the student's perception, and it is not possible to manipulate the object (for example, rotate), which consequently tends to hinder student learning.
- **Concrete material:** these are usually solids built from planned models. Most of the time, they are built with straw (Figure 2) paper (Figure 3) or acrylic pieces (Figure 4).

- **Software:** there are several computer programs aimed at teaching spatial geometry, such as, for example, GeoGebra 3D (beta), Calques 3D, Winplot (Figure 5), among others. They make it possible to view three-dimensional

Figure 3. Spatial geometry with paper concrete material.

objects on the monitor (two-dimensional), showing an alternative to the use of concrete material. However, the teacher, in addition to relying on his knowledge of the software's operating dynamics, also depends on the conditions of use of the school's computer labs (Figure 6).

The use of blackboards and chalk is more available to the teacher since every school has these elements. However, in addition to being a criticized method (mainly because it is not a recent technology), it is understood that the main setback is the impossibility of material manipulating (drawn solids cannot be easily rotated on the blackboard) and, consequently, does not provide a clear view of a three-dimensional object.

The use of concrete material opens the possibility to build the material by the student himself and the possibility of manipulation. However, it concentrates

Figure 4. Spatial geometry with acrylic concrete material.

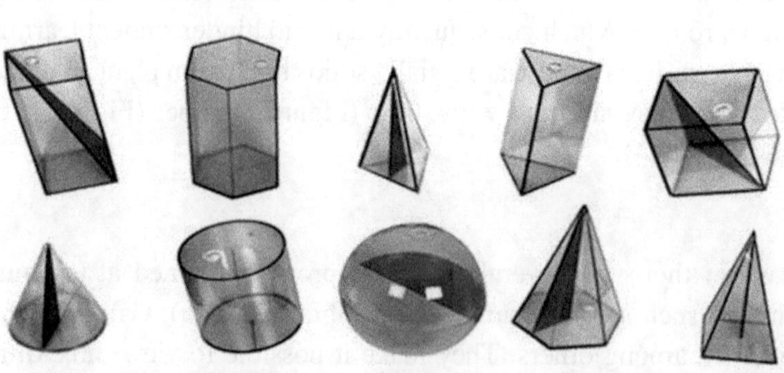

Figure 5. Spatial geometry with software.

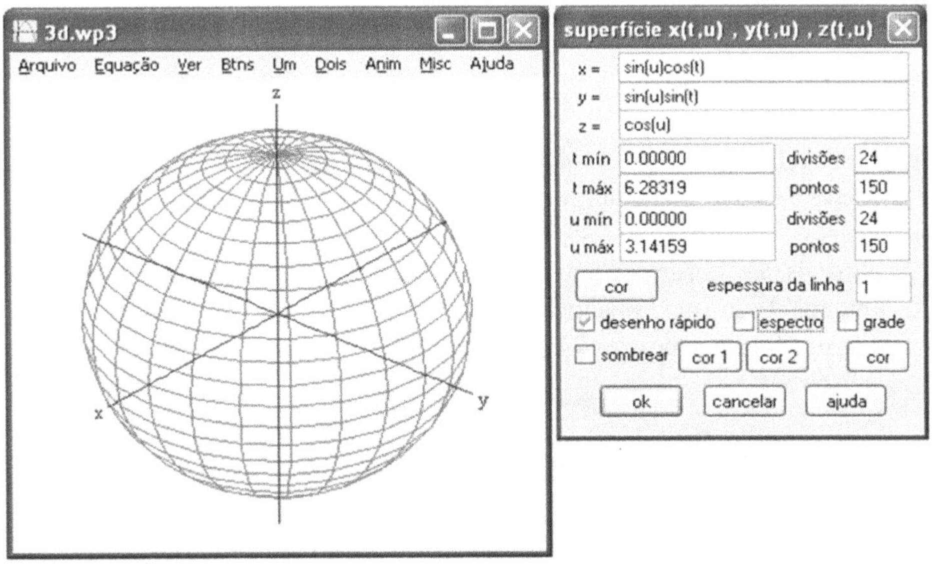

difficulties regarding the necessary construction material, time spent for assembly and storage. Unfortunately, there is usually not enough material, time, and / or storage. There is also the proposal to use software that, despite seeking integration

Figure 6. Public school computer lab.

of technology in the classroom, ends up having a major obstacle: the difficulties arising from computer labs, which are not normally in full operation.

Problem Definition

Considering that the presentation of concrete objects facilitates the understanding of concepts by students, the following question arises.

- What is the impact of approaching high school spatial geometry content through Augmented Reality?
- Is it possible that the use of Augmented Reality can replace the use of concrete objects?

In this way, in this work, the use of Augmented Reality Software is proposed. Thus, there is a disadvantage in learning the tool, but with the following advantages:

- Possibility of manipulating solids and greater ease of visualization and understanding of the object.
- There is no need for physical spaces for storage since all objects are all virtual.
- Independence of computer lab facilities, as it can be used in the classroom with presentation viewing equipment.

RELATED WORKS AND CONCEPTS

In this section, the authors begin with the presentation of concepts involved in the work. Virtual Reality is an area that started with a filmmaker in the 1950s, who created the first device that allowed the user to immerse themselves in a three-dimensional virtual world. The term appeared around the 1980s. Augmented Reality can be defined as the enrichment of the real environment with virtual objects, using some technological device and working in real time (Tori, Kirner, & Siscoutto, 2006).

The main difference between Virtual Reality and Augmented Reality is the fact that the former consists of a virtual environment generated exclusively by a computer and that for a real interaction it needs advanced equipment for interaction between the user and the system (such as gloves for virtual reality). In RVA, virtual images are used to enhance the real environment.

Virtual reality still implies that there will be complete immersion of the user within the generated virtual world. Augmented Reality (AR) can have its complete immersion or not. In this sense, when one thinks of visualizing a world totally generated in 3D and that complete immersion does not occur, then, in this case, we have 3D Visualization. Due to its characteristic of freedom of operation and not requiring specific devices (such as HMD for Virtual Reality), several works are usually found addressing the use of AR and spatial geometry.

There are some applications of Augmented Reality to aid the teaching and learning process in various contents and subjects of elementary and high school, such as Euler's Relation in (Lemos & Carvalho, 2010) and (Araujo, 2017) or in descriptive geometry (Lima, Haguenauer, & Cunha, 2007). There are also works related to educational games, such as (Zorzal, Cardoso, Kirner, & Júnior, 2006) (Deng, et al., 2019) (Lee H.S., 2008) and related to spatial geometry (Rodrigues, et al., 2010) and math in general (Radu, McCarthy, & Kao, 2016). There is also the SISEULER application that uses Augmented Reality as elements of Euler's Relation to visualize Platonic solid, discussed by (Araujo, 2017); the GEOAR that according to (Reis & Kirner, 2012) is an interactive book of Geometry that brings the content linked to images in Augmented Reality; the EASY MATH discussed by (Noval, 2013) seeks to highlight the height and base of polyhedron.

It is noticed in most studies that theoretical questions are presented, often showing that AR has enormous potential to expand and facilitate the teaching of Mathematics, but without going into details about methods or processes.

The work of (França, 2015) presents the use of SketchUp to build figures in three dimensions and the use of FLARAS to visualize them. The work addresses the use in an undergraduate course of a bachelor's degree in Graphic Expression, which differs from the focus of the work of this article: students of the 2nd year of high school.

Augmented Reality With PC

The following devices are required for the use of AR (Figure 7):

- Monitor or screen (presenting viewing equipment), which will be used to view objects.
- A camera, which will serve as an instrument for visualizing the environment.
- Markers are the cards that enable the relationship between augmented reality and the environment.
- Specific software for managing the virtual object.
- A software for the construction of the objects. In this case, SketchUp was chosen.

Figure 7. Augmented Reality schema with PC.

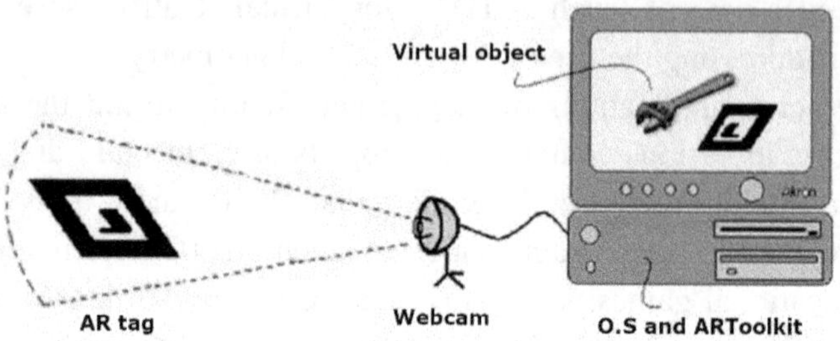

Why Use AR on PC Instead of Smartphone?

With the growing popularity of smartphones, AR has gained space with smartphones. There are several apps that look to make use of it, such as Pokémon Go, IKEA place or YouCam Makeup. Pokémon Go (Niantic, Inc., 2022) addressed the possibility for users to hunt Pokémon in the most diverse environments. Often causing people to move around in search of the desired pokémon. IKEA place (Inter IKEA Systems, 2022) belongs to the IKEA brand and allows buyers to visualize in their spaces how the desired products will look. Finally, YouCam Makeup allows users to evaluate makeup products before purchasing them, "avoiding the need to physically try multiple makeups, as well as being fooled by flashing lights" (Perfect Corp., 2022).

There is also the GeoGebra app (GeoGebra, 2022). Originally the application was limited to a specific group of ready-made objects provided by GeoGebra itself. More recently, space has opened up for greater freedom in creating objects. Despite this recent expansion, the use of GeoGebra implies that each student must have a smartphone capable of running the application. In addition, the teacher would need a connector that allows him to connect to the presentation viewing equipment (e.g., data show) and thus share the image of his smartphone with everyone in the class.

In this way, an application that runs on a PC or notebook and that can easily be connected to a presenter is the solution we have chosen. It is necessary to reinforce those students from public schools in Brazil have a low socio-economic situation. This tends to imply the availability of little access to smartphones or, at most, devices with low processing power. In addition, presenters have reasonable availability in public schools in Brazil.

AUGMENTED REALITY AND SPATIAL GEOMETRY

In this section, the presentation of the FLARAS and SketchUp tools, followed by the method used in the study will be exposed.

SketchUp

Originally, Google SketchUp was free software for creating 2D and 3D objects and spaces. It was used by architects and civil construction engineers. Despite requiring greater knowledge about computing for its use, it was chosen because it is free. The NIEP research group to generate tutorials that would guide the use of the tool by enthusiastic mathematics teachers. Currently the tool belongs to Trimble Navigation (Trimble Inc, 2022) and has paid and free versions, these with some limitations of use.

FLARAS

FLARAS (Flash Augmented Reality Authoring System) was developed by Costa and Douglas, under the guidance of Professor Claudio Kirner. Based on FLARToolKit, it therefore allows applications to run on any computer that has a browser with a Flash Player plug-in. FLARAS allows the insertion and visualization of textures (2D image), videos, 3D objects, and audio. Furthermore, it allows the user to save a file that can be edited later or even export the project, creating an application that can be executed in any browser with the Flash Player plug-in properly installed (Souza & Kirner, 2012). The main advantages of the tool are:

- It presents a good degree of usability.
- Allow the user to create an application in AR, which may contain: 3D virtual objects, audio files, and images.

One unfavorable point for FLARAS was the installation requirement. The process was found to be simple. Even so, the NIEP research group has developed a tutorial to make it easier for a computer enthusiast math teacher to use.

Methodology

The study started with the instructional materials provided by the NIEP Group of the Computing Department of UEPB. The material, easy to understand, showed in an objective and obvious way the step by step to find, create, and use geometric objects. It also brought with it examples for a better understanding of the process.

Subsequently, NIEP students showed examples of the use of FLARAS (Souza & Kirner, 2012) and later there was access to tutorials: 'Tutorial for using FLARAS' and 'Tutorial for downloading virtual objects for SACRA and FLARAS' (for the search for virtual objects); and 'Tutorial for converting virtual objects 3ds in .WRL or .KMZ'.

Search for 3D Virtual Objects

After studying the tutorials, web searches were made for objects that were following the desired parameters of use, to quote:

- Objects that assist the teacher in displaying three-dimensional geometric figures.
- Objects that make it possible to study its intrinsic elements, both on its surface and inside.

Unfortunately, there was no success in searching for these objects in repositories on the Internet. Thus, it was decided to produce them. To this end, a set of textbooks was defined that would serve as a basis for cataloging the images of the objects that would be used. Three textbooks were chosen, normally used in Brazilian Schools, which address Spatial Geometry:

- **Mathematics High School - 2nd grade** (Smole & Diniz, 2019): It is a book that deals with Spatial Geometry in a very theoretical way, without mentioning objects from reality, leaving only the drawings of the book itself. It is seen that, with this reference, many students experience difficulties in understanding and visualizing objects.
- **Fundamentals of Elementary Mathematics - Volume 10** (Dolce & Pompeo, 2019): Classic textbook used by many teachers' formation courses and preparatory courses. Referenced in most high school books.
- **High School Mathematics - Volume 2** (Lima, Carvalho, Wagner, & Morgado, 2022): aimed at high school and widely used in teacher formation courses. It is one of the textbooks of the geometry discipline in the Professional Master´s in Mathematics - PROFMAT.

Basic Methodology Process

Material Constructions:

- Choice of solids to be drawn in SketchUp.

- SketchUp study.
- Solid design.
- Visualization of results in FLARAS.
- Class preparation with an innovative approach.

EXPERIENCE REPORT

In this section, the authors present the dynamics for the development of class materials and are already exposing some difficulties that were encountered and how they were remedied. The discussion continues with the presentation of the dynamics used with Class1 will be presented, which is the traditional and regular dynamics for approaching spatial geometry content for 2nd year high school classes. This is significant to highlight the dynamics achieved with Class2, also 2nd year of high school, in which the approach to dealing with spatial geometry content was with the aid of Augmented Reality and 3D Visualization.

Material Development

Then the study on the use of SketchUp started from the "Tutorial on modeling virtual objects using Google SketchUp" and from video classes made available by the NIEP team.

Construction of 3D Virtual Objects

SketchUp is a free software that allows the user to create objects in 2D and 3D. It was created for the use of architects and engineers in civil construction and is available at http://www.sketchup.com/intl/pt-BR/. Despite being a complex tool and requiring a little more computational skill from the user, it was the software chosen for the construction of the objects. From there, the objects were built via SketchUp with support from the NIEP team.

3D Virtual Object Visualization

Finally, the objects were visualized in the FLARAS Augmented Reality software (Souza & Kirner, 2012). The greatest difficulties met were discussed with the specialist team (NIEP), such as:

- Why was the figure perfect in SketchUp but it did not appear as it should in FLARAS (Figure 8)?

- How to create spherical figures?

Figure 8. (a) SketchUp construction; (b) FLARAS visualization.

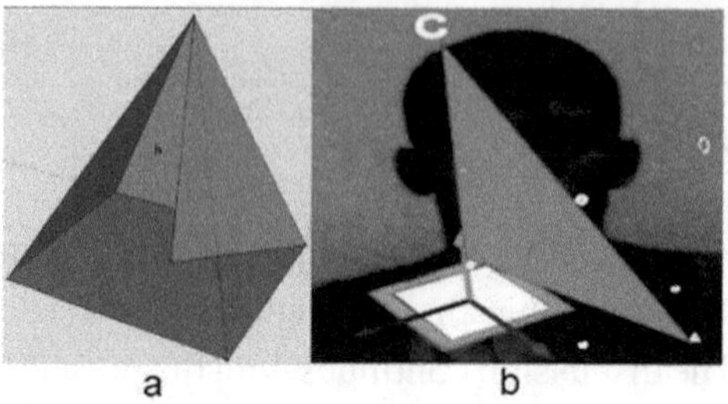

In addition, during the objects developing process, it was noticed that there were some flaws in the program, such as:

- If the object is painted with some colors, at the time of presentation at FLARAS only a part of the object appears, that is, that part that is painted in a certain color.
- There are also some cases where letters, symbols, and numbers do not appear when the virtual object is used in FLARAS.
- Lack of repositories focused on teaching spatial geometry.

Figure 9. Two lines concurrent to the α plane parallel to the β plane, presented by SketchUp.

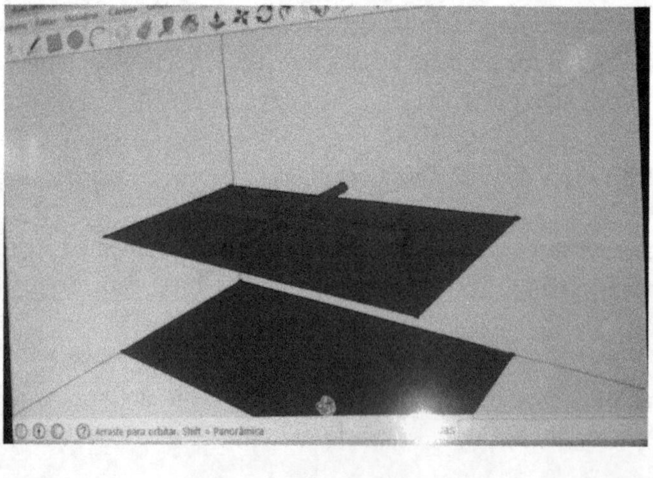

Table 1. Comparison between Class1 and Class2.

	Class1	Class2
Meeting number	• 10	• 4
Material used	• Textbook	• Textbook
	• Chalkboard and Chalk	• Chalkboard and Chalk
	• Paper sheets and pens	• AR (FLARAS) and 3D (SketchUp)

Therefore, a series in deficiencies of the tooling were noticed for visualization (by FLARAS) of the created objects. Therefore, it was noticed that it would be difficult to adjust some of the generated objects so that they were properly presented by FLARAS. Therefore, sometimes it was chosen to use SketchUp directly, as can be seen in (Figure 9).

Use of Material in the Classroom

Based on the experience of previous years and seeking to draw a parallel between the teaching of the content of spatial geometry, through the systematics normally used (chalk and chalk) and the systematics with the use of technology (Augmented Reality), the authors defined the content of spatial geometry in the classroom from the notion of point, line and plane to the part of parallelism, using the same book (Smole & Diniz, 2019) in Class1 and Class2. It is worth noting that:

- Each class lasts forty-five minutes = 1 h/class.
- The classes were taught in the same classroom (both for lessons that used chalk and chalk, as well as for those that used augmented reality).
- There were two groups of students (classes); while for Class1, the content was taught using blackboard and chalk, while for Class2, the content was taught using Augmented Reality with the FLARAS software and the help of SketchUp.
- Due to school transportation problems, the total number of meetings with Class2 was less than the number of meetings that Class1 had.

It is important to reinforce that there are differences in the development of classroom content between Class1 and Class2. There was a time reduction for Class2 due to student public transport issues. It is also necessary to observe that in Class1, the content is presented in the traditional way (textbook + blackboard), while in Class2, the content is presented with the aid of Augmented Reality (with FLARAS software) and 3D visualization (with SketchUp software) (Table 2).

Class1: Content Presented With Blackboard, Chalk, Textbook

In these classes, only the textbook (Smole & Diniz, 2019) and the blackboard were used, in addition to the material found in the room, such as sheets and pens being planes and lines, respectively, to improve visualization. Class1 had a set of 10 meetings of 2 h/class each. The distribution of content by meetings took place as follows:

1st Meeting (2h/Class)

In the first 2h/class, a brief reading of what concept, postulate, and theorem was held, followed by the presentation of the first six postulates of the textbook, which are present the first six postulates of the book.

1. Lines and planes are sets of points.
2. Given two points, there is a single line that contains them.
3. Given three non-collinear points, there is a single plan that contains them.
4. If two points are on a plane, then the line passing through them is contained in that plane.
5. If two planes intersect, their intersection is a line.
6. In space there are infinite points. Every line has infinite points, and every plane has infinite points.

In addition to three theorems exposed by (Lima, Carvalho, Wagner, & Morgado, 2022). Such properties (theorems) can be visually constructed and justified based on the Postulates presented.

- If two lines intersect, their intersection is a single point. The result above comes directly from Postulate 1 and guarantees the existence of one of the possible relative positions between lines: concurrent lines.
- If a line r intersects a α plane and is not contained there, the intersection is a single point. The above statement shows one of the possible relative positions between the line and the plane, in which the line is secant to the plane and is obtained through the analysis of Postulate 3.
- Given a line s and a point P outside it, there is a single plane that contains the point and the line. The construction that justifies the presented result is given by combining Postulates 1 and 2.

All these subjects were seen in the book and with reading and discussion of each topic addressed, all being shown with representations drawn on the blackboard.

It was observed that the students had a lot of difficulty, especially in being able to visualize the objects, since on the blackboard we do not have a three-dimensional perception of what was drawn. One of the two classes was used only with repetitions and tries to find simpler ways for the content to be assimilated satisfactorily.

2nd Meeting (2h/Class)

At the 2nd meeting exercises proposed in the book were discussed. Even with the teacher drawing the objects of the exercises on the blackboard, the students claimed to have difficulty understanding. As students had difficulty in executing even the simplest exercises in the book, this led to a review. In turn, it made it impossible to explore the most complex exercises.

3rd Meeting (2h/Class)

At the 3º meeting a debate was held on Euclid's postulate and relative positions between two lines. Even with the effort to use of sheets and pens, it was not successful. Many of the students could not have a spatial perception of the information presented, nor understand the content clearly. They had difficulties in understanding the definition of reverse lines and some exercises in which a little more spatial perception was needed. The content was reviewed several times until the end of the classes, but even so, there were still some doubts and questions from students about the content covered.

4th Meeting (2h/Class)

It was then realized the need for more 2h/class to try new ways and means of introducing the content about relative positions between two lines. Finally, the evolution in solving the exercises proposed in the book can start, all being shown and visualized on the blackboard. Some improvements were obtained, but it was still clearly perceived that the students had difficulties.

In this part of the content, the difficulty of the students in relation to the visualization of the objects became even more clear, even though they were represented in the book. It was noticed by the interactions of the students that even with the reading, the debate and the figures shown on the blackboard, there was not a satisfactory learning.

The use of sheets as a representation of planes and pens to stand for lines was then approached again; but even so, the difficulty in understanding and visualizing the objects was evident.

5th Meeting (2h/Class)

The class started with a brief explanation of what relative positions between planes are about. As this part of the content is a little smaller, it was possible to approach it in a faster and more practical way, taking only 2h/class, being 1h/class for exercises proposed in the book and some for fixing on the blackboard.

It was noticed that again the visualization of objects was the greatest difficulties of the students. However, there was a slight improvement in understanding compared to previous contents. This is evident when observing that the students during the resolution of the exercises did not have as many difficulties, only in some more complex ones.

6th Meeting (2h/Class)

At this point in the classes, several complaints were already heard from students that the content was boring, monotonous, and exceedingly difficult. The topic of the day was the debate of what would be the relative positions between line and plane. Once again, because the subject is smaller than the others, there were not as many problems to advance.

Again, even with a small content, it took 2h/class for the students to understand what was proposed in the class, because in the part of the exercises without the visualization of the objects, they felt difficulties and even a little frustration for not being able to answer correctly. The exercises.

7th Meeting (2h/Class)

The class began with a brief explanation of what parallelism is, followed by using the textbook for debates and visualization of objects, in addition to the use of sheets and pens to represent, respectively, planes and lines.

Several topics were discussed many times to clarify as much as possible and leave no doubts, even so it was not possible to complete all the content prepared for these classes and this made another meeting to be used to finish the content.

8th Meeting (2h/Class)

Continuing the content of parallelism, once again with the reading and debate of some properties and theorems, and with the use of some materials such as pens and sheets to try to ease learning.

A lot of time was spent explaining the subject, in attempts to use the blackboard as a visualization, and in the use of sheets and pens, as it was never clear to all students. This was easily perceived when solving exercises, in which it was clear that even in the simplest exercises, the students felt difficulties in visualization and consequently in giving a correct answer.

9th Meeting (2h/Class)

The class began with a small explanation of what would be seen in the perpendicularity content, which is certainly one of the biggest parts of the subject's content, and one of greater difficulty in understanding. Added to this the approach of the date of the final exams (bimonthly tests), there were serious difficulties to present the content.

This was followed by reading the properties, theorems, and postulates followed by visualizations on the blackboard and in the book. It was noticed in the students that there was much more difficulty than in previous classes. What was heard was several complaints and discontent, as well as a lack of interest in the content.

The first meeting was used to show the content and discuss what was learned, but it was not possible once again to show all the content proposed for this meeting.

10th Meeting (2h/Class)

In the last meeting before the bimonthly test, the last part of the perpendicularity content was shown and some exercises proposed in the book were solved, all of these using the same method of blackboard and chalk and reading the properties in the text.

A brief review of all spatial geometry content applied so far was conducted, as there would be the end of classes with the bimonthly tests.

What can be observed is that at the end of 10 meetings (totaling 20h/class) the students had great difficulties in:

- Understanding of the content presented through the blackboard and chalk and material present in the textbook of the discipline.
- In solving the exercises proposed in the textbook, however simple they may be,
- In addition to a general feeling of demotivation in the class.

Class2: Content Presented With AR, 3D, and Textbook

Class2 had a set of only four meetings of 2h/class each. This significant reduction in meetings was due to problems with school transport. The approach was through the application of material in AR and 3D visualization, previously developed by the teacher. For the presentation to students, the school's presentation viewing equipment was used, in addition to the teacher's notebook and webcam. The distribution of content by meetings took place as follows:

1st Meeting (2h/Class)

Initially, the technologies that would be used in conjunction with the textbook were presented to the students: computer, webcam, presentation viewing equipment, and

Figure 10. Introducing AR and FLARAS.

SketchUp. The students were very interested and excited. Soon after, a brief notion of what would be Augmented Reality and the FLARAS program was presented, in addition to some examples (Figure 10), which caused some uproar as it was a technology that they had not yet seen.

At the 1st meeting with all students with their books open on the spatial geometry chapter. The class then began with a little explanation of what spatial geometry means and its importance to society.

Soon after, it was discussed a little about what is deduction and then the students were shown the concept of point, line, and plane. It was also discussed what a line segment, vertex of an angle, and polygons would be.

At these points, the students did not experience difficulties, even so each of these topics were approached with the SketchUp tool. It was noticed that they managed to have a positive reaction both in terms of understanding and in a more practical and meaningful approach. The approach of the first postulates described in the book was continued, with the students themselves reading and trying to absorb the content.

There were some difficulties in understanding the concepts, and this made it possible to use SketchUp once again to help with the visualization of the concepts. It was noticed that it was a very constructive experience, due to the dynamics in which they read the postulate, while the teacher created the drawing in the tool. It was observed that this made them have an exceptionally good understanding. Some had difficulties, but when it was shown the second time it was clear to them.

Soon after the postulates were presented, three theorems were read and shown, all with the use of the FLARAS tool in augmented reality, and this tool created a twist, all the students started to comment, and it even generated a little confusion because of the conversation, but silence was asked, and the class proceeded quietly. It was clear that all of the students were more interested because they were interacting with the objects.

As the students were excited about the novelty and also enjoying it, as they proved that they understood the subject more easily, some exercises were done from the book itself. They were asked to do it in the notebook, and then it was solved together using SketchUp. It became even more evident that everyone had a great understanding of the content, since there was an average of 85% correct answers and few doubts.

It was noted that there was an improvement in learning since the same exercises from the previous year were used with the teaching of the blackboard and chalk and the students had a certain ease in responding clearly and quickly. It was also evident that there was a better transition of students' knowledge from the concrete to the abstract.

In preparing the lesson plans, the end of this class would be at this point, but as there was a good response from the students and there was still time for h/class, the next part of the content began: relative positions between two lines.

It was shown what coplanar lines are with the help of FLARAS. It was shown what are parallel lines, Euclid's postulate, concurrent lines, and reverse lines. No complaints or claims were made for not understanding the content; all claimed to understand it clearly.

Soon after, some exercises from the book would be started, but unfortunately the meeting's class time is over. The students themselves asked to be shown a little more of the content, which was not possible, since the teacher of another subject was already waiting to enter the room.

2nd Meeting (2h/Class)

Starting by solving some exercises in the book without using the tool to feel if all the content shown was really being absorbed by the students, a good improvement was noticed than Class1, as there were very few doubts and questions from the students.

The class continued with the demonstration of some more theorems, now of relative positions between two planes, these being shown with the help of FLARAS; the result obtained was particularly good, since in Class1 there were some difficulties, especially when two planes are concurrent, as the students felt exceedingly difficult to visualize.

It was then followed by relative positions between line and plane, and some more theorems, these visualized in SketchUp. It is important to note that in Class1, to reach this point, eight classes had already passed. Therefore, all content was addressed faster and more clearly.

Soon after, some exercises in the book were repeated without the help of the tools. In some of them there was the drawing in the book, and in others there was no drawing, even so, superior results were observed, since in Class1 there were difficulties and lack of interest in solving problems.

In these 2h/class it was shown all the content that had been programmed and even more exercises than expected. This means that once again the use of the tool allowed impressive results, including the students' interest in knowing how the tools were used. Ten minutes of class were used to show students how drawings were made in SketchUp and how they were used in FLARAS.

3rd Meeting (2h/Class)

The class started with the theorem on the properties of parallelism, which is shown in FLARAS. There was a good understanding of the students regarding this issue; we continued with some more properties and more theorems, all of which were shown with SketchUp and with the help of FLARAS.

There were some difficulties in the theorem in which a plane intersects two other planes forming two parallel lines, but with the construction of SketchUp, a considerable improvement in learning was noticed. Soon after all the parallelism content, some exercises proposed in the book were conducted and most of the students were able to solve the problems even without the help of the visualization in the tool. Then after they answered, they were shown the answers with the help of SketchUp.

It was then continued with the properties of perpendicularity, the theorems and properties being read by the students and shown in SketchUp and FLARAS. In this part of the content, there was a little difficulty in understanding the content, considering that it really is a larger part than the others.

With some repetitions and visualizations in SketchUp, success was achieved in learning, since soon after, some more exercises proposed in the book were applied, where students showed little difficulty in reaching the resolution. Even so, it is worth noting that they performed much better than in Class1.

4th Meeting (2h/Class)

As this was the last day of class before the bimonthly tests, the students were presented with basic concepts of polyhedron content, showing their characteristics such as face, edge, and vertex, which were shown in SketchUp in a simple and straightforward way, which generated a reaction student in terms of understanding.

It was then followed by showing some three-dimensional objects and polyhedron mentioned in the book were also created with the help of SketchUp. As there was a satisfactory learning process, nonplanar geometric solids of irregular shapes and nonconvex polyhedron were also shown.

In Class1 we had ten meetings and even, so it was not possible to address the content of the polyhedron, the most that was achieved was to get to the perpendicularity part, with many objections, complaints, and discussions about how this content was boring, sleepy, and exceedingly difficult to understand.

It is observed that, even having a little less than half of the classes of Class1, there was a considerable improvement in the learning, commitment, and interest of the class.

With that, there was time to show some notions of prisms, even if in a superficial and more simplified way: what is height, base, edges, faces and some classifications of straight prisms were also addressed; we also saw pyramids and their classifications, being in these only their shapes were worked, how to recognize parallel and perpendicular lines.

These objects were shown both with the help of FLARAS and with the help of SketchUp. To conclude this content, Plato's five polyhedrons were approached and three were shown with the help of FLARAS: the regular tetrahedron (Figure 11), the regular hexahedron and the regular octahedron. The others are not shown due to the complexity of creating objects in SketchUp.

Figure 11. Regular tetrahedron with FLARAS.

Finally, it was possible to apply, even in a basic and simplified way, some characteristics and classifications of cones and cylinders. After all the content was covered, a question was applied to test whether the students would be able to advance a little further if there were more time; the question was as follows.

Find the diagonal of the base d and the diagonal D of the cube below (Figure 12) knowing that a=8.

Shown with the help of SketchUp, with a little explanation and a little review of the Pythagorean theorem; they were able to understand what was asked and solve the problem on their own without complaints or tribulations.

It should be noted that with Class1 we had ten meetings and even so it was not possible to address the content of polyhedric, the most we could do was to reach

Figure 12. Example exercise using SketchUp as a support.

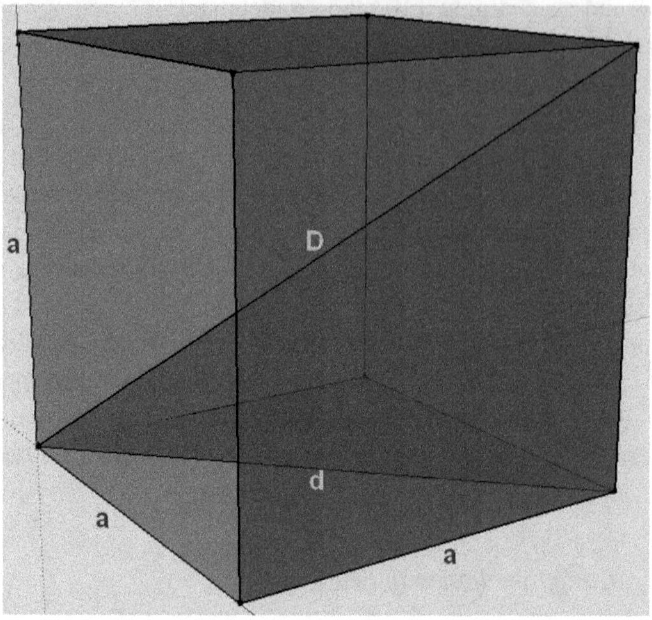

the part of perpendicularity and how many objections, complaints, and discussions of how this content was boring, gave sleep, and difficult for understanding. It is observed that, even having a little less than half of the classes than Class1 had, for this class we achieved a considerable improvement in the learning, commitment, and interest of the class, compared with Class1.

CONCLUSION

The focus of this paper is to present the experience report on the use of Augmented Reality using tutorials developed by NIEP group, aiming to generate personalized material for use in the classroom by high school students in Mathematics, in the teaching/learning of Space Geometry. The results found demonstrate improved learning, better understanding of the content and reduced learning time.

Geometry is a branch of Mathematics that helps us to work with distances, volumes, and areas in the real world. However, learning content related to Spatial Geometry, whose visual appeal should be an invitation to study, presents an unusual obstacle for the student:

- how to understand the elements of a three-dimensional object if they are normally presented in a two-dimensional way (e.g., drawn on the blackboard or book)?

There is several software that can be used in the teaching of Space Geometry. However, in most times, the teacher has no contact with these tools, either due to unavailability of hardware to interact; or due to difficulty in acquiring the software, which in turn may be due to the cost or lack of knowledge of the means to make the acquisition.

In this sense, the authors followed the proposal to use tutorials to facilitate the independence of the mathematics teacher, so that he could build the class following his style and didactics.

The use of technologies that would effectively be available for use was also sought for personal computer, webcam, and presentation viewing equipment.

Despite the difficulties presented, the use of AR with FLARAS and SketchUp tools applied in Class2 proved to be a good proposal for classroom work, both for the teacher in terms of motivation and for the students as a facilitator in understanding the content covered. Since in only four meetings in Class2, all the content that was applied in Class1 was addressed. That is, in 30% of the time spent with Class1, it was possible to explore all the content planned for Class2. In addition to having time to explore and discuss another part of the book that was not programmed in the lesson plans: the study of polyhedron.

SOLUTIONS AND RECOMMENDATIONS

The application of Augmented Reality and 3D visualization was made by the authors in a class (Class2) and compared with another class (Class1) that had the presentation of content in a traditional way (blackboard and chalk). Both classes were from the 2nd year of high school in a public school in Brazil.

Reinforcing, in the first class, called Class1, resources normally available were used: textbook, blackboard, and chalk, as well as sheets and pens to illustrate the concepts of plane and line. In the second class, called Class2, were used, in addition to the textbook, blackboard, and chalk, AR (FLARAS) and RV (SketchUp).

It was expected that with the aid of Augmented Reality, students in Class2 would perform better than Class1. A better understanding of the content was expected since they would have better visualization of the spatial objects. Consequently, better performance in exercises and problems was expected.

However, what was observed on the first day of class with Class2 is that this advance was greater than expected. To teach the first part of the content (point,

Table 2. Comparison between Class1 and Class2.

<table>
<tr><th></th><th>Class1</th><th>Class2</th></tr>
<tr><td>Point, line, and plane</td><td>4 h/class</td><td rowspan="2">2 h/class</td></tr>
<tr><td>Relative positions between two lines</td><td>4 h/class</td></tr>
<tr><td>Relative positions between two planes</td><td>2 h/class</td><td rowspan="2">2 h/class</td></tr>
<tr><td>Relative positions between line and plane</td><td>2 h/class</td></tr>
<tr><td>Parallelism</td><td>4 h/class</td><td rowspan="2">2 h/class</td></tr>
<tr><td>Perpendicularity</td><td>4 h/class</td></tr>
<tr><td>Polyhedrons</td><td>There was no time.</td><td>2 h/class</td></tr>
<tr><td>Total meetings</td><td>10 meetings of 2h/class</td><td>4 meetings of 2h/class</td></tr>
</table>

line, and plane), it was only necessary 25% of the class time. Additionally, it was noticed that the content was learned in class2 much more clearly and objectively than in class1. It was still possible to solve, in the classroom, several more exercises proposed in the textbook.

It can be seen in Table 1 that the Table 1that the distribution of time for each content in each of the classes (Class1 and Class2) is significantly different. It is necessary to remember that Class2 had this time reduction due to students' school transport problems, which directly impacted the amount of time available for the subject's contents during that evaluation bimester.

In the second meeting with Class2, the content that was scheduled for the next meeting began: relative positions between two plans. Then it is observed that it took six hours / class less in Class2 than in Class1 to reach the same content.

In the third meeting with Class2 exercises were applied. And significant changes were observed in the learning quality of Class2 students, since they participated more and had an easier time understanding all the content that was exposed, in addition to interacting more. An improvement in the comprehension of the content and in the resolution of the exercises in the book was noticed, as well as in the questions related to the content, even for the most complex questions.

It should be noted that in just four meetings, that is, in two weeks, all the content that had been applied in Class1 was addressed. In 30% of the time spent with Class 1, it was possible to explore all the planned content. In addition to having time to explore and discuss another part of the book that was not programmed in the lesson plans: the study of polyhedron.

It can be concluded for this first practical experiment that the use of AR and 3D visualization with the proposed tools resulted in the following.

- More productive classes.

- More participatory students.
- With much more advanced understanding than in Class1.

Furthermore, it was observed that students felt more motivated to participate in classes, either by asking questions or when solving exercises. Including requesting that we have more classes and that they are longer than the regular time.

DIFFICULTIES FOUND

Regarding the use of AR technology, the greatest difficulty was the use of the 2.2 MP webcam leadership equipment. In some moments during classes, with the movement, the equipment disconnected and ended up interrupting the execution (crashing) of FLARAS. Therefore, it was necessary to restart the program, which does not require much time, but hinders the continuity of the class.

The equipment was old, both the webcam and the computer. Therefore, the USB port connection was soft and resulted in disconnection when moving the webcam cable. With newer equipment, this does not happen. Another alternative would be a support to fix the webcam and thus move only the AR tag.

There was also difficulty in allocating the presentation viewing equipment, as other teachers wanted to use it as well. It is known that this equipment is still a scarce or missing resource in many schools.

It is observed that over the years Brazilian public schools have received more of this equipment. In addition, the authors understand that, in the reality of Brazilian public schools, it is easier to have equipment for the teacher to collectively present the content to students than for students to have smartphones that run AR applications.

Another difficulty that the authors thought might exist was the inability to maximize the AR presentation screen in FLARAS. It was imagined that the image of the 3D object would be too reduced.

However, the practice proved to be the opposite, since in the presentation viewing equipment (due to a natural low resolution) the image is enlarged and with good visualization.

There were also difficulties regarding the modeling of 3D objects. Originally the proposal was to use only FLARAS, however certain models proved to be too difficult to be conducted, or even, they did not present an adequate result. For example:

- If the object is painted with some colors, at the time of presentation at FLARAS only a part of the object appears, that is, that part that is painted in a certain color.

- There are also some cases where letters, symbols, and numbers appear in SketchUp (Figure 12) but do not appear when the virtual object is used in FLARAS (Figure 13). It is important to observe how the visualization of the 3D object is impaired due to the limitations of rendering of the software and of the visualization in the presentation equipment. In addition to practically all the variables not appearing and the transparency effect being very poorly rendered, there is still great difficulty in visualizing the main element in question: the diagonal D and how it should be understood by students. It is observed that the same visualization problem is seen in Figure 11.
- Lack of repositories focused on teaching spatial geometry.

The solution found was the use of 3D visualization of the objects generated and presented in SketchUp.

Figure 13. AR visualization with FLARAS.

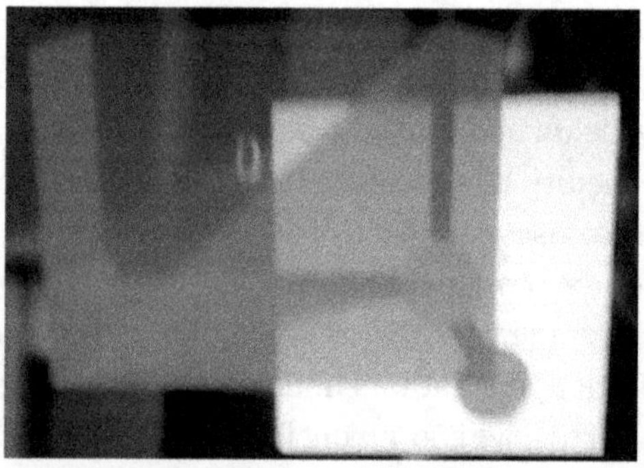

LIMITATIONS

The authors observed that the results achieved were quite expressive. However, it should be noted that more experimentation with new classes is needed. Due to operationalization and temporality issues, the experiment was carried out with only one class.

The authors emphasize that it is important to consider that the class approached was in a Brazilian high school. This context encompasses a type of student profile that normally has a more fragile socio-economic situation. If, on the one hand, this characteristic of the class increases the importance of the result obtained, it also increases the need for new experiments.

Another point to be noted is that the class was considered as a collective and not because of the individual characteristics of the students. Still, at this point, it should be noted that the proposal for viewing 3D objects is not applicable for people with visual impairments. It was also not considered how the technique impacts students on the autistic spectrum.

In the case of students with visual impairments, the authors point out that concrete objects are still needed (Figure 2, Figure 3 and Figure 4).

Regarding students on the autistic spectrum, the authors reinforce the need for specific research for this audience.

Another point to be noted was the time available for Class2, which was significantly reduced and did not allow a complete observation and evaluation of the results achieved with the use of Augmented Reality and 3D Visualization.

Another point to be noted is the mathematics teacher himself. Being an enthusiast and strongly interested in computational technologies, he can generate results that perhaps a less interested teacher would obtain. It is important to emphasize that the teacher had the knowledge to even use the computational tools and generate the examples and constructions in real time. In this sense, it is necessary to expand the experiment to other teacher profiles.

Finally, the authors point out that there is a limitation facing the technology itself. Both from the point of view of there being a need for computer equipment for effective use; as well as the software involved. SketchUp in its latest versions imposes limitations that the version originally used in the experiment did not have. FLARAS is based on an already outdated technology (Flash) and current alternatives for Augmented Reality require equipment that many students and teachers from Brazilian public schools do not have access to.

FUTURE RESEARCH DIRECTIONS

As next steps in the research, the authors point out:

- Apply the approach with other classes to verify that the agility of presentation of the content and its ease of absorption are kept.
- Verify that the use of other AR technologies (O.S. native APIs) do not present the visualization problems encountered.
- Development of a repository with the generated objects, both in its 3D visualization version and in the version visible by an AR application.
- Publication of this object repository so that other teachers can use and expand it.
- Incorporate an AR application running on a smartphone, such as ARCore or ARToolkit, so that students can access objects for self-study of content.

ACKNOWLEDGMENT

The authors are grateful for the space at UEPB so that studies and development of the materials could be carried out.

REFERENCES

Araujo, G. V. (2017). *The Use of Augmented Reality in the Teaching of Regular Convex Polyhedra.* Dourados: UEMS Profmat.

Brito, F. d. (2014). *The use of software in the teaching of positional spatial geometry.* Universidade Federal De Lavras, Programa de Pós- Graduação Profissional em Matemática. Retrieved from http://repositorio.ufla.br/jspui/handle/1/2191

Deng, L., Tian, J., Cornwell, C., Phillips, V., Chen, L., & Alsuwaida, A. (2019). Towards an Augmented Reality-Based Mobile Math Learning Game System. *International Conference on Human-Computer Interaction.* 10.1007/978-3-030-23525-3_28

Dolce, O., & Pompeo, J. N. (2019). *Fundamentals of Elementary Mathematics* (Vol. 10). Saraiva Didáticos.

Fanelli, R. P. (2013). *Alternatives for teaching spatial geometry.* Universidade Estadual de Mato Grosso do Sul, Dourados.

França, J. S. (2015). A didactic proposal of augmented reality in the teaching of sapce geometry. UFPA, Programa pos-graduação em matemática em rede nacional.

GeoGebra. (2022). *Geogebra - the world's favorite, free math tools used by over 100 million students and teachers*. Retrieved from GeoGebra for Teaching and Learning Math: https://www.geogebra.org/

Inter IKEA Systems. (2022). *Inter IKEA Group*. Retrieved from Inter IKEA Group: https://www.inter.ikea.com/en

Lee, H. S. L. J. (2008). Mathematical Education Game Based on Augmented Reality. Technologies for E-Learning and Digital Entertainment.

Lemos, B. M., & Carvalho, C. V. (2010, Julho). Use of augmented reality to support the understanding of the Euler relationship. *Novas Tecnologias na Educação.*

Lima, A. J., Haguenauer, C. J., & Cunha, G. G. (2007). Augmented Reality In Teaching Descriptive Geometry. *VII International Conference on Graphics Engineering for Arts and Design.*

Lima, E. L., Carvalho, P. C., Wagner, E., & Morgado, A. C. (2022). *High School Mathematics* (Vol. 2). SBM.

Moraes, L. d. (2014). *Spatial geometry in high school: A study on the use of concrete material in problem solving*. Universidade Federal do Estado Rio de Janeiro.

Niantic, Inc. (2022). *Pokémon GO*. Retrieved from Pokémon GO: https://pokemongolive.com/en/

Noval, M. D. (2013). *Augmented reality in mathematics teaching: a case study*. Universidade de Trás-os-Montes e Alto Douro. Retrieved from https://catalogo.biblioteca.utad.pt/cgi-bin/koha/opac-detail.pl?biblionumber=66150

Pereira, D. D. (2014). *Use of Augmented Reality as a Support Tool for Teaching Spatial Geometry in the 2nd Year of High School: Use of FLARAS and Google Sketchup Tools*. Universidade Estadual da Paraíba.

Perfect Corp. (2022). *YouCam Makeup: Best Selfie Editor*. Retrieved from YouCam Makeup: Best Selfie Editor: https://www.perfectcorp.com/consumer/apps/ymk

Radu, I., McCarthy, B., & Kao, Y. (2016). Discovering educational augmented reality math applications by prototyping with elementary-school teachers. IEEE Virtual Reality (VR).

Raymundo, M. F. (2010). *Work plan on pyramid and cone*. Colégio Estadual Dr. João Nery. Rio de Janeiro: Formação continuada para professores de matemática Fundação CECIERJ/SEEDUC-RJ. Retrieved from https://www.google.com/url?sa=t&rct=j&q=&esrc=s&source=web&cd=&ved=2ahUKEwjGtsHM26f3AhXHY98KHRzoDOcQFnoECCYQAQ&url=https%3A%2F%2Fcanal.cecierj.edu.br%2Fanexos%2Frecurso_interno%2F12780%2Fdownload%2F057d5b3bfc142f883063f48da78e4ddd&usg=AOvVaw0L8QXs3-xXcRVe

Reis, F. M., & Kirner, T. G. (2012). Students' Perception of the Usability of an Interactive Book with Augmented Reality for Learning Geometry. *RENOTE Revista Novas Tecnologias na Educação*. doi:10.22456/1679-1916.30814

Rodrigues, R. L., Soares, M., Souza, G. G., Lacerda, A., Souza, C., Gomes, A., & Alves, C. (2010). *Augmented Reality for the Teaching of Spatial Geometry*. CBIE.

Smole, K. S., & Diniz, M. I. (2019). *Mathematics - High School - 2nd grade* (Vol. 2). Saraiva Didáticos.

Souza, R. C., & Kirner, C. (2012). *Flaras +*. Retrieved 2015, from http://ckirner.com/flaras2/

Souza, S. d. (2004). *Using Winplot.* UFPB, Matemática. Retrieved from http://www.mat.ufpb.br/sergio/winplot/winplot.html

Tori, R., Kirner, C., & Siscoutto, R. (2006). *Fundamentals and Technologies of Virtual and Augmented Reality*. SBC.

Zorzal, E. R., Cardoso, A., Kirner, C., & Júnior, E. L. (2006). Augmented Reality Applied in Educational Games. *V Workshop de Educação em Computação e Informática do Estado de Minas Gerais.*

KEY TERMS AND DEFINITIONS

3D Visualization: Visualization of computer-created objects on computer or smartphones. There is no overlap of the object in the real environment.

Application (App): Software created for computers or smartphones that make it possible to carry out activities with these devices.

Augmented Reality (AR): Visualization of objects created by the computer and superimposed on the real environment. Usually through a smartphone or using a webcam connected to a computer.

Blackboard: The blackboard is a common device in Brazilian schools. Usually in public schools it is found in the form for using chalk. It can also be found in formica or glass for whiteboard marker use.

Brazilian High School: School environment maintained by public entities, be they Municipality, State or Federal State. Free access school.

FLARAS: Free application created to easily allow the use of Augmented Reality. Runs only on a personal computer.

SketchUp: Application that has a free version and allows the creation of 3D objects.

Spatial Geometry: It is a branch of mathematics that studies the measurements and properties of figures, being divided into two subareas, in addition to spatial geometry: plane geometry (responsible for the study of the plane and space) and analytic geometry (which is related to algebra). and mathematical analysis).

Chapter 9
Virtualization of Laboratories:
Student and Professor Opinions

Diego Vergara
https://orcid.org/0000-0003-3710-4818
Catholic University of Avila, Spain

Pablo Fernández-Arias
Catholic University of Avila, Spain

Jamil Extremera
University of Salamanca, Spain

Álvaro Antón-Sancho
Catholic University of Avila, Spain

ABSTRACT

The use of virtual reality (VR) in the educational sector has increased considerably in the last decade, especially for its direct application in the development of virtual laboratories (VL) that, since the appearance of COVID-19, are being more demanded by universities. Therefore, knowing the opinion of students and professors about VR is essential for VR-based applications to be designed in an appropriate way and to be efficient at an educational level. In this sense, the results of this study, which analyzes the opinion of 420 engineering students and 44 engineering professors, can help future professors or software programmers in general to design VR-based educational resources in an appropriate way and in particular to better design their VLs.

DOI: 10.4018/978-1-6684-3398-0.ch009

INTRODUCTION

New technologies have transformed the world since the end of the 20th century, accelerating the radical change in society and the economy, which these first two decades of the 21st century have identified. An example of this change is the many tasks that were performed manually in the past that have been automated in recent years. And as a result, the labor landscape of today's society has been profoundly altered. Another example of how new technologies have differentiated today's society from that of the 20th century is in the scenario that originated from the COVID-19 pandemic. Indeed, since the pandemic was declared, the use of new technologies has allowed a large part of the economic sectors to continue their activity in a relatively normal and safe way, thanks to remote work. That is, teleworking has been promoted. Currently, most of society uses information and communication technologies (ICT) daily, making a new way of life and social behavior.

Thus, most remote personal communications are carried out through instant messaging services, which is a change from what happened just 30 years ago when the most common communication method was phone calls. In the same way, electronic mail has almost completely replaced postal mail (both in the personal sphere and between institutions or companies); the creation and sharing of images and videos have displaced much of the information that was once shared through text; social networks have created a new concept of the relationship between people from all over the world; etc. Such is the influence of ICTs on society that two new adjectives emerge to define people (Prensky, 2016): (i) digital natives, who are those individuals who were born with the ICT revolution already consolidated; and (ii) digital immigrants, who are those who were born before the ICT revolution began, and from a certain point in their life have had to update their knowledge and adapt their habits to this new reality. Even the first group of digital natives differentiates those who were born without the internet that we know today (millennials or generation Y) and those who were born with the current network of networks (internet generation or generation Z).

The education sector is no stranger to this ICT revolution, being today a sector in which digital transformation is an unstoppable event. In this way, instructors often implement new ICT-based methodologies in the classroom to capture the attention of the students and motivate them to study different subjects, regardless of educational level. In this sense, practical classes traditionally developed in laboratories (e.g., in which experiments are carried out) are moving to virtual worlds (Soliman et al., 2021).

Two of the most promising technologies with the best results when developing virtual laboratories (VLs) are: (i) virtual reality (VR); and (ii) augmented reality (AR). The so-called mixed reality (MR) is a set of technologies that combine VR and AR. Specifically, the MR user interacts with physical and virtual reality objects at the same time (Quint et al., 2015). In technical fields, MR allows, for example, to compare potential developments of a project with its current development, which, in turn, helps to locate problems in the progress of the project and to solve them, or to foresee the evolution of the project (Wu et al., 2018). Likewise, regarding its applicability in educational environments, the literature does not find significant differences between the academic use of VR and MR, although VR is interpreted as a more natural environment for learning than MR (Ergün et al., 2019).

Within VR, a distinction can be made between immersive virtual reality (IVR) and non-immersive virtual reality (NIVR). IVR uses mechanisms, such as special glasses, to provide a complete sensory experience, so that the user acquires the realistic sensation of being immersed in the environment being simulated. NIV allows the user to interact with the virtual world through certain mechanisms, such as the monitor or keyboard, which do not immerse the user in the simulated environment. Both technologies (VR and AR) have revolutionized both the education sector and the professional sector (Kamińska et al., 2017). In the specific case of VR, it has proven to be an effective tool for learning in higher education in various areas of knowledge, including engineering and architecture (Wang et al., 2018; Mirauda et al., 2019; Safikhani et al., 2022), health sciences (King et al., 2018), sciences (Durukan et al., 2020) or arts and humanities (Paatela-Nieminen, 2021). This statement is reinforced by the data illustrated in Figure 1, which shows the number of research works indexed in Scopus that contain the expression "virtual reality" in their title, abstract, or keywords, and that have been published in last decade (2012-2021). This extends the authors' analysis conducted in the areas of engineering and medicine to the year 2021 (Vergara et al., 2021). According to previous papers of the authors (Vergara et al, 2022a), four periods can be distinguished in the present century in relation to the evolution of scientific production related to VR: (i) 2000-2006, from the release of the first VR-based video game ARQuake to the global economic crisis of 2007; (ii) 2006-2012, characterized by a phase of stagnation due to the economic crisis and the high cost of VR devices; (iii) 2012-2016, where Oculus Rift and Google Cardboard were launched; and (iv) 2016-to date, where the development and use of new VR devices (Samsung Gear, Play Station VR, HTC Vive Pro, etc.) has been boosted in almost every field. This way, Figure 1 shows the evolution of the publications indexed in Scopus in this last period, differentiating between the papers, reviews, and book chapter (dashed line), on one hand, and the conference papers and conference reviews (dotted line), on the other hand. In addition, the total number of publications is represented in this Figure 1 (solid line), where a clear increasing trend in VR research is also observed, which evidences the great interest of the scientific community in this topic. Besides, it appears that, except for the last two years, the Scopus database contains a greater number of research works presented at conferences than published in journals. This growing trend also marks

Figure 1. Number of publications indexed in SCOPUS in last decade (2012-2021), which include "virtual reality" in the title, abstract, or keywords.
Source: Own preparation.

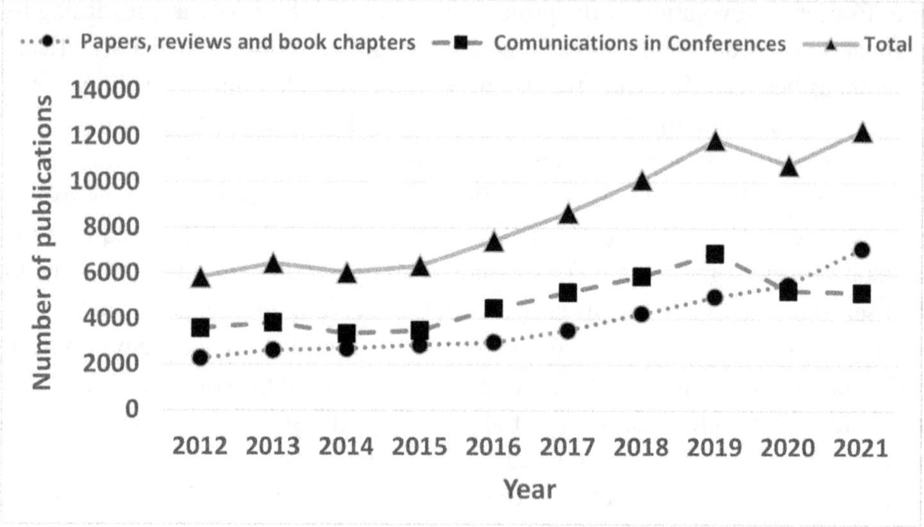

a paradigm shift in university teaching since the use of VR is increasingly relevant at this educational level of teaching. The progressive cheapening of the VR devices has had an impact at a more affordable price for the public and this, in turn, in an expansion of the use of VR devices in different sectors.

In the specific fields of science and technology, the consideration of VLs is of particular interest. VLs allow the student to interact with the objects and procedures of a real laboratory (RL), but through the techniques provided by VR, which overcomes the limitations of RLs, such as the lack of modern and updated laboratory equipment or the high costs of its acquisition (Balamuralithara and Woods, 2009; Potkonjak et al., 2016). The present research is focused on the authors' experience using VLs in the practical teaching of Mechanical and Civil Engineering courses (Figure 2).

The main objective of this research is to analyze the perspective that a set of students and a set of professors of engineering careers have about the didactic use of VR technologies in the classroom. The participants expressed their assessments after conducting a VR experience through VLs. Two surveys were designed to collect opinions, one for students and one for professors, whose answers have been statistically analyzed.

This work is organized as follows: one section presents the theoretical background on the didactic use of VR and LVs in higher education classrooms in the field of engineering and how such resources should be designed and implemented in the

Figure 2. Different examples of equipment used in Mechanical Engineering courses with VLs: a) universal testing machine, b) industrial radiology and c) compression testing machine.
Source: Own preparation.

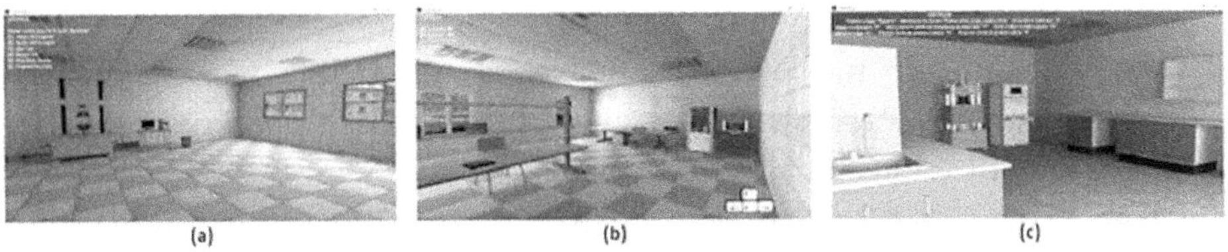

classroom; the next section presents the surveys used to explore the opinions of students and professors of various engineering disciplines (Mechanical Engineering and Civil Engineering) who have participated in the study, presents the results of the statistical analysis carried out on the answers and discusses those results; the final sections present recommendations derived from the results obtained, future lines of research opened by the present work and the main conclusions of the study.

BACKGROUND

The use of VR-based resources in the teaching-learning process has been implemented for several decades (Vergara et al., 2017a) and, although some studies highlight the lack of use of the potential that this type of technology presents, the advantages that VLs present from an educational point of view have been analyzed by different authors in countless articles, some of them are:

- They represent a minimal expense when compared with the investment involved in installing a real lab (RL) and, besides, they do not require a maintenance cost (Román-Ibáñez et al., 2018) to keep them running (although they do have a cost of periodic updating (Balali et al., 2020)).
- Avoid or prevent potential damage that can arise from misuse with a real machine (Vergara and Rubio, 2012).
- Reduce the space occupied by large equipment installed in RLs (Vergara et al., 2017b).
- Avoid problems or accidents that may arise in training carried out in real settings, for example during chemical reactions (Xie and Tinker, 2006), during training in industrial radiology (Vergara and Rubio, 2012), during firefighter training (Cha et al., 2014), during firefighter training technicians working in critical facilities, such as nuclear power plants (Mól et al., 2009),

during training in industrial processes, such as welding (Lee and Cha, 2019), etc.

- Allow access to expensive and sophisticated facilities that would otherwise be virtually impossible to access (Berg and Vance, 2016; Vergara-Rodríguez et al., 2018).
- Allow you to apply transparency options to see hidden parts of a real machine (some machines or tools have protective covers that cannot be removed during a test and, therefore, do not allow you to understand the execution of the test in more details) (Potkonjak et al., 2019).
- Facilitate the instructor's work in large groups of learners since they allow each student to see at his/her own pace the instructor's explanation with the highest level of detail (Vergara et al., 2017b).
- They offer different possibilities that favor the teaching-learning process (Vergara et al., 2018): interactivity options, zone transparency, zooming in to see interesting details, modifying the execution speed of a task to check certain details or obtain related insights, and so on.
- They favor spatial thinking and three-dimensional vision necessary for learning certain technical concepts in some areas, such as materials science (Extremera, 2022).
- They favor the autonomy of the student (Syed et al., 2019) and the personalization of educational practice by facilitating the design desired by the instructor (Llobera et al., 2013).
- Admit to repeating the task as many times as the student wishes (Extremera et al., 2020).
- They include – in many cases – practical exercises that are solved interactively from the virtual laboratory itself, thus completing the process of training the corresponding topic (Vergara et al., 2012; Vergara et al., 2014).
- They promote research opportunities for students who work individually or in a team, guided by an instructor who will need to design pedagogical materials that are effective in terms of content and engagement (Doblack et al., 2014; Meagher et al., 2014; Doblack et al., 2011; Flores et al., 2012).

On the other hand, some drawbacks should be discussed in the present work:

- VL programming, although in general, it does not require the participation of expert programmers, it does need to be carried out by people who have dedicated a considerable amount of time to training in this activity. The same occurs with the creation of virtual environments, which can be modeled by almost anyone who has previously invested some time in learning to handle 3D modeling tools. For these reasons, it is necessary to form a multidisciplinary team to deal with the design of a virtual laboratory (Vergara et al., 2017a) or to hire a specialized company for this purpose.

- Technological obsolescence affects VLs in a relatively quick time, thereby reducing student motivation to use the obsolete tool (Vergara et al., 2020a). Therefore, every few years the instructor must redesign the virtual laboratory so that it continues to be relevant and interesting among the student community.
- Design is essential to achieve optimal results in different educational aspects such as meaningful learning, motivation, etc. (Vergara et al., 2019a; Vergara et al., 2019b), and for this, an essential factor is the instructor's experience (Vergara et al., 2020b), which must be broad for the design to be truly effective at the educational level.
- The training of university faculty regarding their digital competence in general and, in particular, the use of VR, is one of the main disadvantages that hinders the incorporation of VR in the classroom, even if they are engineering professors (Vergara et al., 2022b).
- The cost of VR is an impediment to its implementation in universities regardless of the area of knowledge to which it is applied. This fact is widely reported in the specialized literature (Hilfert, 2016; Halabi, 2020).

The steps to follow to design a virtual laboratory are divided into three levels (Figure 3): (i) determine the usefulness of the virtual laboratory, defining specific objectives – in this case educational – and specific objectives for interactive use; (ii) define the technical design of the virtual laboratory, taking into account the desired levels of realism and interactivity, and (iii) develop and evaluate the virtual laboratory, modifying it as many times as necessary to ensure that the final version of the virtual laboratory meets the objectives desired. It should be noted that the development of a virtual laboratory consists of two different stages: (i) the creation of the 3D virtual environment; and (ii) the programming of the virtual laboratory.

Generally, during the creation of the virtual environment, the rooms, machines, instruments, and other virtual elements are modeled in three-dimensions, materials are applied, and lighting is defined. Although there are different programs that allow these activities to be carried out, some of the most widely used currently are: 3DS Max®, Maya®, and Blender®. Moreover, the programming stage consists of making interactive the virtual environment to allow the students to interact with the virtual laboratory (that is, they can move through the virtual environment, pick up objects, manipulate machines and instruments, receive messages, etc.). Two of the programs most used today at this stage are the Unity 3D® and Unreal Engine 4® game engines.

The implementation procedure in the classroom of the VL is outlined in Figure 4 and consists of the following stages (Vergara et al., 2020):

Figure 3. Flowchart of the VR application design process.
Source: Adapted from Vergara et al. (2017).

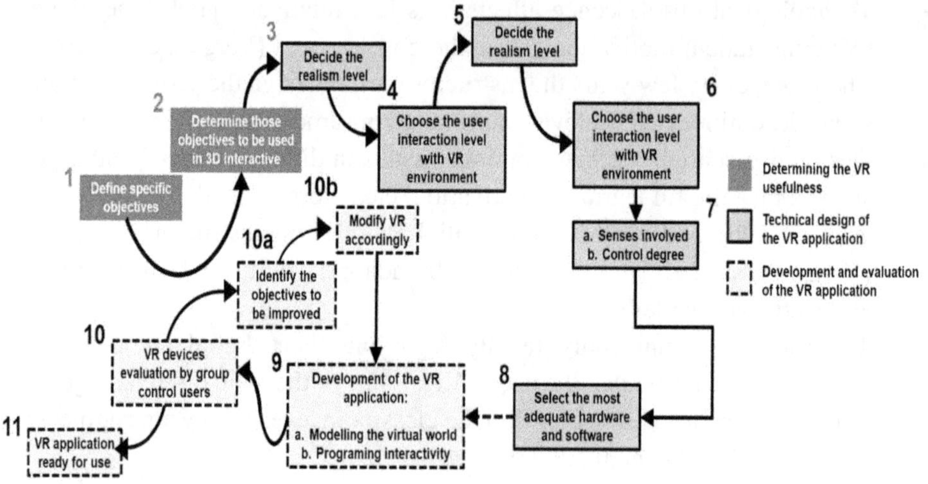

- The instructor of a given subject gives master classes in which he/she explains to the students the concepts related to the laboratory practices that will be carried out. Depending on the subject taught, this stage can last between 2 and 10 hours.
- Each student individually uses a VL under the supervision of the instructor. This stage can last from 30 minutes to 1 hour.
- Students solve practical exercises in groups made up of 2-4 students, which are later commented on and corrected by the instructor. In some subjects this stage, which last approximately 2 hours, can be omitted.
- Once outside the classroom, students have the possibility of using the VL individually (self-study) as many times as they wish.
- Depending on the subject matter under study, the students attend a RL in which they repeat the experiment that they carried out virtually through the VL.
- Students fill out surveys from which data is obtained that is subsequently analyzed to improve the teaching-learning process.

Figure 4. Implementation scheme in the classroom of the VLs.
Source: Adapted from Vergara et al. (2020).

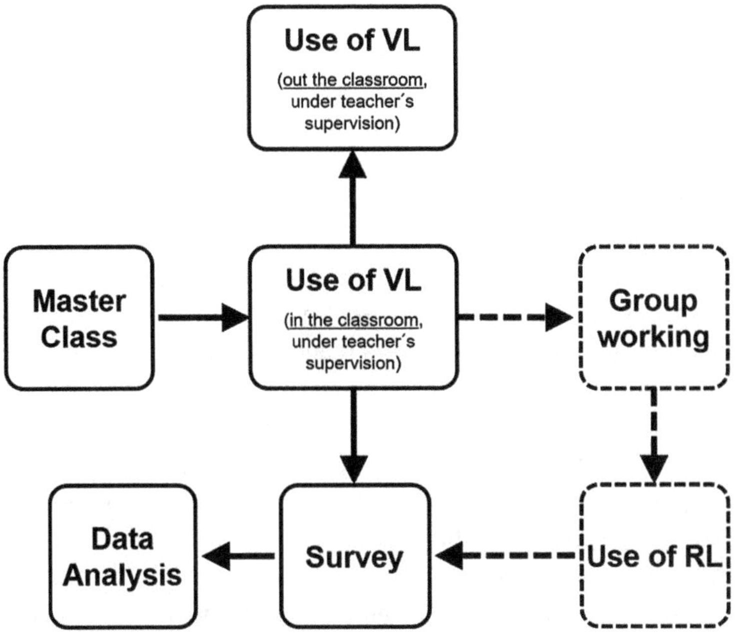

RESULTS AND DISCUSSION

According to the educational experiences lived in recent years with different virtual learning environments, the authors have been able to verify that VR technologies and, specifically, VLs are especially useful for explaining concepts that may be difficult to explain by the instructor in engineering fields, such as situations related to the capacity for spatial vision of the students, in which the instructor is limited to make the students understand something that they are not able to visualize or abstract concepts (e.g. crystallography). In addition, throughout different teaching experiences, the authors have been able to obtain the assessment of 420 students and 44 engineering professors through two different surveys on the use of VR, VLs and RLs to carry out the teaching-learning process. All students were studying Mechanical or Civil Engineering at one of the following universities:

- Spanish universities: (i) Catholic University of Ávila and (ii) University of Salamanca – Higher Polytechnic School of Zamora, Higher Technical School of Industrial Engineering of Béjar, and Higher Polytechnic School of Ávila –.

- Portuguese Polytechnic Institutes, during international teaching stays withing the framework of different LLP Erasmus Programmes: (i) Bragança and (ii) Viseu.

The professors surveyed are also of Spanish or Portuguese nationality and teach at one of the universities mentioned above. From the analysis of the answers of the surveys carried out within the students and professors participating in the study, the IBM SPSS Statistics 25® and Excel® software were used for data curation and as statistical computation tools.

In the case of the students, they answered a survey (Table 1) after having used several VLs in the classroom and also after having practiced in RLs, as it was described in the methodology of implementation of VR and VL in the classroom. As shown in Table 1, the survey used to collect the information is composed by questions related to the effectiveness of the application of the VLs (question 1, Table 1); others were related to the possible methodological changes that the implementation of a virtual laboratory implies (questions 2-4, Table 1); and, finally, a question focused on the design of the VLs (question 5, Table 1).

As results, when asked about the effectiveness of the VLs as methodological resources (question 1, Table 1), the students answered mostly (89%) that the VLs are a useful complement to reinforce and/or clarify the explanations of the instructors (Table 2).

With regard to question 2 (Table 1), students clearly preferred the distribution of practical classes (Table 3). In this case, 89% of the students prefer the combined use of VLs+RLs (option c, question 2 in Table 1), and only 6% prefer the practical classes taught exclusively in the RLs. Among the students who choose this option (89%) – mixed option of VLs+RLs–, all of them decided that most of the hours of the practical classes should take place in real environments (RLs), thus suggesting that virtual environments (VLs) can actually be a complement to the teaching-learning process. The distribution preferred by students (question 3, Table 1) were 71% of practical classes held in a RL and the 29% in the VL (Table 4).

Regarding the preferred distribution of the methodological organization of subject teaching, including practical classes in laboratories (question 4, Table 1), it was found (Table 5) that the master class (MC) is recognized as the most valuable methodology (42%). The problem-solving class (PSC) is valued in second place (28%) as a methodological resource to include when it comes to solving technical concepts, followed by the RLs (14%), VLs (7%), and finally, other virtual resources (9%).

Finally, students were also asked about the basic technical and didactic characteristics of VLs (question 5, Table 1). The results (Table 6) reflect the following ranking in terms of technical aspects of VLs: (i) interactivity: students ranked

Table 1. Questions asked to the students in the survey.

Number	Question	Answer Options
1	In relation to the usefulness of the teaching, you consider that the VL:	a) VLs are a useful complement to reinforce and/or clarify the explanations of the instructor. b) VLs are self-sufficient in explaining the subject matter.
2	In your personal opinion, the practical part of the subject should be taught:	a) Using just VLs. b) Using just the RLs. c) Mixing VLs and RLs, using VLs in the first place. d) Mixing VLs and RLs, using RLs in the first place.
3	If you chose option (c) or (d) in the previous question, what do you consider to be the most appropriate percentage distribution of practical classes?	a) RL: _______% b) VL:_______%
4	In your opinion, what is the most appropriate percentage distribution to be applied in the classroom?	a) Master Classes: ____% b) Problem Solving Classes: ____% c) RL: ____% d) VL: ____% e) Other virtual resources:____%
5	Assess from 1 to 10 the following characteristics of VR technologies when used in learning environments: (a) interactivity; (b) motivation; (c) ease of use; and (d) educational usefulness.	1 to 10 for each aspect.

Source: Adapted from (Vergara et al., 2015).

highest; (ii) ease of use: was ranked second; (iii) motivation: was ranked third; and (iv) educational usefulness: was the least valued. The engineering students valued the interactivity and ease of use with 9.8 mean (μ) out of 10, with a 0.80 standard deviation (σ) and 9.14% of coefficient of variation (C_V). Ease of use resulted 9.3

Table 2. Students' evaluation of VL teaching is useful (Question 1, Table 1).

Answer Option	Results	
	Number of Students (*n*)	Percentage (%)
a) VLs are a useful complement to reinforce and/or clarify the explanations of the instructor.	373	88.81%
b) VLs are self-sufficient in explaining the subject matter	47	11.19%

Source: Own preparation.

Table 3. Students' evaluation of VL teaching is useful (Question 2, Table 1).

Answer Option	Results	
	Number of Students (*n*)	Percentage (%)
a) Using just VLs.	8	1.90%
b) Using just the RLs.	26	6.19%
c) Mixing VLs and RLs, using VLs in the first place.	373	88.81%
d) Mixing VLs and RLs, using RLs in the first place.	13	3.10%

Source: Own preparation.

Table 4. Students' assessment of the methodology followed in the practical classes (Question 3, Table 1).

Answer Option	Results	
	Number of Students (*n*)	Percentage (%)
a) RL	298	70.95%
b) VL	122	29.05%

Source: Own preparation.

mean and 7.90% of coefficient of variation. Motivation resulted in a mean of 8.5 with a standard deviation of 0.64 and 7.54% coefficient of variation. and, finally, in the case of educational usefulness, the evaluation obtained was 8 out of 10, with 0.59 standard deviation and 9.14% coefficient of variation.

The survey that was passed to the professors (Table 7) consists of five questions: (i) self-perception of digital competence; (ii) assessment of immersion, motivation, usability, and educational effectiveness aspects of VR; (iii) valuation of possible

Table 5. Students' evaluation of methodological organization (Question 4, Table 1).

Answer Option	Results	
	Number of Students (*n*)	Percentage (%)
a) Master Classes	176	41.90%
b) Problem Solving Classes	118	28.10%
c) RL	59	14.05%
d) VL	29	6.90%
e) Other virtual resources	38	9.05%

Source: Own preparation.

Table 6. Students' evaluation of technical and didactic aspects of VR technologies (Question 4, Table 1).

Answer Option	Results			
	Mean (μ)	Variance (σ^2)	Standard Deviation (σ)	Coefficient of Variation (C_V)
(a) Interactivity	9.80	0.64	0.80	8.14%
(b) Motivation	8.50	0.41	0.64	7.54%
(c) Ease of use	9.30	0.54	0.73	7.90%
(d) Educational usefulness	8.00	0.34	0.59	7.34%

Source: Own preparation.

disadvantages of using VR in educational settings; (iv) most frequent uses that surveyed participants give to VR; and (v) VR technology most used by the participant in the classroom. The first three questions are Likert-type and are rated from 1 to 10 (where 1 expresses the lowest rating and 10 the highest rating). The last two are polytomous and can take the values indicated in Table 7. The validation of the Likert-type questions part of the survey has been completed with the Cronbach's α parameters (0.7281 for question 1; 0.7470 for question 2; and 0.7731 for question 3), composite reliability (0.7174 for question 1; 0.7369 for question 2; and 0.7702 for question 3), and average variance extracted (0.5024 for question 1; 0.5119 for question 2; and 0.5308 for question 3).

With regard to the first question of the professors' survey (Table 8), they reported intermediate levels of digital competence (5.73 over 10) and lower levels of knowledge of VR technologies (4.50 over 10) and of the training received in this regard (4.59 over 10). However, the dispersion is high, especially in the questions that specifically involve VR, as can be seen in the values of the variance, standard deviation and coefficient of variation. Specifically, the standard deviations are above a quarter of the value of the corresponding mean in all the items studied. This means that there is some insecurity among professors when they talk about their own competence in the use of VR, but they are more confident when they assess their generic digital competence.

The second question posed to the professors, which asks them to assess certain technical and didactic aspects that influence the methodological organization when VR technologies are used (Table 7), is analogous to question 5 of the students' survey (Table 1). All the dimensions of the VR that were asked about were highly valued by the teachers, who gave mean scores above 8.00 out of 10 in all cases (Table 9). The measures of dispersion of the answers are all low (all coefficients of variations are less than 25%), which shows certainty and consensus in the opinions expressed in

Table 7. Questions asked to the professors in the survey.

Number	Question	Answer Options
1	Assess from 1 to 10 your self-perception on the following aspects: (a) digital skills; (b) VR knowledge; (c) training received on VR.	1 to 10 for each aspect.
2	Assess from 1 to 10 the following characteristics of VR technologies when used in learning environments: (a) interactivity; (b) motivation; (c) ease of use; and (d) educational usefulness.	1 to 10 for each characteristic.
3	Assess from 1 to 10 the degree to which the following aspects are disadvantages of using VR in the classroom: (a) costs; (b) shortage of space; (c) required faculty training; and (d) obsolescence of university equipment.	1 to 10 for each disadvantage.
4	Indicate which of the following most influences, in your opinion, the use of VR in the classroom.	a) To enhance student motivation b) To improve the quality of training activities c) For little; it is only a small stimulus
5	Indicate which technology you use most frequently in the classroom.	a) None b) AR c) MR d) IVR e) NIVR

Source: Own preparation.

this regard. Of all the aspects analyzed, the didactic effectiveness of VR is the most highly rated by the teachers (8.82 out of 10). On the other hand, the least valued

Table 8. Professors' assessment of self-perception on their competence on the use of VR (Question 1, Table 7).

Answer Option	Results			
	Mean (μ)	Variance (σ^2)	Standard Deviation (σ)	Coefficient of Variation (C_V)
(a) Digital skills	5.73	3.84	1.96	34.17%
(b) VR knowledge	4.50	4.12	2.03	45.09%
(c) Training received on VR	4.59	6.05	2.46	53.63%

Source: Own preparation.

Table 9. Professors' assessment of technical and didactic aspects of VR technologies (Question 2, Table 7).

Answer Option	Results			
	Mean (μ)	Variance (σ^2)	Standard Deviation (σ)	Coefficient of Variation (C_V)
(a) Interactivity	8.32	3.35	1.83	21.97%
(b) Motivation	8.41	1.80	1.34	15.88%
(c) Ease of use	8.41	3.10	1.76	21.89%
(d) Educational usefulness	8.82	2.66	1.63	18.51%

Source: Own preparation.

aspect is interactivity (8.32 out of 10). The answers on the interactivity of VR are also the most dispersed (with a standard deviation of 1.83 out of 10), which shows that the teachers are less well trained in this concept than the rest.

Comparing the above mean answers with those of the analogous question asked to students (Table 6), it can be observed that professors value the interaction and usability of VR to a lesser extent than students (Figure 5). However, educational effectiveness is more highly valued by professors than by students, and with respect to motivation, the differences are very weak. Thus, students value more the technical aspects linked to VR, while professors emphasize its didactic usefulness over the technical dimensions.

Faculty members' lack of knowledge about the use of VR is, with a mean value of 8.45 out of 10, the biggest disadvantage that professors find to the use of these technologies in the classroom (Table 10). The high costs of VR (mean of 7.63 out of 10) and the obsolescence of the equipment used by universities (mean of 7.77 out of 10) are indicated as disadvantages of VR behind the lack of knowledge. The feature that least negatively influences the didactic use of VR is, in the opinion of the surveyed professors, the space required by these technologies. As expressed by the coefficients of variation, the standard deviations are above a quarter of the mean, but below half the mean value, in the valuations of all the disadvantages, except for lack of knowledge of professors, where the deviation is lower than a quarter of the mean. This suggests that there is a fair amount of consensus and confidence in singling out this feature of VR as the most negative.

Regarding the results of question 4 of the professors' survey, on the aspects of the development of academic activities on which VR has the most decisive influence, the professors indicate mostly, with 61.36%, the increase it causes in the students' motivation towards learning (Table 11). 36.36% believe that the most important effect of VR is not on the student's attitude, but on the quality of the training activities, which is improved. On the other hand, only one participant stated that he did not find essential advantages in the use of VR in the classroom.

Figure 5. Mean values of interaction, motivation, ease of use and educational effectiveness of VR given by students and professors (Tables 6 and 9).
Source: Own preparation.

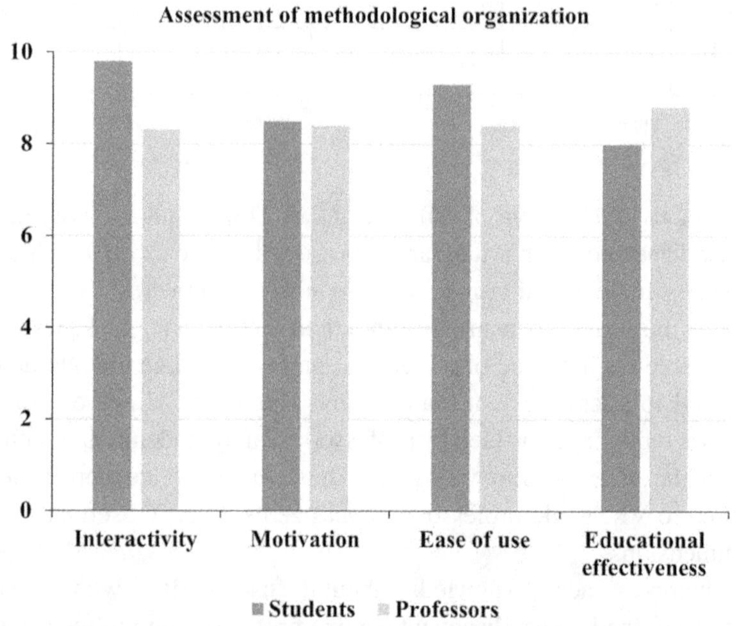

Table 10. Professors' assessment of disadvantages of VR (Question 3, Table 7).

Answer Option	Results			
	Mean (μ)	Variance (σ^2)	Standard Deviation (σ)	Coefficient of Variation (C_V)
(a) Costs	7.64	5.06	2.25	29.50%
(b) Shortage of space	6.09	5.60	2.36	38.76%
(c) Lack of knowledge of professors	8.45	4.24	2.06	24.39%
(d) Obsolescence of university equipment	7.77	4.12	2.03	26.16%

Source: Own preparation.

Table 11. Professors' opinion on the educational aspect that is most strongly influenced by the use of VR (Question 4, Table 7).

Answer Option	Results	
	Number of Professors (n)	Percentage (%)
a) To enhance student motivation.	27	61.36%
b) To improve the quality of training activities.	16	36.36%
c) For little; it is only a small stimulus.	1	2.27%

Source: Own preparation.

Regarding the technology most frequently used in the development of classes (question 5, Table 6), it was found that more than three quarters of the surveyed professors stated that they do not habitually use any of the VR or AR technologies (Table 13). Among those who use any of them, the most frequent is NIVR (although only 4 participants say they use it more regularly than the rest of the technologies), while IVR, AR and MR seem to be less popular technologies among professors (with 2 participants each).

Table 12. Professors' most used technology (Question 5, Table 7).

Answer Option	Results	
	Number of Professors (n)	Percentage (%)
a) None	34	77.27%
b) AR	2	4.55%
c) MR	2	4.55%
d) IVR	2	4.55%
e) NIVR	4	9.10%

Source: Own preparation.

Given the above results, it is possible to affirm that there are evident advantages of using VR technologies and VLs in the classroom of higher education compared to traditional methods and RLs. This fact is supported by both student and professor opinions. In this sense, it is convenient to point out some aspects in which VR and VLs stand out:

- VR is widely demanded by students (Table 6), since from the students' point of view, the experience lived in a virtual world – no matter how sophisticated and detailed it has been designed – is not the same as in the real world. In this sense, new design trends include IVR (Vergara et al., 2017a), by bringing the user closer to the real world.

- The interest generated by laboratory practices in students – at least in engineering students – is especially high in the case of RLs (compared with VLs) (Table 4). In the practices developed in RLs, students perceive a simulation of their future professional development.
- Professors' valuations of VR technologies are also high (Table 9). Professors assess the didactic aspects of VR more highly, while students value its technical aspects more highly (Figure 5). In particular, the aspect of VR most valued by professors is the motivation it generates in students towards learning.
- Despite high assessments, professors report low knowledge about the use of VR technologies and intermediate digital competence (Table 8). This is in line with the results of previous work on the digital competence of professors (Antón-Sancho et al., 2021a; Antón-Sancho et al., 2021b; Fernández-Arias et al., 2021; Vergara et al., 2022). This observation indicates that it is necessary to reinforce faculty training on VR and its didactic use, to increase the educational potential that professors have identified in these technologies.
- The VR knowledge of professors is, precisely, the greatest disadvantage they identify in the use of VR, ahead of the costs of implementing these technologies (Table 10). This probably explains why most professors have not yet implemented any VR technology as a frequent resource in their classrooms (Table 12).

For this reason, it can be ensured that currently, students demand the joint use of VLs and RLs for the delivery of practical teaching and professors value these resources as effective for learning. This confirms what previous articles (Wolfartsberger, 2019) reflect, where it is indicated that VLs are a useful resource to complete the training process, but not a substitute for the traditional. In this sense, although VR and VLs are clearly imposing themselves in the teaching of the 21st century, in the future it is very likely that these technologies and resources will be present in university facilities – at least in those of a classroom nature.

SOLUTIONS AND RECOMMENDATIONS

Throughout the study, it has been shown that there is a certain gap between students' and professors' perceptions of VR. Specifically, students find it easier to use and rate the interactive experience of this resource higher, while professors rate the didactic usefulness of VR higher than professors do. This is probably due to the fact that students are more favorable to the incorporation of digital resources and suggests the need to train professors so that there is a match between the didactic objectives they seek, the training needs of students and the design of didactic situations using VR.

Based on the results of this study, it is recommended that universities develop training plans for engineering professors with a double objective: (i) to increase the digital teaching skills of professors; and (ii) to introduce them to VR technologies and their didactic use. These trainings should be continuous over time and specifically adapted to the different areas that are part of engineering students' learning. This would give professors confidence in the technical aspects of VR, improve the didactic effectiveness of the activities they design and, finally, help to involve students more intensely in their learning process.

It is also recommended that professors introduce VR in combination with other teaching resources in the classroom. The use of VR technologies, even if it involves an initial economic cost, will reduce costs in the long term, especially if the use of VLs is intensified over RLs. In addition, the combination of VR with other resources will prevent students from falling into a routine that decreases their motivation and will also allow them to acquire diverse experiences of the different objects of study.

FUTURE RESEARCH DIRECTIONS

It is proposed as a future line of research to extend the sample of students and professors to include participants from wider geographical areas. In this way, the results obtained could be generalized. It would also be interesting to carry out an analogous study focused on areas of knowledge other than engineering, in order to analyze the perspective of professors and students in these areas, identify possible differences between them and analyze whether the specificities of each area influence the perceptions expressed by the participants. Other research perspectives related to the topic discussed are: (i) the development of VR applications for teaching specific topics in engineering education; (ii) the design of learning assessment tools based on VR technologies; or (iii) carrying out a descriptive study of a comparative type of learning outcomes in engineering students who have used VLs versus those who have used RLs.

CONCLUSION

Considering the technological advances that have occurred in the last part of the 20th century until today, and the positive experiences that are being lived in practical teaching when using virtual reality technologies and virtual laboratories in engineering education – which reflect a series of clear advantages compared to traditional methodologies and practical classes in RLs – the implementation of these didactic resources in the educational sector is an unstoppable fact. This trend has various implications, such as the development of virtual learning environments or the design of digital teaching materials of very different natures. The application of VR to education is part of a very fruitful line of educational innovation that consists of the development of technological applications for learning. The current situation due to the pandemic caused by COVID-19 has only accelerated a process of virtualization of education that had already begun previously. Despite this, university students emphasize the importance for them to be able to use RLs in practical teaching. Engineering professors also give high valuations to the use of VR in the classroom, with special emphasis on the didactic benefits of these technologies but expressing the drawback of the lack of faculty training in this regard.

In view of the current situation, and following the opinion expressed by students and professors, it can be stated that the use of VR technologies is going to increase in the near future and, in particular, both types of laboratories (virtual and real) will coexist in the new post-COVID-19 hybrid educational models, which combine face-to-face and online teaching and learning. This foreseeable increase in the use of VR will be facilitated by the increase in technological development, the progressive migration of educational processes to virtual environments (favored by the COVID-19 pandemic), and the results of numerous research studies that demonstrate the good academic results obtained by the use of these technologies in different areas of knowledge. Among the challenges for the future of VR are lower production and implementation costs, faculty training and the development of policies to facilitate access to these technologies for all students.

ACKNOWLEDGMENT

The authors wish to acknowledge the financial support provided by the Spanish Association “Amigos de la Universidad Católica de Ávila” (Award 2021).

References

Antón-Sancho, Á., Vergara, D., & Fernández-Arias, P. (2021a). Self-assessment of soft skills of university teachers from countries with a low level of digital competence. *Electronics (Basel)*, *10*(20), 2532. doi:10.3390/electronics10202532

Antón-Sancho, Á., Vergara, D., Lamas-Álvarez, V. E., & Fernández-Arias, P. (2021b). Digital content creation tools: American university teachers' perception. *Applied Sciences (Basel, Switzerland)*, *11*(24), 11649. doi:10.3390/app112411649

Balali, V., Zalavadia, A., & Heydarian, A. (2020). Real-time interaction and cost estimating within immersive virtual environments. *Journal of Construction Engineering and Management*, *146*(2), 04019098. doi:10.1061/(ASCE)CO.1943-7862.0001752

Balamuralithara, B., & Woods, P. C. (2009). Virtual laboratories in engineering education: The simulation lab and remote lab. *Computer Applications in Engineering Education*, *17*(1), 108–118. doi:10.1002/cae.20186

Berg, L. P., & Vance, J. M. (2016). Industry use of virtual reality in product design and manufacturing: A survey. *Virtual Reality (Waltham Cross)*, *21*(1), 1–17. doi:10.100710055-016-0293-9

Cha, M., Han, S., Lee, K., & Choi, B. (2014). A virtual reality based fire training simulator integrated with fire dynamics data. *Fire Safety Journal*, *50*, 12–24. doi:10.1016/j.firesaf.2012.01.004

Doblack, B. N., Allis, T., & Davila, L. P. (2014). Novel 3D/VR interactive environment for MD simulations, visualization and analysis. *Journal of Visualized Experiments*, *94*(94), e51384. doi:10.3791/51384 PMID:25549300

Doblack, B. N., Flores, C., Matlock, T., & Dávila, L. P. (2011). The emergence of immersive low-cost 3D virtual reality environments for interactive learning in materials science and engineering. In *Proceedings of Materials Research Society Symposium* (vol. 1320). Cambridge University Press. 10.1557/opl.2011.636

Durukan, A., Artun, H., & Temur, A. (2020). Virtual reality in science education: A descriptive review. *Journal of Science Learning*, *3*(3), 132–142. doi:10.17509/jsl.v3i3.21906

Ergün, O., Akın, Ş., Dino, İ. G., & Surer, E. (2019). Architectural design in virtual reality and mixed reality environments: A comparative analysis. In *Proceedings of the 2019 IEEE Conference on Virtual Reality and 3D User Interfaces (VR)* (vol. 1, pp. 914-915). Osaka, Japan: IEEE. 10.1109/VR.2019.8798180

Extremera, J., Vergara, D., Dávila, L. P., & Rubio, M. P. (2020). Virtual and augmented reality environments to learn the fundamentals of crystallography. *Crystals*, *10*(6), 456. doi:10.3390/cryst10060456

Extremera, J., Vergara, D., Rodríguez, S., & Dávila, L. P. (2022). Reality-virtuality technologies in the field of materials science and engineering. *Applied Sciences (Basel, Switzerland)*, *12*(10), 4968. doi:10.3390/app12104968

Fernández-Arias, P., Antón-Sancho, Á., Vergara, D., & Barrientos, A. (2021). Soft skills of American university teachers: Self-concept. *Sustainability*, *13*(22), 12397. doi:10.3390u132212397

Flores, C., Matlock, T., & Dávila, L. P. (2012). Enhancing materials research through innovative 3D environments and interactive manuals for data visualization and analysis. In *Proceedings of Materials Research Society Symposium* (vol. 1472). Cambridge University Press. 10.1557/opl.2012.1257

Halabi, O. (2020). Immersive virtual reality to enforce teaching in engineering education. *Multimedia Tools and Applications*, *79*(3-4), 2987–3004. doi:10.100711042-019-08214-8

Hilfert, T., & König, M. (2016). Low-cost virtual reality environment for engineering and construction. *Visualization in Engineering*, *4*(2), 1–18. doi:10.118640327-015-0031-5

Kamińska, D., Sapiński, T., Aitken, N., Della Rocca, A., Barańska, M., & Wietsma, R. (2017). Virtual reality as a new trend in mechanical and electrical engineering education. *Open Physics*, *15*(1), 936–941. doi:10.1515/phys-2017-0114

King, D., Tee, S., Falconer, L., Angell, C., Holley, D., & Mills, A. (2018). Virtual health education: Scaling practice to transform student learning: Using virtual reality learning environments in healthcare education to bridge the theory/practice gap and improve patient safety. *Nurse Education Today*, *71*, 7–9. doi:10.1016/j.nedt.2018.08.002 PMID:30205259

Lee, H., & Cha, W. C. (2019). Virtual reality-based ergonomic modeling and evaluation framework for nuclear power plant operation and control. *Sustainability*, *11*(9), 2630. doi:10.3390u11092630

Llobera, J., González-Franco, M., Perez-Marcos, D., Valls-Solé, J., Slater, M., & Sanchez-Vives, M. V. (2013). Virtual reality for assessment of patients suffering chronic pain: A case study. *Experimental Brain Research*, *225*(1), 105–117. doi:10.100700221-012-3352-9 PMID:23223781

Meagher, K. A., Doblack, B. N., Ramírez, M., & Dávila, L. P. (2014). Scalable nanohelices for predictive studies and enhanced 3D visualization. *Journal of Visualized Experiments*, *93*(93), e51372. doi:10.3791/51372 PMID:25407548

Mirauda, D., Capece, N., & Erra, U. (2019). StreamflowVL: A virtual fieldwork laboratory that supports traditional hydraulics engineering learning. *Applied Sciences (Basel, Switzerland)*, *9*(22), 4972. doi:10.3390/app9224972

Mól, A. C. A., Jorge, C. A. F., Couto, P. M., Augusto, S. C., Cunha, G. G., & Landau, L. (2009). Virtual environments simulation for dose assessment in nuclear plants. *Progress in Nuclear Energy*, *51*(2), 382–387. doi:10.1016/j.pnucene.2008.04.003

Paatela-Nieminen, M. (2021). Remixing real and imaginary in art education with fully immersive virtual reality. *International Journal of Education Through Art*, *17*(3), 415–431. doi:10.1386/eta_00077_1

Potkonjak, V., Gardner, M., Callaghan, V., Mattila, P., Guetl, C., Petrovic, V. M., & Jovanovi, K. (2016). Virtual laboratories for education in science, technology, and engineering: A review. *Computers & Education*, *95*, 309–327. doi:10.1016/j.compedu.2016.02.002

Prensky, M. (2016). Digital natives, digital immigrants. Part 1. *On the Horizon*, *9*, 1–6.

Quint, F., Sebastian, K., & Gorecky, D. (2015). A mixed-reality learning environment. *Procedia Computer Science*, *75*, 43–48. doi:10.1016/j.procs.2015.12.199

Román-Ibáñez, V., Pujol-López, F. A., Mora-Mora, H., Pertegal-Felices, M. L., & Jimeno-Morenilla, A. (2018). A low-cost immersive virtual reality system for teaching robotic manipulators programming. *Sustainability*, *9*, 112.

Safikhani, S., Keller, S., Schweiger, G., & Pirker, J. (2022). Immersive virtual reality for extending the potential of building information modeling in architecture, engineering, and construction sector: Systematic review. *International Journal of Digital Earth*, *15*(1), 503–526. doi:10.1080/17538947.2022.2038291

Soliman, M., Pesyridis, A., Dalaymani-Zad, D., Gronfula, M., & Kourmpetis, M. (2021). The application of virtual reality in engineering education. *Applied Sciences (Basel, Switzerland)*, *11*(6), 2879. doi:10.3390/app11062879

Syed, Z. A., Trabookis, Z., Bertrand, J. W., Madathil, K. C., Hartley, R. S., Frady, K. K., Wagner, J. R., & Gramopadhye, A. K. (2019). Evaluation of virtual reality based learning materials as a supplement to the undergraduate mechanical engineering laboratory experience. *International Journal of Engineering Education*, *35*, 1–11.

Vergara, D., Antón-Sancho, Á., Dávila, L. P., & Fernández-Arias, P. (2022b). Virtual reality as a didactic resource from the perspective of engineering teachers. *Computer Applications in Engineering Education*, *30*(4), 1–16. doi:10.1002/cae.22504

Vergara, D., Antón-Sancho, Á., Extremera, J., & Fernández-Arias, P. (2021). Assessment of virtual reality as a didactic resource in higher education. *Sustainability*, *13*(22), 12730. doi:10.3390u132212730

Vergara, D., Extremera, J., Rubio, M. P., & Dávila, L. P. (2019a). Meaningful learning through virtual reality learning environments: A case study in materials engineering. *Applied Sciences (Basel, Switzerland)*, *9*(21), 4625. doi:10.3390/app9214625

Vergara, D., Extremera, J., Rubio, M. P., & Dávila, L. P. (2020a). The technological obsolescence of virtual reality learning environments. *Applied Sciences (Basel, Switzerland)*, *10*(3), 915. doi:10.3390/app10030915

Vergara, D., Extremera, J., Rubio, M. P., & Dávila, L. P. (2020b). The proliferation of virtual laboratories in educational fields. *ADCAIJ: Advances in Distributed Computing and Artificial Intelligence Journal*, *9*(1), 85–97. doi:10.14201/ADCAIJ2020918597

Vergara, D., Fernández-Arias, P., Extremera, J., Dávila, L. P., & Rubio, M. P. (2022a). Educational trends post COVID-19 in engineering: Virtual laboratories. *Materials Today: Proceedings*, *49*, 155–1609. doi:10.1016/j.matpr.2021.07.494 PMID:35018286

Vergara, D., Lorenzo, M., & Rubio, M. P. (2015). Virtual environments in materials science and engineering: the students' opinion. In H. L. Lim (Ed.), *Handbook of research on recent developments in materials science and corrosion engineering education* (pp. 148–165). IGI Global. doi:10.4018/978-1-4666-8183-5.ch008

Vergara, D., & Rubio, M. P. (2012). Active methodologies through interdisciplinary teaching links: Industrial radiography and technical drawing. *The Journal of Materials Education*, *34*, 175–186.

Vergara, D., Rubio, M. P., & Lorenzo, M. (2014). Interactive virtual platform for simulating a concrete compression test. *Key Engineering Materials*, *572*, 582–585. doi:10.4028/www.scientific.net/KEM.572.582

Vergara, D., Rubio, M. P., & Lorenzo, M. (2017a). On the design of virtual reality learning environments in engineering. *Multimodal Technologies and Interaction*, *1*(2), 11. doi:10.3390/mti1020011

Vergara, D., Rubio, M.P. & Lorenzo, M. (2017b). New approach for the teaching of concrete compression tests in large groups of engineering students. *Journal of Professional Issues in Engineering Education and Practice*.

Vergara, D., Rubio, M. P., & Lorenzo, M. (2018). A virtual resource for enhancing the spatial comprehension of crystal lattices. *Education in Science*, *8*(4), 153. doi:10.3390/educsci8040153

Vergara, D., Rubio, M. P., Lorenzo, M., & Rodríguez, S. (2019b). On the importance of the design of virtual reality learning environments. In *Methodologies and Intelligent Systems for Technology Enhanced Learning* (vol. 1007, pp. 146–152). Springer.

Vergara-Rodríguez, D., Antón-Sancho, Á., & Fernández-Arias, P. (2022). Variables influencing professors' adaptation to digital learning environments during the COVID-19 pandemic. *International Journal of Environmental Research and Public Health*, *19*(6), 3732. doi:10.3390/ijerph19063732 PMID:35329422

Vergara-Rodriguez, D., Rodriguez-Martin, M., Rubio-Cavero, M. P., Ferrer-Marin, J., Núñez-Garcia, J., & Moralejo-Lobo, L. (2018). Technical staff training in ultrasonic non-destructive testing using virtual reality. *Dyna*, *94*(1), 150–154. doi:10.6036/8444

Wang, P., Wu, P., Wang, J., Chi, H.-L., & Wang, X. (2018). A critical review of the use of virtual reality in construction engineering education and training. *International Journal of Environmental Research and Public Health*, *15*(6), 1204. doi:10.3390/ijerph15061204 PMID:29890627

Wolfartsberger, J. (2019). Analyzing the potential of virtual reality for engineering design review. *Automation in Construction*, *104*, 27–37. doi:10.1016/j.autcon.2019.03.018

Wu, W., Tesei, A., Ayer, S., London, J., Luo, Y., & Gunji, V. (2018). Closing the skills gap: Construction and engineering education using mixed reality – A case study. In *Proceedings of the 2018 IEEE Frontiers in Education Conference (FIE)* (vol. 1, pp. 1-5). Osaka, Japan: IEEE. 10.1109/FIE.2018.8658992

Xie, Q., & Tinker, R. (2006). Molecular dynamics simulations of chemical reactions for use in education. *Journal of Chemical Education*, *83*(1), 77–83. doi:10.1021/ed083p77

ADDITIONAL READING

Antón-Sancho, Á., Nieto-Sobrino, M., Fernández-Arias, P., & Vergara-Rodríguez, D. (2022). Usability of memes and humorous resources in virtual learning environments. *Education Sciences*, *12*(3), 208. doi:10.3390/educsci12030208

Caserman, P., Garcia-Agundez, A., Konrad, R., Göbel, S., & Steinmetz, R. (2019). Real-time body tracking in virtual reality using a Vive tracker. *Virtual Reality (Waltham Cross)*, *23*(2), 155–168. doi:10.100710055-018-0374-z

Kelly, J. W., Cherep, L. A., & Siegel, Z. D. (2017). Perceived space in the HTC vive. *ACM Transactions on Applied Perception*, *15*(1), 2. doi:10.1145/3106155

Lamas-Álvarez, V. E., Antón-Sancho, Á., Vergara-Rodríguez, D., Gómez-Vallecillo, A. I., Fernández-Arias, P., & Nieto-Sobrino, M. (2021). Using digital teaching materials in university education. In *Proceedings of the XI International Conference on Virtual Campus (JICV) Virtual Campus (JICV)* (vol. 1, pp. 11-13). IEEE. 10.1109/JICV53222.2021.9600432

Thomas, B., Close, B., Donoghue, J., Squires, J., De Bondi, P., Morris, M., & Piekarski, W. (2000). ARQuake: an outdoor/indoor augmented reality first person application. *Digest of Papers. Fourth International Symposium on Wearable Computers* (vol. 1, pp. 139–146). IEEE. 10.1109/ISWC.2000.888480

Vergara, D., & Rubio, M. P. (2015). The application of didactic virtual tools in the instruction of industrial radiography. *The Journal of Materials Education*, *37*(1-2), 17–26.

Vergara, D., Rubio, M. P., Extremera, J., & Lorenzo, M. (2021). Interdisciplinary learning methodology for supporting the teaching of industrial radiology through technical drawing. *Applied Sciences (Basel, Switzerland)*, *11*(12), 5634. doi:10.3390/app11125634

Vergara, D., Rubio, M. P., & Lorenzo, M. (2014). New virtual application for improving the students' understanding of ternary phase diagrams. *Key Engineering Materials*, *572*, 578–581. doi:10.4028/www.scientific.net/KEM.572.578

Vergara, D., Rubio, M. P., & Lorenzo, M. (2015). A virtual environment for enhancing the understanding of ternary phase diagrams. *The Journal of Materials Education*, *37*(3-4), 93–102.

Vergara, D., Rubio, M. P., Prieto, F., & Lorenzo, M. (2016). Enhancing the teaching/learning of materials mechanical characterization by using virtual reality. *The Journal of Materials Education*, *38*(3-4), 63–74.

Vergara-Rodríguez, D., Gómez-Asenjo, A., Fernández-Arias, P., Gómez-Vallecillo, A. I., Lamas-Álvarez, V. E., & Santos-Iglesia, C. (2021). Immersive vs. non-immersive virtual reality learning environments. In *Proceedings of the XI International Conference on Virtual Campus (JICV) Virtual Campus (JICV)* (vol. 1, pp. 8-10). IEEE. 10.1109/JICV53222.2021.9600337

Key Terms And Definitions

Information and Communication Technologies (ICT): A set of technological resources used to create, transmit, exchange, or share information.

Interactive Multimedia Application: A virtual tool that combines diverse content forms in an interactive way, such as audio, animation, text, or video.

Learning Environment: A physical or digital environment in which the teaching and learning process takes place.

Real Laboratory: An environment that provides controlled conditions to carry out scientific or technological testing.

Virtual Laboratory: Computer-simulated environment in which the conditions for experimentation typical of a conventional laboratory are recreated using generic or specific computer software.

Virtual Reality: A set of computer tools that enable the design of simulated environments that allow user interaction by means of appropriate digital devices.

Virtual Resource: Computer systems integrated in a computer-simulated environment.

Chapter 10
The Importance of Social Competence for 21st Century Citizens:
The Use of Mixed Reality for Social Competence Learning in Mainstream Education

Xining Wang
https://orcid.org/0000-0002-5505-5151
Trinity College Dublin, Ireland

Conor McGuckin
Trinity College Dublin, Ireland

Mary Quirke
https://orcid.org/0000-0002-8118-7270
Trinity College Dublin, Ireland

ABSTRACT

This chapter presents the results of a systematic review that investigated the use of mixed reality (MR) technology to assist social competence learning in mainstream education. Social competence represents our ability to interact with others and, therefore, is a key determinant for many of the possibilities that are presented to us across the lifespan. In today's digital world, MR technology has been widely used in special and inclusive education for social competence training purposes but has not yet been generally applied to mainstream education. This systematic review bridges this research gap. Findings support (1) the potential for MR technology as a medium for social competence learning activities and (2) how the MR approach can contribute to a universally designed (UD) learning environment.

DOI: 10.4018/978-1-6684-3398-0.ch010

INTRODUCTION

Education is constantly evolving, from curricula developments to new approaches to teaching, learning, and assessment. Engaging the utility of one recent development of mixed reality (MR) technology to assist in developing important traits that lend students to personal success (social competence) is indeed novel. However, the authors posit that whilst much of this innovative work has been evident in the area of special and inclusive education, future developments should seek to apply MR to a wider variety of educational and training issues, and, importantly, be developed for wider application to the diversity of learners that we encounter in our work. Therefore, we conclude by advocating that such work be conceptualised and operationalised with supporting evidence.

This chapter explores the use of MR for social competence learning (SCL) in mainstream education with universal design. The initial motivation comes from the reflection of key competencies for 21st-century citizens, regarding how individual configures their world through the application of critical soft skills – collaboration, communication, critical thinking, interaction, creativity, emotional understanding, problem-solving, and decision making. The purpose of this research is (i) to discuss the importance of SCL in mainstream education, and (ii) to understand if MR can effectively assist SCL by reviewing previous studies. Next, we propose a hypothesis for the exploration of other relevant research — on reviewing the evidence we can then substantiate that MR could be an effective tool for supporting SCL in mainstream education. Finally, for ease of legibility, the research journey is set out in the following sections:

1. Background - Challenges for Education in a Contemporary World
2. Theoretical Consideration – Introducing Universal Design and Universal Design Learning
3. An Introduction to VR, AR, And MR Technology, and Their Application in Social Competence Education
4. Research Gap Identified
5. Method and Results of Data Analyses
6. Discussion – MR-assisted Soft Skills Improvement
7. Perspectives of Limitations and Challenges

BACKGROUND: CHALLENGES FOR EDUCATION IN THE CONTEMPORARY WORLD

Education systems are ongoing, being reflective of the changing society that they represent, and incorporating the latest knowledge from applied research. One issue that remains constant in education is the need for individuals to develop and hone their "soft skills". Thus, it is necessary to review our understanding of soft skills and the social competencies that students need for success - both now and in the future (Kay & Greenhill, 2011). In a busy school curriculum, the development of these skills can become less urgent in the traditional areas of literacy, numeracy, modern foreign language, and science. What is required is a recognition of the increasing demand for one's social competence as we continue to learn and adapt to various novel situations in life. Such an approach is needed to help the individual to develop social abilities and to cope with new and evolving challenges.

Social competence includes the ability to analyse social situations and enact appropriate responses (American Psychological Association, 2022). It encapsulates the ability to get on with others, to be able to have and maintain close relationships, and to be able to respond in adaptive ways on different social occasions (Orpinas, 2010). Given the complexity of human sociality, social competence covers a wide range of cognitive capacities, emotional and behavioural patterns, social awareness, and personal world values related to interpersonal interactions (Orpinas, 2010). Social competence is a key determinant for success in life, in that it is our social competence that frames our abilities and possibilities, helping us realise our true potential. Where social competence is a curricular outcome, particular skills are required - collaboration, communication, empathy, creativity, critical thinking, problem solving, and decision making (Rodriguez, 2018; Sanabria & Arámburo-Lizárraga, 2017; Wu et al., 2021). Whilst social competence learning (SCL) is a recognised term for this concept, it is not broadly understood in mainstream education.

Education has continually developed since that ". . . today no organization can achieve results without incorporating technology into every aspect of its everyday practices. It's time for schools to maximize the impact of technology as well" (p. 2). Technology has become a necessary part of students' learning experiences (Yoo, 2020) and is a powerful tool for students to engage with educational activities in a digital society (Young et al., 2020). Given the innovation and uniqueness of MR technology and its increasing implications in our twenty-first century digital society (Young et al., 2020), MR technology can present many opportunities for continuously changing learning environments. Thus, educational practitioners, stakeholders, and students need to engage with and harness these digital representations effectively (Niemi & Multisilta, 2016), and they also need to apply them to SCL. MR-assisted SCL has the very potential to enhance current educational approaches. If they are to develop the requisite skills for success in life, educators and students alike will need to embrace such innovations if they are to meet twenty-first century expectations.

THEORETICAL CONSIDERATION: INTRODUCING UNIVERSAL DESIGN AND UNIVERSAL DESIGN LEARNING

There is a recognised and accepted need to enhance the learning experiences that we provide for students. The simultaneous increase in engagement with different technologies among students makes it increasingly apparent that the learning environment itself needs retrofitting and redesigning. The concept of special and inclusive education has contributed constructively to the idea of retrofitting traditional education environments, as they continue to evolve from segregated to congregated education spaces that seek to be inclusive and representative of the variability that we find in terms of "ability" and "disability". To some extent, these philosophical and practical advances have resulted in decisions and adaptations that enable learning for all students, where once such changes were an "add-on" to the curriculum (e.g., a spell-check function on a computer). Contemporary learning experiences and pedagogical practices need to continue to move beyond what was done in the past - if there is a sincere wish to achieve the targets for "inclusion" that have been espoused in the United Nations Sustainable Development Goals (e.g., Goal 4: Quality Education; Goal 10: Reduced Inequalities).

However, despite the ongoing developments that seek to embrace inclusive education theories, inclusion in education still largely operates from a deficit viewpoint (Braunsteiner, & Mariano-Lapidus, 2014) – focusing on the learner's real or perceived impairment and not on what could be attained with the correct approaches and supports. Such developments include the acceptance of new ways of engaging in pedagogical practice, and embracing everything that technology and its innovations can offer in a truly contemporary environment. The corollary of this is that, if educational practitioners and policymakers aim to develop SCL in a meaningful and engaging way, it is time to rethink "new ways of doing things". Technologies have been continuously adapting and delivering SCL in special schools and inclusive educational environments (e.g., special classes) through specific educational modules. However, this is not the approach in mainstream education, even though it is a powerful teaching and learning innovation that could be used to deliver SCL to all our future citizens. When considering this dilemma, we argue that Universal Design (UD) thinking and Universal Design for Learning (UDL) approaches can present a useful solution. Such a solution would design such approaches from the "get-go" and be applicable to the "universality" of learners and the individual differences that every educational setting represents.

Universal Design is about ensuring that change or accommodation is considered from the very outset, i.e. at the inception stage of any ideas and moreover that we need to be aware and considerate as we make inclusive changes (Quirke, McGuckin & Mc Carthy, 2022). Such an approach means "designing for a universality" resulting in greater autonomy for the great diversity of people that make up humankind (Story et al., 1998). Influenced by UD thinking, UDL was developed by CAST in the USA as a pedagogical approach (CAST, 2018), and has been increasingly applied to the broad landscape that makes up learning environments. UDL demands consideration of inclusion and difference from the get-go (Quirke et al, 2018, Quirke & Mc Carthy, 2022). Revisiting the origins of UDL thinking may make it easier for many pedagogues to embrace technological innovations. They can then appreciate the mindset necessary to embrace change in the learning environment and how technological innovation such as MR can enhance SCL for a wider diversity of students. Technological innovations, including MR, have the potential to enable learners to experience, feel, and realise traditional curricula in new ways and moreover, engage with new curricula such as SCL in meaningful ways.

So how and why do we consider technology assisted SCL using the experience of UDL and inclusive practice? Using the approach as espoused in "Inclusion as Process" (Quirke et al. 2022), the authors of this chapter propose:

- Be solution focused with a difference - anticipate a diversity of needs while respecting we must **engage** all in the "design" process, most especially our teachers and educational leaders. Everyone must have an **input**.
- Seek **workable solutions** for all involved - for the universality of people in our learning environments and society. The **output** needs to work for all.
- Are respectful of all approaches as MR, SCL, and UDL require interdisciplinary and multidisciplinary thinking - such thinking necessitates an appreciation of different terminologies, language, an appreciation of different theories - while recognising the **shared commonality** in terms of making the world a better place.
- Recognise that **such innovations, when grounded in "Inclusive thinking", can offer added value** in the learning environment - they are a new and fast way to learn how to problem solve, shorten the cycle of learning – and moreover offer an exciting and engaging learning experience for a wide diversity of learners.

More importantly, the development of SCL in mainstream education is in direct response to social and active inclusion policies and inclusive education policies. On the other hand, with the rapid development of immersive technology, MR has been widely used in education and has a great potential to change communication, collaboration, and the future of the workplace. Therefore, moving this curriculum onto MR platforms, including virtual reality (VR) and augmented reality (AR) while being considerate of designing for inclusion, means that learning can be very real if we are to strive for true inclusion both in education and society.

AN INTRODUCTION TO VR, AR, AND MR TECHNOLOGY, AND THEIR APPLICATION IN SOCIAL COMPETENCE EDUCATION

The Concept of VR and the Sense of Being There

VR is a technology that integrates computer graphics, visual presentations, motion taking, and sensor devices to serve users with a visual multi-sensory experience and a realistic simulated setting (Maples-Keller et al., 2017). It is a highly immersive technology that disconnects users from the surrounding reality. With the continuous improvement of computer-generated graphic technology, the virtual environment has been created as a replacement or extension of the physical world, allowing users to look in any direction and content in a 360-degree space. Moreover, VR can generate a "sensation of being there" in remote places that are displayed by advanced immersive technology, i.e., self-location and action possibilities can be distinguished. In doing so, spatially presented VR can provide users with vivid experiences of being situated in a virtual space and being able to connect with the virtual environment (Hruby, 2019).

The Concept of AR and the Enhanced Physical Experience

AR is a newer technology than VR. It can be defined as a later technological system in which virtual objects are combined with the real world for users' real-time experience (Cipresso et al., 2018). It incorporates four systems: real environment, AR, augmented virtuality, and virtual environment (Milgram & Kishino, 1994). An AR system usually includes a combination of real and virtual objects in a real environment — a system running interactively and in real-time as well as the integration of the real and virtual objects. Technically speaking, although the AR system contains various elements, it usually exhibits three common components: a geospatial datum for the virtual object (e.g., a visual marker), the surface to project virtual elements to the user, and the process of merging graphics and animation (Cipresso et al., 2018). It is a technology that aims to enhance parts of users' physical world experience with computer-generated input.

MR-Assisted Social Competence Education

Simply put, VR immerses users into a simulated real world, while AR enables virtual objects to be superposed in the real world. MR is an authentic setting that facilitates users' interaction with virtual experiences (Maas & Hughes, 2020). It has been recognised as one of the most promising technologies for next-generation mobile platforms (Zhan et al., 2020). The growing development of VR, AR, and MR technologies can be used simultaneously and contribute to an all in one reality framework; that is they can be used independent of each other or evolve into a mixture. MR simulates and interacts with the real world, empowering people to get the most realistic perception of reality in these different integrated systems. Given that this phenomenal advancement is rapidly developing in many ways and increasingly links our reality to the digital world; by focusing on the opportunities the integration of VR, AR, and MR technologies offers learning, we can realise a broader opportunity MR-assisted pedagogy offers across all aspects of education (Zhan et al., 2020). For example, MR has been applied to support social skills teaching and learning activities for clinical interventions and special education (Wang et al., 2021). MR-assisted SCL is a strategic combination of delivering social knowledge (e.g., social skills training, collaboration and communication, empathy fostering, creativity, critical thinking, and problem solving) within a diverse digital environment (e.g., VR and AR). Recent research has demonstrated that both VR and AR generate realistic and credible scenarios and interactive settings so that people can behave and respond in undifferentiated ways within their environments from what they do in the real world (Howard & Gutworth, 2020; Maruhn et al., 2020). Consequently, it allows students to acquire social skills in a safe, realistic simulated, controllable, and interactive setting and practice their acquisitions in real life.

Research Gap Identified

Social competence is a vital part of human development necessary at all stages of the lifespan, instead of only a necessity for individuals with additional needs (American Psychological Association, 2022; Junge et al., 2020; Ma, 2012; Orpinas, 2010). It encompasses complex competencies and plays a critical role for individuals in accomplishing positive developmental outcomes (Wang et al., 2021). When conducting SCL, well-designed MR applications simulate real life conventions and human interactions to support users to have a better understanding of emotional and behavioural patterns (Fagernäs et al., 2021; Pan & Hamilton, 2018).

Emerging studies have highlighted that MR-assisted SCL has been increasingly used for either individuals with physical disabilities, or with mental illnesses in the field of special education (Shema-Shiratzky et al., 2019; Susindar et al., 2019;

Wallace et al., 2017), nevertheless, little research focuses on SCL and/or social skills training in mainstream education or social competence programs for individuals without additional needs. Due to these existing issues, this systematic review aims to bridge the research gap and provide systematic information for future studies.

METHODOLOGY

The Necessity for Conducting a Systematic Review

A systematic review rigorously reviews and sorts the data, formulating evidence and questions clearly and using explicit methods to identify, select, and critically evaluate (O'Brien & Mc Guckin, 2016). Given that the researchers have identified a lacuna between MR technology and SCL in mainstream education after a range of database pre-searching, we utilised a systematic review approach to explore highlighted hypotheses and bridge the research gap. It is a valid way to identify relevant studies and assess their quality and reliability.

Searching Strategy

This study used the Preferred Reporting Items for Systematic Reviews and Meta-Analyses (PRISMA) model (Moher et al., 2009). The following keywords derived from our research questions were employed for the systematic searching: (i) mixed reality, (ii) social competence, and (iii) education. Relevant synonyms are also identified to enrich the search string — virtual reality, augmented reality, extended reality, VR, AR, XR, social, social skills, and educational. Finally, the Boolean "AND" has been used to concatenate keywords, while the "OR" operator has been used to connect synonyms. All searches were completed by 01/04/2022.

Databases

In accordance with the interdisciplinary nature of this study, the selection of databases were those that were related to fields of education, psychology, and technology. Hence, the following eight databases were selected: EBSCOhost, Scopus, PsycInfo, ACM Digital Library, IEEE Xplore Digital Library, ProQuest, Web of Science, and Google Scholar. Since Google Scholar is a platform used to broadly search scholarly literature across a wide variety of disciplines and sources, it was also chosen to work as a complementary tool to retrieve further research.

Searching Strand and Preliminary Searching Results

The searching strand used in our research was the following: "mixed reality or virtual reality or augmented reality or extended reality or MR or VR or AR or XR AND social competence or social AND education or educational".

Preliminary searching results were:

- 17 studies were retrieved by EBSCOhost (2010 to present),
- 20 studies were retrieved by Scoups (2010 to present),
- 250 studies were retrieved by ACM Digital Library (2010 to present),
- 23 studies were retrieved by IEEE Xplore Digital Library (2010 to present),
- 16 studies were retrieved by ProQuest (2010 to present),
- 1 study was retrieved by PsyInfo (2010 to present),
- 1 study was retrieved by Web of Science (2010 to present),
- 114 studies were retrieved by Google Scholar (2010 to present).

Criteria of Selection

Based on previous successful experience, the research harnessed the inclusion criteria and exclusion criteria from the study *A Systematic Review of Virtual Reality Interventions for Children with Social Skills Deficits* (Wang et al., 2021) to develop the scope of final selection. As a result, studies were selected and reviewed if they met the following requirements:

- Studies published in the last twelve years – between 2010 and 2022
- Discussing MR applications
- Targeting the use of MR technology to assist SCL in mainstream education
- Educational activities include discussions on human sociality and social skills
- Written in English

Meantime, research was excluded if studies were in accord with the following criteria:

- Research focuses on using MR to assist special education and/or clinical intervention
- Targeted groups are individuals with special needs
- Research mainly focuses on MR software/platform development and with little discussion and contribution to human development
- Research with a poorly structured methodology or without explicit findings

- Documents cannot be downloaded from the university library portal or are not open access sources

Searching Results

The preliminary retrieve resulted in 442 studies. Next, the first round of screening was implemented to remove duplicated research, which resulted in 124 compliant studies. After excluding studies written in languages other than English, retrieved records listed 112 manuscripts. Then the researchers conducted the third round of

Figure 1. PRISMA searching diagram.

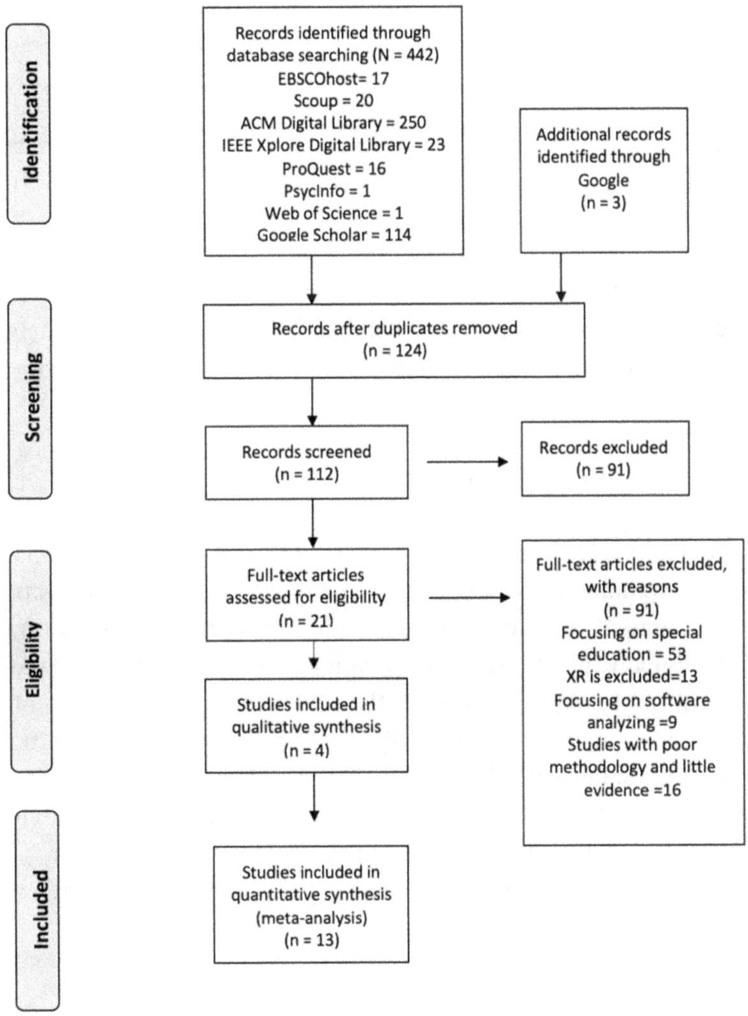

Table 1. Summary of reviewed articles.

Number	Authors, Year	Types of Research	Sample Size	Gender Identity	Average Age	Types of SCL	Types of MR	Main Findings
1	Young et al. (2021)	Empirical study	20	M=11, F=9	34.1	Perspective-taking, mediated empathy, VR empathy, and social empathy building.	VR	VR production techniques could successfully deliver empathy-driven materials.
2	Ip & Li (2015)	Review	NA	NA	NA	Collaborative learning, communication skills and problem solving.	VR	VR provides safe and repeatable environments for students to learn social skills. However, VR education needs to be further investigated via long-term practice.
3	Papanastasiou et al. (2019)	Review	NA	NA	NA	Critical thinking, collaboration, communication, creativity, emotional skills, and social skills.	VR & AR	VR and AR system may create a more cooperative environment and also helps students develop their social competence.
4	Rezende et al. (2017)	Case study	1	NA	NA	Development of cognitive skills, such as perception, attention, and decision making	AR	AR environment is fun for learning, which can increase students' interest and motivation.
5	Mukkawar & Netak (2021)	Technological evaluation	2	NA	NA	Self-awareness, interpersonal skills, communication skills, teamwork, collaboration, leadership, critical thinking, creative thinking, problem-solving, and decision making.	VR & AR	Both VR and AR are promising to create quality applications for SCL.
6	Lorusso et al. (2018)	Empirical study	25	M=12, F=13	4.5	Understanding, strategic behaviors, participation, interaction, conflict, and cooperation.	AR	AR is useful for personal practical skills and social competencies.
7	Young et al. (2020)	Empirical study	39	M=17, F=22	21	Focus, collaboration, sense of responsibility, and decision-making skills.	VR	Students concluded 6 categories of "thinks", "feels", "says", "does", "pains", and "gains" for SCL experience.
8	Wu et al. (2013)	Review	NA	NA	NA	social interactivity	AR	Students' social interactivity could be improved when collaborating through networked AR devices.
9	Dhar et al. (2021)	Review	NA	NA	NA	Understanding, practical skills, and social skills.	AR	AR-based learning improved students' cognitive and practical skills, social skills, innovation, and creativity.
10	Craciun & Bunoiu (2016)	Empirical study	16	M=14, F=2	21.6	collaboration, creativity, and imagination.	AR	Students had a better understanding of concepts and phenomena and gained social skills.
11	Martinez, et al. (2016)	Educational design	2	NA	NA	Development of the ability to understand and regulate emotions.	AR	Learners could a have self-evaluation of their SCL.
12	Wójcik (2016)	Education program	8	NA	NA	Social competencies related to labor market needs.	AR	AR is useful for personal practical skills and social competencies.
13	Perryman et al. (2021)	Empirical study	29	NA	NA	Social communication and social validity.	VR & AR	students reported an increase in their perceived ability to apply social counselling skills.
14	Queiroz et al. (2018)	Group study	70	NA	NA	Social skills development.	VR & AR	There are gaps in the application of VR and AR to specific educational levels
15	Zhang et al. (2020)	Review	NA	NA	NA	Game-based Learning and social skills via VR.	VR & AR	MR exhibit excellent performance in SCE related knowledge presentation and assessment.
16	Bucea-Manea-Țoniș et al. (2020)	Empirical study	1032	M=423, F=609	about 38.9	Social life, collaborative learning, and social media use.	XR	XR supports collaborative learning and offers advantages by facilitating deep comprehensive learning.
17	Ramirez-Montoya et al. (2020)	Educational design	1	NA	NA	Social skills, innovation, and creativity.	VR	The training course has positive impact on competence in social entrepreneurship.
18	Schiffeler et al. (2018)	Review	NA	NA	NA	Social construction of knowledge, social interaction, communication, and collaborative working.	AR	Results show that robots can learn from humans. Also, it is possible to use robots in social learning processes.
19	Herbst et al. (2021)	Empirical study	14	NA	NA	Social distancing guidelines	VR	VR in medical education can improve health care providers' communication skills and practice behaviors.
20	Mosher & Carreon (2021)	Review	NA	NA	NA	Perspective-taking, creativity, and empathy.	VR	VR is useful for providing student engagement and students' new perspective-taking, empathy, and creativity.
21	Papoutsi & Skianis (2021)	Review	NA	NA	NA	Social interaction, emotional skills, and self and social awareness.	VR & AR	VR and AR are effective tools to enhance students' emotional and social skills.

Note. NA=none applicable; M=Male; F=Female.

eligibility review, 91 studies were ruled out since they did not have a structured methodology, robust discussion, and/or validated evidence. Finally, 21 manuscripts were given an in-depth review and detailed analysis in this systematic review (Figure 1 and Table 1).

Summary of Evaluated Studies

The 21 studies include 1211 samples, 1132 participants (477 males and 655 females), 8 educational programs, 9 system designs, and 62 assessments. These studies also incorporate a range of research methods, such as empirical study (n=7), reviews (n=8), technological evaluation (n=2), educational design (n=2), group study (n=1), and case study (n=1). Applied SCL in the reviewed studies consists of various components, i.e., empathy building (14%), collaboration (33%), communication (19%), perspective-taking (9.5%), problem solving (14%), critical thinking (9.5%), interaction (24%), creativity (19%), emotional skills and understanding (24%), decision making (14%), and others (48%). Each component makes up a different proportion, whereas shares similar and indispensable significance to relevant SCL activities (Table 2).

Table 2. Types of applied SCL from the 21 reviewed articles.

Type	Percentage
Empathy Building	14%
Collaboration	33%
Communication	19%
Perspective-taking	9.5%
Problem-solving	14%
Critical thinking	9.5%
Interaction	24%
Creativity	19%
Emotional Skills and Understanding	24%
Decision Making	14%
Others	48%

RESULTS OF DATA ANALYSES

MR Technology for SCL Environment

With the rapid development of cutting-edge technologies, advances in MR open new possibilities for innovative education. It contributes to the understanding of technology-mediated collaborations and tech-based programs, as well as offering new solutions for educational purposes (Wang et al., 2022). Existing MR technologies can further personalize the learning experience in a way that other educational technologies simply cannot (Young et al., 2020). For example, MR education supports students learning by doing instead of learning by listening. Learning in an MR system allows students to touch and control objects, forming a greater understanding of learning tasks. Students can interact with datasets, complex calculations, and abstract concepts that are more difficult to understand through a teacher's verbal instructions (Dhar et al., 2021). At the same time, educational practitioners have also taken the major step of using MR technology to support a variety of educational activities. MR has created new digital platforms that prompt educators to rethink the pros and cons of traditional pedagogies and, furthermore, take advantage of leading-edge technology to create a more inclusive, engaging, and creative environment for students' SCL experience (Dhar et al., 2021). In many educational practices, MR facilitates embedding knowledge and social competence skills in the context of real life, reflecting daily life activities to virtual or augmented reality based scenarios. When compared to traditional contexts in education, it "feels more real" as students can flexibly transport themselves to a creative and effective learning experience within the MR system. The following cases are elaborations of how different MR technologies can positively support diverse learning experiences for mainstream education.

Case 1. VR-based SCL Learning Environment

VR based learning environment is a virtual setting that is developed with educational models. The entire system involves using one or more didactic objectives to demonstrate students' learning experiences, experiences they may not have in the physical world (Herbst et al., 2021). VR-assisted SCL is a pedagogical approach to practice SCL through a VR system. It aims to achieve SCL learning outcomes based on the design of the VR learning system. Because VR simulations enhance SCL for students, the technology enables the learning of complex competencies by allowing the deliberate practice of necessary skills while adhering to current social occasions and social norms (Herbst et al., 2021). The design helps learners to react to social instruction that builds upon their interactions with VR avatars. Also, this learning process can be repeated in VR without extra expenditures, so that learners can gradually acquire social competence in speciðc learning domains (Ip & Li, 2015). It is the way that mainstream education should take advantage to inspire students to form new ideas and solutions for real life situations.

Case 2. SCL Interactive Environment in AR

As a superposition of virtual elements on the real environment, the use of AR in education allows virtual elements to be performed in the real environment, increasing more enrichment and diversification of learning experiences (Craciun & Bunoiu, 2016). AR-assisted educational designs support students to interact with complex platforms and communicate with one another. For instance, AR learning software is compatible with different learning devices, such as smartphones, tablets, laptops, and smartwatches, which directly leads to the result of a more accessible and affordable solution for future education, and a possibility of generalised SCL in mainstream education (Wu et al., 2013). Mukkawar and Netak (2021) have indicated that applying AR technology to education can improve student-teacher interaction and satisfaction. For example, AR-interfaced books provide a respite for students struggling with complicated or dull learning materials. It also can be used as an innovative learning toolkit to visualize and concretize learning resources with rich stereoscopic effects. Another example is that Mukkawar and Netak (2021) conducted an eye contact study and proved that AR-assisted SCL may improve abilities of communication and interaction, such as team group-based learning, real-life participation, and group communication.

Therefore, deducing from the above evidence, the authors believe that MR presents a real possibility to contribute to and enhance most conventional and modern educational methodologies and implementations. Although MR has been identified as an opportunity to revolutionize the way people perceive and interact with complex digital information (Zhan et al., 2020), the technology is not important since it does not cause or facilitate meaningful learning in and of itself. It is worth noting that when new technologies emerge in education, a majority of educators are usually excited about teaching and learning through technology-centred thinking, with little consideration as to "how" learners actually think and learn. Students may have a better sense of "being present" using MR-assisted learning systems, whereas MR cannot lead to better learning efficacy without a thoughtful and productive learning experience that has been well-designed in advance.

DISCUSSION: MR-ASSISTED SOFT SKILLS IMPROVEMENT

Collaboration and Communication

Collaboration and communication are deeply human social competencies that are vital for forming effective communication and obtaining one's needs for normal community functioning (Meadan & Monda-Amaya, 2008). These capabilities increase likeability, productive teamwork and pleasant interpersonal relationships thus leading to improved life quality. It is worth stating that these necessary social skills are not natural or inherited equally by all humans. Collaboration and communication are learned competencies that develop over our lifetime, supported with educational input (Meadan & Monda-Amaya, 2008). Even though collaboration and communication are currently integrated into our education processes, these competencies need to be practiced and adapted intentionally as we go about our daily lives. Squire and Jan (2007) have proved that AR game-based education can be used to engage students in collaborative learning and scientific thinking. Through the use of their AR curriculum — Mad City Mystery, students develop the ability to conduct various scientific discussions. In addition, collaborative learning is a constructivist approach that can invoke collaboration and communication skills among students. Many educational practices have employed MR-based learning programs for both classroom learning and distance learning, which can break through the limitations of traditional education since large scale collaboration can be realized virtually without many physical and geographical constraints (Ip & Li, 2015).

VR and AR have been valued as creative learning aids for twenty-first century education because these technologies enable users to access flexible learning through entertainment-based software and hardware, while also offering diverse support for personalised learning (Rogers, 2019; Sanabria & Arámburo-Lizárraga, 2017). The learning tasks in VR and AR environments require learners to apply and synthesize multiple skills in collaboration, spatial navigation, technology manipulation, interactive capability, and immersion interfaces (Radianti et al., 2020). These collaborative activities through MR platforms can strengthen positive attitudes towards social engagement, social interaction, positive learning, and communication (Beach & Wendt, 2014; Crowell et al., 2020). For example, a previous roleplay experiment illustrated that students were assigned identities to understand the working model of scientiðc investigations and related social situated nature. These identities include social activists, scientists, and environmental investigators. After a series of scene simulations and role-playing via the MR system, students learned how to use different ways of thinking to access information relevant to their roles during the experimental sessions (Squire & Klopfer, 2007). Similarly, participation in MR enables each participant to work as interacting components of the dynamic MR system (Dhar et al., 2021). In turn, interactions among students can affect the outcomes of the computer-human interaction and MR system. Nowadays, collaborative learning is assisting inclusive research and educational challenges during the Covid-19 pandemic (Wang et al., 2022). MR-based collaborative learning, therefore, presents a further advantage to facilitate comprehensive learning and communication.

Critical Thinking and Creativity

Critical thinking is a capacity that refers to a complex process of evaluation and deliberation. It involves a wide range of skills and attitudes, including identifying other people's positions and reviewing the evidence for alternative perspectives (Stella, 2005). Creativity is the ability to generate ideas, and be imaginative while also applying new thinking so that one can efficiently solve problems (Kinga & István, 2012). It encompasses the ability to discover innovative thoughts, plans, and solutions for various issues. Individuals with creativity are good at fostering resilience, happiness, and self-actualization (Kinga & István, 2012). With this ability, students can effectively respond to situations where they encounter both familiar and unfamiliar circumstances, breaking through ineffective learning and building on successful experiences. Applying this concept in SCL, MR applications can be cutting-edge digital toolkits for teachers to foster students' critical thinking and creativity in educational practice, which also gives a chance for students to engage in social events and understand digital life. For example, Craciun and Bunoiu (2016) have demonstrated SCL education in discovery learning and scientific learning activities by using location-aware AR technologies. In these educational activities, AR laboratories have become an innovative place to foster students' creativity and critical thinking. These SCL experiences develop learners' critical thinking while also providing scientific facts and concepts. Students have been encouraged to identify potential issues and find a solution through the AR system. Another example of MR-assisted SCL is the AR field trip in Romania. The AR platform is named Wikitude, which can be used to retrieve destination information through Wikipedia and automatically provides other sightseeing possibilities nearby. All attractions within Wikitude have visualized objects that are particularly designed for these field trips. Having these virtual trips applied in SCL education, students can have options to discover attractions individually or travel as a group, so that they can collaborate and communicate with their peers.

Reviewed studies have illustrated that MR has great potential to stimulate students' critical thinking and creativity in massive learning experiences. For instance, Yang et al. (2018) have indicated that VR can simulate physical settings and realistic experiences, reducing spatial constraints and facilitating creativity through imaginary and immersive settings. The fully immersive VR system has the advantage of "being there" and generating various scenarios that cannot be simply or safely completed in the real world. Likewise, AR combines the real world and the virtual world by following the idea of constructivism learning, which allows learners to make use of unreal objects in an enlarged environment to have critical thinking and learning (Faridi et al., 2021). The controlled classroom environment by MR introduces students to different ways of digital creativity, enabling students to translate their experiences into broader social competence from digital social spaces without unnecessary effort. Therefore the MR-based learning environment may develop a positive impact on students' critical thinking through learning activities. Furthermore, given the novelty of MR and its growing functions in the 21st century's digital society, utilizing VR and AR to support SCL in mainstream education offers many educators and students unique exposures to a virtual and real-life mixed environment (Young et al., 2020). Thus, it is both timely and necessary to propose that all mainstream schools initiate the development of SCL curricula, with consideration and critical discussion of the meanings of digital representations and interactions.

Emotional Skills and Understanding

Emotional skills refer to the ability to regulate one's emotions, thoughts, and behaviours. These skills determine how people manage their feelings, perceptions, as well as their surroundings and engagement (OECD, 2017). Perspectives from psychology demonstrated that understanding is one important aspect of emotional skills. It is related to "the knowledge gained from inside the inter-subjective field formed by the intersection of two different subjectivities" (Orange, 1995). Meantime, understanding is "an intersubjective process of emotional comprehension, of reaching and or developing an understanding with each other" (Orange, 1995). Emotional skills and understanding are dependent upon situational factors and respond to individual and environmental change and development via formal and informal learning experiences. These skills may influence a wide range of personal and societal outcomes throughout one's lifespan (OECD, 2017). MR-assisted SCL makes emotional skills learning exciting for students and the technology makes it easy to generate various scenarios that imitate various social occasions, social activities, and social manners, all of which are key factors for students as they form their emotional understanding.

In some cases, VR applications have been designed to generate body swap illusions. Within these illusions, virtual roles are designed to be controlled and selected. These virtual avatars are developed so that they play the role of social competence tutors, communicating and interacting with users through social skills activities. Immersing into a safe virtual setting, users have reported that they experience less social embarrassment and increased motivation for learning perspective-taking, imagining one's situation, empathic concern, and emotional understanding (Martingano et al., 2021). Huang et al.(2016) have developed an AR botanical garden to support students to immerse in floristic exploration and interaction with AR-enhanced ecological settings. Findings show that this AR application prompted students' willingness to learn more about nature and the local ecological system. Furthermore, they developed a positive attachment with the virtual plants and eco-setting and quickly understood the importance of environmental protection and climate change. Also, the AR system aroused students' emotions for perspective-taking, interest, and happiness (Huang et al., 2016). However, certain types of VR do not trigger an individual's psychological engagement to a sufficient level to arouse empathy, because affordable VR headsets (i.e., Cardboard VR) usually have less immersive and interactive developments. Also, challenges of AR learning settings involve a longer period of training times for students to use AR and low sensitivity to trigger students' empathy and emotional recognition of the avatars. Therefore, it is hard to infer that VR and AR can significantly improve learners' comprehensive emotional skills and understanding since research on MR systems in fostering emotions is still at an early stage, so there is insufficient empirical research to guide and examine relevant MR system designs.

Problem Solving and Decision Making

Problem solving can be defined as a behavioural process which makes a range of responses to deal with a problematic situation and improves the probability of choosing the most effective response from alternatives (D'zurilla & Goldfried, 1971). It enables us to identify the difficulties in the environment and exploit potential opportunities to control the future. Decision making is the process of identifying and selecting alternatives based on the decision maker's values and preferences. The process of decision making refers to how choices are to be made, and in such a case people want to not only find options, but to choose the one that fits most with their goals, objectives, desires, and values (Harris, 1998). In SCL, fostering students with the capacity to solve problems and make decisions is crucial to their success in career and life development. This capacity has become even more significant in the context of educational reform efforts. Reviewed studies demonstrated that MR assisted educational games included problem solving and decision making features in the design (Ip & Li, 2015; Wu et al., 2013; Young et al., 2020). For example, Mathews (2010) employed a mobile device in interdisciplinary studies of language arts. This MR-based design helped students to identify issues within their community, and then recommended relevant GPS-based games that would solve problems both individually and collaboratively. Finally, some games from mobile devices have the potential to teach students and community members to think about learning related issues.

Given that SCL tasks in AR environments require students to exert multiple skills in social inferring, problem solving, and spatial navigation, they can gain the capacity for problem solving and decision making. Similarly, Hoppenstedt et al. (2021) substantiated that AR can assist learners to solve problems effectively during collaborative working experiences. The research team investigated different types of challenges encountered by collaborators as they interacted with a range of learning activities. The groups were divided into non-AR group and AR stimuli group, with the students from the AR group using AR features to address their learning difficulties. Results showed that educators believed AR might be useful for detecting potential learning issues in the classroom and could help students discuss solutions, thus preventing identified problems that negatively impact on future learning.

In conclusion, it is clear that MR offers many great possibilities for a wide variety of educational practices including SCL, allowing teachers and students to participate safely, supported by a virtual and augmented reality system before their learning can then be applied to life in the real world. However, MR is not without its limitations and this can affect user experience making it difficult to be applied in prospective mainstream education. In the next section, we summarise the most significant limitations and challenges for current MR technology, considerations both for the application of MR in education and moreover for future studies - where this analysis can be used as a reference.

PERSPECTIVES OF LIMITATIONS AND CHALLENGES

Challenges for Teachers and Learners

Prior to the rapid development of MR applications for mainstream education, Wu et al. (2013) indicated that AR environments could increase learners' cognitive load, and in fact overload their thinking with a massive increase of information from the system. Also, learners had to learn how to engage with multiple AR devices in a short period of time, where the learning tasks were cumbersome. Meanwhile, in comparison to studies of other sophisticated technologies in education (e.g., information and communications technology-based education and multimedia platforms), MR applications in education are still in an early burgeoning stage. Although evidence shows that MR-assisted teaching and learning appears to show promise for future education approaches, many MR systems still focus mainly on technological updates and creating special effects, media and graphics (Kobayashi et al., 2018; Poux et al., 2020), rather than concentrating on the actual objective and designing the system for educational and human developmental purposes. Furthermore, educators experienced inñexibility in MR systems with teachers unable to make changes to the system content, resulting in them being unable to accommodate individual students' learning interests, demotivation and subsequently not accomplishing their teaching tasks (Wu et al., 2013).

Limitations in Past Research

It must be appreciated that VR and AR are relatively new mediums for educational activities. Most research studies mainly focus on system design, case studies, and pilot studies. There was no research focused on long-term evaluations of MR-assisted knowledge and skills, and the transference of such learning from the virtual system to the students' practice in reality. Most research has been on a small scale, which is limited and as such affects the generalisability and relevance of the findings (Rodriguez, 2018). Furthermore, many studies reported that some students and educators are more likely to use this approach just to enjoy the virtual world without using it as an actual learning tool since the technology is novel, exciting, and rich in multi-sensory stimulations (Huang et al., 2016). Hence, there is a limited understanding of MR's efficacy, as reviewed studies have not presented any results about MR's long-term impact on a wide range of students' performance in both classroom education and/or online education.

Challenges for MR In and Off Itself

Last but not least, when discussing the use of cutting-edge technology in education, it is easy to get carried away by the enthusiasm for new solutions but ignore the reality and real circumstances (Wójcik, 2016). Practically speaking, many studies pointed out that MR education brings students chaos and confusion with virtual environment controls - this unfamiliarity might cause fear and distraction that can weaken students' focus on the learning content. More seriously, users may have side effects from VR, which refers to cybersickness such as headache, nausea, motion sickness, eye strain, pallor, sweating etc (Rodriguez, 2018). In addition, from a macro level, the biggest hurdle faced by MR education is how to make this technology equitable and accessible for all educators and students across the world. The cost of developing and purchasing MR platforms and devices is pricey, which makes this technology impossible for students who live in under-developed regions (Dhar et al., 2021). Therefore, paying more attention to the challenges of MR education and coming up with solutions is essential if we are to consider generalizing this technology to a mainstream level. More importantly, prejudging and diagnosing potential factors that may cause problems in MR education would protect the application from becoming impractical for teaching and learning, eventually assuring new MR platforms serve teachers and students on a daily basis (Wójcik, 2016).

CONCLUSION

In this chapter, the authors discussed the importance of social competence for students as twenty-first century citizens, and conducted a systematic review to analyse the feasibility and effectiveness of using Mixed Reality (MR) to assist Social Competence Learning (SCL) in mainstream education. Findings support collaborations between MR technologies and SCL activities that fit with Universal Design for Learning (UDL) environments - contemporary learning environments that can meet the need of a diversity of students needing to develop social competence traits for today's world. MR-assisted SCL particularly enhances students' collaboration, communication, critical thinking, creativity, problem-solving, and decision making. Although MR technologies are not without their limitations (e.g., increased cognitive load, challenges for educators, limited research as to their efficacy, the gap between basic and advanced MR devices, and side effects of cybersickness), it offers great potential to support students' SCL experience. Although schools do not currently have a designated SCL module or course in mainstream education while the need for such skills continues to increase, MR as an up-and-coming medium could be the solution to increased SCL input across mainstream education. Therefore, the authors suggest that future studies may consider universally designing and conducting comprehensive SCL programs with mainstream schools, enabling engagement on a large scale, while examining its related efficacy across a diverse student population. It is time we recognise the opportunity MR-assisted SCL offers - how it embraces the emerging role of technology in education, respects the importance of inclusion, and demands that we as teachers and learners redesign for approaches to learning - it not only promotes competencies necessary for future work but will also help them to thrive as outstanding twenty-first century citizens.

ACKNOWLEDGMENT

This publication was funded by Trinity College Dublin, Ireland and the China Scholarship Council (TCD-CSC Joint Scholarship). Also, thanks to the University of Copenhagen's humanistic working conditions and harmonious working environment, this chapter can be finished pleasantly and smoothly. We would also like to remember future learners, including Sile- Marie and Eoin, for whom this development is critical.

REFERENCES

American Psychological Association. (2022). *Social Competence*. https://dictionary.apa.org/social-competence

Beach, J., & Wendt, J. (2014). *Social Interaction Development through Immersive Virtual Environments*. ERIC.

CAST. (2018). *Universal Design for Learning Guidelines version 2.2*. Retrieved from http: //udlguidelines.cast.org

Cipresso, P., Giglioli, I. A. C., Raya, M. A., & Riva, G. (2018). The Past, Present, and Future of Virtual and Augmented Reality Research: A Network and Cluster Analysis of the Literature. *Frontiers in Psychology*, *9*, 2086–2086. doi:10.3389/fpsyg.2018.02086 PMID:30459681

Craciun, D., & Bunoiu, M. (2016). *Augmented reality in Romanian science education pros and cons*. doi:10.12753/2066-026X-16-205

Crowell, C., Sayis, B., Benitez, J. P., & Pares, N. (2020, January). Mixed Reality, Full-Body Interactive Experience to Encourage Social Initiation for Autism: Comparison with a Control Nondigital Intervention. *Cyberpsychology, Behavior, and Social Networking*, *23*(1), 5–9. doi:10.1089/cyber.2019.0115 PMID:31644332

D'zurilla, T. J., & Goldfried, M. R. (1971). Problem solving and behavior modification. *Journal of Abnormal Psychology*, *78*(1), 107–126. doi:10.1037/h0031360 PMID:4938262

Dhar, P., Rocks, T., Samarasinghe, R. M., Stephenson, G., & Smith, C. (2021). Augmented reality in medical education: Students' experiences and learning outcomes. *Medical Education Online*, *26*(1), 1953953–1953953. doi:10.1080/10872981.2021.1953953 PMID:34259122

Fagernäs, S., Hamilton, W., Espinoza, N., Miloff, A., Carlbring, P., & Lindner, P. (2021). What do users think about Virtual Reality relaxation applications? A mixed methods study of online user reviews using natural language processing. *Internet Interventions: the Application of Information Technology in Mental and Behavioural Health*, *24*, 100370. doi:10.1016/j.invent.2021.100370 PMID:33665136

Faridi, H., Tuli, N., Mantri, A., Singh, G., & Gargrish, S. (2021). A framework utilizing augmented reality to improve critical thinking ability and learning gain of the students in Physics. *Computer Applications in Engineering Education*, *29*(1), 258–273. doi:10.1002/cae.22342

Harris, R. (1998). *Introduction to decision making*. VirtualSalt. http://www. virtualsalt. com/crebook5. htm

Herbst, R., Rybak, T., Meisman, A., Whitehead, M., Rosen, B., Crosby, L. E., Klein, M. D., & Real, F. J. (2021, June 29). A Virtual Reality Resident Training Curriculum on Behavioral Health Anticipatory Guidance: Development and Usability Study. *JMIR Pediatrics and Parenting*, *4*(2), e29518. doi:10.2196/29518 PMID:34081601

Hoppenstedt, E., Radu, I., Joy, T., & Schneider, B. (2021). Augmented Reality in Collaborative Problem Solving: A Qualitative Study of Challenges and Solutions. *International Conference on Computer Supported Collaborative Learning*.

Howard, M. C., & Gutworth, M. B. (2020). A meta-analysis of virtual reality training programs for social skill development. *Computers & Education*, *144*, 103707.

Hruby, F. (2019). The Sound of Being There: Audiovisual Cartography with Immersive Virtual Environments. *KN - Journal of Cartography and Geographic Information, 69*(1), 19-28. doi:10.1007/s42489-019-00003-5

Huang, T.-C., Chen, C.-C., & Chou, Y.-W. (2016). Animating eco-education: To see, feel, and discover in an augmented reality-based experiential learning environment. *Computers & Education*, *96*, 72–82. doi:10.1016/j.compedu.2016.02.008

Ip, H. H., & Li, C. (2015). Virtual reality-based learning environments: Recent developments and ongoing challenges. *International Conference on Hybrid Learning and Continuing Education*.

Junge, C., Valkenburg, P. M., Deković, M., & Branje, S. (2020). The building blocks of social competence: Contributions of the Consortium of Individual Development. *Developmental Cognitive Neuroscience*, *45*, 100861–100861. doi:10.1016/j.dcn.2020.100861

Kay, K., & Greenhill, V. (2011). Twenty-first century students need 21st century skills. In *Bringing schools into the 21st century* (pp. 41–65). Springer. doi:10.1007/978-94-007-0268-4_3

Kinga, S., & István, S. (2012). Relationship between social creativity and social intelligence, and their cognitive correlates. *Transylvanian Journal of Psychology*, *13*(1), 39–62.

Kobayashi, L., Zhang, X. C., Collins, S. A., Karim, N., & Merck, D. L. (2018). Exploratory Application of Augmented Reality/Mixed Reality Devices for Acute Care Procedure Training. *The Western Journal of Emergency Medicine*, *19*(1), 158–164. doi:10.5811/westjem.2017.10.35026 PMID:29383074

Ma, H. K. (2012). Social competence as a positive youth development construct: A conceptual review. *TheScientificWorldJournal*, *2012*, 287472–287472. doi:10.1100/2012/287472 PMID:22645418

Maas, M. J., & Hughes, J. M. (2020). 2020/03/14). Virtual, augmented and mixed reality in K–12 education: A review of the literature. *Technology, Pedagogy and Education*, *29*(2), 231–249. doi:10.1080/1475939X.2020.1737210

Maples-Keller, J. L., Bunnell, B. E., Kim, S.-J., & Rothbaum, B. O. (2017, May/June). The Use of Virtual Reality Technology in the Treatment of Anxiety and Other Psychiatric Disorders. *Harvard Review of Psychiatry*, *25*(3), 103–113. doi:10.1097/HRP.0000000000000138 PMID:28475502

Martingano, A. J., Hererra, F., & Konrath, S. (2021). *Virtual reality improves emotional but not cognitive empathy: A meta-analysis*. doi:10.1037/tmb0000034

Maruhn, P., Dietrich, A., Prasch, L., & Schneider, S. (2020, March 22-26). Analyzing Pedestrian Behavior in Augmented Reality—Proof of Concept. *2020 IEEE Conference on Virtual Reality and 3D User Interfaces (VR).*

Mathews, J. M. (2010). Using a studio-based pedagogy to engage students in the design of mobile-based media. *English Teaching*, *9*(1), 87–102.

Meadan, H., & Monda-Amaya, L. (2008). Collaboration to Promote Social Competence for Students With Mild Disabilities in the General Classroom: A Structure for Providing Social Support. *Intervention in School and Clinic*, *43*(3), 158–167. doi:10.1177/1053451207311617

Milgram, P., & Kishino, F. (1994). A taxonomy of mixed reality visual displays. *IEICE Transactions on Information and Systems*, *77*(12), 1321–1329.

Moher, D., Liberati, A., Tetzlaff, J., Altman, D. G., & Group, P. (2009). Preferred reporting items for systematic reviews and meta-analyses: The PRISMA statement. *PLoS Medicine*, *6*(7), e1000097. doi:10.1371/journal.pmed.1000097 PMID:19621072

Mukkawar, V. V., & Netak, L. D. (2021). Technological Evaluation of Virtual and Augmented Reality to Impart Social Skills. *International Conference on Intelligent Human Computer Interaction.*

Niemi, H., & Multisilta, J. (2016). Digital storytelling promoting twenty-first century skills and student engagement. *Technology, Pedagogy and Education*, *25*(4), 451–468. doi:10.1080/1475939X.2015.1074610

O'Brien, A. M., & Mc Guckin, C. (2016). *The systematic literature review method: Trials and tribulations of electronic database searching at doctoral level.* SAGE Publications, Ltd. doi:10.4135/978144627305015595381

Orange, D. M. (1995). *Emotional understanding: Studies in psychoanalytic epistemology*. Guilford Press.

Orpinas, P. (2010). Social Competence. In *The Corsini Encyclopedia of Psychology* (pp. 1-2). Academic Press.

Pan, X., & Hamilton, A. F. C. (2018). Why and how to use virtual reality to study human social interaction: The challenges of exploring a new research landscape. *British Journal of Psychology*, *109*(3), 395–417. doi:10.1111/bjop.12290 PMID:29504117

Postman, N. (2011). *Technopoly: The surrender of culture to technology*. Vintage.

Poux, F., Valembois, Q., Mattes, C., Kobbelt, L., & Billen, R. (2020). Initial User-Centered Design of a Virtual Reality Heritage System: Applications for Digital Tourism. *Remote Sensing*, *12*(16), 2583. doi:10.3390/rs12162583

Quirke, M., Mc Guckin, C., & McCarthy, P. (2022). How to adopt an "inclusion as process" approach and navigate ethical challenges in research. In *SAGE Research Methods Cases*. SAGE Publications, Ltd. doi:10.4135/9781529605341

Radianti, J., Majchrzak, T. A., Fromm, J., & Wohlgenannt, I. (2020). 2020/04/01/). A systematic review of immersive virtual reality applications for higher education: Design elements, lessons learned, and research agenda. *Computers & Education*, *147*, 103778. doi:10.1016/j.compedu.2019.103778

Rodriguez, O. J. (2018). *K-12 Regionalization in Connecticut: Pros, Cons and Surprises*. H. F. f. P. Giving. https://www.hfpg.org/files/7915/3013/0299/Regionlization_Report_Draft_as_of_6-27-2018.pdf

Rogers, S. (2019). Virtual reality: The learning aid of the 21st century. *Secondary Virtual reality: The learning aid of the 21st century*.

Rose, D. (2000). Universal Design for Learning. *Journal of Special Education Technology*, *15*(3), 45–49. doi:10.1177/016264340001500307

Sanabria, J. C., & Arámburo-Lizárraga, J. (2017). Enhancing 21st century skills with AR: Using the gradual immersion method to develop collaborative creativity. *Eurasia Journal of Mathematics, Science and Technology Education*, *13*(2), 487–501. doi:10.12973/eurasia.2017.00627a

Shema-Shiratzky, S., Brozgol, M., Cornejo-Thumm, P., Geva-Dayan, K., Rotstein, M., Leitner, Y., Hausdorff, J. M., & Mirelman, A. (2019, August). Virtual reality training to enhance behavior and cognitive function among children with attention-deficit/hyperactivity disorder: Brief report. *Developmental Neurorehabilitation*, *22*(6), 431–436. doi:10.1080/17518423.2018.1476602 PMID:29771624

Squire, K., & Klopfer, E. (2007). Augmented Reality Simulations on Handheld Computers. *Journal of the Learning Sciences*, *16*(3), 371–413. doi:10.1080/10508400701413435

Squire, K. D., & Jan, M. (2007). Mad City Mystery: Developing Scientific Argumentation Skills with a Place-based Augmented Reality Game on Handheld Computers. *Journal of Science Education and Technology*, *16*(1), 5–29. doi:10.100710956-006-9037-z

Stella, C. (2005). *Critical thinking skills/Stella Cottrell*. Palgrave Macmillan.

Story, M. F., Mueller, J. L., & Mace, R. L. (1998). The Universal Design File: Designing for People of All Ages and Abilities. Revised Edition.

Susindar, S., Sadeghi, M., Huntington, L., Singer, A., & Ferris, T. K. (2019). The Feeling is Real: Emotion Elicitation in Virtual Reality. *Proceedings of the Human Factors and Ergonomics Society Annual Meeting*.

Wallace, S., Parsons, S., & Bailey, A. (2017). Self-reported sense of presence and responses to social stimuli by adolescents with autism spectrum disorder in a collaborative virtual reality environment. *Journal of Intellectual & Developmental Disability*, *42*(2), 131–141. doi:10.3109/13668250.2016.1234032

Wang, X., Hodgers, C., McGuckin, C., & Lv, J. (2022). A Conceptual Learning Design in Virtual Reality The Cognitive VR Classroom for Education After the Pandemic Era. *17th Education and Development Conference*. https://www.ed-conference.org/edc2022001.html

Wang, X., Young, G. W., Mc Guckin, C., & Smolic, A. (2021). A Systematic Review of Virtual Reality Interventions for Children with Social Skills Deficits. *2021 IEEE International Conference on Engineering, Technology & Education (TALE)*. 10.1109/TALE52509.2021.9678808

Wójcik, M. (2016). Potential use of Augmented Reality in LIS education. *Education and Information Technologies*, *21*(6), 1555–1569. doi:10.100710639-015-9399-z

Wu, H.-K., Lee, S. W.-Y., Chang, H.-Y., & Liang, J.-C. (2013). Current status, opportunities and challenges of augmented reality in education. *Computers & Education*, *62*, 41–49. doi:10.1016/j.compedu.2012.10.024

Wu, W.-C. V., Manabe, K., Marek, M. W., & Shu, Y. (2021). Enhancing 21st-century competencies via virtual reality digital content creation. *Journal of Research on Technology in Education*, 1–22. doi:10.1080/15391523.2021.1962455

Yang, X., Lin, L., Cheng, P.-Y., Yang, X., Ren, Y., & Huang, Y.-M. (2018). Examining creativity through a virtual reality support system. *Educational Technology Research and Development*, *66*(5), 1231–1254. doi:10.100711423-018-9604-z

Yoo, H. (2020). Research-to-Resource: Use of Technology to Support 21st Century Skills in a Performing Ensemble Program. *Update: Applications of Research in Music Education*, *39*(2), 10–14. doi:10.1177/8755123320953435

Young, G., Stehle, S., Yazgı, B., & Tiri, E. (2020). Exploring Virtual Reality in the Higher Education Classroom: Using VR to Build Knowledge and Understanding. *Journal of Universal Computer Science*, *26*(8), 904–928. doi:10.3897/jucs.2020.049

Zhan, T., Yin, K., Xiong, J., He, Z., & Wu, S.-T. (2020). Augmented Reality and Virtual Reality Displays: Perspectives and Challenges. *iScience*, *23*(8), 101397. doi:10.1016/j.isci.2020.101397 PMID:32759057

KEY TERMS AND DEFINITIONS

Clinical Intervention: An intervention carried out to improve, maintain or assess the health of a person, in a clinical situation.

Inclusive Education: Inclusive education supports all children in the same classrooms and same schools to have equal learning opportunities for groups who have traditionally been excluded – not only children with disabilities, but speakers of minority languages too.

Mainstream Education: Education for all kinds of students regardless of their abilities in regular classes.

Sense of Being There: We are present in an environment - real and/or synthetic - when we are able to intuitively transform our intentions into actions within the setting.

Social Competence Learning: Educational activities for students to obtain the ability to engage in meaningful interactions with others.

Special Education: Special education is the practice of educating students in a way that accommodates their individual differences, disabilities, and special needs.

Twenty-First Century Citizens: Active, informed, engaged citizens with important skills (i.e., collaboration, communication, creativity, critical thinking, and computational thinking) to succeed in today's workplace.

Chapter 11
The New Trends and Applications in E-Learning Environments and E-Technologies

Luis A. Alfaro
https://orcid.org/0000-0002-8576-3861
Universidad Nacional de San Agustin de Arequipa, Peru

Claudia P. Rivera
https://orcid.org/0000-0002-8576-3861
Universidad Nacional de San Agustín de Arequipa, Peru

Jorge Luna-Urquizo
Universidad Nacional de San Agustín de Arequipa, Peru

Castañeda Elisa
Universidad Nacional de San Agustín de Arequipa, Peru

Jesús Zuñiga-Cueva
Universidad Nacional de San Agustín de Arequipa, Peru

Maribel Urquizo-Abril
Universidad Tecnológica del Perú, Peru

ABSTRACT

The importance of the e-technologies available to support teaching and learning in e-learning systems is becoming increasingly evident to educators and system developers. In this chapter, the authors review some of the e-technologies and e-learning that are used to support the individual requirements of teachers, allowing them to provide the best opportunities to students, considering that the current situation, in which educational systems have new immediate claims, derived in part from the COVID-19 pandemic, motivated face-to-face educational practices to give way to remote activities mediated by technological resources. The new contemporary trends in e-learning and e-technologies development and applications

DOI: 10.4018/978-1-6684-3398-0.ch011

utilize a wide range of available technologies, which are framed in web and virtual reality environments among other emerging technologies; therefore, the decision to use a particular technology must be based on solid research and evidence. This chapter reviews many of these e-technologies and provides information on their use, opportunities, and trends in development and applications.

INTRODUCTION

Since the term was first introduced in the late 1990s by Gerhard and Mayre (2002), e-Learning has been defined in various ways. For Tavangarian et al. (2004), e-Learning is "all forms of electronically supported teaching and learning, which are procedural in nature and aim to realize knowledge construction with reference to the individual experience, practice and knowledge of the learner. Information and communication systems, whether networked or not, that serve as specific means to implement the learning process".

Educators must be well informed and familiar with the available technologies used in the teaching/learning process. Also, the technologies available to educators continue to emerge rapidly and those that were not originally considered teaching/learning tools (such as Facebook) are now present in teaching and learning spaces. There are increasing expectations for educators to be proficient in the use of the wide range of technologies available. These expectations put increasing pressure on educators (Orton-Johnson, 2009).

The organization of the document is as follows: Section background, describes the basics of e-Learning; Section e-Technologies, discusses and explores electronic technologies; the next section, discusses some current and future trends and applications in e-Technologies; finally, Section, sets out the conclusions and future recommendations for this work.

METHODS

In this chapter, a systematic review of the literature on e-Learning and its associated emerging technologies is carried out, exploring mainly the Scopus and Web of Science databases, and investigating various works carried out from 2000 to 2022, with the objective of establishing the e-Technologies and e-Learning that are used to support the requirements of teachers, as well as the new trends and applications of these technologies and their effectiveness in the training and education process of higher education students, taking into consideration the factors that may influence their adoption and successful use. As several review studies suggest (Hsu et al., 2012), it is essential to review data sources for high quality articles. To this end,

Table 1. List of venues with number of publications.

Academic Journals	74
Conference paper, conference proceedings	12
Reports (evaluation, research, technical), working papers and policy briefs	1
Graduate dissertations	1
Books and handbooks	14
Total publications	102

articles were selected from different databases for this study, as these contain the most reputable collections of journal articles, as well as printed documents from various publishers and theses from different universities. The results of the consultations ("e-Learning", "adaptive e-learning", "adaptive learning" or "personalized learning", "e-Technologies", "New technologies in learnig", " New trends in e-Learning", "Extended Reality (XR)", "Immersive Virtual Reality (VR) and Augmented Reality (AR) in e-Learning") carried out to the articles in the databases were normally high. The publication period was set at approximately two decades (i.e., 2020 to 2022) to ensure that there was adequate data to observe research trends, and the type of publication was set as "article" as recommended by other study reviews (Lin & Lan, 2015). Since ''adaptive learning'' is also a term in the area of machine learning in computer science, the authors established the category as ''education/ educational research'' in addition to those that existed, with a total of 86 articles found in the consultation results. These articles were truly related to e-learning and associated emerging technologies, which were read and analyzed carefully using the following criteria for inclusion. Each article should be relevant to the understanding of e-learning, adaptive learning supported by technology, VR, AR and (XR) in e-learning. To be specific, each article should be related to the use of e-learning and e-technologies systems to support to teaching a learning functions and activities, as well as e-Technologies, Virtual Reality, Augmented Reality and Extended Reality in e-Learning. Adopting this criteria, irrelevant articles were filtered out, leaving 65 relevant articles for the e-Learning, the VR and AR and ER (XR) in e-Learning, as well as the e-Technologies in e-Learning. The remaining 23 articles formed the final data set for the analysis, to which 10 conference papers, 1 Reports (evaluation, research, technical), working papers and policy briefs, 1 graduate dissertations, and 11 books were added. These results are shown in Table 1. To ensure that the review process is rigorous and valid, the guidelines suggested by Webster and Watson (2002), and Okoli and Schabram (2012) have been followed.

Initially, this search process yielded 240 publications, which were summarized in a metadata matrix and concepts for further analysis in light of a set of exclusion criteria, including research objectives, relevance, time, and place of publication. This quality assessment and evaluation resulted in the retention of 102 publications, most of which were published within the last 20 years.

BACKGROUND

e-Learning

García-Peñalvo and Seoane-Pardo (2105), summarize the evolution of e-Learning, which is defined as the "formative process of intentional or non-intentional nature, oriented to the acquisition of a series of competences and skills in a social context that develops in a technological ecosystem in which different user profiles interact, sharing content, activities and experiences and which, in formal learning situations, must be supervised by teaching staff whose activity contributes to guaranteeing the quality of all the factors involved", (García-Peñalvo & Seoane-Pardo, 2015).

Using the metaphor of generations, stating that the third one is contemporary, characterized by the confluence of two aspects:

The first aspect is the technological one, in which the concept of learning platform or LMS breaks down and remains limited, as the element responsible for the functionalities for online training since with the emergence of Web 2. 0 and tools of a social nature, technology must be understood as an element of a technological ecosystem of learning, defined as a community of living beings or an autopoietic system (Maturana & Varela, 1998), whose main processes are interrelated and whose development is based on the physical factors of the environment (Laanpere, 2012; Pata, 2011; Clark & Mayer, 2012), allow us to have facilities, to offer interactions with greater teaching flexibility to teachers.

The second aspect, focused on the concept of e-Learning, which becomes a more transversal and universal element, placed at the service of the broad formation of the people involved in the teaching-learning processes, or self-learning. At this stage, the penetration of technology in people's daily lives facilitated the elimination of the borders, increasingly diffuse, between formal and informal learning (García-Peñalvo et al., 2012).

A critical issue related to e-Learning, is that it is focused on functionalities, rather than on the student or the educator, since the student is obliged to perform specific activities, with predefined functionalities and established deadlines in addition to not having control over the prerequisites, for the evolution of their own progress in educational activities.

Another weakness of the LMS is the absence of interaction between (i) student - content, (ii) educator - educator (if applicable), (iii) educator - student. Although they include a variety of communication channels support between educators and students, they are only used as document repositories (Kemp & Livingstone, 2006).

On the other hand, only experienced educators use most of the technological resources offered; therefore, e-Learning systems are not fully compatible with online learning. It can also be noted that e-Learning tools do not improve the independence of students because they are not motivated to take responsibility for their own learning. Nor do they allow students to define their own goals and deadlines, and they can be discouraged from organizing their tasks and time. There is the possibility that they avoid cooperation with other users for the creation of documents or multimedia content. Finally, students have to follow a predefined educational path as specified within the e-Learning activities. For Hughes (2001), the support of student skills is a necessary part of personal self-awareness and self-esteem.

Finally, until today, e-Learning, is a widely used term, even though this definition is not universally accepted, but it can be considered as an improved learning technology, in which all kinds of digital technologies are used to support the learning process. Next, the authors will review the literature focused on adaptive e-Learning systems in order to understand the characteristics of these systems and the parameters used for adaptation.

Next, some technologies and resources frequently used by teachers and students for the implementation of e-Learning systems are reviewed.

e-Technologies

Asynchronous Communication

According to Vygotsky's (1978) sociocultural theory, interactions between students and teachers and the students themselves are essential components of the learning process. Therefore, synchronous and asynchronous communication methods are of particular importance. The educational process includes many forms of online communication between teachers and students. The main forms of communication sustainability are: e-mail, forum, chat, social network, blog (Martyushev et al., 2021).

Electronic mail is a technology that has functionalities for sending and receiving electronic messages over a computer network. The operating principle of e-mail virtually replicates the paper mail system: mail, letter, envelope, attachment, box, delivery and other terms. This asynchronous communication resource is widely used in educational environments, for one-to-one or one-to-many online communication. Files including text, graphics and other multimedia content can be attached with or in messages. The strengths of e-mail include the immediacy of this technology, the ability to connect and stay connected, ease of use and flexibility (Dawley, 2007). However, these can be seen as weaknesses, as they create the expectation that the educator will always be connected and accessible. For Koehler et al. (2013), other weaknesses include the high rate of misunderstandings due to the lack of nonverbal triggers, such as tone of voice or mood, as well as the need to set and enforce boundaries and labels.

The forum is one of the most widely used tools in collaborative learning, being necessary to emphasize that participants explicitly and consensually use coordination and collaboration strategies or skills (Barrera et al., 2021). This effort favors the acquisition of cognitive and metacognitive skills, which play an essential role in learning processes (Kupczynski et al., 2011). It has been noted, on the one hand, that participants often do not use the possibilities of communication and collaboration offered by these tools; and on the other hand, that the existence of a high participation of communicative exchanges between participants does not necessarily lead to the development of collaborative learning, nor does it guarantee the achievement of better results (Chávez et al., 2016).

The insertion of the blog in the school context can be based on social education, since this virtual resource collaborates in communication, organization of identity groups and dissemination of topics and debates and discussions; it can be an area of intervention within the context of cyberculture, since "Social education seeks to develop the development of politics in the subject as a human ability to know how to think, act and intervene in the search for spaces of individual and collective autonomy".

The use of social networking sites such as Facebook among others is becoming increasingly ubiquitous among students as they help users connect with relevant people with whom they can share information. Online social networks allow for sustaining meaningful relationships between connected people and have the potential to facilitate students to seek and provide help in solving problems in discussion forums (Po-Yao et al., 2019).

Synchronous Communication

It is focused on synchronous video transmissions (or synchronous webinars) that allow e-Learning listeners to follow a "live" instructor, through a browser or a customized application that incorporates a video player (Vakaloudis, 2014). Although there are numerous tools for the development and implementation of these systems, it is still a multidisciplinary process that involves among other competencies, audiovisual techniques, network engineering, administration and user experience in education.

In the wake of the Covid-19 pandemic, a large number of educational organizations had to initiate distance education activities globally, which prompted the use of synchronous tools to facilitate communication in an environment where government

Figure 1. The differences between asynchronous, synchronous, and quasi-synchronous communication.
Source: Tang and Hew (2022).

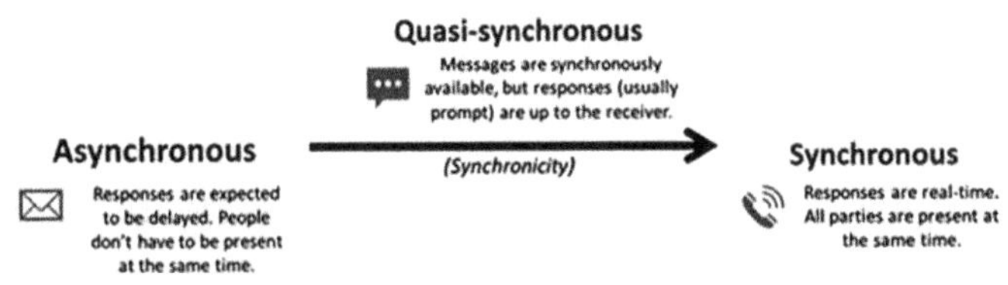

agencies dictated measures to maintain social distancing, as face-to-face education was restricted for some academic periods during the Covid-19 pandemic.

It is also the most technologically compatible mode of communication - the closest to face-to-face communication - and has the element of immediacy that asynchronous communication lacks. It can be text or audio-based and can include video, multimedia and the possibility of using documents and the desktop. This type of communication can be done through chat rooms, instant messaging and videoconferencing which are commonly used in education.

Synchronous online environments allow students and instructors to communicate using video, audio, chat, text, interactive whiteboard, insant polling, application sharing, etc. as if face-to-face in a classroom. Participants can talk, view each other through a webcam, use emoticons, and work together in breakout rooms. Blackboard Collaborate, Zoom, Adobe Connect, Elluminate, and Webex are some of the synchronous online technologies prevalent in higher education. Synchronous technologies can be incorporated into online courses for social learning or community-building and are better suited to discussing less complex issues, getting acquainted, or planning tasks (Hrastinski, 2008). Synchronous online technologies are less flexible in terms of time, but can be accessed from anywhere. They render immediate feedback and allow multi-modality communication (Martin & Parker, 2014)

The differences between synchronous, asynchronous and quasi-asynchronous communication are shown in Figure 1.

Live chat is designed for one-to-one interactions, rather than peer-to-peer interaction or group chat, and is only synchronous (Kang et al., 2015). That is, communication only occurs when both parties are available. There are no studies to date that explore student perceptions of the use of live chat technology within higher education courses (Broadbent & Lodge, 2021). However, in the last decade, live chat has become popular within university library services (Matteson et al., 2011).

Tang and Fon (2022), compared the effects of mobile instant messaging (MIM) with asynchronous online discussion (AOD), finding that the use of MIM could better facilitate interaction and the development of interpersonal relationships. A learning environment with higher levels of intimacy and interactivity that can help satisfy the psychological need for motivation. They also found that when MIM was used in optional task development, in which students could choose whether and how they would participate in a discussion, MIM appeared to enable a higher level of cognitive engagement, as shown by some indicators of idea exchange and creativity, and today emerges as a promising tool for engaging students in social learning activities and for fostering higher-level thinking through interaction. The findings of these researchers provide evidence for improving the instructional design of MIM-supported learning experiences and for promoting theoretical understanding of student engagement.

Although some researchers have suggested that there are differences in the use of synchronous tools depending on factors such as cultural (Huang & Yang, 2009), social, and economic factors, others have argued that the use of such tools can cross these potential barriers. Rutter (2009) suggests that the use of synchronous communication tools brings benefits to student support through more efficient communication. These tools can also be used to promote cooperation between students working individually on their computers from home, which can cross national and cultural boundaries. The immediacy of synchronous tools to facilitate classroom communications offers a number of benefits to students that asynchronous communication tools do not.

The effects are also examined for several moderating methodological, pedagogical, and demographical factors. Following a systematic identification and screening procedure there was a statistically significant small effect in favor of synchronous online learning versus asynchronous online learning for cognitive outcomes (Martin et al., 2021).

Evaluation Tools

The tools for formative and summative assessment used in higher education include: questionnaires and surveys, e-Examinations and those for visualization and development of activities, whose conception and design were focused on encouraging student learning and to allow a better understanding of their behavior and progress. Online surveys or questionnaires are generated for testing purposes or as a learning tool that enable automatic feedback. Surveys can be created through an LMS or through Web-based survey tools. Angus and Watson (2009), found that the use of such online instruments leads to increased student learning.

The use of online exams, or e-Examinations, is becoming more and more prevalent and there are efforts to move from multiple choice questions to more sophisticated software tools, including question banks, randomized test generators, etc. Applications of this type, focused on mobile technology, can simplify exam processes, save a lot of time and resources and have functionalities, which allow students to check their current grade or previous exam results, download exam questions and access the exam by providing a valid key code generated by the teacher (Rifin et al., 2018).

Finally, there are a variety of visualization tools that help teachers better understand students, like a Kinect-based 3D gesture recognition system for interactive manipulation of 3D objects in educational visualization software, where the teachers can visualize cognitive levels and their progress through learning concepts and using materials. Although these tools are not focused on student assessment, they are a means to better understand behavioral patterns, which allows for improved assessment processes.

Digital Repositories

These technologies categorize the different content management systems and search engines that index them. Digital repositories incorporate on-line bibliographic databases that provide abstracts and indexing of global scientific and technical documents from various disciplines. Today there are too much databases, including: Web of Science, Scopus, IEEE Xplore, Google Scholar, Web of Knowledge, PubMed, among others, which can be easily accessed through institutional libraries. Research on hybrid e-Learning applications uses Pedagogical Agent Harvesting technology, such as the architecture proposed by Ivanovic et al. (2015), which provides students with agents that facilitate automated information search.

Another type of digital repository is a learning repository created from combinations of internal and third-party resources, allowing scholars to retrieve and share these resources.

The e-Portfolio is a type of digital repository that focuses on an individual's collection of artifacts and facilitates the process of collecting, sharing, and presenting learning outcomes and other professional achievements through a digital medium. Currently, innovative use of e-Portfolios is being made in areas that link education to the domain of planning, professional development, and are even used as resources for summative assessment in the educational process, as well as in work-integrated learning. Wakimoto and Lewis (2014) found that students valued the e-portfolio construction process and considered it beneficial for monitoring and reflecting on their learning strategies and behavior. Additionally, self-regulated learning seemed to be positively related to the quality of the e-portfolios (Händel et al., 2020).

In this context, Dorninger and Schrack (2008), emphasize the importance of having a common framework of content and technical environments claims.

Podcasts and Streaming

A podcast is an audio or video file which in this case is used as an educational resource, and which can be created and made available for download from the Internet to a computer or mobile device that is capable of playing MP3 or MP4 files on demand. Streaming files with data sent in a compressed format which are played in real time at the destination, are used as an alternative resource to podcasts. This media is being widely used in educational activities, especially in distance education, and is even used globally in prestigious universities, which provide educational services with lectures that incorporate these resources. The use of teacher- and student-generated podcasts in LMS has been investigated considerably and Hew (2009), argues that the most common use of podcasts is in the delivery of lectures and supplementary recordings.

The consolidation of smartphones as the dominant devices for accessing information and digital entertainment has redefined the production and marketing processes of the cultural communication industries. The nature of these devices, which prioritize visual content over sound, now determines the nature of marketing strategies in the audio market: radio operators, streaming music services and podcast creators need to adapt their value chains to the habits derived from this mediatization, especially with the younger audience (Pedrero-Esteban et al., 2019). Other studies investigated and demonstrated the versatility and effectiveness of podcasts as a means of engaging students in their own learning. For Hew (2009), some barriers to the sustainable use of podcasts in education include lack of awareness of the technology and, especially, the perception that it would have little relevance to teaching-learning, as well as lack of time to prepare podcasts. Middleton (2009) highlights as obstacles to the institutional scalability of podcasting, the lack of technical support, knowledge and technical confidence of users. For Sutton-Brady et al. (2009), they suggested that "most students felt they benefited from learning from podcasts, and also highlighted the flexibility of the medium".

Management and Administration Tools

Tools for teaching and managing learners, as well as for managing their learning, include those for managing grades, reporting their progress, as well as plagiarism detection (Zimba & Gasparyan, 2021). Tools to support group formation and to support group work, such as private discussion spaces and document sharing, are included. The electronic student information system, or gradebook, stores demographic data and allows the recording of grades and other data that can be edited, published for viewing, and exported. According to Dawley (2007), "Students really value the ability to see their overall progress at any point in the development of a course". Also, it is important to highlight media report tracking tools to monitor student access to course components or completion of assignments.

On the other hand, according to Sheridan et al. (2005), the global open access movement has made it possible to easily reveal most cases of plagiarism, including the copying of text and graphics in old and digitized digital documents to new sources. Otherwise, unethical articles have predominantly affected authors from different areas of China, India and Iran, particularly those publishing in low impact journals (Wang et al., 2019). Digitization of editorial management and regular scanning of countless online platforms has enabled detection of unethical reuse in peer-reviewed manuscripts (Heaven, 2018). The digitization of peer review has also allowed exposure of instances of theft of ideas and materials that are intended for confidential and privileged evaluation by reviewers (Mehregan, 2019). In that context, online plagiarism detection software can be used to encourage students to use referencing standards correctly and write assignments in their own words and above all respecting the ideas and intellectual property of other authors. For teachers, it is a screening tool to verify the authorship of work submitted by students. The software for plagiarism detection software and databases in high schools and universities are using, one of them is Turnitin, and other alternatives such as the one proposed by Chao et al. (2009), which can be used in conjunction with Cross Reference.

Categorized technologies should be used by teachers within the framework of educational theories of educational sciences, educational psychology and knowledge management, as well as teaching and learning practices, to enable the development and proper use of educational technologies that support the educational process more efficiently; however, research is required on e-Learning systems, focusing on making them more attractive in pedagogical terms, in which they can focus from an adaptive perspective, as well as on the use of media as tools to improve communication and interaction with students.

Several AI applications have been implemented in higher education worldwide (Salas-Pilco et al., 2022), for example:

AI Predictive modeling in education, estimate educational processes using large educational datasets (Brooks & Tompson, 2017), is beneficial because it gives accurate insight into educational questions and allows decisions to be made in advance; it is also time-saving and cost-efective. For example, course performance (Bojorque & Pesántez-Avilés, 2020), students' dropout rates (Palacios et al., 2021) and academic performance (Castrillón et al., 2020). Of the predictive models in the reviewed studies, the most common algorithm was the Multilayer Perceptron Artificial Neural Network (MLP-ANN), which also achieved a high average accuracy.

AI computer-assisted content analysis is now being adopted. Te use of natural language processing brings many opportunities in areas that involve an immense amount of textual data (Lu, 2018). Regarding content analysis, studies showed that

AI algorithms have been applied in higher education for student online assessment (Mendoza, 2020), for extracting information from university documents to generate a dataset that can provide answers to queries (Sayama et al., 2019), and for evaluating teacher performance through student comments (Gutiérrez et al., 2018) or the analysis of syllabuses (Okoye et al., 2020).

Next, the authors focus on establishing some of the current and future trends in the development of e-Learning systems, many of which incorporate the approach of some of the e-Technologies.

SOME CURRENT AND FUTURE TRENDS IN THE DEVELOPMENT AND APPLICATIONS OF E-TECHNOLOGIES AND E-LEARNING SYSTEMS

As a result of the COVID-19 pandemic, an unexpected situation, important critical steps were taken towards the integration of technology in the classroom environment in previously unimaginable methods, which have incorporated on-line and off-line learning into the teaching/learning process for instructors, collaborators and students in higher education institutions around the world (Anthes et al., 2016; Akcayir & Akcayir, 2017).

Immersive learning was developed to meet part of these needs and has been scientifically validated for two decades (Hew, 2009; Middleton, 2009). The following is a review of these technologies and applications developed in this context.

Extended Reality (XR)

XR is a term referring to the changing and growing field of human-computer interaction (HCI) (Palmas et al., 2019). It is a technology or application that combines various realities such as virtual worlds (VW), virtual reality (VR), augmented reality (AR) and mixed reality (MR) referred to as extended reality (XR) or cross-reality (Southgate, 2020).

Due to significant disagreements among experts, the terms metaverse, virtual reality (VR), mixed reality (MR), and cross reality (XR) refer to the same thing (Stein & Ohler, 2017). The interchangeability of terminology is a distinctive feature of a technology in its early stages of development in this area (Shams & Seitz, 2008). The meaning "XR" refers to all immersive experiences of any kind. All of these designations refer to situations in which a person has a virtual reality experience that has significant technological advances (Conijn, 2017). Historically, VR has been more widely used than XR (Alam, 2021), due to the interconnected nature of user experience (UX), instructional design (ID), and human-computer interface (HCI).

Figure 2. System model for using immersive technologies in adaptative e-Learning environments.
Source: Alfaro et al. (2021a).

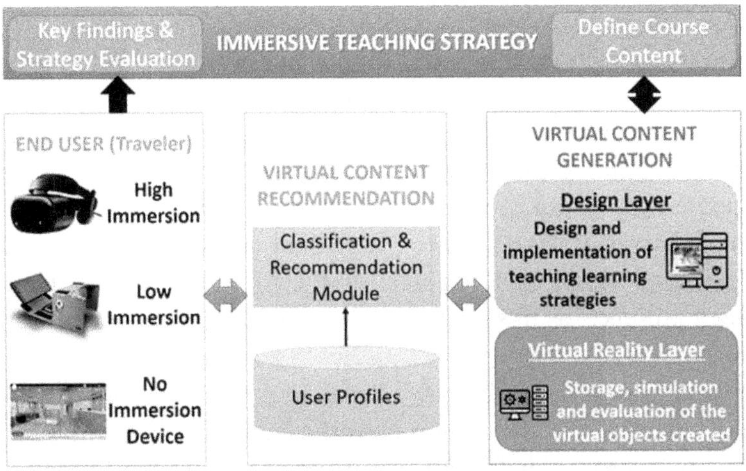

The System model for using different VR technologies in adaptative e-Learning environments using some its definitions was proposed by Alfaro et al. (2021a), and is show in Figure 2.

VR is related to a three-dimensional world in which users interact with the virtual world through different types of knowledge building experiences that are not available in the real world; however, it can have enormous potential in education and training focusing on the concepts called "Dimension", "Transduction" and "Reification" (Alfaro et al., 2021b), or can also be embodied as avatars that interact with each other and with the virtual world.

In Gutiérrez et al. (2008), it is stated that the three key elements that characterize VR are sensory immersion, where the user has the ability to look around, usually with the use of a head-mounted immersive helmet; interactive simulation, which consists of a simulation in the sense of recreating a virtual world, which only exists as a digital representation of physical objects on a computer; implicit interaction, which allows a certain degree of control over the experiences, usually achieved with sensors and input devices such as joysticks or keyboards.

Immersive learning emphasizes the continuity of experiences, from a computer augmenting an educator's reality with overlapping information, to a computer transferring a learner to another place and time through manipulation of sight and sound (Hayes & Johnson, 2019).

All immersive learning environments (ILE) have one characteristic: they provide context for the technical and narrative aspects that are challenging (Batmaz et al.,

2020). The term "Virtual Reality" is often used to refer to self-guided immersive experiences facilitated by immersive headset technology (Anthes et al., 2016), through some concepts such as:

- **Presence:** students generally state that the main feature of XR is the feeling of being there (Shuo et al., 2015). The pandemic that physically separates many people can provide pathways to social connections, while instilling a sense of belonging and pleasure in disease-affected societies. Presence could be defined as the psychological state in which virtual objects enable experiences that are experienced as real objects in sensory or non-sensory ways, a concept that has been widely explored on a variety of levels. VR users should have a sense of presence, as this is a suggested practice for pandemic times (Ray & Srivastava, 2020).
- **Storytelling:** can be defined as a dynamic presentation through the use of stories or narratives that evoke powerful audience emotions and insights about one's ideas, beliefs, personal experiences and life lessons. Through experience, stories educate learners and also address critical questions: Students are more likely to abandon an experience if they do not understand or know why they are being compelled to do so (Markowitz et al., 2018). Through the use of experiences, storytelling is connected to close-to-real experiences through VR (Railean, 2017).

VR can be partnered with Artificial Intelligence (AI) in innovative experiences, which currently can be found only in a little research; however, they can contribute towards enhanced learning, because they enable direct experiences of real or even imaginary world phenomena (Alfaro et al., 2019a; Alfaro et al., 2019b). As the design and development of VR and AI become more accessible to institutions, the levels of use and dissemination may be greater as research, evidence and experience are currently limited, some of these being the following: In Ballu et al. (2016), they propose a prototype virtual laboratory, dedicated to dimensional and geometric metrology, with simulated traditional measuring devices (caliper, micrometer, etc.) and coordinate measuring machines. Measurement simulation can be performed in a 3D environment, starting from models of parts with dimensional, orientation, position and shape errors (shape mask model) and from models of measuring devices, which present measurement uncertainties. In Chiu (2015), a paper was proposed, focusing on the particular advantages that virtual laboratories have to support experimentation of non-observable phenomena such as thermodynamics, chemical reactions or electricity. The authors argue that reality can be adapted, i.e., the properties of the mathematical model underlying the virtual laboratory can be changed to facilitate the interpretation of certain phenomena.

Finally, the incorporation of XR in higher education has already established a solid research base for experiences that blend interactivity, materiality, and permanence (Haraway, 2006).

Hybrid e-Learning Systems

A pedagogical agent is an intelligent agent with a pedagogical agenda (Haake, 2009), and refers to characters generated by computational resources to be used in educational environments, for the purpose of performing pedagogical activities. A pedagogical agent is an anthropomorphic virtual character (Veletsianos, 2010), used in an online learning environment for educational purposes and to serve as a learning support tool, providing help and guidance, demonstrating principles, procedures and examples to help students understand, process and store knowledge and information, enabling them to learn anytime and anywhere. From the point of view of e-learning, there are two types of agents that are of particular interest to researchers (Ivanovic et al., 2015): collectors and pedagogues. Collecting agents gather learning material from heterogeneous online repositories. The core properties of agent technology (e.g., parallel and distributed execution, mobility, and inter-agent communication) can bring significant benefits to the collection process. In Ivanovic et al. (2015), a standalone e-learning architecture is proposed called HArvester as well as a pedagogical agent-based e-learning (HAPA) system, which are designed to assist learners during the solving of programming tasks (Figure 3).

HAPA has three main components: harvesting agents, classifier module and pedagogical agents. The harvesting agents collect appropriate learning material from the Web, which is then entered into the Classifier module, which performs automatic classification of individual learning objects. Two specially designed pedagogical agents are also used, one helpful and one deceptive, to interact with learners and guide them in understanding the learning material. The helpful pedagogical agent provides useful hints to solve the problem at hand. The misleading pedagogical agent guides the learning process in the wrong direction. Because the learner is never sure which agent(s) he or she is interacting with, this novel approach encourages learners not to blindly follow the agent/tutor's instructions, but to employ critical thinking.

The authors of this architecture believe that this "softstress" environment could help students to cope with really stressful and competitive work environments. This proposal suggests a hybrid system, associating an LMS to a Pedagogical Agent, which together with collection agents can collect additional learning material (Ivanovic et al., 2014). Collection agents are also defined as web crawlers, specialized in information gathering. The proposal includes tools to elaborate useful and misleading suggestions, and the implementation of visual representation of pedagogical agents.

Figure 3. A high-level overview of the HAPA system.
Source: Chao et al. (2009).

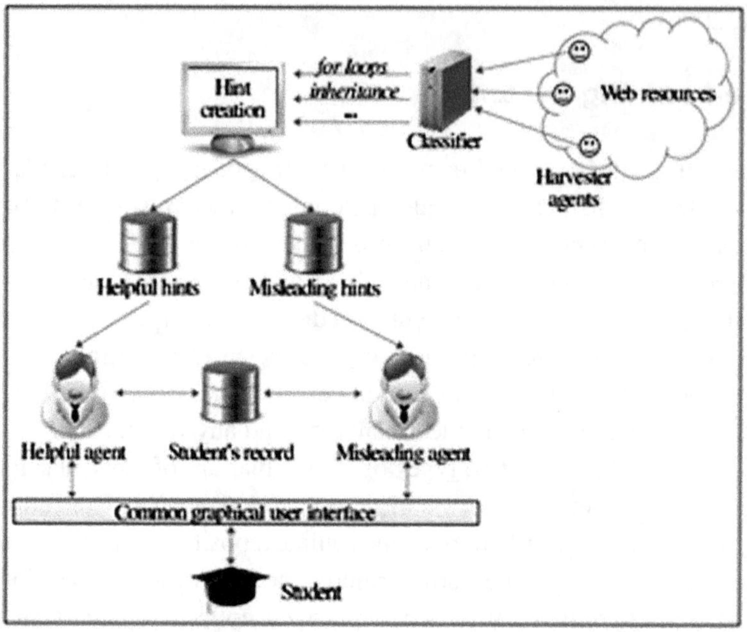

Collaborative e-Learning

Collaborative learning as an object of research and the benefits that such forms of work produce on student learning, has a long tradition within the educational sciences; the empirical approach to this topic has been developed, for example, from the fields of educational psychology, pedagogy, didactics and curriculum, among others (Pástor et al., 2018). Research focused on how computers could involve groups of students to improve their learning (Verdú et al., 2008), forming learning communities in small groups. Framed in the theories of social constructivism (Jameson & Gajos, 2020), this paradigm offers opportunities in the educational construction process. In a Computer Social Collaborative Learning (CSCL) environment, students learn in groups, through interactions that include asking questions, explaining and justifying opinions, explaining their reasoning, and presenting to their peers (Verdú et al., 2008).

The main form of collaboration is network-based support, with resources such as videoconferencing, e-mail, chat, social networks, forums and 3D environments. Likewise, Collaborative Virtual Environments (CVE), can be Immersive simulators.

Interesting CSCL implementations are currently emerging in tutoring systems to show the benefits obtained from the interaction between students during problem solving, as in the proposal of (Liao et al., 2014), stating that in the face of an increase in the number of students versus a lower growth rate of teachers, educational problems have arisen due to the lack of sufficient support in e-Learning activities to students, suggesting as a solution to the problem, collaborative learning, a collaborative model of e-Learning using Cloud Computing, having proposed a prototype whose empirical evaluations demonstrated the effectiveness of the proposed approach.

On the other hand, Masud (2016) proposes a collaborative e-learning content management environment, arguing that the heterogeneity of data in different Learning Management Systems (LMSs), presents many difficulties for data sharing, such as how to integrate data, produce results to address user queries and find the data, for which the authors present a solution for semantic data interoperability, distributed metadata management and an agent-based query processing approach to support the sharing of learning content from different LMSs. The authors also present an empirical evaluation of user acceptance of the proposed solutions to find qualitative measures of user acceptance and satisfaction, which show high user satisfaction.

Semantic Web Technologies (SWT) and Ontologies in the Design and Development of e-Learning Systems

A key aspect of e-Learning is instructional design, which allows the creation of online courses. Several studies have been conducted on the use of ontologies and other semantic web technologies in open e-Learning platforms, which indicate several advantages in terms of improved learning and better organization of teaching practices (Pástor et al., 2018). Semantic web technologies have had a positive impact on several areas of administrative knowledge, being remarkable that of the educational field, in which many sub-areas have been identified, such as adaptive learning, learning objects, collaborative learning, instructional design and authoring tools.

The integration of e-Learning and the Semantic Web has led to some important results (Isotani et al., 2013) in e-Learning research, highlighting the combination of Semantic Web Technologies (SWT) with educational theories and teaching and learning practices for the development of educational technologies, which incorporate and use teaching/learning theories, which support the educational process in a more efficient way. The e-learning environment uses media as well as tools to enhance communication and interaction with students. Studies conducted by Aroyo and Dicheva (2004), in relation to ontologies and the semantic Web for e-Learning, stand out for the use and management of ontologies used for their ability to be shared and reused, and are necessary to facilitate semantic interoperability in which there are many technologies involved, which are increasingly important in the design and development of pedagogical applications (Dicheva, 2008). Other studies have focused on issues related to interoperability, annotation, reuse and intelligent/

adaptive systems, such as Cuéllar et al. (2011), which allows the integration of different systems and learning through SWT.

Al-Chalabi and Hussein (2020), point out that the domain ontologies in adaptive e-learning systems help to determine the extensible representation of knowledge related to particular domains, since it is possible to address their requirements in an adaptive and personalized way, according to the characteristics, interests of the learners and learning objects available in the system. There are also studies that propose innovative approaches to recommend SWT-based e-learning content (Castellanos-Nieves et al., 2011).

Finally, according to the review by Pastor et al. (2018), there is a greater growth in the number of research papers related to the construction and use of ontologies and technologies within the context of instructional design, compared to research papers related to models, frameworks, tools and standards in the context of identification. Most of the studies analyzed showed little interest in the representation of certain aspects of instructional design using semantic web technologies. This refers specifically to those works that did not consider the pedagogical approach, instructional design standards or specifications, and compatibility with virtual learning environments. This could be due to the complexity of representing these aspects through ontologies and semantic web technologies, suggesting that the systems incorporate features of WS technologies in virtual learning environments.

Learning Analytics

Learning Analytics proposes a promising approach for digital and adaptive learning environments (Aguilar, 2018). Through Learning Analytics and the possibility of using large amounts of data associated with the teaching strategies used in educational action and the results that these strategies help to achieve in students, new fields of research associated with the analysis of student action data open up, which can help to define educational policies and to predict, among other things, school dropout (Morais et al., 2017). The main motivations for the use of Learning Analytics include preventing school failure, providing better feedback to students, obtaining data on students' attention and improving the teaching-learning process.

Learning analytics uses static and dynamic information about learners and learning environments, assessing, eliciting and analyzing it to model, predict and optimize learning processes (Duin & Tham, 2020), learning environments and educational decision making in real time (Misiejuk et al., 2021). The goal is to improve the satisfaction of learners' needs by providing individual learning paths, adaptive assessments and recommendations, or adaptive and Just-in-Time feedback, according to the motivations of learner states, individual characteristics and learning objectives.

However, a better understanding of how learning processes are related is required and can be captured through the data available in today's digital learning environments (Wilson et al., 2017). Therefore, learning analytics approaches may be appropriate, as they allow additional information about online learning behavior to be obtained without being intrusive (Vieira et al., 2018). Current approaches to learning analytics focus on behavioral indicators in the digital learning environment, such as time spent online, access to various types of resources, or reading and writing publications that relate them to learning performance (Mah, 2016). In addition, few approaches are enriched with learner characteristics, such as demographics or assessment results, to predict study success (Vieira et al., 2018).

Remote Labs

Laboratories were initially conceived to conduct research and generate knowledge. Laboratories were introduced as part of the student curriculum in the late 19th century in the United States (Morales-Menendez et al., 2019), and are considered absolutely essential in engineering education in the sense that the theoretical knowledge imparted to students in the classroom is adequately supplemented with practical experiences through laboratory experiments.

Social distancing measures resulting from the COVID-19 pandemic have disrupted many regular teaching activities, especially laboratory sessions. Curricula at many institutions have been at risk or have lost the experiential learning laboratory practices that have usually been conducted over the past several years. Many of the laboratory activities at various institutions were adapted to allow students to work remotely and synchronously on-line (Wee-Seng, 2021).

The term "remote laboratory" describes laboratory experiments that can be remotely controlled and monitored from a distant location (Grodotzki et al., 2018). This offers numerous advantages in educational settings compared to a classical laboratory. Remote laboratories and virtual reality are widely discussed tools in the educational context. They offer a practical and motivating way to teach students and are therefore an interesting topic for scientific research (Hermann et al., 2016).

Wee-Seng (2021), conducted an analysis showing that while many students perceived that face-to-face laboratories provided them with better hands-on skills training compared to online laboratories, they could function well as complements to face-to-face physical laboratories, according to tests that measured the level of understanding of the principles taught. Thus, online laboratories are effective in retaining hands-on experiential learning, although not ideal; they may be a suitable substitute for physical in-person labs when the latter must be limited due to safety and health concerns. Provisioning take-home kits with necessary equipment and components also allows more proactive students to test activities outside of class hours, which can enhance overall learning experiences.

CONCLUSION

The literature of recent years was reviewed, linked to e-Learning systems, e-Technologies and development trends in these promising areas of research and development, a period in which there were many innovations and changes in various aspects, such as the technological and methodological, which became a component of a much more complex technological ecosystem, based on services that interoperate with each other and that focus on meeting the demands of institutions and individuals.

The emerging problems of research and development in e-Learning were also reviewed, focusing on the factors that influence these development trends.

On the other hand, teachers and students are faced with a large amount of bibliographic material to study and research and in many cases do not know how to filter it, which discourages interaction with the system. In this case, some e-Technologies and especially adaptive e-Learning can be very useful, since they constitute a kind of personal tutor and in this way there are many challenges in relation to the appropriate methods and strategies to be applied to meet the needs of students.

Finally, this work, which is the result of a brief review of e-Learning and e-Technologies systems, allowed to focus on some technological and operational aspects, a fact that can contribute to the conception, design and innovation of these systems, which will undoubtedly facilitate the work of students and teachers and designers of e-Learning and e-Technologies systems.

ACKNOWLEDGMENT

The authors would like to thank National University of San Agustin (UNSA) – Arequipa, Peru, and Technological University of Peru – Arequipa, Peru.

REFERENCES

Aguilar, S. J. (2018). Learning Analytics: At the Nexus of Big Data, Digital Innovation, and Social Justice in Education. *TechTrends*, *62*(1), 37–45. doi:10.100711528-017-0226-9

Akcayir, M., & Akcayir, G. (2017). Advantages and challenges associated with augmented reality for education: A systematic review of the literature. *Educational Research Review*, *20*(1), 1–11. doi:10.1016/j.edurev.2016.11.002

Al-Chalabi, H., & Hussein, A. (2020). Ontologies and Personalization Parameters in Adaptive E-learning Systems [Review]. *Journal of Applied Computer Science & Mathematics*, *14*(1), 14–19. doi:10.4316/JACSM.202001002

Alam, A. (2021). Designing XR into Higher Education using Immersive Learning. *2021 International Conference on Advances in Computing, Communication, and Control (ICAC3).*

Alfaro, L., Rivera, C., Luna-Urquizo, J., Alfaro, S., & Fialho, F. (2019a). Knowledge construction by immersion in virtual reality environments. *International Journal of Advanced Computer Science and Applications*, *10*(12). Advance online publication. doi:10.14569/IJACSA.2019.0101278

Alfaro, L., Rivera, C., Luna-Urquizo, J., Alfaro, S., & Fialho, F. (2019b). Virtual reality full immersion techniques for enhancing workers performance, 20 years Later: A review and a reformulation. *International Journal of Advanced Computer Science and Applications*, *10*(10). Advance online publication. doi:10.14569/IJACSA.2019.0101066

Alfaro, L., Rivera, C., Luna-Urquizo, J., Castañeda, E., Zuñiga-Cueva, J., & Rivera-Chavez, M. (2021a). Work in Progress: Adaptive e-Learning software architecture based on immersive technologies. *2021 IEEE World Conference on Engineering Education (EDUNINE).* 10.1109/EDUNINE51952.2021.9429149

Alfaro, L., Rivera, C., Luna-Urquizo, J., Castañeda, E., Zuñiga Cueva, J., Rivera-Chavez, M., & Fialho, F. (2021b). A review of 20 years of adaptive e-learning. In D. Kolbaek (Ed.), *Challenges and Opportunities of Online Learning* (pp. 275–315). Nova Science Publishers Inc.

Angus, S. D., & Watson, J. (2009). Does regular online testing enhance student learning in the numerical sciences? Robust evidence from a large data set. *British Journal of Educational Technology*, *40*(2), 255–272. doi:10.1111/j.1467-8535.2008.00916.x

Anthes, C., Garcia-Hernandez, R. J., Wiedemann, M., & Kranzlmuller, D. (2016). State of the art of virtual reality technology. *2016 IEEE Aerospace Conference*, 1-19. 10.1109/AERO.2016.7500674

Aroyo, L., & Dicheva, D. (2004). The new challenges for e-learning: The Educational Semantic Web. *Journal of Educational Technology & Society*, *7*(4), 59–69.

Ballu, A., Yan, X., Blanchard, A., Clet, T., Mouton, S., & Niandou, H. (2016). Virtual Metrology Laboratory for e-Learning. *Procedia CIRP*, *43*, 148–153. doi:10.1016/j.procir.2016.02.110

Barrera, R., Montaño, R., Marín, P., & Chávez, J. (2021). Trabajo colaborativo y la ecología del aprendizaje. *Formación Universitaria*, *14*(6), 3–12. doi:10.4067/S0718-50062021000600003

Batmaz, A., Mutasim, A., & Stuerzlinger, W. (2020). Precision vs. ower grip: A comparison of pen grip styles for selection in virtual reality. *2020 IEEE Conference on Virtual Reality and 3D User Interfaces Abstracts and Workshops (VRW).*

Bojorque, R., & Pesántez-Avilés, F. (2020). Academic quality management system audit using artifcial intelligence tech- niques. In T. Ahram (Ed.), *Advances in artificial intelligence, software and systems engineering (AHFE 2019)* (Vol. 965, pp. 275–283). Springer. doi:10.1007/978-3-030-20454-9_28

Broadbent, J., & Lodge, J. (2021). Use of live chat in higher education to support self-regulated help seeking behaviours: A comparison of online and blended learner perspectives. *International Journal of Educational Technology on Higher Education*, *18*(17), 17. doi:10.118641239-021-00253-2 PMID:34778522

Brooks, C., & Thompson, C. (2017). Predictive modelling in teaching and learning. In C. Lang, G. Siemens, A. Wise, & D. Gašević (Eds.), *Handbook of learning analytics* (pp. 61–68). Society for Learning Analytics Research. doi:10.18608/hla17.005

Castellanos-Nieves, D., Fernández-Breis, J. T., Valencia-García, R., Martínez-Béjar, R., & Iniesta-Moreno, M. (2011). Semantic Web Technologies for supporting learning assessment. *Information Sciences*, *181*(9), 1517–1537. doi:10.1016/j.ins.2011.01.010

Castrillón, O. D., Sarache, W., & Ruiz-Herrera, S. (2020). Predicción del rendimiento académico por medio de técnicas de inteligencia artificial [Prediction of academic performance through artificial intelligence techniques]. *Formación Universitaria*, *13*(1), 93–102. doi:10.4067/S0718-50062020000100093

Chao, C.-A., Wilhelm, W. J., & Neureuther, B. D. (2009). A study of electronic detection and pedagogical approaches for reducing plagiarism. *Journal of Research in Business Education*, *51*(1), 31–42.

Chávez, J., Montaño, R., & Barrera, R. (2016). Structure and content of messages in an online environment: An approach from participation. *Computers in Human Behavior*, *54*(1), 560–568. doi:10.1016/j.chb.2015.08.046

Chiu, J. L., Dejaegher, C. J., & Chao, J. (2015). The effects of augmented virtual science laboratories on middle school students' understanding of gas properties. *Computers & Education*, *85*, 59–73. doi:10.1016/j.compedu.2015.02.007

Clark, R. C., & Mayer, R. E. (2012). e-Learning and the Science of Instruction: Proven Guidelines for Consumers and Designers of Multimedia Learning (3rd ed.). John Wiley & Sons. doi:10.1002/9781118255971

Conijn, R., Snijders, C., Kleingeld, A., & Matzat, U. (2017). Predicting student performance from LMS data: A comparison of 17 blended courses using moodle LMS. *IEEE Transactions on Learning Technologies*, *10*(1), 17–29. doi:10.1109/TLT.2016.2616312

Cuéllar, M. P., Delgado, M., & Pegalajar, M. C. (2011). A common framework for information sharing in e-learning management systems. *Expert Systems with Applications*, *38*(3), 2260–2270. doi:10.1016/j.eswa.2010.08.014

Dawley, L. (2007). The tools for successful online teaching? *British Journal of Educational Technology*, *38*(5), 949–950. doi:10.1111/j.1467-8535.2007.00749_8.x

Dicheva, D. (2008). Ontologies and Semantic Web for E-Learning. In *Handbook on Information Technologies for Education and Training* (pp. 47–65). Springer. doi:10.1007/978-3-540-74155-8_3

Dorninger, C., & Schrack, C. (2008). Future learning strategy and e-Portfolios in education. *International Journal of Emerging Technologies in Learning*, *3*(1), 11–14.

Duin, A. H., & Tham, J. (2020). The Current State of Analytics: Implications for Learning Management System (LMS) Use in Writing Pedagogy. *Computers and Composition*, *55*, 55. doi:10.1016/j.compcom.2020.102544

García-Peñalvo, F. J., Colomo-Palacios, R., & Lytras, M. D. (2012). Informal learning in work environments: Training with the Social Web in the workplace. *Behaviour & Information Technology*, *31*(8), 753–755. doi:10.1080/0144929X.2012.661548

García-Peñalvo, F. J., & Pardo, A. M. (2015). Una revisión actualizada del concepto de eLearning: Décimo Aniversario. *Education in the Knowledge Society*, *16*(1), 119–144. doi:10.14201/eks2015161119144

Gerhard, J., & Mayr, P. (2002). Competing in the e-learning environment strategies for universities. In *Proceedings of the Annual Hawaii International Conference on System Sciences* (pp. 3270–3279). 10.1109/HICSS.2002.994405

Grodotzki, J., Ortelt, T. R., & Tekkaya, A. E. (2018). Remote and Virtual Labs for Engineering Education 4.0: Achievements of the ELLI project at the TU Dortmund University. *Procedia Manufacturing*, *26*, 1349–1360. doi:10.1016/j.promfg.2018.07.126

Gutiérrez, M. A., Vexo, A. F., & Thalmann, D. (2008). *Stepping into virtual reality*. Springer-Verlag. doi:10.1007/978-1-84800-117-6

Haake, M. (2009). *Embodied Pedagogical Agents: From Visual Impact to Pedagogical Implications* [Doctoral Thesis]. Lund University.

Händel, M., Wimmer, B., & Ziegler, A. (2020). E-portfolio use and its effects on exam performance – A field study. *Studies in Higher Education*, *45*(2), 258–270. doi:10.1080/03075079.2018.1510388

Haraway, D. (2006). A cyborg manifesto: Science technology and socialist feminism in the late 20th century. In *The international handbook of virtual learning environments* (pp. 117–158). Springer. doi:10.1007/978-1-4020-3803-7_4

Hayes, A., & Johnson, K. (2019). Cultural embodiment in virtual reality education and training: A reflection on representation of diversity. In *Foundations and Trends in Smart learning* (pp. 93–96). Springer. doi:10.1007/978-981-13-6908-7_13

Heaven, D. (2018). AI peer reviewers unleashed to ease publishing grind. *Nature*, *563*(7733), 609–610. doi:10.1038/d41586-018-07245-9 PMID:30482927

Hermann, M., Pentek, T., & Otto, B. (2016). Design principles for industrie 4.0 scenarios. In *Proceedings of the Annual Hawaii International Conference on System Sciences* (pp. 3928–3937). 10.1109/HICSS.2016.488

Hew, K. F. (2009). Use of audio podcast in K-12 and higher education: A review of research topics and methodologies. *Educational Technology Research and Development*, *57*(3), 333–357. doi:10.100711423-008-9108-3

Hrastinski, S. (2008). Asynchronous and synchronous e-learning. *EDUCAUSE Quarterly*, *31*(4), 51–55. https://er.educause.edu/articles/2008/11/asynchronous-and-synchronous-elearning

Hsu, Y.-C., Ho, H., Tsai, C.-C., Hwang, G.-J., Chu, H.-C., Wang, C.-Y., & Chen, N.-S. (2012). Research Trends in Technology-based Learning from 2000 to 2009: A content analysis of publications in selected journals. *Journal of Educational Technology & Society*, *15*(2), 354–370.

Huang, S. L., & Yang, C. W. (2009). Designing a semantic bliki system to support different types of knowledge and adaptive learning. *Computers & Education, 53*(3), 701–712. doi:10.1016/j.compedu.2009.04.011

Hughes, P. (2001). Developing independent learning skills. In *University of Hertfordshire* (p. 2001). University of Hertfordshire.

Isotani, S., Mizoguchi, R., Isotani, S., Capeli, O. M., Isotani, N., de Albuquerque, A. R. P. L., Bittencourt, I., & Jaques, P. (2013). A Semantic Web-based authoring tool to facilitate the planning of collaborative learning scenarios compliant with learning theories. *Computers & Education, 63*, 267–284. doi:10.1016/j.compedu.2012.12.009

Ivanovic, M., Mitrovic, D., Budimac, Z., Jerinic, L., & Badica, C. (2015). HAPA: Harvester and pedagogical agents in e-learning environments. *International Journal of Computers, Communications & Control, 10*(2), 200–210. doi:10.15837/ijccc.2015.2.1753

Ivanovic, M., Mitrović, D., Budimac, Z., Vesin, B., & Jerinić, L. (2014). Different roles of agents in personalized programming learning environment. In Lecture Notes in Computer Science (vol. 7697, pp. 161–170). Springer. doi:10.1007/978-3-662-43454-3_17

Jameson, A., & Gajos, K. Z. (2020). Systems That Adapt to Their Users. In *The Human–Computer Interaction Handbook* (pp. 431–456). Springer.

Kang, L., Wang, X., Tan, C., & Zhao, J. (2015). Understanding the antecedents and consequences of live chat use in electronic markets. *Journal of Organizational Computing and Electronic Commerce, 25*(2), 117–139. doi:10.1080/10919392.2015.1033935

Kemp, J., & Livingstone, D. (2006). Putting a Second Life "Metaverse" Skin on Learning Management Systems. In *Proceedings of the Second Life Education Workshop* (Vol. 2006, pp. 13–18). 10.1145/1235511.1235517

Koehler, M. J., Mishra, P., & Cain, W. (2013). What is Technological Pedagogical Content Knowledge (TPACK)? *Journal of Education, 193*(3), 13–19. doi:10.1177/002205741319300303

Kupczynski, L., Gibson, A. M., Ice, P., Richardson, J., & Challoo, L. (2011). The Impact of Frequency on Achievement in Online Courses: A Study from a South Texas University. *Journal of Interactive Online Learning, 10*(3), 141–149.

Laanpere, M. (2012). Digital Learning Ecosystems: rethinking virtual learning environments in the age of social media. In IFIP-OST'12 conference 2012 (p. 12). Academic Press.

Lee, J., Gu, H., Kim, H., Kim, J., Kim, H., & Kim, H. (2013). Interactive manipulation of 3D objects using Kinect for visualization tools in education. In *13th International Conference on Control, Automation and Systems (ICCAS 2013)*. 10.1109/ICCAS.2013.6704175

Liao, J., Wang, M., Ran, W., & Yang, S. J. H. (2014). Collaborative cloud: A new model for e-learning. *Innovations in Education and Teaching International*, *51*(3), 338–351. doi:10.1080/14703297.2013.791554

Lin, T.-J., & Lan, Y.-J. (2015). Language Learning in Virtual Reality Environments: Past, Present, and Future. *Journal of Educational Technology & Society*, *18*(4), 486–497.

Lu, X. (2018). Natural language processing and intelligent computer-assisted language learning (ICALL). In J. I. Liontas (Ed.), *The TESOL encyclopedia of English language teaching* (pp. 1–6). Wiley Blackwell. doi:10.1002/9781118784235.eelt0422

Mah, D. K. (2016). Learning Analytics and Digital Badges: Potential Impact on Student Retention in Higher Education. *Technology. Knowledge and Learning*, *21*(3), 285–305. doi:10.100710758-016-9286-8

Markowitz, D. M., Laha, R., Perone, B. P., Pea, R. D., & Bailenson, J. (2018). Immersive virtual reality field trips facilitate learning about climate change. *Frontiers in Psychology*, *9*(1), 2364. doi:10.3389/fpsyg.2018.02364 PMID:30555387

Martin, F., & Parker, M. A. (2014). Use of synchronous virtual classrooms: Why, who and how? *Journal of Online Learning and Teaching*, *10*(2), 192–210. https://jolt.merlot.org/vol10no2/martin_0614.pdf

Martin, F., Sun, T., Turk, M., & Ritzhaupt, D. (2021). A Meta-Analysis on the Effects of Synchronous Online Learning on Cognitive and Affective Educational Outcomes. *The International Review of Research in Open and Distributed Learning*, *22*(3), 205–242. doi:10.19173/irrodl.v22i3.5263

Martyushev, N., Shutaleva, A., Malushko, E., Nikonova, Z., & Savchenko, I. (2021). Online Communication Tools in Teaching Foreign Languages for Education Sustainability. *Sustainability*, *13*(19), 11127. doi:10.3390u131911127

Masud, M. (2016). Collaborative e-learning systems using semantic data interoperability. *Computers in Human Behavior, 61*, 127–135. doi:10.1016/j.chb.2016.02.094

Matteson, M. L., Salamon, J., & Brewster, L. (2011). A systematic review of research on live chat service. *Reference and User Services Quarterly, 51*(2), 172–190. doi:10.5860/rusq.51n2.172

Maturana, H. R., & Varela, F. J. (1998). *De máquinas y seres vivos; una teoría sobre la organización biológia.* Santiago de Chile: Editorial Universitaria.

Mehregan, M. (2019). Ethical Reviewers are Essential for Scholarly Journals for Timely Processing of Submissions and Avoiding Retractions. *Journal of Korean Medical Science, 34*(5, e41), e41. doi:10.3346/jkms.2019.34.e41 PMID:30718993

Mendoza, H. (2020). Modelos de redes neuronales artifciales, como sustento evaluativo al crecimiento pedagógico virtual en Educación Superior [Artifcial neural network models, as evaluative support to virtual pedagogical growth in Higher Education]. *Educación Superior, 7*(2), 25–36. https://www.scielo.org.bo/pdf/escepies/v7n2/v7n2_a06.pdf

Middleton, A. (2009). Beyond podcasting: Creative approaches to designing educational audio. *Alt-J, 17*(2), 143–155. doi:10.1080/09687760903033082

Misiejuk, K., Wasson, B., & Egelandsdal, K. (2021). Using learning analytics to understand student perceptions of peer feedback. *Computers in Human Behavior, 117*, 106658. Advance online publication. doi:10.1016/j.chb.2020.106658

Morais, C., Alvis, P., & Miranda, L. (2017). Learning analytics and performance indicators in higher education. *Proceedings of the 12th Iberian Conference on Information Systems and Technologies AISTI.* 10.23919/CISTI.2017.7975812

Morales-Menendez, R., Ramírez-Mendoza, R. A., & Guevara, A. J. V. (2019). Virtual/Remote Labs for Automation Teaching: A Cost Effective Approach. *IFAC-PapersOnLine, 52*(9), 306–311. doi:10.1016/j.ifacol.2019.08.219

Okoli, C., & Schabram, K. (2012). A guide to conducting a Systematic Literature Review of Information Systems Research. SSRN *Electronic Journal.* doi:10.2139/ssrn.2115818

Okoye, K., Arrona-Palacios, A., Camacho-Zuñiga, C., Hammout, N., Nakamura, E. L., Escamilla, J., & Hosseini, S. (2020). Impact of students' evaluation of teaching: A text analysis of the teachers' qualities by gender. *International Journal of Educational Technology in Higher Education, 17*(1), 1–27. doi:10.118641239-020-00224-z

Orton-Johnson, K. (2009). I've stuck to the path I'm afraid': Exploring student non-use of blended learning. *British Journal of Educational Technology*, *40*(5), 837–847. doi:10.1111/j.1467-8535.2008.00860.x

Palmas, F., Labode, D., Plecher, D. A., & Klinker, G. (2019). Comparison of a Gamified and Non-Gamified Virtual Reality Training Assembly Task. In *Proceedings of IEEE 11th International Conference on Virtual Worlds and Games for Serious Applications: VS-Games* (pp. 1-8). 10.1109/VS-Games.2019.8864583

Pástor, D., Jiménez, J., Gómez, O., & Isotani, S. (2018). New Perspectives in Instructional Design using Semantic Web Technologies: A Systematic Literature Review. *Ingeniería y Desarrollo. Universidad del Norte*, *36*(1), 215–239.

Pata, K. (2011). An ecological meta-design framework for open learning ecosystems. In *Mupple2011* (pp. 13–16). Open University of London.

Pedrero-Esteban. L., Barrios-Rubio, A., Medina-Avila, V. (2019). Teenagers, Smartphones and digital audio consumption in the age of spotify. *Media Education Reseach Journal, Comunicar, 27*(60).

Po-Yao, Ch., Lai, R., Chen-Chung, L., & Hung-Ming, L. (2019). Strengthening Social Networks in Online Discussion Forums to Facilitate Help Seeking for Solving Problems. *Journal of Educational Technology & Society*, *21*(4), 39–50.

Railean, E. A. (2017). Metacognition in Higher Education: Successful Learning Strategies and Tactics for Sustainability. In E. Railean, A. Elci, & A. Elci (Eds.), *Metacognition and Successful Learning Strategies in Higher Education* (p. 121). IGI Global. doi:10.4018/978-1-5225-2218-8.ch001

Ray, S., & Srivastava, S. (2020). Virtualization of science education: A lesson from the COVID-19 pandemic. *Journal of Proteins and Proteomics*, *11*(2), 77–80. doi:10.100742485-020-00038-7 PMID:33132627

Rifin, R., Fang, T. E., Abidin, A. F. Z., Adam, A., Majid, M. A., Zainuddin, A., Mohammad, S. H., Harun, M. H., & Rizman, Z. I. (2018). Examwiz: A development and implementation of an android based examination. *Journal of Fundamental and Applied Sciences*, *10*(6S), 965–976.

Rutter, M. (2009). Messenger in The Barn: Networking in a learning environment. *Alt-J*, *17*(1), 33–47. doi:10.1080/09687760802649863

Salas-Pilco, S., & Yang, Y. (2022). Artificial intelligence applications in Latin American higher education: A systematic review. *International Journal of Educational Technology in Higher Education*, *19*(1), 21. doi:10.118641239-022-00326-w

Shams, L., & Seitz, A. R. (2008). Benefits of multisensory learning. *Trends in Cognitive Sciences, 12*(11), 411–417. doi:10.1016/j.tics.2008.07.006 PMID:18805039

Sheridan, J., Alany, R., & Brake, D. J. (2005). Pharmacy students' views and experiences of Turnitin - An online tool for detecting academic dishonesty. *Pharmacy Education, 5*(3–4), 241–250. doi:10.1080/15602210500288977

Shuo, R., McKenzie, F. D., Chaturvedi, S. K., Prabhakaran, R., Jaewan, Y., & Katsioloudis, P. J. (2015). Design and Comparison of Immersive Interactive Learning and Instructional Techniques for 3D Virtual Laboratories. *Presence (Cambridge, Mass.), 24*(2), 93–112. doi:10.1162/PRES_a_00221

Southgate, E. (2020). *Virtual reality in curriculum and pedagogy: Evidence from secondary classrooms*. Routledge. doi:10.4324/9780429291982

Stein, J. P., & Ohler, P. (2017). Venturing into the uncanny valley of mind - The influence of mind attribution on the acceptance of human-like characters in a virtual reality setting. *Cognition, 160*(1), 43–50. doi:10.1016/j.cognition.2016.12.010 PMID:28043026

Sutton-Brady, C., Scott, K. M., Taylor, L., Carabetta, G., & Clark, S. (2009). The value of using short-format podcasts to enhance learning and teaching. *Alt-J, 17*(3), 219–232. doi:10.1080/09687760903247609

Tang, Y., & Hew, K. F. (2022). Effects of using mobile instant messaging on student behavioral, emotional, and cognitive engagement: A quasi-experimental study. *International Journal of Educational Technology in Higher Education, 19*(3), 3. Advance online publication. doi:10.118641239-021-00306-6 PMID:35036520

Tavangarian, D., Leypold, M. E., Nölting, K., Röser, M., & Voigt, D. (2004). Is e-Learning the Solution for Individual Learning? *Electronic Journal of e-Learning, 2*(2), 273–280.

Vakaloudis, A. (2014). A Framework for Rating Synchronous Video e- Learning Applications. *Science and Information Conference 2014*. 10.1109/SAI.2014.6918293

Veletsianos, G. (2010). Contextually relevant pedagogical agents: Visual appearance, stereotypes, and first impressions and their impact on learning. *Computers & Education, 55*(2), 576–585. doi:10.1016/j.compedu.2010.02.019

Verdú, E., Regueras, L. M., Verdú, M. J., De Castro, J. P., & Pérez, M. A. (2008). An analysis of the research on adaptive Learning: The next generation of e-learning. *WSEAS Transactions on Information Sciences and Applications, 5*(6), 859–868.

Vieira, C., Parsons, P., & Byrd, V. (2018). Visual learning analytics of educational data: A systematic literature review and research agenda. *Computers & Education, 122*, 119–135. doi:10.1016/j.compedu.2018.03.018

Vygotsky, L. S. (1978). *Mind in society: The development of higher psychological processes.* Harvard University Press.

Wakimoto, D., & Lewis, E. (2014). Graduate Student Perceptions of Eportfolios: Uses for Reflection, Development, and Assessment. *The Internet and Higher Education, 21*, 53–58. doi:10.1016/j.iheduc.2014.01.002

Wang, T., Xing, Q. R., Wang, H., & Chen, W. (2019). Retracted Publications in the biomedical Literature from Open Access Journals. *Science and Engineering Ethics, 25*(3), 855–868. doi:10.100711948-018-0040-6 PMID:29516389

Webster, J., & Watson, R. (2002). Analyzing the Past to Prepare for the Future: Writing a Literature Review. *Management Information Systems Quarterly, 26*(2), xiii–xxiii.

Wee-Seng, S. (2021). Experiential Learning Through Remote Electrical Engineering Labs During the COVID-19 Pandemic. *2021 IEEE International Conference on Engineering, Technology & Education (TALE).*

Wilson, A., Watson, C., Thompson, T. L., Drew, V., & Doyle, S. (2017). Learning analytics: Challenges and limitations. *Teaching in Higher Education, 22*(8), 991–1007. doi:10.1080/13562517.2017.1332026

Zimba, O., & Gasparyan, A. (2021). Plagiarism detection and prevention: A primer for researchers. *Reumatologia, 59*(3), 132–137. doi:10.5114/reum.2021.105974 PMID:34538939

KEY TERMS AND DEFINITIONS

Cyberculture: Contemporary culture structured by digital network technologies.

Pedagogical Agent: Is an intelligent agent with a pedagogical agenda.

Presence/Immersion: Both presence and immersion are used interchangeably to describe the sensation of feeling physically present within a virtual experience, as opposed to the detachment experienced when experiencing content through a conventional screen-based medium.

Semantic Web: Sometimes known as Web 3.0, is an extension of the World Wide Web through standards set by the World Wide Web Consortium (W3C). The goal of the Semantic Web is to make Internet data machine-readable.

Significant Learning: Which can be related, in a non-arbitrary and substantial way (not verbatim), to what the student already knows.

Social Interaction: Relations of the subject with their social environment.

Social Networking: Refers to the use of internet-based social media sites to stay connected with friends, family, colleagues, customers, or clients.

Streaming Files: Method of transmitting a media file in a continuous stream of data that can be processed by the receiving computer before the entire file has been completely sent.

System: Any distinguishable set of components that are specified as constituting a unit.

Compilation of References

DVista. (n.d.). *3DVista*. Retrieved November 29, 2021, from https://www.3dvista.com/

Ackerman, M. S., & Starr, B. (1995, December). Social activity indicators: interface components for CSCW systems. *Proceedings of the 8th annual ACM symposium*, 159–168. 10.1145/215585.215969

Adelman, C. (1993). Kurt Lewin and the origins of action research. *Educational Action Research*, *1*(1), 7–24. doi:10.1080/0965079930010102

Aggarwal, R., Grantcharov, T., Moorthy, K., Hance, J., & Darzi, A. (2006). A competency-based virtual reality training curriculum for the acquisition of laparoscopic psychomotor skill. *American Journal of Surgery*, *191*(1), 128–133. https://doi.org/10.1016/j.amjsurg.2005.10.014

Aguilar, S. J. (2018). Learning Analytics: At the Nexus of Big Data, Digital Innovation, and Social Justice in Education. *TechTrends*, *62*(1), 37–45. doi:10.100711528-017-0226-9

Akcayir, M., & Akcayir, G. (2017). Advantages and challenges associated with augmented reality for education: A systematic review of the literature. *Educational Research Review*, *20*(1), 1–11. doi:10.1016/j.edurev.2016.11.002

Akour, I. A., Al-Maroof, R. S., Alfaisal, R., & Salloum, S. (2022). A conceptual framework for determining metaverse adoption in higher institutions of gulf area: An empirical study using hybrid SEM-ANN approach. *Computers and Education: Artificial Intelligence*, *3*, 100052. doi:10.1016/j.caeai.2022.100052

Alam, A. (2021). Designing XR into Higher Education using Immersive Learning. *2021 International Conference on Advances in Computing, Communication, and Control (ICAC3).*

Al-Chalabi, H., & Hussein, A. (2020). Ontologies and Personalization Parameters in Adaptive E-learning Systems [Review]. *Journal of Applied Computer Science & Mathematics*, *14*(1), 14–19. doi:10.4316/JACSM.202001002

Alfaro, L., Rivera, C., Luna-Urquizo, J., Alfaro, S., & Fialho, F. (2019a). Knowledge construction by immersion in virtual reality environments. *International Journal of Advanced Computer Science and Applications*, *10*(12). Advance online publication. doi:10.14569/IJACSA.2019.0101278

Alfaro, L., Rivera, C., Luna-Urquizo, J., Alfaro, S., & Fialho, F. (2019b). Virtual reality full immersion techniques for enhancing workers performance, 20 years Later: A review and a reformulation. *International Journal of Advanced Computer Science and Applications, 10*(10). Advance online publication. doi:10.14569/IJACSA.2019.0101066

Alfaro, L., Rivera, C., Luna-Urquizo, J., Castañeda, E., Zuñiga Cueva, J., Rivera-Chavez, M., & Fialho, F. (2021b). A review of 20 years of adaptive e-learning. In D. Kolbaek (Ed.), *Challenges and Opportunities of Online Learning* (pp. 275–315). Nova Science Publishers Inc.

Alfaro, L., Rivera, C., Luna-Urquizo, J., Castañeda, E., Zuñiga-Cueva, J., & Rivera-Chavez, M. (2021a). Work in Progress: Adaptive e-Learning software architecture based on immersive technologies. *2021 IEEE World Conference on Engineering Education (EDUNINE).* 10.1109/EDUNINE51952.2021.9429149

Alnagrat, A. J. A., Ismail, R. C., & Idrus, S. Z. S. (2021, May). Extended Reality (XR) in Virtual Laboratories: A Review of Challenges and Future Training Directions. In *Journal of Physics: Conference Series* (Vol. 1874, No. 1, p. 012031). IOP Publishing.

Alonso, S., López, D., Puente, A., Romero, A., Álvarez, I. M., & Manero, B. (2021). Evaluation of a motion capture and virtual reality classroom for Secondary school teacher training. In *Proceedings of the 29th International Conference on Computers in Education*. Asia-Pacific Society for Computers in Education. https://icce2021.apsce.net/proceedings/volume1/

Alvarez, I. M., González-Parera, M., & Manero, B. (2022). The role of emotions in classroom conflict management. Case studies geared towards improving teacher training. *Frontiers in Psychology, 13*, 818431. Advance online publication. doi:10.3389/fpsyg.2022.818431 PMID:35369238

American Psychological Association. (2022). *Social Competence.* https://dictionary.apa.org/social-competence

Amin, D., & Govilkar, S. (2015). Comparative study of augmented reality SDKs. *International Journal on Computational Science & Applications, 5*(1), 11–26. doi:10.5121/ijcsa.2015.5102

Anderson, L., Peter, K., Airasian, D., Cruikshank, K., Mayer, R., Pintrich, P., Raths, J., & Wittrock, M. (2001). *Taxonomy for learning, teaching, and assessing: a revision of Bloom's taxonomy of educational objectives.* Addison Wesley Longman.

Andolsek, D. L. (1995). Virtual reality in education and training. *International Journal of Instructional Media, 22*(2), 145–155. https://www.learntechlib.org/p/85408/

Angus, S. D., & Watson, J. (2009). Does regular online testing enhance student learning in the numerical sciences? Robust evidence from a large data set. *British Journal of Educational Technology, 40*(2), 255–272. doi:10.1111/j.1467-8535.2008.00916.x

Anthes, C., Garcia-Hernandez, R. J., Wiedemann, M., & Kranzlmuller, D. (2016). State of the art of virtual reality technology. *2016 IEEE Aerospace Conference*, 1-19. 10.1109/AERO.2016.7500674

Antón-Sancho, Á., Vergara, D., & Fernández-Arias, P. (2021a). Self-assessment of soft skills of university teachers from countries with a low level of digital competence. *Electronics (Basel), 10*(20), 2532. doi:10.3390/electronics10202532

Antón-Sancho, Á., Vergara, D., Lamas-Álvarez, V. E., & Fernández-Arias, P. (2021b). Digital content creation tools: American university teachers' perception. *Applied Sciences (Basel, Switzerland), 11*(24), 11649. doi:10.3390/app112411649

Araujo, G. V. (2017). *The Use of Augmented Reality in the Teaching of Regular Convex Polyhedra.* Dourados: UEMS Profmat.

Arias, S., Wahlqvist, J., Nilsson, D., Ronchi, E., & Frantzich, H. (2021). Pursuing behavioral realism in virtual reality for fire evacuation research. *Fire and Materials, 45*(4), 462–472. doi:10.1002/fam.2922

Aroyo, L., & Dicheva, D. (2004). The new challenges for e-learning: The Educational Semantic Web. *Journal of Educational Technology & Society, 7*(4), 59–69.

Åslund, O., & Rooth, D. (2007). Do When and Where Matter? Initial Labour Market Conditions and Immigrant Earnings. *Economic Journal (London), 117*(518), 422–448. https://doi.org/10.1111/j.1468-0297.2007.02024.x

Baía Reis, A., & Coelho, A. F. V. C. C. (2018). Virtual Reality and Journalism: A gateway to conceptualizing immersive journalism. *Digital Journalism, 6*(8), 1090-1100.

Balali, V., Zalavadia, A., & Heydarian, A. (2020). Real-time interaction and cost estimating within immersive virtual environments. *Journal of Construction Engineering and Management, 146*(2), 04019098. doi:10.1061/(ASCE)CO.1943-7862.0001752

Balamuralithara, B., & Woods, P. C. (2009). Virtual laboratories in engineering education: The simulation lab and remote lab. *Computer Applications in Engineering Education, 17*(1), 108–118. doi:10.1002/cae.20186

Ballu, A., Yan, X., Blanchard, A., Clet, T., Mouton, S., & Niandou, H. (2016). Virtual Metrology Laboratory for e-Learning. *Procedia CIRP, 43*, 148–153. doi:10.1016/j.procir.2016.02.110

Barnett, R., & Jackson, N. (Eds.). (2019). *Ecologies for learning and practice: Emerging ideas, sightings, and possibilities.* Routledge. doi:10.4324/9781351020268

Barrera, R., Montaño, R., Marín, P., & Chávez, J. (2021). Trabajo colaborativo y la ecología del aprendizaje. *Formación Universitaria, 14*(6), 3–12. doi:10.4067/S0718-50062021000600003

Barr, J. J. (2011). The relationship between teachers' empathy and perceptions of school culture. *Educational Studies, 37*(3), 365–369. doi:10.1080/03055698.2010.506342

Batey, M., Hughes, D. J., Crick, L., & Toader, A. (2021). Designing creative spaces: An experimental examination of the effect of a nature poster on divergent thinking. *Ergonomics, 64*(1), 139–146. doi:10.1080/00140139.2020.1811398 PMID:32819209

Batmaz, A., Mutasim, A., & Stuerzlinger, W. (2020). Precision vs. ower grip: A comparison of pen grip styles for selection in virtual reality. *2020 IEEE Conference on Virtual Reality and 3D User Interfaces Abstracts and Workshops (VRW).*

Beach, J., & Wendt, J. (2014). *Social Interaction Development through Immersive Virtual Environments*. ERIC.

Benítez de Gracia, M. J., Herrera Damas, S., & Benítez de Gracia, E. (2019). Analysis of the immersive social content feature in the Spanish news media. *Revista Latina de Comunicación Social*, *74*, 1655-1679.

Berg, L. P., & Vance, J. M. (2016). Industry use of virtual reality in product design and manufacturing: A survey. *Virtual Reality (Waltham Cross)*, *21*(1), 1–17. doi:10.100710055-016-0293-9

Berkman, M. I., & Akan, E. (2019). *Presence and Immersion in Virtual Reality*. Springer International Publishing. doi:10.1007/978-3-319-08234-9_162-1

Bianchi-Berthouze, N., Kim, W. W., & Patel, D. (2007). Does body movement engage you more in digital game play? and why? In A. C. R. Paiva, R. Prada, & R. W. Picard (Eds.), *International conference on affective computing and intelligent interaction* (pp. 102–113). Berlin: Springer.

Biocca, F. (1992). Virtual reality technology: A tutorial. *Journal of Communication*, *42*(4), 23–72. doi:10.1111/j.1460-2466.1992.tb00811.x

Blaga, A., & Tamas, L. (2018). Augmented reality for digital manufacturing. *2018 26th Mediterranean Conference on Control and Automation (MED)*, 173-178.

Bloom, B., Engelhart, M., Furst, E., Hill, W., & Krathwohl, D. (1956). *Taxonomy of educational objectives. Book 1 Cognitive domain*. Longmans.

Bocos-Corredor, M., Diaz-Nieto, A., Lopez-Garcia, A., Romero-Hernandez, A., Alvarez, I. M., & Manero, B. (2020). A VR game to improve communication skills in Secondary -school teachers. In *Proceedings of EDULEARN20. 12th International Conference on Education and New Learning Technologies* (pp. 8701–8710). IATED Academy.

Bojorque, R., & Pesántez-Avilés, F. (2020). Academic quality management system audit using artifcial intelligence tech- niques. In T. Ahram (Ed.), *Advances in artificial intelligence, software and systems engineering (AHFE 2019)* (Vol. 965, pp. 275–283). Springer. doi:10.1007/978-3-030-20454-9_28

Bombari, D., Schmid Mast, M., Canadas, E., & Bachmann, M. (2015). Studying social interactions through immersive virtual environment technology: Virtues and challenges. *Frontiers in Psychology*, *6*, 6. doi:10.3389/fpsyg.2015.00869 PMID:26157414

Bonilla, V. P. (2020). *Design of industrial robot control systems based on industry 4.0* [Diseño de sistemas de control industrial de robots basados en industria 4.0]. Universidad técnica de ambato. https://repositorio.uta.edu.ec/bitstream/123456789/31221/1/t1698id.pdf

Bösch, M., Gensch, S., & Rath-Wiggins, L. (2018). Immersive Journalism: How Virtual Reality Impacts Investigative Storytelling. In Digital Investigative Journalism (pp. 103-111). Palgrave Macmillan.

Boulos, M. N. K., Hetherington, L., & Wheeler, S. (2007). Second life: An overview of the 9otential of 3-D virtual worlds in medical and health education. *Health Information and Libraries Journal, 24*(4), 233–245. doi:10.1111/j.1471-1842.2007.00733.x PMID:18005298

Brito, F. d. (2014). *The use of software in the teaching of positional spatial geometry.* Universidade Federal De Lavras, Programa de Pós- Graduação Profissional em Matemática. Retrieved from http://repositorio.ufla.br/jspui/handle/1/2191

Broadbent, J., & Lodge, J. (2021). Use of live chat in higher education to support self-regulated help seeking behaviours: A comparison of online and blended learner perspectives. *International Journal of Educational Technology on Higher Education, 18*(17), 17. doi:10.118641239-021-00253-2 PMID:34778522

Brooke, J. (1996). SUS: A 'quick and dirty' usability scale. *Usability Evaluation in Industry, 189.*

Brooks, C., & Thompson, C. (2017). Predictive modelling in teaching and learning. In C. Lang, G. Siemens, A. Wise, & D. Gašević (Eds.), *Handbook of learning analytics* (pp. 61–68). Society for Learning Analytics Research. doi:10.18608/hla17.005

Bujic, M., & Hamari, J. (2020, January). Satisfaction and willingness to consume immersive journalism: experiment of differences between VR, 360 video, and article. In *Proceedings of the 23rd International Conference on Academic Mindtrek* (pp. 120-125). Academic Press.

Buttussi, F., & Chittaro, L. (2021). A comparison of procedural safety training in three conditions: Virtual reality headset, smartphone, and printed materials. *IEEE Transactions on Learning Technologies, 14*(1), 1–15. doi:10.1109/TLT.2020.3033766

Calandra, D., Pratticò, F. G., Migliorini, M., Verda, V., & Lamberti, F. (2021). A Multi-role, Multi-user, Multi-technology Virtual Reality-based Road Tunnel Fire Simulator for Training Purposes. In *Proceedings of the 16th International Joint Conference on Computer Vision, Imaging and Computer Graphics Theory and Applications – GRAPP* (pp. 96–105). SciTePress.

Calandra, D., Pratticò, F., Migliorini, M., Verda, V., & Lamberti, F. (2021). A multi-role, multi-user, multi-technology virtual reality-based road tunnel fire simulator for training purposes. In *Proceedings of the 16th International Joint Conference on Computer Vision, Imaging and Computer Graphics Theory and Applications* (vol. 1, pp. 96-105). 10.5220/0010319400960105

Cant, R., Cooper, S., & Ryan, C. (2022, March 8). Using virtual simulation to teach evidence-based practice in nursing curricula: A rapid review. *Worldviews on Evidence-Based Nursing.* Advance online publication. doi:10.1111/wvn.12572 PMID:35261156

Carrier, M., & Gartzlaff, M. (2020). Responsible research and innovation: Hopes and fears in the scientific community in Europe. *Journal of Responsible Innovation, 7*(2), 149–169. doi:10.1080/23299460.2019.1692571

Carron, L. (2019, March 19). *Yahoo News announces innovative XR partner program and world's first XR aggregator for users*. Verizon News Center. https://vz.to/3vS5Md7

CAST. (2018). *Universal Design for Learning Guidelines version 2.2*. Retrieved from http: // udlguidelines.cast.org

Castellanos-Nieves, D., Fernández-Breis, J. T., Valencia-García, R., Martínez-Béjar, R., & Iniesta-Moreno, M. (2011). Semantic Web Technologies for supporting learning assessment. *Information Sciences*, *181*(9), 1517–1537. doi:10.1016/j.ins.2011.01.010

Castrillón, O. D., Sarache, W., & Ruiz-Herrera, S. (2020). Predicción del rendimiento académico por medio de técnicas de inteligencia artificial [Prediction of academic performance through artificial intelligence techniques]. *Formación Universitaria*, *13*(1), 93–102. doi:10.4067/S0718-50062020000100093

Cha, M., Han, S., Lee, K., & Choi, B. (2014). A virtual reality based fire training simulator integrated with fire dynamics data. *Fire Safety Journal*, *50*, 12–24. doi:10.1016/j.firesaf.2012.01.004

Chang, E., Kim, H. T., & Yoo, B. (2020). Virtual Reality Sickness: A Review of Causes and Measurements. *International Journal of Human-Computer Interaction*, *36*(7), 1658–1682. doi: 10.1080/10447318.2020.1778351

Chang, M.-L., & Taxer, J. (2020). Teacher emotion regulation strategies in response to classroom misbehaviour. *Teachers and Teaching*, *27*(5), 353–369. doi:10.1080/13540602.2020.1740198

Chao, C.-A., Wilhelm, W. J., & Neureuther, B. D. (2009). A study of electronic detection and pedagogical approaches for reducing plagiarism. *Journal of Research in Business Education*, *51*(1), 31–42.

Chávez, J., Montaño, R., & Barrera, R. (2016). Structure and content of messages in an online environment: An approach from participation. *Computers in Human Behavior*, *54*(1), 560–568. doi:10.1016/j.chb.2015.08.046

Chesher, C. (1994). Colonizing virtual reality: Construction of the discourse of virtual reality. *Cultronix*, *1*(1), 1–27.

Chirico, A., Cipresso, P., Yaden, D. B., Biassoni, F., Riva, G., & Gaggioli, A. (2017). Effectiveness of immersive videos in inducing awe: An experimental study. *Scientific Reports*, *7*(1), 1–11. doi:10.103841598-017-01242-0 PMID:28450730

Chittaro, L., & Buttussi, F. (2022). Learning safety through public serious games: A study of "Prepare for Impact" on a very large, international sample of players. *IEEE Transactions on Visualization and Computer Graphics*, *28*(3), 1573–1574. doi:10.1109/TVCG.2020.3022340 PMID:32894716

Chiu, J. L., Dejaegher, C. J., & Chao, J. (2015). The effects of augmented virtual science laboratories on middle school students' understanding of gas properties. *Computers & Education*, *85*, 59–73. doi:10.1016/j.compedu.2015.02.007

Chi-Yuan, Ch. (2022). Immersive virtual reality to train preservice teachers in managing students' challenging behaviours: A pilot study. *British Journal of Educational Technology*, *53*(4), 998–1024. Advance online publication. doi:10.1111/bjet.13181

Cipresso, P., Giglioli, I. A. C., Raya, M. A., & Riva, G. (2018). The Past, Present, and Future of Virtual and Augmented Reality Research: A Network and Cluster Analysis of the Literature. *Frontiers in Psychology*, *9*, 2086–2086. doi:10.3389/fpsyg.2018.02086 PMID:30459681

Clarà, M., Mauri, T., Colombiana, R., & Onrubia, J. (2019). Supporting collaborative reflection in teacher education: A case study. *European Journal of Teacher Education*, *42*(2), 175–191. doi:10.1080/02619768.2019.1576626

Clark, R. C., & Mayer, R. E. (2012). e-Learning and the Science of Instruction: Proven Guidelines for Consumers and Designers of Multimedia Learning (3rd ed.). John Wiley & Sons. doi:10.1002/9781118255971

Clarysse, B., Wright, M., Bruneel, J., & Mahajan, A. (2014). Creating value in ecosystems: Crossing the chasm between knowledge and business ecosystems. *Research Policy*, *43*(7), 1164–1176. https://doi.org/10.1016/j.respol.2014.04.014

Conijn, R., Snijders, C., Kleingeld, A., & Matzat, U. (2017). Predicting student performance from LMS data: A comparison of 17 blended courses using moodle LMS. *IEEE Transactions on Learning Technologies*, *10*(1), 17–29. doi:10.1109/TLT.2016.2616312

Craciun, D., & Bunoiu, M. (2016). *Augmented reality in Romanian science education pros and cons*. doi:10.12753/2066-026X-16-205

CRESCEnt Project. (2021). *Mind the Gap in media coverage and strategic communication in case of security threats*. Erasmus+ 2018-1-RO01-KA202-049449. https://crescentproject.eu

Creswell, J. W. (2002). *Educational research: Planning conducting and evaluating quantitative and qualitative research*. Pearson.

Crowell, C., Sayis, B., Benitez, J. P., & Pares, N. (2020, January). Mixed Reality, Full-Body Interactive Experience to Encourage Social Initiation for Autism: Comparison with a Control Nondigital Intervention. *Cyberpsychology, Behavior, and Social Networking*, *23*(1), 5–9. doi:10.1089/cyber.2019.0115 PMID:31644332

Cuéllar, M. P., Delgado, M., & Pegalajar, M. C. (2011). A common framework for information sharing in e-learning management systems. *Expert Systems with Applications*, *38*(3), 2260–2270. doi:10.1016/j.eswa.2010.08.014

Cummings, J. J., & Bailenson, J. N. (2016). How immersive is enough? A meta-analysis of the effect of immersive technology on user presence. *Media Psychology*, *19*(2), 272–309. doi:10.1080/15213269.2015.1015740

D'zurilla, T. J., & Goldfried, M. R. (1971). Problem solving and behavior modification. *Journal of Abnormal Psychology*, *78*(1), 107–126. doi:10.1037/h0031360 PMID:4938262

Dalgarno, B., Hedberg, J., & Harper, B. (2002). The Contribution of 3D Environments To Conceptual Understanding. *19th Annual Conference of the Australasian Society for Computers in Learning in Tertiary Education (ASCILITE 2002), 1*, 149–158. http://ascilite.org.au/conferences/auckland02/proceedings/papers/051.pdf

Dalgarno, B., & Lee, M. J. (2010). What are the learning affordances of 3-D virtual environments? *British Journal of Educational Technology, 41*(1), 10–32. doi:10.1111/j.1467-8535.2009.01038.x

Damásio, A. (1999). *The feeling of what happens: body and emotion in the making of consciousness.* Harcourt Brace & Company.

Dann, R. (2019). Feedback as a relational concept in the classroom. *Curriculum Journal, 30*(4), 352–374. doi:10.1080/09585176.2019.1636839

Davis, F. D. (1989). Perceived usefulness, perceived ease of use, and user acceptance of information technology. *Management Information Systems Quarterly, 13*(3), 319–340. doi:10.2307/249008

Dawley, L. (2007). The tools for successful online teaching? *British Journal of Educational Technology, 38*(5), 949–950. doi:10.1111/j.1467-8535.2007.00749_8.x

Dawley, L., & Dede, C. (2014). Situated Learning in Virtual Worlds and Immersive Simulations. In J. M. Spector, M. D. Merrill, J. Elen, & M. J. Bishop (Eds.), *Handbook of Research on Educational Communications and Technology* (pp. 723–734). Springer. doi:10.1007/978-1-4614-3185-5_58

De Lorenzis, F., Pratticò, F. G., & Lamberti, F. (2022). Hcp–vr: Training first responders through a virtual reality application for hydrogeological risk management. *HUCAPP, 2022*, 273–280.

De-la-Peña, N., Weil, P., Llobera, J., Giannopoulos, E., Pomés, A., Spaniang, B., Friedman, D., Sánchez-Vives, M. V., & Slater, M. (2010). Immersive journalism: Immersive virtual reality for the first-person experience of news. *Presence (Cambridge, Mass.), 19*(4), 291–301. doi:10.1162/PRES_a_00005

Deng, L., Tian, J., Cornwell, C., Phillips, V., Chen, L., & Alsuwaida, A. (2019). Towards an Augmented Reality-Based Mobile Math Learning Game System. *International Conference on Human-Computer Interaction.* 10.1007/978-3-030-23525-3_28

Deterding, S., Dixon, D., Khaled, R., & Nacke, L. (2011, September). From game design elements to gamefulness: defining 'gamification. *MindTrek'11: Proceedings of the 15th International Academic MindTrek conference: Envisioning Future Media Environments*, 9-15.

Dhar, P., Rocks, T., Samarasinghe, R. M., Stephenson, G., & Smith, C. (2021). Augmented reality in medical education: Students' experiences and learning outcomes. *Medical Education Online, 26*(1), 1953953–1953953. doi:10.1080/10872981.2021.1953953 PMID:34259122

Dicheva, D. (2008). Ontologies and Semantic Web for E-Learning. In *Handbook on Information Technologies for Education and Training* (pp. 47–65). Springer. doi:10.1007/978-3-540-74155-8_3

Disney. (n. d.). Stitch [Imagen]. ClipArtMag. https://clipartmag.com/download-clipart-image#stitch-drawing-ohana-36.jpg

Doblack, B. N., Allis, T., & Davila, L. P. (2014). Novel 3D/VR interactive environment for MD simulations, visualization and analysis. *Journal of Visualized Experiments, 94*(94), e51384. doi:10.3791/51384 PMID:25549300

Doblack, B. N., Flores, C., Matlock, T., & Dávila, L. P. (2011). The emergence of immersive low-cost 3D virtual reality environments for interactive learning in materials science and engineering. In *Proceedings of Materials Research Society Symposium* (vol. 1320). Cambridge University Press. 10.1557/opl.2011.636

Dolce, O., & Pompeo, J. N. (2019). *Fundamentals of Elementary Mathematics* (Vol. 10). Saraiva Didáticos.

Dorninger, C., & Schrack, C. (2008). Future learning strategy and e-Portfolios in education. *International Journal of Emerging Technologies in Learning, 3*(1), 11–14.

Doyle, W. (2006). Ecological approaches to classroom management. In C. M. Evertson & C. S. Weinstein (Eds.), Handbook of classroom management: Research, practice, and contemporary issues (pp. 97-125). Mahwah, NJ: Erlbaum.

Drake, M. (2019). Embedding virtual reality into competence recognition. *16th International Conference on Cognition and Exploratory Learning in Digital Age, CELDA 2019,* 465–467. doi:10.33965/celda2019_201911r064

Drake, M., & Kauppinen, R. (2021). *New Technology - A New Approach to Further Vocational Training?* doi:10.21125/iceri.2021.1811

Duin, A. H., & Tham, J. (2020). The Current State of Analytics: Implications for Learning Management System (LMS) Use in Writing Pedagogy. *Computers and Composition, 55*, 55. doi:10.1016/j.compcom.2020.102544

Dumlao, R. (2018). *A guide to collaborative communication for service-learning and community engagement partners*. Stylus Publishing, LLC.

Durukan, A., Artun, H., & Temur, A. (2020). Virtual reality in science education: A descriptive review. *Journal of Science Learning, 3*(3), 132–142. doi:10.17509/jsl.v3i3.21906

Easymodbus, T. C. P. (2022). *Communication library and professional tools for industrial communication*. Easymodbustcp. http://easymodbustcp.net/en/

Ekman, R. (1985). *Telling Lies*. Berkley Books.

Ergün, O., Akın, Ş., Dino, İ. G., & Surer, E. (2019). Architectural design in virtual reality and mixed reality environments: A comparative analysis. In *Proceedings of the 2019 IEEE Conference on Virtual Reality and 3D User Interfaces (VR)* (vol. 1, pp. 914-915). Osaka, Japan: IEEE. 10.1109/VR.2019.8798180

Eronen, A., Härmälä, V., Jauhiainen, S., Karikallio, H., Karinen, R., Kosunen, A., Laamanen, J.-P., & Lahtinen, M. (2014). *Maahanmuuttajien työllistyminen : taustatekijät, työnhaku ja työvoimapalvelut* [Labour Market of Immigrants in Finland]. Publications of Ministry of Economic Affairs and Employment. http://linda.linneanet.fi/F/?func=direct&doc_number=006622519&local_base=fin01%5Cnhttp://www.tem.fi/files/38664/TEMjul_6_2014_web_10022014.pdf

European Commission. (2019). *ESCO handbook* (2nd ed.). Directorate-General for Employment, Social Affairs and Inclusion.

Evertson, C., & Poole, I. (2008). Proactive classroom management. In T. Good (Ed.), 21st century education: A reference handbook (pp. I-131-I-140). Thousand Oaks, CA: SAGE Publications, Inc. doi:10.4135/9781412964012.n14

Evertson, M., & Weinstein, C. S. (Eds.). (2006). *Handbook of classroom management: Research, practice, and contemporary issues*. Erlbaum.

Extremera, J., Vergara, D., Dávila, L. P., & Rubio, M. P. (2020). Virtual and augmented reality environments to learn the fundamentals of crystallography. *Crystals*, *10*(6), 456. doi:10.3390/cryst10060456

Extremera, J., Vergara, D., Rodríguez, S., & Dávila, L. P. (2022). Reality-virtuality technologies in the field of materials science and engineering. *Applied Sciences (Basel, Switzerland)*, *12*(10), 4968. doi:10.3390/app12104968

Fadda, P., & Sullivan, P. (2013). Using interactive video to develop preservice teachers' classroom awareness. *Contemporary Issues in Technology & Teacher Education*, *13*(2), 156–174.

Fagernäs, S., Hamilton, W., Espinoza, N., Miloff, A., Carlbring, P., & Lindner, P. (2021). What do users think about Virtual Reality relaxation applications? A mixed methods study of online user reviews using natural language processing. *Internet Interventions: the Application of Information Technology in Mental and Behavioural Health*, *24*, 100370. doi:10.1016/j.invent.2021.100370 PMID:33665136

Fanelli, R. P. (2013). *Alternatives for teaching spatial geometry*. Universidade Estadual de Mato Grosso do Sul, Dourados.

Fang, H., Khim, S., & Nee, A. (2009). *Robot Programming Using Augmented Reality*. IEEE Conference Publication. https://ieeexplore.ieee.org/document/5279717

Faridi, H., Tuli, N., Mantri, A., Singh, G., & Gargrish, S. (2021). A framework utilizing augmented reality to improve critical thinking ability and learning gain of the students in Physics. *Computer Applications in Engineering Education*, *29*(1), 258–273. doi:10.1002/cae.22342

Feng, Y., Duives, D. C., & Hoogendoorn, S. P. (2021). Using virtual reality to study pedestrian exit choice behaviour during evacuations. *Safety Science*, *137*, 105158. doi:10.1016/j.ssci.2021.105158

Feng, Z., González, V. A., Amor, R., Lovreglio, R., & Cabrera-Guerrero, G. (2018). Immersive virtual reality serious games for evacuation training and research: A systematic literature review. *Computers & Education*, *127*, 252–266.

Feng, Z., González, V. A., Amor, R., Spearpoint, M., Thomas, J., Sacks, R., Lovreglio, R., & Cabrera-Guerrero, G. (2020a). An immersive virtual reality serious game to enhance earthquake behavioral responses and post-earthquake evacuation preparedness in buildings. *Advanced Engineering Informatics*, *45*, 101118. doi:10.1016/j.aei.2020.101118

Feng, Z., González, V. A., Mutch, C., Amor, R., Rahouti, A., Baghouz, A., Li, N., & Cabrera-Guerrero, G. (2020b). Towards a customizable immersive virtual reality serious game for earthquake emergency training. *Advanced Engineering Informatics*, *46*, 101134. doi:10.1016/j.aei.2020.101134

Fernández-Arias, P., Antón-Sancho, Á., Vergara, D., & Barrientos, A. (2021). Soft skills of American university teachers: Self-concept. *Sustainability*, *13*(22), 12397. doi:10.3390u132212397

Fink, L. D. (2003). *Creating significant learning experiences for EAL learners*. Jossey-Bass.

Finnish Food Authority. (2020). *Hygienie Passport*. https://www.ruokavirasto.fi/en/private-persons/hygiene-passport/

Flores, C., Matlock, T., & Dávila, L. P. (2012). Enhancing materials research through innovative 3D environments and interactive manuals for data visualization and analysis. In *Proceedings of Materials Research Society Symposium* (vol. 1472). Cambridge University Press. 10.1557/opl.2012.1257

França, J. S. (2015). A didactic proposal of augmented reality in the teaching of sapce geometry. UFPA, Programa pos-graduação em matemática em rede nacional.

Freeman, G., & Maloney, D. (2020). Body, Avatar, and Me: The Presentation and Perception of Self in Social Virtual Reality. *Proceedings of the ACM on Human- Computer Interaction*, *4*.

Freina, L., & Ott, M. (2015, April). A literature review on immersive virtual reality in education: state of the art and perspectives. In The international scientific conference eLearning and software for education (Vol. 1, No. 133, pp. 10-1007). Academic Press.

Frenzel, A. C., Daniels, L., & Burić, I. (2021). Teacher emotions in the classroom and their implications for students. *Educationnels Psychologist*, *56*(4), 250–264. doi:10.1080/00461520.2021.1985501

Fu, M., Liu, R., & Zhang, Y. (2021). Do people follow neighbors? An immersive virtual reality experimental study of social influence on individual risky decisions during evacuations. *Automation in Construction*, *126*, 103644. doi:10.1016/j.autcon.2021.103644

García, A. A., Bobadilla, I. G., Arroyo-Figueroa, G., Pérez-Ramírez, M., & Román, J. (2015). Virtual reality training system for maintenance and operation of high-voltage overhead power lines. *Virtual Reality (Waltham Cross)*, *20*(1), 27–40. doi:10.100710055-015-0280-6

García-Magariño, I., Cerezo, E., Plaza, I., & Chittaro, L. (2019). A mobile application to report and detect 3D body emotional poses. *Expert Systems with Applications*, *122*, 207–216. doi:10.1016/j.eswa.2019.01.021

García-Peñalvo, F. J., Colomo-Palacios, R., & Lytras, M. D. (2012). Informal learning in work environments: Training with the Social Web in the workplace. *Behaviour & Information Technology, 31*(8), 753–755. doi:10.1080/0144929X.2012.661548

García-Peñalvo, F. J., & Pardo, A. M. (2015). Una revisión actualizada del concepto de eLearning: Décimo Aniversario. *Education in the Knowledge Society, 16*(1), 119–144. doi:10.14201/eks2015161119144

GeoGebra. (2022). *Geogebra - the world's favorite, free math tools used by over 100 million students and teachers*. Retrieved from GeoGebra for Teaching and Learning Math: https://www.geogebra.org/

Gerhard, J., & Mayr, P. (2002). Competing in the e-learning environment strategies for universities. In *Proceedings of the Annual Hawaii International Conference on System Sciences* (pp. 3270–3279). 10.1109/HICSS.2002.994405

Girvan, C. (2018). What is a virtual world? Definition and classification. *Educational Technology Research and Development, 6*(5), 1087–1100. doi:10.100711423-018-9577-y

Gisler, J., Hift, C., Kunz, A., & Holzwarth, V. (2020). Designing virtual training environments: Does immersion increase task performance? In *2020 International Conference on Cyberworlds (CW)* (pp. 125–128). 10.1109/CW49994.2020.00026

Gladden, M. E. (2019). Novel forms of "magical" human-computer interaction within the cyber-physical smart workplace: Implications for usability and user experience. *International Journal of Research Studies in Management, 8*(1), 25–48. doi:10.5861/ijrsm.2019.4001

Goda, Y., & Mitsuhara, H. (2021). Learning experiences in a full 3D conference: Relationships with 3D factors and innovative mindsets. In *Proceedings of 2021 IEEE International Conference on Engineering, Technology and Education* (pp.119-125). 10.1109/TALE52509.2021.9678846

Gorini, A., Griez, E., Petrova, A., & Riva, G. (2010). Assessment of the emotional responses produced by exposure to real food, virtual food and photographs of food in patients affected by eating disorders. *Annals of General Psychiatry, 9*(30). http://www.annals-general-psychiatry.com/content/9/1/30

Goyette, G., & Lessard, H. M. (1988). *La investigación-acción. Funciones, fundamentos e instrumentación*. Alertes.

Granja Oramas, M. V. (2014). *Modeling and analysis of the direct and inverse kinematics of the Stanford manipulator of six degrees of freedom* [Modelación y análisis de la cinemática directa e inversa del manipulador Stanford de seis grados de libertad]. Repositorio Digital Institucional de la Escuela Politécnica Nacional. https://bibdigital.epn.edu.ec/handle/15000/8693

Graus, M., van de Broek, A., Hennissen, P., & Schils, T. (2022). Disentangling aspects of teacher identity learning from reflective blogs: The development of a category system. *Teaching and Teacher Education, 111*, 103624. Advance online publication. doi:10.1016/j.tate.2021.103624

Grodotzki, J., Ortelt, T. R., & Tekkaya, A. E. (2018). Remote and Virtual Labs for Engineering Education 4.0: Achievements of the ELLI project at the TU Dortmund University. *Procedia Manufacturing*, *26*, 1349–1360. doi:10.1016/j.promfg.2018.07.126

Gutiérrez, M. A., Vexo, A. F., & Thalmann, D. (2008). *Stepping into virtual reality*. Springer-Verlag. doi:10.1007/978-1-84800-117-6

Haake, M. (2009). *Embodied Pedagogical Agents: From Visual Impact to Pedagogical Implications* [Doctoral Thesis]. Lund University.

Häfner, P., Häfner, V., & Ovtcharova, J. (2013). Teaching Methodology for Virtual Reality Practical Course in Engineering Education. *Procedia Computer Science*, *25*, 251–269. doi:10.1016/j.procs.2013.11.031

Halabi, O. (2020). Immersive virtual reality to enforce teaching in engineering education. *Multimedia Tools and Applications*, *79*(3-4), 2987–3004. doi:10.100711042-019-08214-8

Hamit, O., & Yildirim, R. (2020). Teacher perspectives on classroom management. *International Journal of Contemporary Educational Research*, *7*(1), 99–113. doi:10.33200/ijcer.645818

Han, B., Liu, Y., & Qian, F. (2020, April). ViVo: Visibility-aware mobile volumetric video streaming. In *Proceedings of the 26th Annual International Conference on Mobile Computing and Networking* (pp. 1-13). Academic Press.

Händel, M., Wimmer, B., & Ziegler, A. (2020). E-portfolio use and its effects on exam performance – A field study. *Studies in Higher Education*, *45*(2), 258–270. doi:10.1080/03075079.2018.1510388

Han, E., Miller, M. R., Ram, N., Nowak, K. L., & Bailenson, J. N. (2022, May 26-30). Understanding Group Behavior in Virtual Reality: A Large-Scale, Longitudinal Study in the Metaverse. *72nd Annual International Communication Association Conference*.

Haraway, D. (2006). A cyborg manifesto: Science technology and socialist feminism in the late 20th century. In *The international handbook of virtual learning environments* (pp. 117–158). Springer. doi:10.1007/978-1-4020-3803-7_4

Harmer, J., Gisslén, L., del Val, J., Holst, H., Bergdahl, J., Olsson, T., Sjoo, K., & Nordin, M. (2018). Imitation learning with concurrent actions in 3d games. In *2018 IEEE Conference on Computational Intelligence and Games (CIG)*. IEEE. 10.1109/CIG.2018.8490398

Harris, R. (1998). *Introduction to decision making*. VirtualSalt. http://www. virtualsalt. com/crebook5. htm

Hassenzahl, M., Koller, F., & Burmester, M. (2008). Der user experience (UX) auf der spur: Zum einsatz von. In H. Brau, S. Diefenbach, M. Hassenzahl, F. Koller, M. Peissner, & K. Rose (Eds.), *Tagungsband UP08* (pp. 78–82). Fraunhofer Verlag. www.attrakdiff.de

Hayes, A., & Johnson, K. (2019). Cultural embodiment in virtual reality education and training: A reflection on representation of diversity. In *Foundations and Trends in Smart learning* (pp. 93–96). Springer. doi:10.1007/978-981-13-6908-7_13

Heaven, D. (2018). AI peer reviewers unleashed to ease publishing grind. *Nature, 563*(7733), 609–610. doi:10.1038/d41586-018-07245-9 PMID:30482927

Heras, L., & Villarreal, B. (2004). *Augmented reality: a technology waiting for users* [La realidad aumentada: una tecnología en espera de usuarios]. https://www.revista.unam.mx/vol.8/num6/art48/jun_art48.pdf

Herbst, R., Rybak, T., Meisman, A., Whitehead, M., Rosen, B., Crosby, L. E., Klein, M. D., & Real, F. J. (2021, June 29). A Virtual Reality Resident Training Curriculum on Behavioral Health Anticipatory Guidance: Development and Usability Study. *JMIR Pediatrics and Parenting*, *4*(2), e29518. doi:10.2196/29518 PMID:34081601

Hermann, M., Pentek, T., & Otto, B. (2016). Design principles for industrie 4.0 scenarios. In *Proceedings of the Annual Hawaii International Conference on System Sciences* (pp. 3928–3937). 10.1109/HICSS.2016.488

Herrmann, L. & Schilling. (2013). A spatial augmented reality system for intuitive display of robotic data. *Int. Conf. Human-Robot Interact.* doi: 10.1109/HRI.2013.6483560

Hew, K. F. (2009). Use of audio podcast in K-12 and higher education: A review of research topics and methodologies. *Educational Technology Research and Development*, *57*(3), 333–357. doi:10.100711423-008-9108-3

Hilfert, T., & König, M. (2016). Low-cost virtual reality environment for engineering and construction. *Visualization in Engineering*, *4*(2), 1–18. doi:10.118640327-015-0031-5

Hocker, J., & Wilmot, W. W. (2014). *Interpersonal conflict* (9th ed.). McGraw-Hill.

Hoppenstedt, E., Radu, I., Joy, T., & Schneider, B. (2021). Augmented Reality in Collaborative Problem Solving: A Qualitative Study of Challenges and Solutions. *International Conference on Computer Supported Collaborative Learning.*

Howard, M. C., & Gutworth, M. B. (2020). A meta-analysis of virtual reality training programs for social skill development. *Computers & Education*, *144*, 103707.

Hrastinski, S. (2008). Asynchronous and synchronous e-learning. *EDUCAUSE Quarterly*, *31*(4), 51–55. https://er.educause.edu/articles/2008/11/asynchronous-and-synchronous-elearning

Hruby, F. (2019). The Sound of Being There: Audiovisual Cartography with Immersive Virtual Environments. *KN - Journal of Cartography and Geographic Information, 69*(1), 19-28. doi:10.1007/s42489-019-00003-5

Hsu, Y.-C., Ho, H., Tsai, C.-C., Hwang, G.-J., Chu, H.-C., Wang, C.-Y., & Chen, N.-S. (2012). Research Trends in Technology-based Learning from 2000 to 2009: A content analysis of publications in selected journals. *Journal of Educational Technology & Society*, *15*(2), 354–370.

Huang, H. M., Rauch, U., & Liaw, S.-S. (2010). Investigating learners' attitudes toward virtual reality learning environments: Based on a constructivist approach. *Computers & Education*, *55*(3), 1171–1182. doi:10.1016/j.compedu.2010.05.014

Huang, S. L., & Yang, C. W. (2009). Designing a semantic bliki system to support different types of knowledge and adaptive learning. *Computers & Education*, *53*(3), 701–712. doi:10.1016/j.compedu.2009.04.011

Huang, T.-C., Chen, C.-C., & Chou, Y.-W. (2016). Animating eco-education: To see, feel, and discover in an augmented reality-based experiential learning environment. *Computers & Education*, *96*, 72–82. doi:10.1016/j.compedu.2016.02.008

Huang, Z., Li, T., Chen, W., Zhao, Y., Xing, J., LeGendre, C., & Li, H. (2018). Deep volumetric video from very sparse multi-view performance capture. In *Proceedings of the European Conference on Computer Vision* (pp. 336–354). ECCV. doi:10.1007/978-3-030-01270-0_21

Hughes, P. (2001). Developing independent learning skills. In *University of Hertfordshire* (p. 2001). University of Hertfordshire.

Hurkmans, B., & Rajagopal, K. (2020). The use of extended reality technologies for learning in industry. *EdMedia+ Innovate Learning*, 900-903. https://www.learntechlib.org/p/217460/

Hyre, A., Harris, G., Osho, J., Pantelidakis, M., Mykoniatis, K., & Liu, J. (2022). Digital Twins: Representation, Replication, Reality, and Relational (4Rs). *Manufacturing Letters*, *31*, 20–23.

IAT. (2020). *Augmented reality. What is it? Features and types* [Realidad aumentada. ¿Qué es? Características y tipos]. IAT. https://iat.es/tecnologias/realidad-aumentada/#:~:text=La%20realidad%20aumentada%20es%20aquella,ofreciendo%20as%C3%AD%20una%20realidad%20transformada

Inter IKEA Systems. (2022). *Inter IKEA Group*. Retrieved from Inter IKEA Group: https://www.inter.ikea.com/en

Ip, H. H., & Li, C. (2015). Virtual reality-based learning environments: Recent developments and ongoing challenges. *International Conference on Hybrid Learning and Continuing Education.*

Isotani, S., Mizoguchi, R., Isotani, S., Capeli, O. M., Isotani, N., de Albuquerque, A. R. P. L., Bittencourt, I., & Jaques, P. (2013). A Semantic Web-based authoring tool to facilitate the planning of collaborative learning scenarios compliant with learning theories. *Computers & Education*, *63*, 267–284. doi:10.1016/j.compedu.2012.12.009

Ivanovic, M., Mitrović, D., Budimac, Z., Vesin, B., & Jerinić, L. (2014). Different roles of agents in personalized programming learning environment. In Lecture Notes in Computer Science (vol. 7697, pp. 161–170). Springer. doi:10.1007/978-3-662-43454-3_17

Ivanovic, M., Mitrovic, D., Budimac, Z., Jerinic, L., & Badica, C. (2015). HAPA: Harvester and pedagogical agents in e-learning environments. *International Journal of Computers, Communications & Control*, *10*(2), 200–210. doi:10.15837/ijccc.2015.2.1753

Jaligama, V., & Liarokapis, F. (2011). An Online Virtual Learning Environment for Higher Education. *Third International Conference on Games and Virtual Worlds for Serious Applications*, 207–214. 10.1109/VS-GAMES.2011.44

Jameson, A., & Gajos, K. Z. (2020). Systems That Adapt to Their Users. In *The Human–Computer Interaction Handbook* (pp. 431–456). Springer.

Janke, E., & Dumlao, R. J. (2019). Developing Communication Repertoires to Address Conflict in Community Engagement Work. *Journal of Higher Education Outreach & Engagement, 23*, 35–56. https://eric.ed.gov/?id=EJ1212501

Japan Meteorological Agency (JMA). (2022). https://www.jma.go.jp/jma/indexe.html

Jennings, P. A., & Greenberg, M. T. (2009). The prosocial classroom: Teacher social and emotional competence in relation to student and classroom outcomes. *Review of Educational Research, 79*(1), 491–525. doi:10.3102/0034654308325693

Jerald., J. (2016). *The VR Book: Human-Centred Design for Virtual Reality*. ACM Books.

Jing, W., Goh, C. F., Rajaraman, M., Gao, F., Park, S., Liu, Y., & Shimada, K. (2018). *A Computational Framework for Automatic Online Path Generation of Robotic Inspection Tasks via Coverage Planning and Reinforcement Learning*. IEEE Xplore. https://ieeexplore.ieee.org/stamp/stamp.jsp?arnumber=8476296

Jones, T. S. (2000). Emotional communication in conflict: Essence and impact. In W. Eadie & P. Nelson (Eds.), *The language of conflict and resolution* (pp. 81–104). Sage. doi:10.4135/9781452205496.n6

Jovanović, A., & Milosavljević, A. (2022). VoRtex metaverse platform for gamified collaborative learning. *Electronics (Basel), 11*(3), 317. doi:10.3390/electronics11030317

Junge, C., Valkenburg, P. M., Deković, M., & Branje, S. (2020). The building blocks of social competence: Contributions of the Consortium of Individual Development. *Developmental Cognitive Neuroscience, 45*, 100861–100861. doi:10.1016/j.dcn.2020.100861

Kalawsky, R. S. (1999). VRUSE – A computerised diagnostic tool: For usability evaluation of virtual/synthetic environment systems. *Applied Ergonomics, 30*(1), 11–25. doi:10.1016/S0003-6870(98)00047-7 PMID:10098813

Kaluschke, M., Weller, R., Zachmann, G., Pelliccia, L., Lorenz, M., Killmant, P., Knopp, S., & Hatze, J. P. G. (2018). Hips - a virtual reality hip prosthesis implantation simulator. In *2018 IEEE Conference on Virtual Reality and 3D User Interfaces (VR)* (pp. 591–592). IEEE.

Kamińska, D., Sapiński, T., Aitken, N., Della Rocca, A., Barańska, M., & Wietsma, R. (2017). Virtual reality as a new trend in mechanical and electrical engineering education. *Open Physics, 15*(1), 936–941. doi:10.1515/phys-2017-0114

Kangasniemi, J. (2021, August 3) *What we can learn from the best examples of immersive journalism.* Reuters Institute Research. https://bit.ly/3ybXD54

Kang, L., Wang, X., Tan, C., & Zhao, J. (2015). Understanding the antecedents and consequences of live chat use in electronic markets. *Journal of Organizational Computing and Electronic Commerce, 25*(2), 117–139. doi:10.1080/10919392.2015.1033935

Kaputsos, S. (2020, March 25). *Hacking Reality*. MIT Media Lab. https://bit.ly/3kLclbj

Kauppinen, R., & Drake, M. (2020a). Recognizing competencies of immigrants for restaurant work using virtual reality. *ICERI2020 Proceedings*, 2707–2017. doi:10.21125/iceri.2020.0629

Kauppinen, R., & Drake, M. (2020b). Virtual reality in competence recognition for immigrants. *INTED2020 Proceedings, 1*(March), 5578–5582. doi:10.21125/inted.2020.1515

Kauppinen, R., Drake, M., Anttila, K., & Lindgren, E. (2021). Implementing Virtual Reality Based Competence Recognition. *2021 9th International Conference on Information and Education Technology (ICIET)*, 415–422. doi:10.1109/ICIET51873.2021.9419617

Kavanagh, S., Luxton-Reilly, A., Wuensche, B., & Plimmer, B. (2017). A Systematic Review of Virtual Reality in Education. *Themes in Science and Technology Education, 10*(2), 85–119.

Kay, K., & Greenhill, V. (2011). Twenty-first century students need 21st century skills. In *Bringing schools into the 21st century* (pp. 41–65). Springer. doi:10.1007/978-94-007-0268-4_3

Kazama, M., & Noda, T. (2012). Damage statistics (Summary of the 2011 off the Pacific Coast of Tohoku Earthquake damage). *Soil and Foundation, 52*(5), 780–792. doi:10.1016/j.sandf.2012.11.003

Ke, F., Pachman, M., & Dai, Z. (2020). Investigating educational affordances of virtual reality for simulation-based teaching training with graduate teaching assistants. *Journal of Computing in Higher Education, 32*(3), 607–627. doi:10.100712528-020-09249-9

Keller, J. (2010). *Motivational Design for Learning and Performance: The ARCS Model Approach*. Academic Press.

Keller, M. M., & Becker, E. S. (2020). Teachers' emotions and emotional authenticity: Do they matter to students' emotional responses in the classroom? *Teachers and Teaching, 27*(5), 404–422. doi:10.1080/13540602.2020.1834380

Kelly, A. (2013). *Mobile robotics: mathematics, models, and methods*. Cambridge University Press.

Kemp, J., & Livingstone, D. (2006). Putting a Second Life "Metaverse" Skin on Learning Management Systems. In *Proceedings of the Second Life Education Workshop* (Vol. 2006, pp. 13–18). 10.1145/1235511.1235517

Khanal, S., Medasetti, U. S., Mashal, M., Savage, B., & Khadka, R. (2022). Virtual and augmented reality in the disaster management technology: A literature review of the past 11 years. *Frontiers in Virtual Reality, 3*, 843195. doi:10.3389/frvir.2022.843195

Kim, M. J., Lee, C. K., & Jung, T. (2020). Exploring Consumer Behavior in Virtual Reality Tourism Using an Extended Stimulus-Organism-Response Model. *Journal of Travel Research, 59*(1), 69–89. https://doi.org/10.1177/0047287518818915

Kinga, S., & István, S. (2012). Relationship between social creativity and social intelligence, and their cognitive correlates. *Transylvanian Journal of Psychology, 13*(1), 39–62.

King, D., Tee, S., Falconer, L., Angell, C., Holley, D., & Mills, A. (2018). Virtual health education: Scaling practice to transform student learning: Using virtual reality learning environments in healthcare education to bridge the theory/practice gap and improve patient safety. *Nurse Education Today*, *71*, 7–9. doi:10.1016/j.nedt.2018.08.002 PMID:30205259

Kleinknecht, M., & Gröschner, A. (2016). Fostering preservice teachers' noticing with structured video feedback: Results of an online- and video-based intervention study. *Teaching and Teacher Education*, *59*, 45–46. doi:10.1016/j.tate.2016.05.020

Kobayashi, L., Zhang, X. C., Collins, S. A., Karim, N., & Merck, D. L. (2018). Exploratory Application of Augmented Reality/Mixed Reality Devices for Acute Care Procedure Training. *The Western Journal of Emergency Medicine*, *19*(1), 158–164. doi:10.5811/westjem.2017.10.35026 PMID:29383074

Koehler, M. J., Mishra, P., & Cain, W. (2013). What is Technological Pedagogical Content Knowledge (TPACK)? *Journal of Education*, *193*(3), 13–19. doi:10.1177/002205741319300303

Kool, H. (2016). The ethics of immersive journalism: A rhetorical analysis of news storytelling with virtual reality technology. *Intersect: The Stanford Journal of Science, Technology, and Society*, *9*(3).

Krokos, E., Plaisant, C., & Varshney, A. (2019). Virtual memory palaces: Immersion aids recall. *Virtual Reality (Waltham Cross)*, *23*(1), 1–15. doi:10.100710055-018-0346-3

Kulik, A., Kunert, A., Beck, S., & Fröhlich, B. (2017). Collaborative Virtual Reality for Joint Learning Experiences. *12th International Conference on Computer Supported Collaborative Learning (CSCL 2017)*, 721–722.

Kupczynski, L., Gibson, A. M., Ice, P., Richardson, J., & Challoo, L. (2011). The Impact of Frequency on Achievement in Online Courses: A Study from a South Texas University. *Journal of Interactive Online Learning*, *10*(3), 141–149.

Kuznetcova, I., & Glassman, M. (2020). Rethinking the use of multi-user virtual environments in education. *Technology, Pedagogy and Education*, *29*(8), 1–17. doi:10.1080/1475939X.2020.1768141

Laanpere, M. (2012). Digital Learning Ecosystems: rethinking virtual learning environments in the age of social media. In IFIP-OST'12 conference 2012 (p. 12). Academic Press.

Lamberti, F., De Lorenzis, F., Pratticò, F. G., & Migliorini, M. (2021). An immersive virtual reality platform for training CBRN operators. In *Proceedings of 2021 IEEE 45th Annual Computers, Software, and Applications Conference (COMPSAC)* (pp. 133–137). 10.1109/COMPSAC51774.2021.00030

Lauermann, F., & Butler, R. (2021). The elusive links between teachers' teaching-related emotions, motivations, and self-regulation and students' educational outcomes. *Educational Psychologist*, *56*(4), 243–249. doi:10.1080/00461520.2021.1991800

Lau, K. W., & Lee, P. Y. (2015). The use of virtual reality for creating unusual environmental stimulation to motivate students to explore creative ideas. *Interactive Learning Environments, 23*(1), 3–18. doi:10.1080/10494820.2012.745426

Laws, A. L. S. (2019). *Conceptualising immersive journalism.* Routledge.

Lawson, G., & Burnett, G. E. (2015). Simulation and Digital Human Modelling. In J. Wilson & S. Sharples (Eds.), *Evaluation of Human Work* (4th ed., pp. 201–220). CRC Press.

Lee, H. S. L. J. (2008). Mathematical Education Game Based on Augmented Reality. Technologies for E-Learning and Digital Entertainment.

Lee, L. H., Braud, T., Zhou, P., Wang, L., Xu, D., Lin, Z., Kumar, A., Bermejo, C., & Hui, P. (2021). *All one needs to know about metaverse: A complete survey on technological singularity, virtual ecosystem, and research agenda.* https://arxiv.org/abs/2110.05352

Lee, E. A. L., & Wong, K. W. (2014). Learning with desktop virtual reality: Low spatial ability learners are more positively affected. *Computers & Education, 79*, 49–58. doi:10.1016/j.compedu.2014.07.010

Lee, H., & Cha, W. C. (2019). Virtual reality-based ergonomic modeling and evaluation framework for nuclear power plant operation and control. *Sustainability, 11*(9), 2630. doi:10.3390u11092630

Lee, J., Gu, H., Kim, H., Kim, J., Kim, H., & Kim, H. (2013). Interactive manipulation of 3D objects using Kinect for visualization tools in education. In *13th International Conference on Control, Automation and Systems (lCCAS 2013).* 10.1109/ICCAS.2013.6704175

Lee, M. J. W., Georgieva, M., Alexander, B., Craig, E., & Richter, J. (2021). *State of XR & Immersive Learning Outlook Report 2021.* Immersive Learning Research Network.

Leminen, S., Rajahonka, M., & Westerlund, M. (2017). Towards Third-Generation Living Lab Networks in Cities. *Technology Innovation Management Review, 7*(11), 21–35. doi:10.22215/timreview/1118

Lemos, B. M., & Carvalho, C. V. (2010, Julho). Use of augmented reality to support the understanding of the Euler relationship. *Novas Tecnologias na Educação.*

Lewin, K. (1946). Action research and minority problems. *The Journal of Social Issues, 2*(4), 34–46. doi:10.1111/j.1540-4560.1946.tb02295.x

Liao, J., Wang, M., Ran, W., & Yang, S. J. H. (2014). Collaborative cloud: A new model for e-learning. *Innovations in Education and Teaching International, 51*(3), 338–351. doi:10.1080/14703297.2013.791554

Li, C., Liang, W., Quigley, C., Zhao, Y., & Yu, L. F. (2017). Earthquake safety training through virtual drills. *IEEE Transactions on Visualization and Computer Graphics, 23*(4), 1275–1284. doi:10.1109/TVCG.2017.2656958 PMID:28129163

Lima, A. J., Haguenauer, C. J., & Cunha, G. G. (2007). Augmented Reality In Teaching Descriptive Geometry. *VII International Conference on Graphics Engineering for Arts and Design.*

Lima, E. L., Carvalho, P. C., Wagner, E., & Morgado, A. C. (2022). *High School Mathematics* (Vol. 2). SBM.

Li, N., Sun, N., Cao, C., Hou, S., & Gong, Y. (2022). Review on visualization technology in simulation training system for major natural disasters. *Natural Hazards, 112*(3), 1–32. doi:10.100711069-022-05277-z PMID:35308193

Lin, T.-J., & Lan, Y.-J. (2015). Language Learning in Virtual Reality Environments: Past, Present, and Future. *Journal of Educational Technology & Society, 18*(4), 486–497.

Llobera, J., González-Franco, M., Perez-Marcos, D., Valls-Solé, J., Slater, M., & Sanchez-Vives, M. V. (2013). Virtual reality for assessment of patients suffering chronic pain: A case study. *Experimental Brain Research, 225*(1), 105–117. doi:10.100700221-012-3352-9 PMID:23223781

Lopezosa, C., Codina, L., Fernández-Planells, A., & Freixa, P. (2021). Journalistic innovation: How new formats of digital journalism are perceived in the academic literature. *Journalism.* Advance online publication. doi:10.1177/14648849211033434

Loukas, C., Nikiteas, N., Kanakis, M., & Georgiou, E. (2011). Deconstructing laparoscopic competence in a virtual reality simulation environment. *Surgery, 149*(6), 750–760. https://doi.org/10.1016/j.surg.2010.11.012

Lovreglio, R., Duan, X., Rahouti, A., Phipps, R., & Nilsson, D. (2021). Comparing the effectiveness of fire extinguisher virtual reality and video training. *Virtual Reality (Waltham Cross), 25*(1), 133–145. doi:10.100710055-020-00447-5

Lu, X. (2018). Natural language processing and intelligent computer-assisted language learning (ICALL). In J. I. Liontas (Ed.), *The TESOL encyclopedia of English language teaching* (pp. 1–6). Wiley Blackwell. doi:10.1002/9781118784235.eelt0422

Maas, M. J., & Hughes, J. M. (2020). 2020/03/14). Virtual, augmented and mixed reality in K–12 education: A review of the literature. *Technology, Pedagogy and Education, 29*(2), 231–249. doi:10.1080/1475939X.2020.1737210

Mabrook, R., & Singer, J. B. (2019). Virtual reality, 360 video, and journalism studies: Conceptual approaches to immersive technologies. *Journalism Studies, 20*(14), 2096–2112. doi:10.1080/1461670X.2019.1568203

Maciejewski, P., Gawlik-Kobylińska, M., Lebiedź, J., Ostant, W., & Aydın, D. (2020). To Survive in a CBRN Hostile Environment: Application of CAVE Automatic Virtual Environments in First Responder Training. In *Proceedings of the 3rd International Conference on Applications of Intelligent Systems (APPIS 2020).* Association for Computing Machinery. 10.1145/3378184.3378212

Ma, H. K. (2012). Social competence as a positive youth development construct: A conceptual review. *TheScientificWorldJournal, 2012*, 287472–287472. doi:10.1100/2012/287472 PMID:22645418

Mah, D. K. (2016). Learning Analytics and Digital Badges: Potential Impact on Student Retention in Higher Education. *Technology. Knowledge and Learning*, *21*(3), 285–305. doi:10.100710758-016-9286-8

Makris, S., Karagiannis, P., Koukas, S., & Matthaiakis, A. (2016). Augmented reality system for operator support in human–robot collaborative assembly. *CIRP Annals*. https://www.sciencedirect.com/science/article/abs/pii/S0007850616300385

Malone, T. W. (1981). Toward a Theory of Intrinsically Motivating Instruction. *Cognitive Science*, *5*(4), 333–369. doi:10.120715516709cog0504_2

Manero, B., Alvarez, I. M., Romero, A., & Cárdenas, M. (2022). Adopting an immersive virtual reality system to enhance Pre-service teachers' communicative competence. *Proceedings. IEEE 22nd International Conference on Advanced Learning Technologies ICALT 2022.*

Manifesto. (2020). *Digital estates within Higher Education – A white paper.* Manifesto. https://pages.manifesto.co.uk/higher-education-guide

Maples-Keller, J. L., Bunnell, B. E., Kim, S.-J., & Rothbaum, B. O. (2017, May/June). The Use of Virtual Reality Technology in the Treatment of Anxiety and Other Psychiatric Disorders. *Harvard Review of Psychiatry*, *25*(3), 103–113. doi:10.1097/HRP.0000000000000138 PMID:28475502

Marconi, F., & Nakagawa, T. (2017). *Report: How virtual reality will impact journalism.* Associated Press. https://bit.ly/3s9NnGp

Markowitz, D. M., Laha, R., Perone, B. P., Pea, R. D., & Bailenson, J. (2018). Immersive virtual reality field trips facilitate learning about climate change. *Frontiers in Psychology*, *9*(1), 2364. doi:10.3389/fpsyg.2018.02364 PMID:30555387

Martínez, J. (2012). *Integration of augmented reality by vision in applications for an industrial robot* [Integración de realidad aumentada por visión en aplicaciones para un robot industrial] (1st ed.). Universidad Politécnica de Valencia. https://riunet.upv.es/bitstream/handle/10251/18013/Tesina.pdf?sequence=1

Martínez, M. B., Chacón, J. C., Díaz-Aguado, M. J., Martín, J., & Martínez, R. (2020). Disruptive behavior in compulsory Secondary education classrooms: A multi-informant analysis of the perception of teachers and students. *Pulso. Review of Education*, *43*, 15–34. https://revistas.cardenalcisneros.es/index.php/PULSO/article/view/380

Martin, F., & Parker, M. A. (2014). Use of synchronous virtual classrooms: Why, who and how? *Journal of Online Learning and Teaching*, *10*(2), 192–210. https://jolt.merlot.org/vol10no2/martin_0614.pdf

Martin, F., Sun, T., Turk, M., & Ritzhaupt, D. (2021). A Meta-Analysis on the Effects of Synchronous Online Learning on Cognitive and Affective Educational Outcomes. *The International Review of Research in Open and Distributed Learning*, *22*(3), 205–242. doi:10.19173/irrodl.v22i3.5263

Martingano, A. J., Hererra, F., & Konrath, S. (2021). *Virtual reality improves emotional but not cognitive empathy: A meta-analysis.* doi:10.1037/tmb0000034

Martyushev, N., Shutaleva, A., Malushko, E., Nikonova, Z., & Savchenko, I. (2021). Online Communication Tools in Teaching Foreign Languages for Education Sustainability. *Sustainability, 13*(19), 11127. doi:10.3390u131911127

Maruhn, P., Dietrich, A., Prasch, L., & Schneider, S. (2020, March 22-26). Analyzing Pedestrian Behavior in Augmented Reality—Proof of Concept. *2020 IEEE Conference on Virtual Reality and 3D User Interfaces (VR).*

Marzano, R. J., & Kendall, J. S. (2007). *The New Taxonomy of Educational Objectives* (2nd ed.). Corwin Press.

Maschio, T. (2017, July 28). *Storyliving: An Ethnographic Study of How Audiences Experience VR and What That Means for Journalists*. Retrieved December 12, 2017, from https://newslab.withgoogle.com/assets/docs/ storyliving-a-study-of-vr-in-journalism.pdf

Masó, I. (2022). Los conflictos en el aula de secundaria y las competencias comunicativas del profesorado [Conflict in the Secondary school classroom and teachers' communication skills]. In J.A. Marín, J.C. de la Cruz, S. Pozo, & G. Gómez (Eds.), Investigación e innovación educativa frente a los retos para el desarrollo sostenible (pp. 1383-1398). Andalucía: Dylinson. sl.

Masud, M. (2016). Collaborative e-learning systems using semantic data interoperability. *Computers in Human Behavior, 61*, 127–135. doi:10.1016/j.chb.2016.02.094

Mathews, J. M. (2010). Using a studio-based pedagogy to engage students in the design of mobile-based media. *English Teaching, 9*(1), 87–102.

Matteson, M. L., Salamon, J., & Brewster, L. (2011). A systematic review of research on live chat service. *Reference and User Services Quarterly, 51*(2), 172–190. doi:10.5860/rusq.51n2.172

Maturana, H. R., & Varela, F. J. (1998). *De máquinas y seres vivos; una teoría sobre la organización biológia.* Santiago de Chile: Editorial Universitaria.

McGarr, O. (2021). The use of virtual simulations in teacher education to develop pre-service teachers' behaviour and classroom management skills: Implications for reflective practice. *Journal of Education for Teaching, 47*(2), 274–286. doi:10.1080/02607476.2020.1733398

McGrath, J. L., Taekman, J. M., Dev, P., Danforth, D. R., Mohan, D., Kman, N., Crichlow, A., & Bond, W. F. (2018). Using Virtual Reality Simulation Environments to Assess Competence for Emergency Medicine Learners. *Academic Emergency Medicine, 25*(2), 186–195. https://doi.org/10.1111/acem.13308

McGrath, K. F., & Van Bergen, P. (2019). Attributions and emotional competence: Why some teachers experience close relationships with disruptive students (and others don't). *Teachers and Teaching, 25*(3), 334–357. doi:10.1080/13540602.2019.1569511

Meadan, H., & Monda-Amaya, L. (2008). Collaboration to Promote Social Competence for Students With Mild Disabilities in the General Classroom: A Structure for Providing Social Support. *Intervention in School and Clinic, 43*(3), 158–167. doi:10.1177/1053451207311617

Meagher, K. A., Doblack, B. N., Ramírez, M., & Dávila, L. P. (2014). Scalable nanohelices for predictive studies and enhanced 3D visualization. *Journal of Visualized Experiments*, *93*(93), e51372. doi:10.3791/51372 PMID:25407548

Mehregan, M. (2019). Ethical Reviewers are Essential for Scholarly Journals for Timely Processing of Submissions and Avoiding Retractions. *Journal of Korean Medical Science*, *34*(5, e41), e41. doi:10.3346/jkms.2019.34.e41 PMID:30718993

Melo, M., Bentley, E., McAllister, K. S., & Cortez, J. (2019). Pedagogy of Productive Failure: Navigating the Challenges of Integrating VR into the Classroom. *Journal of Virtual Worlds Research*, *12*(1), 1–21. https://doi.org/10.4101/jvwr.v12i1.7318

Mendoza, H. (2020). Modelos de redes neuronales artifciales, como sustento evaluativo al crecimiento pedagógico virtual en Educación Superior [Artifcial neural network models, as evaluative support to virtual pedagogical growth in Higher Education]. *Educación Superior*, *7*(2), 25–36. https://www.scielo.org.bo/pdf/escepies/v7n2/v7n2_a06.pdf

Middleton, A. (2009). Beyond podcasting: Creative approaches to designing educational audio. *Alt-J*, *17*(2), 143–155. doi:10.1080/09687760903033082

Milgram, P., & Kishino, F. (1994). A taxonomy of mixed reality visual displays. *IEICE Transactions on Information and Systems*, *77*(12), 1321–1329.

Ministry of Education and Vocational Training. (2020). *Facts and figures - School year 19/20*. https://sede.educacion.gob.es/publiventa/datos-y-cifras-curso-escolar-20192020/ensenanza-estadisticas/23109

Ministry of Education. (2010). *Royal Decree 132/2010, of February 12, 2010, which establishes the minimum requirements for the centers that teach the second cycle of early childhood education, Primary education and Secondary education*. Available at https://www.boe.es/buscar/pdf/2010/BOE-A-2010-4132-consolidado.pdf

Mirauda, D., Capece, N., & Erra, U. (2019). StreamflowVL: A virtual fieldwork laboratory that supports traditional hydraulics engineering learning. *Applied Sciences (Basel, Switzerland)*, *9*(22), 4972. doi:10.3390/app9224972

Misiejuk, K., Wasson, B., & Egelandsdal, K. (2021). Using learning analytics to understand student perceptions of peer feedback. *Computers in Human Behavior*, *117*, 106658. Advance online publication. doi:10.1016/j.chb.2020.106658

Mitsuhara, H., Tanioka, I., & Shishibori, M. (2021). Observing evacuation behaviours of surprised participants in virtual reality earthquake simulator. In *Proceedings of the 29th International Conference on Computers in Education* (*vol. 2*, pp. 576-582). Academic Press.

Mitsuhara, H., Inoue, T., Yamaguchi, K., Takechi, Y., Morimoto, M., Iwaka, K., Kozuki, Y., & Shishibori, M. (2015). Web-based system for designing game-based evacuation drills. *Procedia Computer Science*, *72*, 277–284. doi:10.1016/j.procs.2015.12.141

Mitsuhara, H., & Shishibori, M. (2022). Tsunami evacuation drill system focusing on mobile devices. *International Journal of Interactive Mobile Technologies*, *16*(6), 4–20. doi:10.3991/ijim.v16i06.23419

Mitsuhara, H., Tanimura, C., Nemoto, J., & Shishibori, M. (2019). Failure-enhanced evacuation training using a VR-based disaster simulator: A comparative experiment with simulated evacuees. *Procedia Computer Science*, *159*, 1670–1679. doi:10.1016/j.procs.2019.09.337

Moher, D., Liberati, A., Tetzlaff, J., Altman, D. G., & Group, P. (2009). Preferred reporting items for systematic reviews and meta-analyses: The PRISMA statement. *PLoS Medicine*, *6*(7), e1000097. doi:10.1371/journal.pmed.1000097 PMID:19621072

Mól, A. C. A., Jorge, C. A. F., Couto, P. M., Augusto, S. C., Cunha, G. G., & Landau, L. (2009). Virtual environments simulation for dose assessment in nuclear plants. *Progress in Nuclear Energy*, *51*(2), 382–387. doi:10.1016/j.pnucene.2008.04.003

Molka-Danielsen, J., Prasolova-Forland, E., Fominykh, M., & Lamb, K. (2018) Use of a collaborative virtual reality simulation for multi-professional training in emergency management communications. In *Proceedings of the 2018 IEEE International Conference on Teaching, Assessment, Learning and Engineering* (pp. 408-415). 10.1109/TALE.2018.8615147

Moraes, L. d. (2014). *Spatial geometry in high school: A study on the use of concrete material in problem solving*. Universidade Federal do Estado Rio de Janeiro.

Morais, C., Alvis, P., & Miranda, L. (2017). Learning analytics and performance indicators in higher education. *Proceedings of the 12th Iberian Conference on Information Systems and Technologies AISTI*. 10.23919/CISTI.2017.7975812

Morales-Menendez, R., Ramírez-Mendoza, R. A., & Guevara, A. J. V. (2019). Virtual/Remote Labs for Automation Teaching: A Cost Effective Approach. *IFAC-PapersOnLine*, *52*(9), 306–311. doi:10.1016/j.ifacol.2019.08.219

Mossel, A., Peer, A., Goellner, J., & Kaufmann, H. (2015). Towards an immersive virtual reality training system for CBRN disaster preparedness. *5th International Defense and Homeland Security Simulation Workshop, DHSS 2015*, 23 – 32.

Moynihan, M., Ruano, S., & Smolic, A. (2021). Autonomous tracking for volumetric video sequences. In *Proceedings of the IEEE/CVF Winter Conference on Applications of Computer Vision* (pp. 1660-1669). https://bit.ly/3ym431E

Mukkawar, V. V., & Netak, L. D. (2021). Technological Evaluation of Virtual and Augmented Reality to Impart Social Skills. *International Conference on Intelligent Human Computer Interaction.*

Mulders, M., Buchner, J., & Kerres, M. (2020). A Framework for the Use of Immersive Virtual Reality in Learning Environments. *International Journal of Emerging Technologies in Learning*, *15*(24), 208–224. doi:10.3991/ijet.v15i24.16615

Muñoz, P., & Moctezuma. (2015). PD+G set-Point Controller for the Second and Third Joint of a ER-4u Scorbot Robot. In *Int. Conf. Mechatronics, Electron. Automot. Eng*. ICMEAE. doi:10.1109/ICMEAE.2014.36

Mystakidis, S., Besharat, J., Papantzikos, G., Christopoulos, A., Stylios, C., Agorgianitis, S., & Tselentis, D. (2022). Design, development, and evaluation of a virtual reality serious game for school fire preparedness training. *Education Sciences*, *12*(4), 281. doi:10.3390/educsci12040281

Natale, A. F. D., Repetta, C., Rova, G., & Villani, D. (2020). Immersive virtual reality in K-12 and higher education: A 10-year systematic review of empirical research. *British Journal of Educational Technology*, *51*(6), 2003–2033. doi:10.1111/bjet.13030

NATO. (2018). *Commander's guide on medical support to chemical, biological, radiological, and nuclear (cbrn) defensive operations*. https://www.coemed.org/files/stanags/03_AMEDP/AMedP-7.6_EDA_V1_E_2873.pdf

Neves, J., & Hewitt, R. (2021). *Student Academic Experience Survey 2021*. Higher Education Policy Institute. https://www.hepi.ac.uk/2021/06/24/the-student-academic-experience-survey-2021/

Newman, N. (2021). *Journalism, media, and technology trends and predictions 2021*. Reuters Institute. https://bit.ly/3FcwrV1

Niantic, Inc. (2022). *Pokémon GO*. Retrieved from Pokémon GO: https://pokemongolive.com/en/

Nielsen, S. L., & Sheets, P. (2021). Virtual hype meets reality: Users' perception of immersive journalism. *Journalism*, *22*(10), 2637–2653. doi:10.1177/1464884919869399

Niemi, H., & Multisilta, J. (2016). Digital storytelling promoting twenty-first century skills and student engagement. *Technology, Pedagogy and Education*, *25*(4), 451–468. doi:10.1080/1475939X.2015.1074610

Nirhamo, N. (2019). *XR Studio created virtual learning environment with Hololens for Perho Culinary, Tourism & Business College*. Softability.

Noval, M. D. (2013). *Augmented reality in mathematics teaching: a case study*. Universidade de Trás-os-Montes e Alto Douro. Retrieved from https://catalogo.biblioteca.utad.pt/cgi-bin/koha/opac-detail.pl?biblionumber=66150

Nowak, K. L., & Biocca, F. (2003). The Effect of the Agency and Anthropomorphism on Users' Sense of Telepresence, Copresence, and Social Presence in Virtual Environments. *Presence (Cambridge, Mass.)*, *12*(5), 481–494. doi:10.1162/105474603322761289

Nowak, K. L., & Fox, J. (2018). Avatars and computer-mediated communication: A review of the definitions, uses, and effects of digital representations. *Review of Communication Research*, *6*, 30–53. doi:10.12840/issn.2255-4165.2018.06.01.015

O'Brien, A. M., & Mc Guckin, C. (2016). *The systematic literature review method: Trials and tribulations of electronic database searching at doctoral level*. SAGE Publications, Ltd. doi:10.4135/978144627305015595381

Object Management Group. (2021). *Unified Modelling Language*. https://www.uml.org/

OECD. (2018). *Working Together: Skills and Labour Market Integration of Immigrants and their Children in Finland*. OECD. doi:10.1787/9789264305250-en

Oh, D.-S., Phillips, F., Park, S., & Lee, E. (2016). Innovation ecosystems: A critical examination. *Technovation*, *54*, 1–6. https://doi.org/10.1016/j.technovation.2016.02.004

Okoli, C., & Schabram, K. (2012). A guide to conducting a Systematic Literature Review of Information Systems Research. SSRN *Electronic Journal*. doi:10.2139/ssrn.2115818

Okoye, K., Arrona-Palacios, A., Camacho-Zuñiga, C., Hammout, N., Nakamura, E. L., Escamilla, J., & Hosseini, S. (2020). Impact of students' evaluation of teaching: A text analysis of the teachers' qualities by gender. *International Journal of Educational Technology in Higher Education*, *17*(1), 1–27. doi:10.118641239-020-00224-z

Orange, D. M. (1995). *Emotional understanding: Studies in psychoanalytic epistemology*. Guilford Press.

Orpinas, P. (2010). Social Competence. In *The Corsini Encyclopedia of Psychology* (pp. 1-2). Academic Press.

Orton-Johnson, K. (2009). I've stuck to the path I'm afraid': Exploring student non-use of blended learning. *British Journal of Educational Technology*, *40*(5), 837–847. doi:10.1111/j.1467-8535.2008.00860.x

Ota, D., Loftin, B., Saito, T., Lea, R., & Keller, J. (1995). Virtual reality in surgical education. *Computers in Biology and Medicine*, *25*(2), 127–137. https://doi.org/10.1016/0010-4825(94)00009-F

Paatela-Nieminen, M. (2021). Remixing real and imaginary in art education with fully immersive virtual reality. *International Journal of Education Through Art*, *17*(3), 415–431. doi:10.1386/eta_00077_1

Paino Ambrosio, A., & Rodríguez Fidalgo, M. I. (2021). Proposal for a new communicative model in immersive journalism. *Journalism*, *22*(10), 2600–2617. doi:10.1177/1464884919869710

Pallot, M., Trousse, B., Senach, B., & Scapin, D. (2011). *Living Lab Research Landscape : From User Centred Design and User Experience towards User Cocreation. In First European Summer School 'Living Labs', Inria (ICT Usage Lab), Userlab, EsoceNet*. Universcience.

Palmas, F., & Klinker, G. (2020, July). Defining Extended Reality Training: A Long-Term Definition for All Industries. In *2020 IEEE 20th International Conference on Advanced Learning Technologies (ICALT)* (pp. 322-324). IEEE.

Palmas, F., & Klinker, G. (2020, July). Defining Extended Reality Training: A Long-Term Definition for All Industries. *Proceedings of the 2020 IEEE 20th International Conference on Advanced Learning Technologies (ICALT)*, 322–324. 10.1109/ICALT49669.2020.00103

Palmas, F., Labode, D., Plecher, D. A., & Klinker, G. (2019). Comparison of a Gamified and Non-Gamified Virtual Reality Training Assembly Task. In *Proceedings of IEEE 11th International Conference on Virtual Worlds and Games for Serious Applications: VS-Games* (pp. 1-8). 10.1109/VS-Games.2019.8864583

Pandey, S. C., & Pattnaik, P. N. (2015). University Research Ecosystem: A Conceptual Understanding. *Review of Economic and Business Studies*, *8*(1), 169–181. https://doi.org/10.1515/rebs-2016-0021

Pan, X., & Hamilton, A. F. C. (2018). Why and how to use virtual reality to study human social interaction: The challenges of exploring a new research landscape. *British Journal of Psychology*, *109*(3), 395–417. doi:10.1111/bjop.12290 PMID:29504117

Parker, J. (2015). 'You become a witness'—Nonny de la Peña's immersive journalism. *Ochre.* https://bit.ly/3FtmYZU

Park, S. M., & Kim, Y. G. (2021). A metaverse: Taxonomy, components, applications, and open challenges. *IEEE Access: Practical Innovations, Open Solutions*, *10*, 4209–4251. doi:10.1109/ACCESS.2021.3140175

Pasila, A., & Sutela, H. (2019, April 12). *Ulkomaalaistaustaisten työllisyysaste eroaa rekisteri- ja haastattelupohjaisissa tilastoissa* [Employment rate of immigrants is different in statistics based on registers and interviews]. https://www.stat.fi/tietotrendit/blogit/2019/ulkomaalaistaustaisten-tyollisyysaste-eroaa-rekisteri-ja-haastattelupohjaisissa-tilastoissa/

Pástor, D., Jiménez, J., Gómez, O., & Isotani, S. (2018). New Perspectives in Instructional Design using Semantic Web Technologies: A Systematic Literature Review. *Ingeniería y Desarrollo. Universidad del Norte*, *36*(1), 215–239.

Pata, K. (2011). An ecological meta-design framework for open learning ecosystems. In *Mupple2011* (pp. 13–16). Open University of London.

Pavlik, J. V. (2020). Drones, augmented reality and virtual reality journalism: Mapping their role in immersive news content. *Media and Communication*, *8*(3), 137–146. doi:10.17645/mac.v8i3.3031

Pedrero-Esteban. L., Barrios-Rubio, A., Medina-Avila, V. (2019). Teenagers, Smartphones and digital audio consumption in the age of spotify. *Media Education Reseach Journal, Comunicar, 27*(60).

Pelegrí, J. (2020). *What are the differences between a cobot and an industrial robot?* [¿Cuáles son las diferencias entre un cobot y un robot industrial?]. https://blog.universal-robots.com/es/cobots-vs-robots-industriales

Pereira, D. D. (2014). *Use of Augmented Reality as a Support Tool for Teaching Spatial Geometry in the 2nd Year of High School: Use of FLARAS and Google Sketchup Tools*. Universidade Estadual da Paraíba.

Pérez, L., Diez, E., Usamentiaga, R., & García, D. F. (2019). Industrial robot control and operator training using virtual reality interfaces. *Computers in Industry*, *109*, 114–120. doi:10.1016/j.compind.2019.05.001

Pérez-Sanagustín, M., Muñoz-Merino, P. J., Alario-Hoyos, C., Soldani, X., & Delgado Kloos, C. (2015). Lessons learned from the design of situated learning environments to support collaborative knowledge construction. *Computers & Education*, *87*, 70–82. doi:10.1016/j.compedu.2015.03.019

Perfect Corp. (2022). *YouCam Makeup: Best Selfie Editor*. Retrieved from YouCam Makeup: Best Selfie Editor: https://www.perfectcorp.com/consumer/apps/ymk

Picciano, A. G. (2002). Beyond Student Perceptions: Issues of Interaction, Presence, and Performance in an Online Course. *Journal of Asynchronous Learning Networks*, *6*(1).

Postman, N. (2011). *Technopoly: The surrender of culture to technology*. Vintage.

Potkonjak, V., Gardner, M., Callaghan, V., Mattila, P., Guetl, C., Petrovic, V. M., & Jovanovi, K. (2016). Virtual laboratories for education in science, technology, and engineering: A review. *Computers & Education*, *95*, 309–327. doi:10.1016/j.compedu.2016.02.002

Poux, F., Valembois, Q., Mattes, C., Kobbelt, L., & Billen, R. (2020). Initial User-Centered Design of a Virtual Reality Heritage System: Applications for Digital Tourism. *Remote Sensing*, *12*(16), 2583. doi:10.3390/rs12162583

Po-Yao, Ch., Lai, R., Chen-Chung, L., & Hung-Ming, L. (2019). Strengthening Social Networks in Online Discussion Forums to Facilitate Help Seeking for Solving Problems. *Journal of Educational Technology & Society*, *21*(4), 39–50.

Prattticò, F. G., De Lorenzis, F., Calandra, D., Cannavò, A., & Lamberti, F. (2021). Exploring simulation-based virtual reality as a mock-up tool to support the design of first responders training. *Applied Sciences (Basel, Switzerland)*, *11*(16), 1–13. doi:10.3390/app11167527

Pratticò, F. G., & Lamberti, F. (2021). Towards the adoption of virtual reality training systems for the self-tuition of industrial robot operators: A case study at kuka. *Computers in Industry*, *129*, 129. doi:10.1016/j.compind.2021.103446

Prensky, M. (2016). Digital natives, digital immigrants. Part 1. *On the Horizon*, *9*, 1–6.

Psotka, J. (1995). Immersive training systems: Virtual reality and education and training. *Instructional Science*, *23*(5), 405–431. doi:10.1007/BF00896880

Qi, Q., Tao, F., Hu, T., Anwer, N., Liu, A., Wei, Y., & Nee, A. Y. (2021). Enabling technologies and tools for digital twin. *Journal of Manufacturing Systems*, *58*, 3–21.

Quint, F., Sebastian, K., & Gorecky, D. (2015). A mixed-reality learning environment. *Procedia Computer Science*, *75*, 43–48. doi:10.1016/j.procs.2015.12.199

Quirke, M., Mc Guckin, C., & McCarthy, P. (2022). How to adopt an "inclusion as process" approach and navigate ethical challenges in research. In *SAGE Research Methods Cases*. SAGE Publications, Ltd. doi:10.4135/9781529605341

Radianti, J., Majchrzak, T. A., Fromm, J., & Wohlgenannt, I. (2020). A systematic review of immersive virtual reality applications for higher education: Design elements, lessons learned, and research agenda. *Computers & Education*, *147*, 103778. Advance online publication. doi:10.1016/j.compedu.2019.103778

Radu, I., McCarthy, B., & Kao, Y. (2016). Discovering educational augmented reality math applications by prototyping with elementary-school teachers. IEEE Virtual Reality (VR).

Rahouti, A., Lovreglio, R., Datoussaid, S., & Descamps, T. (2021). Prototyping and validating a non-immersive virtual reality serious game for healthcare fire safety training. *Fire Technology*, *57*(6), 3041–3078. doi:10.100710694-021-01098-x

Railean, E. A. (2017). Metacognition in Higher Education: Successful Learning Strategies and Tactics for Sustainability. In E. Railean, A. Elci, & A. Elci (Eds.), *Metacognition and Successful Learning Strategies in Higher Education* (p. 121). IGI Global. doi:10.4018/978-1-5225-2218-8.ch001

Ramírez, J., & Rubiano, A. (2018). *Mathematical modeling of the direct and inverse kinematics of a manipulative robot of three degrees of freedom* [Modelamiento matemático de la cinemática directa e inversa de un robot manipulador de tres grados de libertad]. Ingeniería Solidaria. https://revistas.ucc.edu.co/index.php/in/article/download/47/48/

Rantanen, E. M., & Talleur, D. A. (2005). Incremental transfer and cost effectiveness of groundbased flight trainers in university aviation programs. *Proceedings of the Human Factors and Ergonomics Society Annual Meeting*, *49*(7), 764–768. doi:10.1177/154193120504900705

Rao, D., & Verweij, G. (2017). *Sizing the prize What's the real value of AI for your business and how can you capitalise?* PWC.

Raymundo, M. F. (2010). *Work plan on pyramid and cone.* Colégio Estadual Dr. João Nery. Rio de Janeiro: Formação continuada para professores de matemática Fundação CECIERJ/SEEDUC-RJ. Retrieved from https://www.google.com/url?sa=t&rct=j&q=&esrc=s&source=web&cd=&ved=2ahUKEwjGtsHM26f3AhXHY98KHRzoDOcQFnoECCYQAQ&url=https%3A%2F%2Fcanal.cecierj.edu.br%2Fanexos%2Frecurso_interno%2F12780%2Fdownload%2F057d5b3bfc142f883063f48da78e4ddd&usg=AOvVaw0L8QXs3-xXcRVe

Ray, S., & Srivastava, S. (2020). Virtualization of science education: A lesson from the COVID-19 pandemic. *Journal of Proteins and Proteomics*, *11*(2), 77–80. doi:10.100742485-020-00038-7 PMID:33132627

Reis, F. M., & Kirner, T. G. (2012). Students' Perception of the Usability of an Interactive Book with Augmented Reality for Learning Geometry. *RENOTE Revista Novas Tecnologias na Educação*. doi:10.22456/1679-1916.30814

Rifin, R., Fang, T. E., Abidin, A. F. Z., Adam, A., Majid, M. A., Zainuddin, A., Mohammad, S. H., Harun, M. H., & Rizman, Z. I. (2018). Examwiz: A development and implementation of an android based examination. *Journal of Fundamental and Applied Sciences, 10*(6S), 965–976.

Ripipsa. (2020). *History of Collaborative Robot* [Historia de los Robots Colaborativos]. Ripipsa Cobots. https://ripipsacobots.com/historia-robots-colaborativos/

Ritala, P., & Almpanopoulou, A. (2017). In defense of 'eco' in innovation ecosystem. *Technovation, 60–61*, 39–42. doi:10.1016/j.technovation.2017.01.004

Rodrigues, R. L., Soares, M., Souza, G. G., Lacerda, A., Souza, C., Gomes, A., & Alves, C. (2010). *Augmented Reality for the Teaching of Spatial Geometry*. CBIE.

Rodríguez, L., Paredes, C., & Martell, F. (2021). *Forward and Inverse Kinematics Control of a Collaborative 6-DOF Robot for an Augmented Reality Educational System.* https://ieeexplore.ieee.org/document/9590903

Rodriguez, O. J. (2018). *K-12 Regionalization in Connecticut: Pros, Cons and Surprises*. H. F. f. P. Giving. https://www.hfpg.org/files/7915/3013/0299/Regionlization_Report_Draft_as_of_6-27-2018.pdf

Rodríguez-Fidalgo, M. I., & Paino-Ambrosio, A. (2020). Use of virtual reality and 360° video as narrative resources in the documentary genre: Towards a new immersive social documentary? *Catalan Journal of Communication & Cultural Studies, 12*(2), 239-253.

Roettl, J., & Truter, R. (2018). The same video game in 2D, 3D or virtual reality – How does technology impact game evaluation and brand placements? *PLoS One, 13*(7), e0200724. Advance online publication. doi:10.1371/journal.pone.0200724 PMID:30028839

Rogers, S. (2019). Virtual reality: The learning aid of the 21st century. *Secondary Virtual reality: The learning aid of the 21st century.*

Román-Ibáñez, V., Pujol-López, F. A., Mora-Mora, H., Pertegal-Felices, M. L., & Jimeno-Morenilla, A. (2018). A low-cost immersive virtual reality system for teaching robotic manipulators programming. *Sustainability, 9*, 112.

Rose, D. (2000). Universal Design for Learning. *Journal of Special Education Technology, 15*(3), 45–49. doi:10.1177/016264340001500307

Rubio-Tamayo, J. L. (2019). Realidad extendida, interactividad y entornos inmersivos 3d: Revisión de la literatura y proyecciones. *Actas Icono 14, 1*(1), 396-415. https://bit.ly/3skNPSi

Rutter, M. (2009). Messenger in The Barn: Networking in a learning environment. *Alt-J, 17*(1), 33–47. doi:10.1080/09687760802649863

Safikhani, S., Keller, S., Schweiger, G., & Pirker, J. (2022). Immersive virtual reality for extending the potential of building information modeling in architecture, engineering, and construction sector: Systematic review. *International Journal of Digital Earth, 15*(1), 503–526. doi:10.1080/17538947.2022.2038291

Salas-Pilco, S., & Yang, Y. (2022). Artificial intelligence applications in Latin American higher education: A systematic review. *International Journal of Educational Technology in Higher Education, 19*(1), 21. doi:10.118641239-022-00326-w

Sanabria, J. C., & Arámburo-Lizárraga, J. (2017). Enhancing 21st century skills with AR: Using the gradual immersion method to develop collaborative creativity. *Eurasia Journal of Mathematics, Science and Technology Education, 13*(2), 487–501. doi:10.12973/eurasia.2017.00627a

Sánchez-Acedo, A., & Gertrudix, M. (2020). Comunicar la ciencia con vídeos 360. In M. Gertrudix & M. Rajas (Eds.), *Comunicar la ciencia. Guía para una comunicación eficiente y responsable de la investigación e innovación científica*. Gedisa.

Sandars, J. (2010). The importance of usability testing to allow e-learning to reach its potential for medical education. *Education for Primary Care, 21*(1), 6–8. doi:10.1080/14739879.2010.11493869 PMID:20202315

Sangrá, A., Raffaghelli, J. E., & Guitert-Catasús, M. (2019). Learning ecologies through a lens: Ontological, methodological and applicative issues. A systematic review of the literature. *British Journal of Educational Technology, 50*(4), 1619–1638. doi:10.1111/bjet.12795

Sarcedo-Gorgoso, M. C., Santos-González, M. C., & Rego-Agraso, L. (2020). Las competencias docentes en la formación del profesorado de educación secundaria. *Profesorado. Revista de Currículum y Formación de Profesorado, 24*(3), 401–421. doi:10.30827/profesorado.v24i3.8260

Scavarelli, A., Arya, A., & Teather, R. J. (2020). Virtual reality and augmented reality in social learning spaces: A literature review. *Virtual Reality (Waltham Cross), 25*(1), 257–277. doi:10.100710055-020-00444-8

Schleicher, A. (2020). *Teaching and Learning International Survey. TALIS 2018. Insights and Interpretations*. OCDE. https://www.oecd.org/education/talis/

Schnädelbach, H., Penn, A., Steadman, P., Benford, S., Koleva, B., & Rodden, T. (2006, November). Moving office: inhabiting a dynamic building. In *Proceedings of the 2006 20th anniversary conference on Computer supported cooperative work* (pp. 313-322). 10.1145/1180875.1180924

Schönauer, C., Bösch, C., Wechdorn, T., Göllner, J., Peer, A., Mossel, A., & Kaufmann, H. (2020). Physical object interaction in first responder mixed reality training. *Proceedings of SPIE - The International Society for Optical Engineering, 11426*. 10.1117/12.2557396

Schreer, O., Feldmann, I., Renault, S., Zepp, M., Worchel, M., Eisert, P., & Kauff, P. (2019, September). Capture and 3D video processing of volumetric video. In *2019 IEEE International conference on image processing (ICIP)* (pp. 4310-4314). IEEE. https://bit.ly/3LIf5SD

Schwarz, S., Hannuksela, M. M., Fakour-Sevom, V., & Sheikhi-Pour, N. (2018, June). 2D video coding of volumetric video data. In *2018 Picture Coding Symposium (PCS)* (pp. 61-65). IEEE.

Seufert, C., Oberdörfer, S., Roth, A., Grafe, S., Lugrin, J. L., & Latoschik, M. E. (2022). Classroom management competency enhancement for student teachers using a fully immersive virtual classroom. *Computers & Education, 179*, 104410. doi:10.1016/j.compedu.2021.104410

Shams, L., & Seitz, A. R. (2008). Benefits of multisensory learning. *Trends in Cognitive Sciences*, *12*(11), 411–417. doi:10.1016/j.tics.2008.07.006 PMID:18805039

Sharma, S. (2020). Improving emergency response training and decision making using a collaborative virtual reality environment for building evacuation. In C. Stephanidis, J. Y. C. Chen, & G. Fragomeni (Eds.), Lecture Notes in Computer Science: Vol. 12428. *HCI International 2020– Late Breaking Papers: Virtual and Augmented Reality* (pp. 213–224). Springer. doi:10.1007/978-3-030-59990-4_17

Sharma, S., Jerripothula, S., Mackey, S., & Soumare, O. (2014). Immersive virtual reality environment of a subway evacuation on a cloud for disaster preparedness and response training. In *2014 IEEE Symposium on Computational Intelligence for Human-like Intelligence* (pp. 1–6). 10.1109/CIHLI.2014.7013380

Shema-Shiratzky, S., Brozgol, M., Cornejo-Thumm, P., Geva-Dayan, K., Rotstein, M., Leitner, Y., Hausdorff, J. M., & Mirelman, A. (2019, August). Virtual reality training to enhance behavior and cognitive function among children with attention-deficit/hyperactivity disorder: Brief report. *Developmental Neurorehabilitation*, *22*(6), 431–436. doi:10.1080/17518423.2018.1476602 PMID:29771624

Sheridan, J., Alany, R., & Brake, D. J. (2005). Pharmacy students' views and experiences of Turnitin - An online tool for detecting academic dishonesty. *Pharmacy Education*, *5*(3–4), 241–250. doi:10.1080/15602210500288977

Sheridan, T. B. (2000). Interaction, imagination and immersion some research needs. *Proceedings of the ACM symposium on Virtual reality software and technology*, 1–7. 10.1145/502390.502392

Shuo, R., McKenzie, F. D., Chaturvedi, S. K., Prabhakaran, R., Jaewan, Y., & Katsioloudis, P. J. (2015). Design and Comparison of Immersive Interactive Learning and Instructional Techniques for 3D Virtual Laboratories. *Presence (Cambridge, Mass.)*, *24*(2), 93–112. doi:10.1162/PRES_a_00221

Slater, M., & Wilbur, S. (1997). A framework for immersive virtual environments (FIVE): Speculations on the role of presence in virtual environments. *Presence (Cambridge, Mass.)*, *6*(6), 603–616. doi:10.1162/pres.1997.6.6.603

Smith, S. M. (1979). Remembering in and out of context. *Journal of Experimental Psychology. Human Learning and Memory*, *5*(5), 460–471. doi:10.1037/0278-7393.5.5.460

Smole, K. S., & Diniz, M. I. (2019). *Mathematics - High School - 2nd grade* (Vol. 2). Saraiva Didáticos.

Snopková, D., Ugwitz, P., Stachoň, Z., Hladík, J., Juřík, V., Kvarda, O., & Kubíček, P. (2022). Retracing evacuation strategy: A virtual reality game-based investigation into the influence of building's spatial configuration in an emergency. *Spatial Cognition and Computation*, *22*(1-2), 30–50. doi:10.1080/13875868.2021.1913497

Soliman, M., Pesyridis, A., Dalaymani-Zad, D., Gronfula, M., & Kourmpetis, M. (2021). The application of virtual reality in engineering education. *Applied Sciences (Basel, Switzerland), 11*(6), 2879. doi:10.3390/app11062879

Song, J., Yamauchi, H., Oguchi, T., & Ogura, T. (2022). Application of web hazard maps to high school education for disaster risk reduction. *International Journal of Disaster Risk Reduction, 72*, 102866. doi:10.1016/j.ijdrr.2022.102866

Sora, C. (2017). Una inmersión en el audiovisual VR y 360. *Serie DigiDoc-EPI*, 1. https://bit.ly/3LV0S4R

Sorensen, P. (2014). Collaboration, dialogue and expansive learning: The use of paired and multiple placements in the school practicum. *Teaching and Teacher Education, 44*, 128–137. doi:10.1016/j.tate.2014.08.010

Southgate, E. (2020). *Virtual reality in curriculum and pedagogy: Evidence from secondary classrooms*. Routledge. doi:10.4324/9780429291982

Souza, R. C., & Kirner, C. (2012). *Flaras +*. Retrieved 2015, from http://ckirner.com/flaras2/

Souza, S. d. (2004). *Using Winplot.* UFPB, Matemática. Retrieved from http://www.mat.ufpb.br/sergio/winplot/winplot.html

Squire, K. D., & Jan, M. (2007). Mad City Mystery: Developing Scientific Argumentation Skills with a Place-based Augmented Reality Game on Handheld Computers. *Journal of Science Education and Technology, 16*(1), 5–29. doi:10.100710956-006-9037-z

Squire, K., & Klopfer, E. (2007). Augmented Reality Simulations on Handheld Computers. *Journal of the Learning Sciences, 16*(3), 371–413. doi:10.1080/10508400701413435

Ståhlbröst, A., & Holst, M. (2021). *The Living Lab Methodology Handbook.* https://www.ltu.se/cms_fs/1.101555!/file/LivingLabsMethodologyBook_web.pdf

Statistics Finland. (2021). *Persons with foreign background.* https://www.stat.fi/tup/maahanmuutto/maahanmuuttajat-vaestossa/ulkomaalaistaustaiset_en.html

Stavroulia, K., Christofi, M., Baka, E., Michael-Grigoriou, D., Magnenat-Thalmann, N., & Lanitis, A. (2019). Assessing the emotional impact of virtual reality-based teacher training. *The International Journal of Information and Learning Technology, 36*(3), 192–217. doi:10.1108/IJILT-11-2018-0127

Steen, K., & van Bueren, E. (2017). The Defining Characteristics of Urban Living Labs. *Technology Innovation Management Review, 7*(7), 21–33. doi:10.22215/timreview/1088

Stein, J. P., & Ohler, P. (2017). Venturing into the uncanny valley of mind - The influence of mind attribution on the acceptance of human-like characters in a virtual reality setting. *Cognition, 160*(1), 43–50. doi:10.1016/j.cognition.2016.12.010 PMID:28043026

Stella, C. (2005). *Critical thinking skills/Stella Cottrell.* Palgrave Macmillan.

Stone, R., & Glover, I. (2021). *Adapting HE teaching for an online environment: A practical guide*. Sage Publications Ltd.

Story, M. F., Mueller, J. L., & Mace, R. L. (1998). The Universal Design File: Designing for People of All Ages and Abilities. Revised Edition.

Stubbs, B. (2018). Virtual reality journalism: Ethics, grammar and the state of play. *Australian Journalism Review*, *40*(1), 81–90. https://bit.ly/3P494Sh

Sundar, S. S., Kang, J., & Oprean, D. (2017). Being there in the midst of the story: How immersive journalism affects our perceptions and cognitions. *Cyberpsychology, Behavior, and Social Networking*, *20*(11), 672–682. doi:10.1089/cyber.2017.0271 PMID:29125787

Susindar, S., Sadeghi, M., Huntington, L., Singer, A., & Ferris, T. K. (2019). The Feeling is Real: Emotion Elicitation in Virtual Reality. *Proceedings of the Human Factors and Ergonomics Society Annual Meeting*.

Sutton-Brady, C., Scott, K. M., Taylor, L., Carabetta, G., & Clark, S. (2009). The value of using short-format podcasts to enhance learning and teaching. *Alt-J*, *17*(3), 219–232. doi:10.1080/09687760903247609

Sutton, R. E. (2004). Emotional regulation goals and strategies of teachers. *Social Psychology of Education*, *7*(4), 379–398. doi:10.100711218-004-4229-y

Syberfeldt, A., Danielsson, O., & Gustavsson, P. (2017). *Augmented reality smart glasses in the smart factory: Product evaluation guidelines and review of available products*. IEEE.

Syed, Z. A., Trabookis, Z., Bertrand, J. W., Madathil, K. C., Hartley, R. S., Frady, K. K., Wagner, J. R., & Gramopadhye, A. K. (2019). Evaluation of virtual reality based learning materials as a supplement to the undergraduate mechanical engineering laboratory experience. *International Journal of Engineering Education*, *35*, 1–11.

Tang, Y., & Hew, K. F. (2022). Effects of using mobile instant messaging on student behavioral, emotional, and cognitive engagement: A quasi-experimental study. *International Journal of Educational Technology in Higher Education*, *19*(3), 3. Advance online publication. doi:10.118641239-021-00306-6 PMID:35036520

TarréR. (2019). *UPC*. https://upcommons.upc.edu/bi tstream/handle/2117/174167/Samper_Marc_memoria_TFG%20%282%29.pdf?sequence=1&isAllowed=y

Tavangarian, D., Leypold, M. E., Nölting, K., Röser, M., & Voigt, D. (2004). Is e-Learning the Solution for Individual Learning? *Electronic Journal of e-Learning*, *2*(2), 273–280.

Tejedor-Calvo, S., Romero-Rodríguez, L. M., Moncada-Moncada, A. J., & Alencar-Dornelles, M. (2020). Journalism that tells the future: Possibilities and journalistic scenarios for augmented reality. *El Profesional de la Información*, *29*(6), e290602. doi:10.3145/epi.2020.nov.02

Terroni, N. N. (2009). La comunicación y la asertividad del discurso durante las interacciones grupales presenciales y por computadora [Communication and discourse assertiveness during face-to-face and computer-based group interactions]. *Psico-USF*, *14*(1), 35–46. doi:10.1590/S1413-82712009000100005

Tori, R., Kirner, C., & Siscoutto, R. (2006). *Fundamentals and Technologies of Virtual and Augmented Reality*. SBC.

Torrico, D. D., Han, Y., Sharma, C., Fuentes, S., Gonzalez Viejo, C., & Dunshea, F. R. (2020). Effects of Context and Virtual Reality Environments on the Wine Tasting Experience, Acceptability, and Emotional Responses of Consumers. *Foods*, *9*(2), 191. https://doi.org/10.3390/foods9020191

Toursel, A., & Philippe, U. (2019). Immersive Journalism, a "New Frontier" of Information Experience? *Brazilian Journalism Research, 15*(2), 336-357.

Tsujimoto, M., Kajikawa, Y., Tomita, J., & Matsumoto, Y. (2018). A review of the ecosystem concept— Towards coherent ecosystem design. *Technological Forecasting and Social Change*, *136*, 49–58. https://doi.org/10.1016/j.techfore.2017.06.032

Uchida, O., Tajima, S., Kajita, Y., Utsu, K., Murakami, Y., & Yamada, S. (2021). Development and implementation of an ICT-based disaster prevention and mitigation education program for the young generation. *Information Systems Frontiers*, *23*(5), 1115–1125. doi:10.100710796-020-10082-9

United States Geological Survey (USGS). (2022). *The USGS Earthquake Hazards Program*. https://earthquake.usgs.gov/

Unity. (n.d.). *Unity*. Retrieved November 29, 2021, from https://unity.com/

Universidad Nacional de Cuyo. (2016). *Industrial application of ethernet networks* [Aplicación industrial de redes ethernet]. https://sistemamid.com/panel/uploads/biblioteca/2017-08-03_04-22-46141559.pdf

URJC. (2022). *Master in Journalistic Investigation, New Narratives, Data, Fact-checking and Transparency*. https://mastermaldita.es

Uskali, T., Gynnild, A., Jones, S., & Sirkkunen, E. (2021). *Immersive Journalism as Storytelling: Ethics, Production, and Design*. Taylor & Francis. doi:10.4324/9780429437748

Uskali, T., & Ikonen, P. (2021). Teaching immersive journalism. In *Immersive Journalism as Storytelling. Ethics, Production, and Design* (pp. 163–175). Routledge. doi:10.4324/9780429437748-18

Vakaloudis, A. (2014). A Framework for Rating Synchronous Video e- Learning Applications. *Science and Information Conference 2014*. 10.1109/SAI.2014.6918293

Van Damme, K., All, A., De Marez, L., & Van Leuven, S. (2019). 360 video journalism: Experimental study on the effect of immersion on news experience and distant suffering. *Journalism Studies*, *20*(14), 2053–2076. doi:10.1080/1461670X.2018.1561208 van der Land, S., Schouten, A. P., Feldberg, F., van den Hooff, B., & Huysman, M. (2013). Lost in space? Cognitive fit and cognitive load in 3D virtual environments. *Computers in Human Behavior, 29*(3), 1054–1064. doi:10.1016/j.chb.2012.09.006

van der Spek, E. D., van Oostendorp, H., & Meyer, Ch. (2013). Introducing surprising events can stimulate deep learning in a serious game. *British Journal of Educational Technology, 44*(1), 156–169. doi:10.1111/j.1467-8535.2011.01282.x

Vázquez-Herrero, J., & López-García, X. (2017, April). Immersive journalism through mobile devices: How virtual reality apps are changing news consumption. In *World Conference on Information Systems and Technologies* (pp. 3–12). Springer. doi:10.1007/978-3-319-56541-5_1

Veletsianos, G. (2010). Contextually relevant pedagogical agents: Visual appearance, stereotypes, and first impressions and their impact on learning. *Computers & Education, 55*(2), 576–585. doi:10.1016/j.compedu.2010.02.019

Verdú, E., Regueras, L. M., Verdú, M. J., De Castro, J. P., & Pérez, M. A. (2008). An analysis of the research on adaptive Learning: The next generation of e-learning. *WSEAS Transactions on Information Sciences and Applications, 5*(6), 859–868.

Vergara, D., Rubio, M. P., Lorenzo, M., & Rodríguez, S. (2019b). On the importance of the design of virtual reality learning environments. In *Methodologies and Intelligent Systems for Technology Enhanced Learning* (vol. 1007, pp. 146–152). Springer.

Vergara, D., Rubio, M.P. & Lorenzo, M. (2017b). New approach for the teaching of concrete compression tests in large groups of engineering students. *Journal of Professional Issues in Engineering Education and Practice.*

Vergara, D., Antón-Sancho, Á., Dávila, L. P., & Fernández-Arias, P. (2022b). Virtual reality as a didactic resource from the perspective of engineering teachers. *Computer Applications in Engineering Education, 30*(4), 1–16. doi:10.1002/cae.22504

Vergara, D., Antón-Sancho, Á., Extremera, J., & Fernández-Arias, P. (2021). Assessment of virtual reality as a didactic resource in higher education. *Sustainability, 13*(22), 12730. doi:10.3390u132212730

Vergara, D., Extremera, J., & Dávila, L. (2019). Meaningful Learning Through Virtual Reality Learning Environments: Case Study in Materials Engineering. *Applied Sciences (Basel, Switzerland), 9*(21), 4625. doi:10.3390/app9214625

Vergara, D., Extremera, J., Rubio, M. P., & Dávila, L. P. (2020a). The technological obsolescence of virtual reality learning environments. *Applied Sciences (Basel, Switzerland), 10*(3), 915. doi:10.3390/app10030915

Vergara, D., Extremera, J., Rubio, M. P., & Dávila, L. P. (2020b). The proliferation of virtual laboratories in educational fields. *ADCAIJ: Advances in Distributed Computing and Artificial Intelligence Journal, 9*(1), 85–97. doi:10.14201/ADCAIJ2020918597

Vergara, D., Fernández-Arias, P., Extremera, J., Dávila, L. P., & Rubio, M. P. (2022a). Educational trends post COVID-19 in engineering: Virtual laboratories. *Materials Today: Proceedings*, *49*, 155–1609. doi:10.1016/j.matpr.2021.07.494 PMID:35018286

Vergara, D., Lorenzo, M., & Rubio, M. P. (2015). Virtual environments in materials science and engineering: the students' opinion. In H. L. Lim (Ed.), *Handbook of research on recent developments in materials science and corrosion engineering education* (pp. 148–165). IGI Global. doi:10.4018/978-1-4666-8183-5.ch008

Vergara, D., & Rubio, M. P. (2012). Active methodologies through interdisciplinary teaching links: Industrial radiography and technical drawing. *The Journal of Materials Education*, *34*, 175–186.

Vergara, D., Rubio, M. P., & Lorenzo, M. (2014). Interactive virtual platform for simulating a concrete compression test. *Key Engineering Materials*, *572*, 582–585. doi:10.4028/www.scientific.net/KEM.572.582

Vergara, D., Rubio, M. P., & Lorenzo, M. (2017a). On the design of virtual reality learning environments in engineering. *Multimodal Technologies and Interaction*, *1*(2), 11. doi:10.3390/mti1020011

Vergara, D., Rubio, M. P., & Lorenzo, M. (2018). A virtual resource for enhancing the spatial comprehension of crystal lattices. *Education in Science*, *8*(4), 153. doi:10.3390/educsci8040153

Vergara-Rodríguez, D., Antón-Sancho, Á., & Fernández-Arias, P. (2022). Variables influencing professors' adaptation to digital learning environments during the COVID-19 pandemic. *International Journal of Environmental Research and Public Health*, *19*(6), 3732. doi:10.3390/ijerph19063732 PMID:35329422

Vergara-Rodriguez, D., Rodriguez-Martin, M., Rubio-Cavero, M. P., Ferrer-Marin, J., Núñez-Garcia, J., & Moralejo-Lobo, L. (2018). Technical staff training in ultrasonic non-destructive testing using virtual reality. *Dyna*, *94*(1), 150–154. doi:10.6036/8444

Vieira, C., Parsons, P., & Byrd, V. (2018). Visual learning analytics of educational data: A systematic literature review and research agenda. *Computers & Education*, *122*, 119–135. doi:10.1016/j.compedu.2018.03.018

Vienne, C., Sorin, L., Blondé, L., Huynh-Thu, Q., & Mamassian, P. (2014). Effect of the accommodation-vergence conflict on vergence eye movements. *Vision Research*, *100*, 124–133. doi:10.1016/j.visres.2014.04.017 PMID:24835799

Villalobos, J., Sanchez, I. Y., & Martell, F. (2021). Statistical comparison of Denavit-Hartenberg based inverse kinematic solutions of the UR5 robotic manipulator. *2021 International Conference on Electrical, Computer, Communications and Mechatronics Engineering (ICECCME)*. doi:10.1109/iceccme52200.2021.9591104

VR Fast Track Project. (2021a). *Health Care VR Implementation (video)*. https://video.haaga-helia.fi/media/VR - Assisted Living/0_l1mgekua

VR Fast Track Project. (2021b). *Restaurant Work VR Implementation (video).* https://video.haaga-helia.fi/media/VR - Restaurant Work/0_3hp1qcp1

VR Fast Track Project. (2021c). *VR implementation for cleaning (video).* https://video.haaga-helia.fi/media/t/0_7wrayri7

VR Fast Track Project. (2021d). *VR implementation for medication dispension (video).* https://video.haaga-helia.fi/media/t/0_ccy3580i

Vuforia. (2020). *Market-Leading Enterprise AR-PTC.* https://www.ptc.com/en/products/augmented-reality/vuforia

Vygotsky, L. S. (1978). *Mind in society: The development of higher psychological processes.* Harvard University Press.

Wakimoto, D., & Lewis, E. (2014). Graduate Student Perceptions of Eportfolios: Uses for Reflection, Development, and Assessment. *The Internet and Higher Education, 21*, 53–58. doi:10.1016/j.iheduc.2014.01.002

Wallace, S., Parsons, S., & Bailey, A. (2017). Self-reported sense of presence and responses to social stimuli by adolescents with autism spectrum disorder in a collaborative virtual reality environment. *Journal of Intellectual & Developmental Disability, 42*(2), 131–141. doi:10.3109/13668250.2016.1234032

Wallach, H. S., Safir, M. P., Samana, R., Almog, I., & Horef, R. (2011). How can presence in psychotherapy employing VR be increased? Chapter for inclusion in: Systems in health care using agents and virtual reality. *Studies in Computational Intelligence, 337*(2009), 129–147. doi:10.1007/978-3-642-17824-5_7

Wang, X., Hodgers, C., McGuckin, C., & Lv, J. (2022). A Conceptual Learning Design in Virtual Reality The Cognitive VR Classroom for Education After the Pandemic Era. *17th Education and Development Conference.* https://www.ed-conference.org/edc2022001.html

Wang, P., Wu, P., Wang, J., Chi, H.-L., & Wang, X. (2018). A critical review of the use of virtual reality in construction engineering education and training. *International Journal of Environmental Research and Public Health, 15*(6), 1204. doi:10.3390/ijerph15061204 PMID:29890627

Wang, T., Xing, Q. R., Wang, H., & Chen, W. (2019). Retracted Publications in the biomedical Literature from Open Access Journals. *Science and Engineering Ethics, 25*(3), 855–868. doi:10.100711948-018-0040-6 PMID:29516389

Wang, X., Young, G. W., Mc Guckin, C., & Smolic, A. (2021). A Systematic Review of Virtual Reality Interventions for Children with Social Skills Deficits. *2021 IEEE International Conference on Engineering, Technology & Education (TALE).* 10.1109/TALE52509.2021.9678808

Warburton, S. (2009). Second life in higher education: Assessing the potential for and the barriers to deploying virtual worlds in learning and teaching. *British Journal of Educational Technology, 40*(3), 414–426. doi:10.1111/j.1467-8535.2009.00952.x

Watanabe, H., & Ujike, H. (2008). The activity of ISO/study group on "image safety" and three biological effect. *Proceedings of the 2nd International Symposium on Universal Communication, ISUC 2008*, 210–214. 10.1109/ISUC.2008.11

Webster, J., & Watson, R. (2002). Analyzing the Past to Prepare for the Future: Writing a Literature Review. *Management Information Systems Quarterly*, *26*(2), xiii–xxiii.

Wee-Seng, S. (2021). Experiential Learning Through Remote Electrical Engineering Labs During the COVID-19 Pandemic. *2021 IEEE International Conference on Engineering, Technology & Education (TALE).*

Wiggins, G., & McTighe, J. (2006). *Understanding by design* (2nd ed.). Perason Education.

William, M., García, C., Naranjo, J., Ortiz, A., & García, M. (2020). *Tele-operation system for Mobile Robots in the Oil and Gas industry* [Sistema de Tele-operación para Robots Móviles en la industria del Petróleo y Gas]. Revista Ibérica de Sistemas e Tecnologias de Información. https://www.researchgate.net/profile/Jose-E-Naranjo-2/publication/341522855_Sistema_de_Tele-operacion_para_Robots_Moviles_en_la_industria_del_Petroleo_y_Gas/links/5fc46ee0458515b7978932fb/Sistema-de-Tele-operacion-para-Robots-Moviles-en-la-industria-del-Petroleo-y-Gas.pdf

Williamson, J. R., Li, J., Vinayagamoorthy, V., Shamma, D. A., & Cesar, P. (2021, May). Proxemics and Social Interactions in an Instrumented Virtual Reality Workshop. *CHI '21.*

Wilson, A., Watson, C., Thompson, T. L., Drew, V., & Doyle, S. (2017). Learning analytics: Challenges and limitations. *Teaching in Higher Education*, *22*(8), 991–1007. doi:10.1080/13562517.2017.1332026

Winstone, N. E., Nash, R. A., Parker, M. P., & Rowntree, J. (2017). Supporting learners' agentic engagement with feedback: A systematic review and a taxonomy of recipience processes. *Educational Psychologist*, *52*(1), 17–37. doi:10.1080/00461520.2016.1207538

Witting, M. (2019, September 16). *Korkeasti koulutettuja ja vähän koulutettuja – ulkomaalaistaustaisten koulutuksesta tulossa tarkempaa tietoa* [Highly educated and less educated - additional information on the education level of immigrants coming up]. https://www.stat.fi/tietotrendit/blogit/2019/korkeasti-koulutettuja-ja-vahan-koulutettuja-ulkomaalaistaustaisten-koulutuksesta-tulossa-tarkempaa-tietoa/

Wójcik, M. (2016). Potential use of Augmented Reality in LIS education. *Education and Information Technologies*, *21*(6), 1555–1569. doi:10.100710639-015-9399-z

Wolfartsberger, J. (2019). Analyzing the potential of virtual reality for engineering design review. *Automation in Construction*, *104*, 27–37. doi:10.1016/j.autcon.2019.03.018

Won, A. S., Bailey, J. O., & Yi, S. (2020, June). Learning about Virtual Worlds in Virtual Worlds: How Remote Learning in a Pandemic Can Inform Future Teaching. *6th International Conference of the Immersive Learning Research Network (iLRN)*, 377–380. 10.23919/iLRN47897.2020.9155201

World Economy Forum. (2020). *Jobs of Tomorrow: Mapping Opportunity in the New Economy.* Author.

World Meteorological Organization (WMO). (2022). https://public.wmo.int/en

Wu, H.-K., Lee, S. W.-Y., Chang, H.-Y., & Liang, J.-C. (2013). Current status, opportunities and challenges of augmented reality in education. *Computers & Education, 62*, 41–49. doi:10.1016/j.compedu.2012.10.024

Wu, W.-C. V., Manabe, K., Marek, M. W., & Shu, Y. (2021). Enhancing 21st-century competencies via virtual reality digital content creation. *Journal of Research on Technology in Education*, 1–22. doi:10.1080/15391523.2021.1962455

Wu, W., Tesei, A., Ayer, S., London, J., Luo, Y., & Gunji, V. (2018). Closing the skills gap: Construction and engineering education using mixed reality – A case study. In *Proceedings of the 2018 IEEE Frontiers in Education Conference (FIE)* (vol. 1, pp. 1-5). Osaka, Japan: IEEE. 10.1109/FIE.2018.8658992

Xie, Q., & Tinker, R. (2006). Molecular dynamics simulations of chemical reactions for use in education. *Journal of Chemical Education, 83*(1), 77–83. doi:10.1021/ed083p77

Yamori, K., & Sugiyama, T. (2020). Development and social implementation of smartphone app Nige-Tore for improving tsunami evacuation drills: Synergistic effects between commitment and contingency. *International Journal of Disaster Risk Science, 11*(6), 751–761. doi:10.100713753-020-00319-1

Yang, X., Lin, L., Cheng, P.-Y., Yang, X., Ren, Y., & Huang, Y.-M. (2018). Examining creativity through a virtual reality support system. *Educational Technology Research and Development, 66*(5), 1231–1254. doi:10.100711423-018-9604-z

Yang, Y., Xu, Z., Wu, Y., Wei, W., & Song, R. (2021). Virtual fire evacuation drills through a web-based serious game. *Applied Sciences (Basel, Switzerland), 11*(23), 11284. doi:10.3390/app112311284

Yen, C. J., & Tu, C. H. (2008). Online Social Presence: A Study of Score Validity of the Computer-Mediated Communication Questionnaire. *Quarterly Review of Distance Learning, 9*(3), 297–310.

Yoo, H. (2020). Research-to-Resource: Use of Technology to Support 21st Century Skills in a Performing Ensemble Program. *Update: Applications of Research in Music Education, 39*(2), 10–14. doi:10.1177/8755123320953435

Young, G., Stehle, S., Yazgı, B., & Tiri, E. (2020). Exploring Virtual Reality in the Higher Education Classroom: Using VR to Build Knowledge and Understanding. *Journal of Universal Computer Science, 26*(8), 904–928. doi:10.3897/jucs.2020.049

Zerman, E., Ozcinar, C., Gao, P., & Smolic, A. (2020, May). *Textured mesh vs coloured point cloud: A subjective study for volumetric video compression. In 2020 Twelfth International Conference on Quality of Multimedia Experience (QoMEX).* IEEE.

Zhang, A., Wang, C., Han, B., & Qian, F. (2021, February). Efficient volumetric video streaming through super resolution. In *Proceedings of the 22nd International Workshop on Mobile Computing Systems and Applications* (pp. 106-111). Academic Press.

Zhan, T., Yin, K., Xiong, J., He, Z., & Wu, S.-T. (2020). Augmented Reality and Virtual Reality Displays: Perspectives and Challenges. *iScience*, *23*(8), 101397. doi:10.1016/j.isci.2020.101397 PMID:32759057

Zhu, Y., & Li, N. (2021). Virtual and augmented reality technologies for emergency management in the built environments: A state-of-the-art review. *Journal of Safety Science and Resilience*, *2*(1), 1–10. doi:10.1016/j.jnlssr.2020.11.004

Zibrek, K., & McDonnell, R. (2019). Social presence and place illusion are affected by photorealism in embodied VR. In *MIG '19* (pp. 1–7). Motion, Interaction and Games. doi:10.1145/3359566.3360064

Zimba, O., & Gasparyan, A. (2021). Plagiarism detection and prevention: A primer for researchers. *Reumatologia*, *59*(3), 132–137. doi:10.5114/reum.2021.105974 PMID:34538939

Zorzal, E. R., Cardoso, A., Kirner, C., & Júnior, E. L. (2006). Augmented Reality Applied in Educational Games. *V Workshop de Educação em Computação e Informática do Estado de Minas Gerais*.

Zwoliński, G., Kamińska, D., Laska-Leśniewicz, A., Haamer, R. E., Vairinhos, M., Raposo, R., Urem, F., & Reisinho, P. (2022). Extended Reality in Education and Training: Case Studies in Management Education. *Electronics (Basel)*, *11*(3), 336. doi:10.3390/electronics11030336

About the Contributors

Anacleto Correia (M) is an Associate Professor and lecturer of Management and Information Systems subjects at the Portuguese Navy Academy. He holds a Ph.D. in Computer Science, an M.Sc. in Statistics and Information Management, a B.Sc. degree in Management, and also a B.Sc. at Portuguese Naval Academy. His research interests are focused on requirements engineering, software engineering, process modeling, data mining, machine learning, and business engineering. He has also more than 20 years of experience in industry-leading projects and architecting large software development projects and is the author of dozens of scientific papers in journals and conference proceedings.

Vítor Viegas (M'16 SM'22) works as a Researcher at the Instituto de Telecomunicações, Instrumentation and Measurement Group, Lisboa; as an Assistant Professor at the Escola Naval, Almada; and as an Invited Adjunct Professor at the Polytechnic Institute of Setúbal, Setúbal, Portugal. His research interests concern electronic instrumentation, measurement systems and industrial informatics. He is the author of national patents, book chapters, articles in peer-reviewed indexed journals, and papers in international conference proceedings. He has been involved in several research projects financed by the Portuguese State and the European Union.

* * *

Luis Alfaro Casas graduated in 1984 with a degree in Industrial Engineering from the National University of San Agustín of Arequipa in 1984, and obtained a Master's degree in Production Engineering from the Universidad Federal de Santa Catarina - SC - Brazil, in 1994. He obtained a Doctorate degree in Production Engineering at the Federal University of Santa Catarina - SC - Brazil in 1999. His areas of interest include research methodology at undergraduate and graduate level, Artificial Intelligence, and Adaptive e-Learning Systems, Immersive Reality applied to education and Marketing. He is research professor, and develops the disciplines of Thesis Workshop, Research Methodology, Artificial Intelligence,

Object-Oriented Analysis at the undergraduate level of the National University of San Agustin and at the graduate level in several universities in Peru. He has been Lecturer in national and international events in the areas of Computer Science and Immersive Reality in Peru, Brazil, Chile, Bolivia and Ecuador, has written more than five books, and has had over 60 articles published in national and international magazines and congresses.

Ibis Alvarez is a PhD in Educational Psychology. Senior lecturer at Department of Basic, Evolutionary and Education Psychology. Universitat Autònoma de Barcelona. Consultant instructor. Psychology and Education Science Studies, Universitat Oberta de Catalunya. Her research focuses on cultural aspects of learning and psychological development and in the collaborative and active learning.

Álvaro Antón-Sancho is Associate Professor at the Department of Mathematics of the School of Education Fray Luis de Leon and at the Catholic University of Avila (Spain). He completed his PhD in Mathematics at the Spanish National Research Council and at the Complutense University of Madrid. He has published numerous research articles in recognized journals on algebraic geometry and didactics of mathematics. In addition, he has been a visitor in several foreign universities, participated in different research projects and organized some events on geometry.

Gary Burnett is a Professor in Transport Human Factors in the Faculty of Engineering at the University of Nottingham in the UK. He leads a team of researchers and PhD students focussed on automotive human factors – in particular the design and evaluation of the Human-Machine Interfaces for future vehicles. For several years, Professor Burnett has taught students on the use of simulation and Virtual Reality (VR) in engineering design – and, recently has pioneered the use of social VR as means to engage with students wholly in virtual worlds.

Miriela Cárdenas graduated from Grand Canyon University, Phoenix, Arizona from both a MS in Psychology with an emphasis in Organizational and Industrial Psychology and a MA in English Language and Education, Linguist and English as a second Language Teacher, currently pursuing a PhD in Educational Psychology at Universitat Autònoma de Barcelona. Her research focuses on the use of Computer Information Technology (CIT) to improve teachers' competences.

Matteo Cultrera received the B.Sc. and the M.Sc. degrees in Computer Engineering at the Politecnico di Torino University, in Italy, in 2017 and 2020, respectively.

Federico De Lorenzis received the B.Sc. and M.Sc. degrees in computer engineering from Politecnico di Torino University, in Italy, in 2016 and 2019, respectively. Currently, he is a Ph.D. student at the Dipartimento di Automatica e Informatica of the Politecnico di Torino. His research activities include the design and development of real-time immersive applications, with a focus on the use of virtual reality for the training of users.

Merja Drake's (PhD in Communication) areas of expertise are online journalism, communication, research methods and future research. She has a long experience leading research and innovation projects. She is interested in XR Technology and especially virtual reality and its benefits i.e. in learning. In addition, she has been participating in projects promoting gender equality, developing new pedagogy concepts and researching social media. She has been working at Haaga-Helia University of Applied Sciences as a principal lecturer since 2006.

Castañeda Elisa has a PhD in Production Engineering, and works as a Researcher at Renacyt M1, and as Principal Professor at the National University of San Agustín de Arequipa.

Jamil Extremera is currently a PhD student at the University of Salamanca. He completed his Mechanical Engineering Degree at Catholic University of Ávila (Spain) and his Master in Mathematical and Computation Engineering at International University of La Rioja (Spain). He has participated as co-author in several papers published in recognized international conferences and journals.

Pablo Fernández-Arias holds a degree in Industrial Engineering from the University of Salamanca and Industrial Engineering from the University Alfonso X el Sabio. He later obtained his PhD degree from the University of Salamanca, in the PhD program in Social Studies of Science and Technology. He has more than 10 years of professional experience in the energy sector. He has had different professional profiles, including Nuclear Power Plant Operation Instructor, Technological Development and Innovation Manager and Technological Leader. Expert in new educational environments, disruptive technologies for training and active learning methodologies. Since 2019, he has been working as a Teacher and Researcher at the Catholic University of Avila (Spain).

Manuel Gértrudix Barrio is Professor of Digital Communication at the Rey Juan Carlos University, coordinator of the Cyberimaginary research group, and co-editor of the scientific journal Icono14. Specialist in digital communication and elearning he has been IP of 8 competitive national and international research projects and has participated in more than 20. He has been Vice Chancellor for Quality, Ethics and Good Governance of the URJC (2018 -2021), Academic Director of the Center for Innovation in Digital Education of the URJC (2013-2017), Technical Advisor of New Technologies (2003-2007) and Head of Service of distance education of the Ministry of Education (Spain). He has taught at Universidad Complutense de Madrid (1999-2002), Universidad Francisco de Vitoria (1999-2003) and Universidad Carlos III de Madrid (2003-2007).

Catherine Harvey is an Assistant Professor in the Human Factors Research Group (Faculty of Engineering, University of Nottingham). Her academic background is in UX evaluation, Human Factors methods and HCI and she has applied this knowledge in the automotive domain and other transport contexts. She teaches a number of modules using a mix of both face-to-face and virtual interaction methods. Dr Harvey has recently completed a PGCHE, which included a research study of peer-to-peer and peer-to-staff interactions in virtual teaching and learning environments.

Thiciany Iwano graduated in Mathematics from the Federal University of Alagoas (2001) and Master's in Mathematics from the Federal University of Campina Grande (2005). She is currently an assistant professor at the State University of Paraíba. She has experience in Mathematics, with an emphasis on Applied Mathematics, working mainly on the following subjects: applied mathematics and educational informatics.

Raine Kauppinen's (Master of Science) areas of expertise include business and ICT cooperation, information management and software development. In addition to this, he has an experience in areas such as public administration software development and information system procurement, project management and architectures. Current areas of interest include digitalisation, development methods of information systems and exploitation of augmented reality (XR).

Rebekah Kay is an MEng Mechanical Engineering graduate, who developed a passion for Virtual Reality (VR) during her master's thesis, where she explored collaborative VR within higher education. Now working within technology consultancy, she has a keen focus on advancing Virtual Reality (VR) solutions and use cases within corporate and educational sectors.

Fabrizio Lamberti is a full professor at the Dipartimento di Automatica e Informatica of Politecnico di Torino. His interests pertain computer graphics, human-machine interaction, and computational intelligence. He is an Associate Editor of IEEE Transactions on Computers, IEEE Transactions on Learning Technologies, IEEE Transactions on Consumer Electronics, IEEE Consumer Electronics Magazine and International Journal of Human-Computer Studies. He is a senior member of the IEEE, IEEE Computer Society and IEEE Consumer Technology Society. He is serving as VP Technical Activities of IEEE Consumer Technology Society (BoG Member-at-Large 2021–2023).

Jorge Luna-Urquizo is a specialist in project management under the approaches of PMBook, CMMI, and agile project management with SCRUM methodology. Her main areas of interest are Artificial Intelligence, image processing, and e-Learning systems, with various publications indexed in these areas. She has worked in the analysis, design and development of various computer systems in the aforementioned areas, as well as in the formulation and execution of various research and innovation projects, both for academia and for applications in industry.

Borja Manero is a PhD in Computer Science, Senior lecturer at Department of Artificial Intelligence, actor and theater director. His research focused on the potential of the artificial intelligence and video games to improve artistic education and communication skills. His line of research deals with the use of new technologies (virtual reality and artificial intelligence) in the teaching of public speaking and the arts.

Fernando Martell Chávez was born in Delicias, Chihuahua, Mexico in 1971. He received the B.S. degree in electronic engineering in 1993, the M.S. degree in energy/electrical engineering in 2007, and the Ph.D. degree in information and communications technology in 2012, from Tecnologico de Monterrey, Monterrey, N.L., Mexico. From 1994 to 2002 he worked for AMIGE International, implementing automation, industrial informatics and energy optimization projects, in 2002 he founded Ingenieria Mecatronica, SA de CV and worked in this company as engineering manager. Since 2017, he has been a engineering researcher at the Centro de Investigaciones en Optica, AC, Aguascalientes, Mexico working on technology development in topics such as power electronics for renewable energies and modelling and control of mechatronics and cyber-physical systems.

Conor McGuckin, PhD, is an Associate Professor of Educational Psychology in the School of Education at Trinity College Dublin, Ireland. Conor convenes the Inclusion in Education and Society Research Group and is the founding editor of the International Journal of Inclusion in Education and Society. Conor's research interests include: psychology applied to educational policy and practices, technology in education, bully/victim problems among children and adults, and special and inclusive education. Conor is an Associate Fellow of both the British Psychological Society (BPS) and the Psychological Society of Ireland (PSI). Conor a Chartered

Psychologist with both the BPS and PSI, and is a Chartered Scientist with the UK Science Council.

Massimo Migliorini since 2005 has worked at SiTI's (now part of LINKS) Security & Safety department, focusing his activities on risk assessment of sensitive assets including cultural heritage. From 2019 he is responsible for the virtual reality LAB hosted by LINKS.

Hiroyuki Mitsuhara received the B.E. and M.E. degrees from Kindai University in 1998 and 2000, and then he received the Ph.D. degree from Tokushima University in 2003. He is currently an associate professor at Tokushima University. His interest includes VR/AR, game-based learning, mobile learning systems and disaster education.

Carlos Alberto Paredes Orta was born in the state of Mexico in 1883. He is a computer systems engineer graduated from ITQ (Technology Institute of the state of Querétaro). He has a master's degree and a doctorate in mechatronics engineering from the Center for Industrial Research and Development (CIDESI). From 2017 to the present, he is a CONACYT professor at the Optics Research Center (CIO). His research lines are image processing, mixed realities and mathematical morphology.

Dayvson Pereira graduated in Mathematics from the State University of Paraíba. He is a teacher in the public education network.

Filippo Gabriele Pratticò is a Ph.D. candidate at Politecnico di Torino, where he carries out research in the areas of extended reality, human-computer and human-robot interaction, serious games, and user experience design. He is a member of the IEEE and the IEEE Consumer Technology Society.

Mary Quirke is a qualified guidance counsellor, for over 20 years. Mary is also a PhD candidate in Trinity College Dublin with a research interest in Guidance Counselling, Universal Design (UD), Universal Design for Learning (UDL), Inclusion and Disability. She has experience with the HSE, REHAB, FETAC, AHEAD and the Institute of Guidance Counsellors. Consequently, Mary has a depth of knowledge and this has been further complemented by her active engagement in the inclusion agenda across learning and work environments, both nationally and internationally over the years.

Claudia Patricia Rivera Chavez graduated in 1995 in Business Administration from the Universidad Católica de Santa María in Arequipa - Peru. She obtained a Master's degree in Administration with a mention in Marketing from the Universidade Federal do Rio Grande do Sul in Porto Alegre - Brazil, and in 1999 she obtained a Doctorate degree in Production Engineering from the National University of San Agustín in Arequipa, Peru, in 2018. Her areas of interest include: E-learning systems, ICT applications in marketing, Virtual Reality in marketing, Sales Point Management. She teaches research at the undergraduate level, and develops the disciplines of Administration, Information Systems, Marketing, Product Strategy and Organizational Behavior; and at the graduate level Management Information Systems Technology at the National University of San Agustín in Arequipa. She has more than ten articles published in national and international journals and conferences.

Lorena Rodríguez Islas was born in Mexico City in 1997. She is a mechatronics engineer and completed her master's degree (August 2022) in the interinstitutional postgraduate degree in science and technology in the specialty of mechatronics, with the project called "Virtual twin of a collaborative robotic arm with 6 degrees of freedom under the technique of augmented reality." This master's degree is located at the Center for Research in Optics (CIO, for its acronym in Spanish), which belongs to one of the CONACyT centers (National Council of Science and Technology, for its acronym in Spanish) and also belongs to the National Institute Program of Postgraduate Quality (PNPC, for its acronym in Spanish).

Alejandro Romero-Hernández has a degree in computer engineering and the master's degree in digital letters (advanced studies in electronic textualities) from the Complutense University of Madrid (UCM), in 2016, where he is currently pursuing the Ph.D. degree in computer engineering. Since 2015, he has been dedicated to the development of artistic videogames for their application in the educational world. His main research interest includes developing different artistic tools using new technologies as videogames or different types of extended realities in order to increase the interest of the general public of these different arts.

José Rubio-Tamayo is a PhD (European Mention, Fine Arts) by Complutense University of Madrid, Bachelor Degree in Fine Arts (Complutense University of Madrid) and Master in Media Engineering (Univerity of Poitiers). His research work addresses the convergence between media, technology, art, design and science communication. He is currently researcher at Ciberimaginario Research Group, and, since 2016, lecturer at URJC. He has been also lecturer at UNED (Spain) and worked for several institutions, such as National Institute for Educational Technologies (Spain). He has also done various research stays in univiersities such as Univertity of Arts, UdK (Berlin), University of Los Lagos (Chile), University of Montreal (Montreal, Quebec, Canada) and has also been guest teacher in institutions such as the OAMK

(Oulu, Finland) and the University of Porto, and the Research Centre for Science and Technology of the Arts (CITAR, UCP, Portugal), among others.

Alberto Sanchez-Acedo has a Bachelor's Degree in Audiovisual Communication and a Master's Degree in Teacher Training specializing in Processes and Audiovisual Communication. He did his university internship at the Ciberimaginario group, where he notoriously carried out her Final Degree Project, which concluded with a meritorious immersive audiovisual product. Thanks to which he acquired professional knowledge regarding immersive technology such as 360 technology or Virtual Reality. Currently, he is starting his doctoral thesis, which also focuses on the world of Virtual Reality.

Daniel Scherer is a PhD in Electrical Engineering from the Federal University of Campina Grande (2010) and a Master's in Informatics from the Federal University of Campina Grande (2004). He is currently a professor at the State University of Paraíba. He has experience in Computer Science, with emphasis on Human Machine Interface, working mainly on the following topics: usability, human-system interface, virtual and augmented reality, educational computing, and educational robotics.

Masami Shishibori received his BS Degree in 1991, his MS Degree in 1993 and PhD Degree in 1997, from Tokushima University, Japan. He is currently a full professor at Tokushima University, Japan. His research interests include multimedia processing, information retrieval and natural language processing.

Maribel Urquizo-Abril is a Systems Engineer graduated from the Santa María Catholic University, Master in Systems Engineering with a mention in Information Technology Management, degree obtained from the National University of San Agustín. She is currently the academic coordinator of the Systems Engineering and Informatics career at the Technological University of Peru, with more than 10 years of experience in university teaching. She has experience in the development of information systems oriented to the electricity and mining sector in both public and private companies.

Diego Vergara-Rodríguez is Associate Professor in the Department of Mechanical Engineering at the Catholic University of Avila (Spain). He completed his PhD studies at the University of Salamanca, where he also obtained the degrees of both Civil Engineering and Materials Engineering. He has participated as co-author in more than 200 papers published in recognized international conferences and journals, as well as in several research projects. It is worth mentioning his activity as a reviewer of prestigious journals.

Xining Wang is a PhD candidate at Trinity College Dublin, Ireland. Also, a guest PhD candidate at the virtual reality learning lab, the University of Copenhagen, Denmark. Her research interests include utilizing immersive technology (mixed reality) in Education and Psychology, reducing educational inequalities, and enhancing students' well-being.

Daniel Wuebben is a Marie Curie Fellow with the GET-Energy COFUND program. He earned a Ph.D. in Literature from the Graduate Center of the City University of New York and has held full-time teaching positions with the City College Center for Worker Education, the University of California Santa Barbara Writing Program, and the Goodrich Scholarship Program at the University of Nebraska Omaha, where he was also director of the Nebraska Post-Secondary Prison Education Program. He has published nine single authored and two co-authored journal articles on a range of topics including floral codes, viral videos, and critical surf studies. His book, Power-lined: Electricity, Landscape, and the American Mind, shows that as longer, taller, and more interconnected lines coalesced on the margins of the modern environment, the meanings of electricity and landscape charged physical spaces and popular consciousness. His current research examines scientific communication, public engagement, and the energy transition in Spain and the rest of the EU.

Jesús Zúñiga-Cueva graduated in 1988 in Industrial Engineering, and in Economics, in 2010 at the National University of San Agustín de Arequipa - Peru. He obtained a Master´s degree in Production Engineering at the National University of San Agustín of Arequipa - Peru, in 2015. His areas of interest include academic research methodology in the areas of educational computing, information systems, adaptive e-Learning, enterprenureship and formative research. He is the Director of the Academic Department of Systems Engineering and Computer Science at the National University of San Agustín of Arequipa and teaches the Thesis Workshop, Research Methodology and Software Engineering at the undergraduate level at the National University of San Agustín. He has had articles published in national and international journals and conferences.

Index

W

X

Ensure Quality Research is Introduced to the Academic Community

Become an Evaluator for IGI Global Authored Book Projects

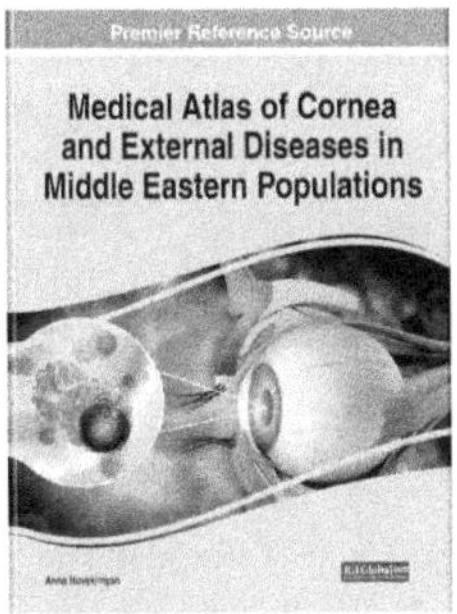

The overall success of an authored book project is dependent on quality and timely manuscript evaluations.

Applications and Inquiries may be sent to:
development@igi-global.com

Applicants must have a doctorate (or equivalent degree) as well as publishing, research, and reviewing experience. Authored Book Evaluators are appointed for one-year terms and are expected to complete at least three evaluations per term. Upon successful completion of this term, evaluators can be considered for an additional term.

If you have a colleague that may be interested in this opportunity, we encourage you to share this information with them.

www.ingramcontent.com/pod-product-compliance
Lightning Source LLC
LaVergne TN
LVHW081332021026
849161LV00008BA/2090
* 9 7 8 1 6 6 8 4 3 3 9 8 0 *